THE
LEISU
ETHI

WORK AND F

IN AMERICA

LITERATUR

1840–1940

THE LEISURE ETHIC

WORK AND PLAY

IN AMERICAN

LITERATURE,

1840–1940

WILLIAM A. GLEASON

STANFORD UNIVERSITY PRESS

STANFORD, CALIFORNIA

1999

Stanford University Press
Stanford, California
© 1999 by the Board of Trustees of the
Leland Stanford Junior University

Printed in the United States of America

CIP data appear at the end of the book

FOR ANDREA AND JEFFREY

PREFACE

This is a book about why play mattered so intensely to Americans at the turn of the last century. It is about leisure as serious business—as, paradoxically, the culture's most vital work. More specifically, it is about a period in American history—and American literary history—when discussions (and representations) of parks, playgrounds, and ball fields opened ineluctably onto the most pressing social issues of the age: immigration, industrial capitalism, women's rights, public health, race relations, consumption, mass culture, and perhaps most important, the nature and meaning of work itself.

Play did not always matter this intensely. But as the spread of factory labor slowly bankrupted the Protestant work ethic—leading more and more Americans to seek fulfillment in nonwork forms—the cultural significance of play rose accordingly. In *The Leisure Ethic* I consider the impact of these developments on nineteenth- and early-twentieth-century American literature and argue that American writers from Henry David Thoreau to Zora Neale Hurston have grappled with the changing meanings of leisure more strenuously, and to greater effect, than we have understood. Tracing the ways these writers helped draw ideas of play into a national discourse of cultural identity and also the ways they engaged and redefined ideas of work, particularly the work of immigrants, women, and African Americans, I argue that these concerns indeed animate their very narratives.

To a large extent, these writers responded not only to the temper of the times but also to an array of other narratives that hoped to direct the discourse on leisure and labor. Those included the writings of the play theorists, an eclectic mix of educators, social philosophers, and playground organizers who, in the face of the continuing decline of meaningful work, envisioned themselves rebuilding American society "from the play group up."[1] More than simply do-gooders taking charge of children's sandboxes, the play theorists spoke from the heart of the turn-of-the-century reform movement and exerted considerable influence on matters of social policy. They looked on literature itself, moreover, as a powerful instrument of instruction and invoked it as the common culture that in part made possible what they called "corporate consciousness." This book examines the multiple points of crossing between these theorists' own writings and a broad range of literary texts—including the work of Thoreau, Mark Twain, Abraham Cahan, Ole Rölvaag, Charlotte Perkins Gilman, Edna Ferber, James Weldon Johnson, F. Scott Fitzgerald, Theodore Dreiser, Richard Wright, William Faulkner, and Hurston—that often challenge the assumptions, implications, and in particular the corporate ethos, of play theory.[2]

By examining these crossings I intend to reorient current approaches to the study of play in American literature. Instead of focusing on sports fiction or on paradigms of "game-play" in American writing—long the main interest of studies in the field—I investigate the specific social, political, and economic histories that accompanied, and sometimes enabled, the rise of modern leisure. This is a necessary step, I would claim, if we are to achieve a fuller understanding of play and representation. We have seen this kind of interpretive practice turned to instructive use in studies of work and literature in an industrializing America. But play and leisure have yet to receive the same depth of attention, a fact I suspect has everything to do with the same hierarchizing impulse that tends to elevate labor over leisure because it is more "serious." *The Leisure Ethic* argues that we need to take the study of play in American culture as seriously as we do the study of work—and that we need to ground such investigations in more concrete contexts. We also need to move beyond the current dichotomy of leisure versus labor—not simply to avoid the stigma of hierarchy, but because what a careful look at the role of play reveals is precisely the historical inextricability of leisure and labor, both in the culture at large and, more specifically, in the textual representations that wrestle with, and then give utterance to, their meanings.[3]

My intention is thus to bring to bear on the literary analysis of play the methods and materials of American studies, cultural studies, and the "new" historicism. Accordingly, the contexts called forth here are many. I look, for example, not merely at the extensive literature on play practice and theory but at the spectrum of cultural forms into whose structures and meanings the new philosophy of leisure quickly insinuated itself, including advertisements, boys' books, photography, Fourth of July orations, household advice books, popular journalism, pageantry, and editorial cartoons. I also take up such pertinent subjects as city planning and the national park movement; domestic service and urban factories; club life and camping; professional sports and church-sponsored recreation. I stop to examine the social and literary responses to each and especially the places where those responses intersect—all in the name of exploring the ways that literary texts, as one critic has put it, "get involved" with, and in turn affect, critical social questions.[4]

The chapters that follow trace the influence on those texts of the simultaneous rise of corporate capitalism and play theory. After a brief introduction that situates recreation reform in its historical and ideological contexts, the first section, "Escape, Evasion, Ambivalence," examines the uneasy engagement of Thoreau and Twain—the two nineteenth-century American writers who would have the greatest influence on later iterations of play theory—with the early phases of both industrialization and recreation reform.[5] Chapter 1 reads Thoreau's visionary fusion of work and play at Walden Pond in relation to his deliberate and troubled exclusion of the immigrant Irish laborer from that very formulation, an anxious gesture that cuts to the heart of Thoreau's rhetorical identity in *Walden* and anticipates the later exclusions (and obsessions) of play theory itself. Chapter 2 looks beneath the surface playfulness of Twain's texts of American travel, *Roughing It* and *Life on the Mississippi*, to uncover a dead-serious concern with the effects of corporate capitalism and wage labor on the forms and values of both work and play. In particular, it charts Twain's growing identification with the independent American artisan struggling to maintain control over his means of production, consumption, and recreation. What Thoreau and Twain alert us to, I argue, writing as they did in an era still firmly pledged to the work ethic but beginning, in the face of an emerging industrial economy, to imagine new forms of self-making through leisure, is the possibility that there are no such forms of self-making that are not already tainted by the very labor relations they would seek to escape.

The second section, "Alternative Articulations," looks at reactions to play theory at the height of its organizational influence—roughly the years 1880 to 1920—and pays particular attention to critiques of reformist fantasies of assimilation, colonization, and control. Chapter 3, for example, examines the resistances articulated in Cahan's *The Rise of David Levinsky* and Röl-vaag's *Giants in the Earth* to play theory's reconception of American leisure as the new (immigrant) frontier. I argue that these two novels cogently crit-icize the reformers' ideals of selfhood and teamwork, ideals that drew on a suspect corporate vision of "team" identity that clashed sharply with immi-grant notions of ethnic identity, citizenship, and communal experience. Chapter 4 describes the merging trajectories of the originally parallel move-ments to reform girls' play and women's work in order to show how two very different "feminist" texts—Gilman's *Herland* and Ferber's *Emma McChes-ney & Co.*—challenge the strategies of recontainment that women seeking liberation encountered from theorists of both play and work. One might well ask why in each of these chapters I have paired texts from the same side of the debate, as it were; why not instead compare an immigrant text with a mainstream work or a feminist text with a patriarchal one? In one sense, of course, I have already done so: in each chapter the texts of the play the-orists serve as the mainstream voices against which I consider alternative ex-pressions of resistance. But by pairing Cahan with Rölvaag and Gilman with Ferber, I also mean to suggest the range of positions inhabited by writ-ers of ostensibly similar ideologies. As will become clear, the texts under consideration here (as in the next section) are in dialogue with each other as much as they are with play theory. Such pairings also reduce the tempta-tion to make any one text stand in for necessarily more diverse traditions.[6]

In the final section, "Whose Golden Age?," I track the continued resistance to play theory's homogenizing impulses as they moved resolutely off the playgrounds and campsites into the culture at large. This section examines both the so-called golden age of 1920s American leisure and its implosive legacy, the 1930s, two decades I see organized in part by a cultural fascination with the intersection of race and leisure, best exemplified in the age's urgent appropriation of blackness as a sign of liberating play. Here each chapter thus pairs two more writers, one African American, one white. Each chapter also confirms what the first four suggest: that no matter how much the play theorists might bemoan the soul-stunting effects of industrial labor, their proposed alternatives remained so indebted to the values of corporate capitalism that they compromised the reformers' claim that play would offer all Americans the autonomy, creativity, and control that work, in theory, had once supplied. Chapter 5 probes the critique of the implicit whiteness of the theorists' "ideal" body in Johnson's *Autobiography of an Ex-Coloured Man* and Fitzgerald's *The Great Gatsby*, texts that show the dependence of that ideal on the laboring bodies of racialized others by interrogating the dialectic of exhibition and concealment that structured the 1920s racial politics of leisure. Chapter 6 shifts focus to the working class itself to argue that the implicitly white body of play theory was also the implicitly white body of consolidated capitalism. Pairing Dreiser's *An American Tragedy* with Wright's *Native Son* in order to illuminate the noisy debate in the 1920s and 1930s over the "proper" disbursement of spare American time, money, and energy, this chapter shows how these texts narrate play theory's failure to reimagine the class and race relations nurtured by capitalist ideology. The final chapter compares the abilities of the female protagonists of Faulkner's *Sanctuary* and Hurston's *Their Eyes Were Watching God* to escape the crippling implications of play theory's enthusiasm for superintendence, ultimately suggesting that even in the midst of play theory's (and capitalism's) worst nightmare—the enforced idleness of the Depression—one might still, by turning to history and one's own imagination, discover both meaningful work and liberating play.

If this book hopes to redirect the study of leisure and literature, it also hopes to provide fresh contexts for reading some very familiar American texts—and at the same time to bring less well-known texts into the cultural conversation surrounding leisure, a conversation I have tried to expand so that it might touch, as play theory touched, the most urgent questions of the late-nineteenth and early-twentieth centuries. "The problem of civilization is the problem of leisure," insisted reformer Joseph Lee in 1915.[7] However critically *The Leisure Ethic* may at times evaluate the play theorists' motives or methods, its chief goal is to take play as seriously as the reformers did themselves.

ACKNOWLEDGMENTS

This book has been many years in the making and helped at each step by generous friends and colleagues, none more so (on both counts) than the incomparable Martha Banta, whose sustaining intelligence, unflagging energy, and inspiring example have shaped this project from first idea to last revision. Special thanks are also due Eric Sundquist, whose careful readings and thoughtful advice have made this a better book. Many others have read portions of the work that follows, talked about it with me, or provided the kind of support or guidance without which such projects rarely begin and never reach completion. In particular I thank Oliver Arnold, Eduardo Cadava, Michael Colacurcio, John Dalton, Barbara Galvin, Michael Goldman, Lisa Gordis, William Howarth, Carla Kaplan, Marge Kingsley, Kenneth Lincoln, Wahneema Lubiano, Debra MacComb, Douglas Mao, Michael Merrill, Lee Mitchell, Barbara Packer, Bruce Schulman, Elaine Showalter, Cécile Whiting, Stephen Yenser, and my colleagues in the American Studies Program at Princeton. In addition, I am grateful for the engaging commentary of audiences at the University of California at Los Angeles, Princeton University, McGill University, the University of Nebraska, the American Studies Association, and the Northeast Modern Language Association. My sincere thanks go also to my editor, Laura Bloch, for her caring attention to this project; to Michael Oriard and an anonymous reader for Stanford University Press for their extremely helpful reports on the manuscript; and to my copy editor, Janet Mowery, for her expert ear.

I would like to thank Amherst College, the University of California, and Princeton University for research and fellowship support throughout this project. Additional thanks go to the cheerful staffs of the University Research Library at the University of California at Los Angeles and the Firestone Library at Princeton.

Portions of this book have been previously published and I am grateful for permission to reproduce them here. An earlier version of Chapter 1 first appeared in *American Literature* 65 (Dec. 1993); a version of Chapter 4 first appeared in *Prospects: An Annual of American Cultural Studies* 21 (1996).

Finally, deep gratitude goes to my family for nurturing in me a love of learning, reading, and writing. And my very deepest appreciation is reserved for Andrea Malcolm, my spirited partner in work and leisure, and our son Jeffrey, who in the past two years has taught me all over again what it means to take play seriously.

CONTENTS

FIGURES

THE LEISURE ETHIC

WORK AND PLAY IN AMERICAN LITERATURE, 1840–1940

Introduction

Why is it that everybody is taking play so seriously to-day? Our
fathers considered it permissible within limits, something which
we might indulge in, something necessary, even, for young people in order that they might be the better prepared for work. . . .
But despite these admissions no one would have dreamed, a
generation ago, of a National Playground Association, or of
groups of sober adults taking counsel together in prayerful spirit
and with missionary zeal, to the end that they might spread
abroad the gospel of play! To our fathers that would have
sounded as blasphemous as a gospel of laxity, as absurd
as a gospel of sweetmeats.

RICHARD CABOT, *What Men Live By* (1914)

BORN FROM THE DEATHBED of the work ethic, spurred by laborers'
demands for more free time and the Progressive Era's belief that right recreation held the key to national regeneration, the American "gospel of play"
quickly became a matter of cultural necessity as well as public policy. What
would presumably have sounded blasphemous or absurd to Richard Cabot's
forefathers—the notion that one might shape a satisfying sense of self primarily through one's leisure activities instead of one's job—was fast becoming an article of American common sense. "It is true there are still many
occupations that are widely expressive of the human instincts," reflected
play theorist Joseph Lee in 1915. "But in the main, under our industrial civilization, it must with the great majority be otherwise. For every man for
whom there is a place among the expressive trades there are ten for whom
no such place exists." In the modern world of soul-deadening wage labor,

concluded Lee's colleague Luther Gulick, it is play that "has a greater shaping power over the character and nature of man than has any one other activity."[1]

The Leisure Ethic investigates not merely the turn to play, but the ways that American writers, in both implicit and explicit response to the play theorists themselves, struggled to make sense of the rapidly changing forms and functions of recreation, leisure, and sport. How, it asks, did these writers react to the hollowing out of the work ethic over the latter half of the nineteenth century? How did they greet the new modes and theories of play muscling their way into American cities, schools, and homes? How did they understand, and in turn represent, the effects of the shift from a gospel of work to a gospel of play on the ongoing formation of national values and "American" selves? Posed in this fashion these questions run the risk of making the cultural transition from work to play seem not only straightforward but natural, inevitable. It was anything but. Throughout the period covered by this study—1840 to 1940, the years that marked the rise, consolidation, and general acceptance of the leisure ethic—Americans engaged in contentious debates over the nature, meaning, and relative shaping power of work and play. The work ethic, if it went at all, went screaming and kicking. As Michael Oriard has argued, if cultural change in America has traditionally "been a matter of fits and starts, gropings and hesitations, sudden advances and abrupt recoilings," the history of the rise of play was no exception.[2]

One reason that I want to avoid the narrative of a simple shift from work to play—as dangerously crude a model of cultural change, Mark Seltzer would suggest, as "the claim that people grew things in the first half of the nineteenth century and ate them in the second"[3]—is that the turn to play simply did not unfold the same way for everyone. From the start, middle- and upper-class Americans had more time and money to spend on leisure than their working-class neighbors, whose own recreations they also frequently sought to police. White racism at all levels restricted access and opportunity, in play as in work, for racially and ethnically defined minorities.

For many American women, long trapped in culturally enforced lives of leisure (or idealized as leading such lives), meaningful work, not increased play, remained their most compelling goal. Women of color often rightly suspected that they would be among the last invited to join the nation's search for constructive play. As the American literary writers whose works this study examines hastened to point out, despite the earnest claims of play theory, modern leisure did not necessarily provide all Americans—particularly immigrants, women, and racial minorities—the "fullest attainable expression" of selfhood.[4]

Before turning to the texts of the literary writers themselves, however, we need to look more closely at the origins and organizing principles of play theory. Crucial to the chapters ahead is a clear sense of the ideological desires and practical methods of the late-nineteenth- and early-twentieth-century recreation reformers who, in the oxymoronic combination of sobriety and zeal that so astonished Richard Cabot, sought to give the American "gospel of play" its widest possible hearing. Lamenting the physical, moral, and spiritual decline brought on by the growth of cramped urban centers, the spread of unskilled labor, and the emphasis in American schools on head work instead of body work, these theorists urged constructive play as the nation's most important work.[5] Neither their laments nor their cures, of course, were turn-of-the-century inventions. Many of the play theorists' ideas and anxieties saw their first organized expression in the mid-nineteenth century, as health and fitness advocates struggled to guide a society being swiftly reorganized by changes in work and class status. It was at that moment, as the critic Michael Newbury has argued, that "exercise and sport came to be imagined among health reformers . . . not only as physically therapeutic but also as morally imperative, as a strenuous activity through which both the character and body of the newly affluent middle-class men and women might be conditioned."[6]

Catharine Beecher and Elizabeth Blackwell were two such mid-century reformers. Beecher argued throughout her career for the benefits of exercise on middle-class American bodies and souls. Both Beecher and Black-

well were particularly attentive to women's exercise, and Blackwell (antici-
pating the turn-of-the-century play reformers) was also interested in the activities of school-age children. Blackwell's 1852 collection of lectures, *The
Laws of Life, with Special Reference to the Physical Education of Girls*, voices
a number of concerns that the later play theorists would echo and amplify.
In it Blackwell argues, for example, that urbanization injures more than the
physical self. Besides producing the "shrunken limbs, crooked spines, weak
joints, and disproportioned bodies" one meets on "our crowded Broadway"—a common complaint about the bodily state of Americans by the
1850s—city living multiplies the "fearful amount of vice, misery, and disease" that "grows with our growth. . . . The larger we build our fair cities,
the more fearful becomes this pestilence of evil."[7] Like the later play reformers, Blackwell also criticized contemporary schools for their one-sided
devotion to the mind.

The Laws of Life similarly anticipates the ideological underpinnings of
play theory. Blackwell frames her project, for example, as a racial imperative
(meaning, for her, "American," but more specifically Anglo-Saxon and
Christian) and implores American mothers to "render" their daughters
"healthy and strong in body" so that as fit mothers themselves they might
reverse the rapid "degeneracy of the race." As we shall see, play theory
would conceive its mission in analogous terms. Blackwell also argues that
there is one "true order of growth" for all existences, especially human be-
ings, an order whose natural phases (of "preparation," "active use," and "decline") we disrupt at our peril and whose progressive model, as later re-
fracted through the child development theories of psychologist G. Stanley
Hall, the recreation reformers would mirror. Finally, the spirit of Blackwell's
urgent call for a "rational system" of gymnastic training as "the *basis* of a
sound education" would animate the theorists' passion for organizing and
systematizing children's play as the first step toward the vigorous revitalization of American society as a whole.[8]

But although one can trace many of the turn-of-the-century play theorists' concerns to mid-nineteenth-century critics like Beecher and Black-

well, there is still considerable philosophical distance between the two moments. Social, economic, and political changes over the latter half of the nineteenth century—changes with which writers like Thoreau and Twain struggled mightily—did much to shape the later theorists' principles. For one, "play," in and of itself, was never a mid-century objective; Beecher's and Blackwell's programs were largely restorative, designed to recover lost vitality, redress present imbalances (particularly of body and mind), or shore up uncertain class positions, but not in the name of play, which for most still connoted excessive indulgence or frivolity.[9] It was another thirty to forty years—as Americans fought for a shorter workday, grew more comfortable experimenting with leisure, and saw their work skills further devalued by the precipitate quest for technological and managerial efficiency—before an actual *ethic* of play could be taken seriously, not just for its value to the body but as itself a body of values.

There are also important practical differences between mid- and late-nineteenth-century approaches to leisure and recreation. The gymnastic training that Blackwell singled out for praise as "the noblest development of the subject of exercise which we have yet had" was the program of Swedish philosopher Peter Ling. But to later reformers, Ling's system laid "insufficient emphasis upon endurance, that capacity of heart and lung which we have seen to be of great importance."[10] Indeed, none of the popular gymnastic programs of the mid-nineteenth century met with the play theorists' approval. "Uninteresting" and "unnatural," sniffed Henry Curtis, cofounder in 1906 of the Playground Association of America. Operating largely by repetitive instruction and drill, gymnastics seemed the very antithesis of the play spirit. They might satisfy "the German people," Curtis opined—gymnastics first came to the United States via mid-nineteenth-century German immigrants—but not "us." And rather than achieve Blackwell's admirable goal of uniting physical and mental energy, argued Joseph Lee, gymnastics will not relate muscles to minds in the same way that play will. "The arm of a gymnast is a good arm in its anatomical aspect, but it is not the boxer's arm, nor the carpenter's, nor the violinist's," Lee explained. "It has large muscles; but it is not, except in the evolutions that produced it, the trained servant of the brain."[11]

One of the most fascinating documents to emerge on the road from Blackwell's desire for a "due balance" of body and mind to Lee's interest in trained muscles that serve minds is J. E. Frobisher's *Blood and Breath*. Issued in 1876 by the Goodyear Rubber Curler Company—and subtitled *A System of Exercise for the Lungs and Limbs. With Illustrations from Life, to Accompany Goodyear's Pocket Gymnasium*—Frobisher's ninety-five-page handbook is equal parts exercise manual, product brochure, and orator's anthology. Its multiple and sometimes contradictory agendas dramatize changing attitudes toward the place of leisure in American life in the later nineteenth century as well as the array of possible trajectories that the turn to play might, and in many cases would, take. Situated at the rough midpoint between *The Laws of Life* and the first codifications of Progressive Era play theory, *The Blood and Breath* signals the advent of new philosophies of play while nonetheless making vivid the ideological distance yet to be traversed. The Pocket Gymnasium itself was quite simple: a thin, flexible rubber tube with solid handles at each end that could be ordered in any of seven strengths. Basic exercises consisted of stretching the tube with one or both hands, either while standing in place or while bending the body, as in calisthenics. More elaborate routines might involve a second person (and a second tube) or require attaching one or more tubes to a wall with screweyes and hooks (included free of charge with model #7). "Be sure to breathe well, and to be in earnest," the manual instructs.[12]

Or better yet—orate. Frobisher, author of *Voice and Action*, wrote *The Blood and Breath* after discovering (according to his preface) that Goodyear's rubber tube outperformed other nineteenth-century "expedients" (including "Indian clubs, dumb-bells, and other appliances") in "restoring the power constantly expended in teaching Elocution" (3).[13] "It seemed to contain all that could possibly be desired," Frobisher recalls. "It was strengthening far beyond mere restoration, . . . not stiffening to the muscles and rendering them rigid and inflexible, like many other instrumentalities; but, being, like the muscles, elastic, it naturally kept them so. It also added suppleness. It was exercise of the true kind" (4). Frobisher devotes half the book to physical exertion, the other half to vocal, including a dozen selections of poetry, prose, and oratory whose daily recitation would "keep the lungs in good condition" (10). The most advantageous use of the book, he suggests, would be to do both forms of exercise at once: "to shout aloud, in *pure tone*, the sounds of the vowels or consonants, even words and sentences, and whole paragraphs" while flexing the tube (30). "See 'The Charge of the Light Brigade,'" he directs. "Recite it in full voice while exercising. . . . The lungs in this manner will be doubly strengthened against disease and the voice made richer and fuller, and more powerful" (30).

Frobisher's vocal training selections are themselves a study in (aptly enough) the arts of breathing and bleeding. The pulsing account of nobly met death in "The Charge of the Light Brigade" is almost fully representative: more than half of the remaining poems, for example, narrate gory battles and poignant ends. The complete mix muses broadly over questions of masculinity and nationalism. These were not surprising preoccupations in the country's centennial year, scarcely a decade removed from the Civil War, or, one might argue, in a fitness manual; what better stimulant to the reluctant exerciser than dramatic tales of nations and individuals turning their own powerful muscles to noble service? The patriotic stance of these narratives is graphically anticipated by the manly frontispiece depicting "Young America in Condition" (see Figure 1), an iconography that itself anticipates the turn-of-the-century robustness of a figure like Theodore Roosevelt, himself a young American in prime condition (recovered from childhood infirmities and just starting college in 1876) who would soon become an important spokesperson for—and virile icon of—the nascent national play movement.[14] One might also see the book's implicit interest in defining "True Americanism" (the title of an address by editor and politician Carl Schurz included as a vocal exercise) as a marker of the play theorists' subsequent efforts to Americanize immigrant children on their melting pot playgrounds. Certainly a recurrent emotion called forth by Frobisher's se-

THE COMPLETE GYMNASIUM.—YOUNG AMERICA IN CONDITION.

FIGURE 1. "Young America in Condition." Frontispiece to Frobisher, *The Blood and Breath* (1876).

lections is the sense of loss at the death of a child, particularly a male child, an emotion that might be said to underlie the play theorists' interest in shepherding American children (especially boys) through playful youth into productive adulthood.

Women and girls also appear in *The Blood and Breath*, both in the figure drawings that illustrate the tube exercises and in the oratorical selections, though these representations tend to work at cross purposes. The physical exercise portion of the book, for example, takes care not to segregate women from men or to sexualize them, unlike many later exercise manuals. Frobisher refers to his models as "persons" and illustrates a handful of the thirty-odd movements with female figures. The vocal exercises, however, depict women in more stereotypical guises: as patient spouses, for example (in Edward Falconer's poem "Anne Hathaway," about Shakespeare's wife), or garrulous shrews (in David Legare's "National Peculiarities"). One notable exception is the satirical verse "She Would be a Mason," which pokes merciless fun at "this ridiculous Mrs. Byrde," who wants to wear her husband's "pantaloons" and go to his lodge meeting, but nonetheless presents a woman eager to imagine herself outside expected roles. Much like the later play reformers, however, many of whom would seek to redirect women's extra-domestic energies into the safer channels of home-play and housework, *The Blood and Breath*'s final message to women is Goodyear's, not Frobisher's: the last page of the manual is a full-page ad for flexible rubber hair curlers.

It is in *The Blood and Breath*'s class interests that we may mark a crucial difference between the Reconstruction Era understanding of "the leisure problem" and the later play theorists' understanding, particularly in relation to changes in American labor. As in the antebellum period, health and fitness reform in the 1870s addressed a primarily middle-class audience. The chief concern of *The Blood and Breath* is the decreased vitality of the merchant and professional classes, whose increasingly sedentary, office-based brain labor (prepared for by equally sedentary student hours) was felt in no wise to substitute for the more vigorous work of the outdoor trades in maintaining physical health. One can surmise as much from the introductory pages of Frobisher's book, which include several illustrations keyed to no specific exercises but depicting middle-class men flexing their Pocket Gymnasiums at home or at work, while seated. One man, dressed in a lounging robe and slippers, leans back in a comfortable chair, arms overhead, assiduously stretching the tube (see Figure 2). Another drawing—which one

FIGURE 2. Exercising man in robe. From Frobisher, *The Blood and Breath* (1876).

FIGURE 3. Exercising clerk. From Frobisher, *The Blood and Breath* (1876).

might be tempted to call "If only Bartleby had a Pocket Gym"—shows a clerk interrupting his office labors to reinvigorate his outer muscles (see Figure 3).

What these illustrations and the surrounding text tell us is that in the 1870s health and fitness reformers imagined (or still wanted to imagine) that the leisure problem was a white-collar problem. Despite overwhelming evidence by 1876 that work in America had not simply shifted from the farm to the office but had been increasingly shunted into the factory and specifically into unskilled labor—a fundamental dislocation that Twain, for one, reluctantly confronted in his own work in the 1870s—*The Blood and Breath* offers its program as a cure for the "diminish[ment]" of "general manual labor" brought about by the transition from a brawny pioneer economy to the physically undemanding era of trade (26). But by the turn of the century, when the play theorists came to write their own manuals, it was impossible to ignore the very real presence (and effects) of widespread unskilled work. The recreation reformers knew full well that if "general manual labor" had diminished, *specialized* manual labor—under the pressure of unprecedented immigration and industrialization and bearing virtually none of general manual labor's supposed physical, moral, or spiritual merits—had massively increased. This does not mean that the play reformers stopped praising the benefits of manual labor, or that their play ethic, particularly its emphasis on "team play" and the "corporate personality," did not at times look suspiciously like the work ethic in disguise.[15] Nor does it mean that the play reformers did not address their handbooks largely to middle-class audiences. But it does mean, for example, that the reformers also turned their attention to the play of the working classes and sought explicitly to direct it. And most signally for my purposes, it means that as the changes to work in the latter half of the nineteenth century precipitated a crisis of self-identity for a growing number of American workers at virtually all levels of society, the play theorists met that crisis—with their playgrounds, school programs, and handbooks—by offering both the sites for and the legitimizing narratives of an alternative system of self-making though play. They did so not merely to provide what Michael Newbury rightly terms "recreational labor" for the middle classes—as one might say of Blackwell's *Laws of Life* and Frobisher's *Blood and Breath*—but to shape new ways of thinking about pressing questions of selfhood, citizenship, and national identity, questions that American writers were also beginning to connect to changes in leisure and labor. At stake was not the health of a class, but the soul of a nation.

■

I want to take up one more aspect of Frobisher's remarkable book before turning to a fuller discussion of the play theorists themselves and then letting (in the chapters that follow) the writers have their say. Although I have characterized the exercises in *The Blood and Breath* as forms of "recreational labor" for the middle classes—physical work that is not itself labor but that is meant to restore the "moral, corporal, and spiritual benefits" once provided by work[16]—Frobisher's handbook comes close in places to depicting the spirit of joyful, self-sustaining play lauded by the recreation reformers.

Consider again the middle-class exercisers depicted in Figures 2 and 3. Their heads lean back in almost dreamy stares; neither man is particularly focused on the actual exercise (with the possible exception of the robed man) but instead on some other space of self-expansion, self-discovery. Even the muscular "Young America in Condition" in Figure 1 seems to have his eyes and mind elsewhere, as though in anticipation of the "instinct toward an ideal" that Joseph Lee would later attribute to the play drive.[17]

If the men in these illustrations look figuratively toward a cultural moment that would take the ideal of recreation seriously, however, the more patterned drawings that guide readers through *The Blood and Breath*'s specific tube exercises anticipate a very different cultural turn—though one that would also find expression within the play reformers' systems. Looking only straight ahead or at their own motions, the men and women depicted in Figure 4 lack the dreamy stares of self-expansion common to the earlier illustrations. They are also not as individualized. Where one can easily distinguish "Young America in Condition" from "robed man" and "exercising clerk," these other figures are standardized replicas, the same people performing different exercises of one long routine. In their fixed stances and carefully arranged motions the pattern figures in *The Blood and Breath* begin to resemble nothing so much as the turn-of-the-century drawings that would emerge from the time and motion studies of industrial efficiency experts. Here's the best pattern; follow it. In this light, even Frobisher's directions begin to sound like factory floor protocols:

> Place r. h. firmly over, and arm resting on the head, with l. h. by side. Pull with r. h. above head to full extent and back. Then pull up again, and gradually raising l. h., and allow r. h. while tube is full tension to follow dotted line to side of body. This brings the l. h. to + on r. of, and the l. arm on the head. Now pull back reversely, full tension, to first position. Repeat five times. (35)

This could be a set of instructions for running a steam press. Indeed, many of the figures look as though they might be performing work, not exercising, as in "Fig. 5," "Fig. 15," and "Fig. 17." Some of the figures do illustrate

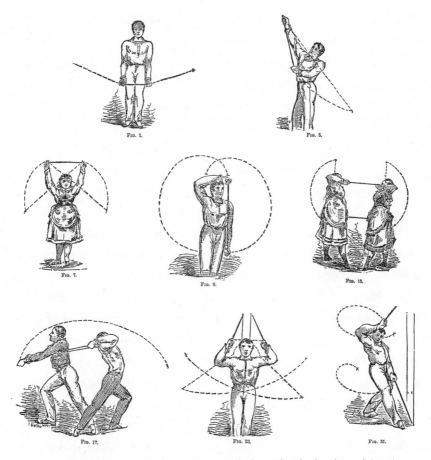

FIGURE 4. Tube exercise figures. From Frobisher, *The Blood and Breath* (1876).

more dynamic motions ("Fig. 31" has a particularly individualistic flair), but even those follow precise formulas.

In a number of striking ways, in other words, *The Blood and Breath* is torn between prescribing individual self-control on the one hand and larger-scale systems of management on the other. The tension between these directives gave Frobisher's book cultural resonance in the 1870s, when the United States was grappling, in sometimes bloody labor-management standoffs, with the implications of its eager embrace of boom and bust industrial capitalism. In *The Blood and Breath*'s prose as well as its illustrations, encomiums to self-regulation appear almost side by side with calls for institutional control. Even Frobisher's own exercise descriptions exhibit this inner tension. Though worded programmatically, the directions for some movements close by encouraging improvisation: "Add others to these," Frobisher directs in one (32). "Now change with palms as before, and pull, making up different exercises at will" (33). Or simply: "Additional exercises can be invented" (40). Perhaps the individual imagination can still come into play, these directions suggest; here's the system—but you are not necessarily bound to it.

In the 1870s, of course, the super-systems of "Taylorism" were still the inchoate dream of an apprentice pattern maker in Pennsylvania. But by the 1890s Frederick Winslow Taylor's efficiency studies were changing the calibration and organization of factory tasks throughout the country, and when the play reformers undertook to design recreational programs for playgrounds and schools they did so from deep within the culture of management, under whose guiding philosophy they sought to resolve in their own way the competing claims of work and play, self and system.[18] The play theorists not only brought an unmistakable zeal for organization to their recreation programs; they were also generally optimistic about work's role in the shaping of American selves and thus often slow to criticize the failures of modern labor. Curtis, for example, while admitting that monotonous industrial labor "is deadly to all that is best in man," protested that it is "only a stage," sure to pass as technology develops "more complicated machines" that will need tending by "skilled mechanics."[19] Others proposed more active interventions. Joseph Lee, recognizing that "even when we have done our best . . . there will still be many occupations in which the best part of the worker's nature will remain unfulfilled," argued that society must provide time, space, and structure for play, the only activity that will keep our souls "alive" when our paid callings deprive us of an "expressive life." And play is more than that: "Play is the word that best covers the things which [man] was wound up to do," insisted Lee (in an ironically mechanical metaphor), "in the doing of which he is most himself."[20]

Despite their rhetoric of self-actualization, the play theorists—Lee emphatically included—were not prepared to give the play instincts of individuals free rein. Inheritors of the same tension between self-expression and obedience to system that *The Blood and Breath* proved unable to resolve, the recreation reformers ultimately backed organization over improvisation. They could (and did) cheer the self-in-the-making that play helped to nourish and could celebrate the freedom, power, and creativity that, in the modern world, only the play-made self was felt to achieve; but they could simultaneously insist that that self was best constructed through the organizational and supervisory ethos of the planned play programs that they themselves designed. (This was felt to be particularly true for children's play, but the recreation reformers' social agenda was always much more ambitious.)[21] Even when they styled themselves as mere "play promoters" or as protectors of the small and weak from bullying "young loafers" who are "likely to smoke and swear and tell obscene tales" and into whose hands "the undirected playground is likely to fall," the play theorists could not disguise their commitment to a freedom tempered—always—by the needs of the social order.[22]

If I seem to criticize these reformers, I do not mean to villainize them; that job has already been capably done.[23] But in understanding the power of the cultural narrative the play theorists so strongly helped to shape—and that the writers in this study so strenuously sought to revise—it is important to be clear about both their ideas and their limitations. Why, for example, did the theorists insist on directed play? First, despite the widespread organization and specialization "going on everywhere," according to Gulick, "recreation remains the one great activity in America which has not fully felt that genius for organization which brings to play the advantages of human co-operation so characteristic of this century."[24] Second, although many Americans seem loath to admit it, American children, the play reformers held, do not know what to play. ("Teach the children to play? You might as well talk about teaching the little lambs to skip and gambol on the hillsides," sputtered an apoplectic congressman when asked to appropriate federal funds for play supervision. Replied Curtis: "When we have opened playgrounds in the great cities, the children have often come in and stood around the edges or sat down in the corners.")[25] Third, and most important, the play theorists regarded not the individual but the team, and its ethic of belonging and subordination—best nurtured, they felt, on the organized playground—as the most evolved human form. The "utter losing of [one]self in the team, merging [one's] own individuality in the common consciousness, is . . . an exhilarating experience," Lee asserts. It is "an experience not of self-sacrifice, but of self-fulfillment. It is the breaking of a band, expansion to a larger personality." As Lee says at the end of his chapter "The Larger Units of Membership" in *Play in Education*: "It is to the ennobling of the state in all its manifestations that we, the citizens of to-day, should consecrate our lives."[26] This is how the play theorists ultimately reconciled the conflicting demands of self and system: by redefining one's highest self to mean "team," not "individual," and insisting that the team-self is best created through systematic management.

For the recreation theorists, then, the gospel of play was itself subordinate to the gospels of belonging, of loyalty, and ultimately of civic membership. Consecrating oneself to the "ennobling of the state" might seem excessively nationalistic to our ears, but the play reformers were certainly not alone in praising the collective over the individual. Charlotte Perkins Gilman, for example, whose writings I consider in Chapter 4—and whose socialist feminism put her at the opposite end of the political spectrum from conservatives like Lee—often articulated the evolutionary significance of "society" in quite similar terms. "To feel the extending light of common consciousness as Society comes alive!" she exclaims on the last page of *Human Work* (1904) "—the tingling 'I' that reaches wider and wider in every age, that is sweeping through the world to-day like an electric current, that lifts and lights and enlarges the human soul in kindling majesty: To feel the power! the endless power!"[27]

And yet in the case of the play theorists, their white, middle-class, and predominantly male conceptions of just which "tingling 'I's" might be so lifted and enlarged to feel that power proved all too often distressingly small. It is of course true that few Americans at the turn of the century (as now) could be said to be free of out-group biases; Gilman herself could seem particularly obtuse in her attitudes toward black Americans.[28] But we should not wave away the play reformers' constricted sense of group membership simply because it was not extraordinary. Its ordinariness is what makes it so important—it is central to the culture that embraced the theorists' narratives of work, play, and the self. When the recreation reformers imagined collective civic life in America, for example, many of them pictured an Anglo-Saxon nation nurtured on Anglo-Saxon team games. Joseph Lee might have declared in theoretical terms that America can tolerate "no possibility of an excluded caste," but in practice he scattered ethnic and dialect humor through his recreation opus and crusaded noisily in public for the tightest possible restrictions on immigration. Those whom he could not convince the government to turn away, the "self-fulfilling" group ideals of play theory would (in theory) turn into obedient, Anglo-Saxonized Americans.[29] It was, after all, urban immigrant neighborhoods into which the play reformers poured the bulk of their financial, political, and organizational resources.

Though never in such direct ways, racial minorities were another constituency non grata for the recreation reformers. It is thus not surprising to find ideas of race at play theory's imaginative core. Lee dubbed the crucial preloyalty stage in play theory's developmental sequence (roughly ages six to eleven) the "Big Injun Age—the age in which the child wants . . . to show himself great and glorious and to be acknowledged as such." To achieve this greatness the child calls on the full force of his or her "primitive" energies and "predatory" instincts. It is the age of barbarism and anarchy, driven by a "sheer craving to exploit the bodily powers" and to experience the "visceral sensations."[30] By racializing this "natural" and expressly bodily rebelliousness as "Injun," the play theorists followed a long tradition in Anglo-American culture (in this case by "redding up") of projecting onto racial minorities a welter of fears, desires, and values that are intimately and complexly tied to white subjectivity, particularly white male subjectivity.[31] Viewed this way (as we shall see in more detail in Chapters 3, 5, and 6), play theory seems as invested in shaping turn-of-the-century notions of whiteness—under the strain of intensified racial antagonism and the immigration of "inferior" peoples from Europe—as it does in guiding play.

That this investment in whiteness (and permissible white "play") emerges in tandem with growing fears about the aggressive rise of industrial labor is by no means surprising. Historians have suggested that one of the functions of blackface minstrelsy, for example, was to present an uncomfortably industrializing white society with (in George Lipsitz's words) "a representation of the natural self at odds with the normative self of industrial culture." David Roediger argues that "minstrelsy's genius was then to be able to both display and reject the 'natural self,' to be able to take on blackness convincingly and to take off blackness convincingly."[32] Play theory's genius— in a society increasingly fearful that the normative industrial self might be *all there was*—was to turn this display and rejection of the "natural" self from an occasional act of cultural performance into an absolutely necessary stage in the socio- and psychobiological growth of the (Anglo-Saxon) subject. In play theory's strict developmental sequence one does not repeatedly assume and discard "Big Injun"-ness but instead puts it on to evolve to a higher stage of Anglo-Saxon "team" belonging, leaving behind "red" anarchy, in other words, for "white" citizenship. Pinning on a 1909 President Taft "I am for Playgrounds" button (see Figure 5) might have made this political embodiment both concrete and personal for the wearer; coupled with Taft's imposing image, his powerful (white, male, elected) "I" would not only represent the playground supporter's position but would literally speak for the wearer himself.

Girl citizens—who perhaps had a harder time speaking through Taft's "I"—had their own body politics to negotiate under the recreation reformers' systems. (Girls were held to follow the same developmental sequence as boys until at about age fourteen they veered off toward the "budding" of

FIGURE 5. The Washington Playground button. From the *Playground* (Oct. 1909).

"young-ladyhood.")[33] I elaborate play theory's conception of gender roles in Chapter 4; suffice it to say here that the narrative of American play was in the end no more comfortable with the "American girl" (or woman) than it was with peasant-caste immigrants from Europe or with America's "native" racial others. Though the often well-intentioned reformers professed to seek freedom, power, and self-fulfillment for all, the carefully organized recreations of the play movement all too frequently offered cramped conceptions of (and opportunities for) the actual selves it hoped to transform. One need look no further than Figure 6, a 1916 photograph of inner-city toddlers at the beach from the popular journal the *Outlook*, to see this contradiction on

FIGURE 6. "Fresh Air for City Children." From the *Outlook*, July 12, 1916.

unintentionally comic display. While no doubt these "tiny residents of New York's east side" were renewed by Coney's fresh air, I suspect that even the patient play monitor at the photo's left margin would acknowledge the irony of her charges' (tiny though they are) tightly basketed "sea breeze" outing.

■

If the Taft button testifies to the recreation reform movement's ability to mobilize political support at the highest level—and the "tiny residents" photo to play theory's ironic tendency to immobilize certain of its intended beneficiaries—both illustrate the reformers' knowing use of public relations and contemporary sign systems to advance their cause. Taft's imprimatur assured Americans that the recreation movement—which in 1906 had tapped then-President Roosevelt as the head of its own first honorary board—continued to merit national approval. The sea breeze outing picture was one of a flood of favorable photographs and articles about the movement's doings that found their way into mass-circulation magazines like the *Outlook*, perhaps not at the behest but certainly through the energies of spokespersons like Gulick, who understood the importance of symbols and knew how to make them stick. (Having designed the triangle emblem of the YMCA in the 1880s, for instance, only to see its adoption blocked, Gulick converted the holdouts by starting a magazine called the *Triangle* and distributing a thousand silver triangle pins to association convention-goers.)[34] Gulick himself wrote articles on play for the *Outlook*, as he did time and again for dozens of publications, ranging from specialized physical education journals (such as *American Physical Education Review* and *Physical Training*), to medical and scientific periodicals (including the *Journal of the American Medical Association* and *Popular Science*), to journals of news and opinion (*World's Work* and *North American Review*), to some of the most widely read magazines of the day (both *Ladies Home Journal* and *Good Housekeeping*). When he was not writing articles, he was popularizing the movement's core ideas through his well-received advice books, including *The Efficient Life* (1907) and *Mind and Work* (1908). Joseph Lee, for his part, was a vigorous pamphleteer.

This recognition of the power of words and images carried over into the reformers' own play manuals, for despite the often overwhelming emphasis on physical activities and the mechanics of games, the reformers' handbooks placed considerable importance on the role of art, and specifically literature, in shaping the ludic self. "Art is play in its intensest, most sublimated form," declared Lee; and literature "is as much an element in growth as air or food."[35] The play reformers not only praised literature in their texts but repeatedly invoked it, referring to fictional characters in one chapter, including a stanza of poetry in another. Sometimes literary references turn up in the unlikeliest places. *Campward Ho! A Manual for Girl Scout Camps*, for example, offers the opening lines of the *Canterbury Tales* as its surprising, if fitting, epigraph: "When that Aprille with his schowres swoote / The drought of March hath perced to the roote / . . . Thanne longen folk to gon on pilgrimages. . . . "[36]

It would be easy to write these references off as class markers, though surely they speak to the educated personas that the theorists wanted to project (and to the readers that they imagined as theirs). But these references work more complexly, for the theorists use them not merely to look well-read but to rekindle specific memories in their readers and, in the process, to activate potent emotions, beliefs, and values shaped by the common culture of reading. "You remember the rapture with which David Copperfield greeted the first sight of Mr. Peggotty's boat residence," prods William Forbush in his 1914 *Manual of Play* as he tries to explain the importance of imaginative play in childhood development.[37] What follows is a nearly paragraph-long quotation from Dickens's novel; you remember it, Forbush suggests—and here it is again. Not only did the play reformers regard literature as a resource and an ally, ably expressing (often in advance) the tenets of play theory; such moments of common recognition in part made the theorists' goal of a play-built "corporate" consciousness possible. At other times the reformers encouraged their readers to remember how they had once imagined themselves as the characters in their favorite fictions.[38] Literary citations in the play reformers' texts thus function as cultural reminders and social guides. They provide examples, confirm hypotheses, create analogies and, almost literally, convey authority. Writers and their texts are cited with such frequency in Lee's *Play in Education* that they stand on virtually equal footing with the scientific experts who more typically "authorize" the handbooks on play. Where literary citations were few, literary techniques were plentiful. Gulick, though not as frequent a quoter as Lee, told countless of his own stories to illustrate his points. Well aware that their books required "scientific" seriousness but that they also aspired to shape cultural values, the play reformers liked to emphasize that, like artists, they were interpreting the world, not merely recording it.[39]

But as *The Leisure Ethic* will demonstrate, the play reformers had no monopoly on either the interpretive imaginings or the real-world shapings of this cultural moment. Nor was literature always the ally they imagined. Into the fray came related but separate recreation movements (physical culture, social dancing); play sponsors from other fields (churches, industry); commercial rivals for America's spare time (professional sports, motion pictures, advertising); and, at every step of the way, equally powerful narrative imaginers of the meanings of work and play in American culture—literary writers themselves. Generally less optimistic and almost always less utopian than the play theorists and their predecessors, American authors told often strikingly different stories about the "proper" evolution from self to team, about the positions of immigrants, women, and racial minorities in the economies of labor and leisure, and about the relation of play to matters of selfhood, citizenship, and freedom. I am not proposing my own story of "good" writers and "bad" theorists, though most of the authors I examine do contest play theory's assumptions about work, play, and the self. What lies ahead is instead a close look at the contentions and confusions that the shift to play unstoppered and, in particular, the ways in which that shift came to focus the American literary imagination.

The literary writers whose texts I discuss represent no single viewpoint, style, or tradition. What they do share is a deep interest in assessing the capacity of both modern leisure and the new ideology of play to substitute for the fading American ideals of—or more precisely, the vanishing American opportunities for—individual autonomy, creativity, and agency. Each text, some more successfully than others, offers narrative solutions for the social, economic, and political pressures that the transition from "work's century" to "play's century" produced, often by strategically rewriting the narratives of the reformers themselves.[40] In what follows I am thus attentive not only to the push and shove of cultural contestation but also to the multiple and often idiosyncratic ways that literary engagement in such contests affects the shape and style of the texts themselves, even texts we think we already know well. It is this "due balance" (as Elizabeth Blackwell might say) of social history and literary criticism at which the ensuing chapters aim.

PART I

ESCAPE, EVASION, AMBIVALENCE

CHAPTER ONE

Re-Creating *Walden*
Thoreau's Economy of Work and Play

It is in obedience to an uninterrupted usage in our community
that, on this Sabbath of the Nation, we have all put aside the
common cares of life, and seized a respite from the
never-ending toils of labour.

CHARLES SUMNER, *The True Grandeur of Nations*

ON JULY 4, 1845, AS THOREAU ("by accident") "took up [his] abode
in the woods,"[1] Charles Sumner exhorted Sabbath-seizing Bostonians to
honor the "venerable forms" of the "Fathers of the Republic." "Let us imitate what in them was lofty, pure and good," declared Sumner. "Let us from
them learn to bear hardship and privation."[2] Although in one sense
Thoreau was engaged in precisely the opposite project—rejecting the "wisdom" of his "Mentors" (9) by beginning (on the national day of rest) his
own "experiment" (84) in living "sturdily and Spartan-like" (91)—he might
have approved Sumner's subsequent call for national introspection: "It becomes us, on this occasion, . . . to turn our thoughts inward, as the good
man dedicates his birth-day, to the consideration of his character and the
mode in which its vices may be corrected and its virtues strengthened.
Avoiding, then, all exultation in the prosperity that has enriched our
land, . . . let us consider what we can do to elevate our character . . . and
to attain to that righteousness which exalteth a nation."[3] How to "elevate
our character" had become a national preoccupation for 1840s America.
Thoreau biographer Robert Richardson suggests that Longfellow's Harvard
lectures on Goethe and William Ellery Channing's 1838 speech "Self-

Culture" helped spur this concern in New England. Critics have long read *Walden* as a record of Thoreau's own attempt at self-cultivation. Richardson, echoing Sherman Paul, asserted in 1986 that "self-culture became a major concern, perhaps the major concern of [Thoreau's] life, and increasingly he tried to reach behind the metaphor of cultivation to the reality."[4]

What Thoreau critics insufficiently acknowledge, however, is *Walden*'s more complex social and cultural heritage.[5] For Thoreau's ostensibly private retreat involved him in a series of very public debates over the cultivation of not only the individual self but also the "self" of the nation. At mid-century the United States was struggling to cope with profound changes in traditional economic and social arrangements brought on by the shift from an agricultural to an industrial economy. Along with other cultural critics such as Channing and Catharine Beecher—although typically in opposition to them—Thoreau tried to articulate a new conception of the relationship between labor, leisure, and self-culture in the face of the emergent industrial society. We can see this attempt even in the earliest draft of *Walden*, which he began at the pond late in 1846. But after 1846 the pace of change quickened dramatically, and a crucial accelerating factor was the massive influx of cheap farm and factory labor in the form of destitute Irish immigrants. In the eyes of many "native" Americans, these immigrants were welcome as useful hands but considerably more suspect as whole bodies. Seen as a demoralizing influence on the health and the very self or character of the nation, the Irish were simultaneously ignored and exploited, and sometimes even deported.

This chapter tracks Thoreau to Walden in order to read his visionary fusion of work and play against the more conventional imaginings of his contemporaries—and then to gauge the impact of Irish immigration on that vision itself. Where Channing and Beecher looked to bolster American attitudes toward mechanical and domestic labor by (in part) encouraging the therapeutic "exercise" of mind and body, Thoreau offers a fundamental rethinking of the relationship between work and play, refusing to subordinate one to the other but insisting that only their merger might truly regenerate the mid-century American character. As we shall see, by going further than his peers in granting play a meaningful role in the shaping of healthy selves, Thoreau anticipates by forty years much of the core philosophy of turn-of-the-century recreation reform and play theory. But of equal importance to Thoreau's status as the mid-century's most potent imaginer of constructive play—and what makes *Walden* a crucial starting point for this book—is his simultaneous anticipation of play theory's vexed relationship with American "others." For complicated social, personal, and rhetorical reasons, Thoreau discovers through the successive drafts of *Walden* that he must bar the arriving Irish from his new ideology of work and play, even as he comes increasingly to suspect that they may be the very laborers most in need of re-creation through leisure.[6]

For however much we tend to think of Thoreau as transcending the petty prejudices of his neighbors, the final version of *Walden* betrays a considerable anxiety about the Irish, particularly their influence on his reconception of labor and leisure. That economic pressures of another sort (namely, the poor sales of *A Week on the Concord and Merrimack Rivers*) forced Thoreau to revise *Walden* several times between 1847 and 1854—the peak years of Irish immigration and nativist anxiety—is in this instance fortunate, for it makes *Walden* an excellent test case for measuring the strain that mid-century immigration could put not merely on social critics but on their very texts. Anxiety about the Irish manifested itself in at times unusual ways; for Thoreau, it meant that while on the one hand (or, we might say, with one hand) he could in private write a letter for an Irishman "sending for his wife in Ireland to come to this country,"[7] on (or with) the other he could later that year publish as a central chapter in *Walden* the distressingly nativist-sounding "Baker Farm." What follows is an exploration of the social and rhetorical tensions that surrounded not only Thoreau's radical reimagining of work and play but also his careful reshaping of the mature but undeniably troubled text of *Walden*.

■

Early in Channing's 1838 speech he defines self-culture as "the care which every man owes to himself, to the unfolding and perfecting of his nature." This linking of economic ("every man owes") and organic ("unfolding") metaphors recurs throughout the talk. Every man must "cultivate himself," Channing says, to discover "within him capacities of growth which deserve and will reward intense, unrelaxing toil."[8] Despite the physical and financial resonance of "growth," this self-development for Channing is principally intellectual, moral, and religious. Thoreau himself had worked similar tropes into his Harvard commencement address a year earlier to caution against the rising spirit of business in the United States: "Let men, true to their natures, cultivate the moral affections, lead manly and independent lives; let them make riches the means and not the end of existence, and we shall hear no more of the commercial spirit."[9]

Although both Channing and Thoreau encourage a "manliness" that seems metaphorically grounded in physical strength—Channing urges his listeners to "build up" their "strength of mind" and "enlarge" themselves through "vigorous purpose"—each man at first resists making actual physical development a meaningful component of self-culture.[10] Yet in the 1840s Thoreau began to expand his earlier notion of a "manly" and "independent" life to include a healthy body. "I never feel that I am inspired," he punned on June 21, 1840, "unless my body is also—It too spurns a tame and commonplace life. . . . The body is the first proselyte the Soul makes" (*PJ* 1: 137–38). Six months later, near the end of January 1841, Thoreau turns this feeling into a directive: "We should strengthen, and beautify, and industriously mould our bodies to be fit companions of the soul.—Assist them to grow up like trees, and be agreeable and wholesome objects in nature" (*PJ* 1: 232). "Industriously mould our bodies" explicitly transforms Channing's earlier exhortation in "Self-Culture" to "strenuously . . . form and elevate our own minds,"[11] with Thoreau's bodies/trees subtly "elevated" by growing "up." Thoreau was gradually coming to insist in his journal that physical culture was a vital element of self-culture. By February 1841 he could further pun, "The care of the body is the highest exercise of prudence" (*PJ* 1: 272).

Thoreau's growing appreciation for bodily health mirrors the efforts of avant-garde educators who had been supplementing their otherwise traditionally intellectual and theological curriculums with new forms of exercise and physical activity since the 1820s. In the *Prospectus* for the progressive Round Hill School in Northampton, Massachusetts, for example, founders George Bancroft and Joseph Cogswell announced that they were "deeply impressed with the necessity of uniting physical with moral education," and they incorporated calisthenics, tumbling, and long walking trips into the daily schedule of the academy. Reform-minded scholars, especially émigrés familiar with the latest European educational practices, gradually established gymnasiums and exercise programs in other schools and communities. The gym at Harvard, for example, was founded in 1826 by German scholar Charles Follen, a professor of literature and close friend of Channing's. The German gymnastic method was hailed as a particularly appropriate model for an American educational system that was devoted to the study of classical literature and that already showed the influence of German idealism. "Look at Germany," one 1830s educator urged. "The same necessity which sent Plato and Aristotle to the gymnasium after severe mental labor, still exists with the hard students of our day."[12]

Although the formalized physical training associated with German gymnastics was waning in popularity when Thoreau attended Harvard in the mid-1830s,[13] taking its place were the nascent forms of more playful, game-oriented sports such as football, baseball, and cricket. And while Thoreau not surprisingly preferred the more solitary pursuit of energetic walking to the team sports breaking out at places like Harvard, his early writings show an enthusiasm for play that matches his growing interest in physical culture. Indeed, of all the transcendentalists, Thoreau seems most concerned with play. Orestes Brownson, with whom Thoreau lived for a short time, did give a lecture entitled the "Necessity and Means of Physical Education" in the 1830s.[14] And Emerson frequently incorporated metaphors of sport and gaming into his writing. "Be a football to time and chance," he exhorts in his journal in 1837; "the world-spirit is a good swimmer, and storms and waves cannot drown him," he writes at the end of "Montaigne." But even Emerson acknowledged that Thoreau put into more vigorous and playful action what the senior writer of Concord thought and felt: "In reading him," Emerson notes, "I find the same thought, the same spirit that is in me, but he takes a step beyond, and illustrates by excellent images that which I should have conveyed in a sleepy generality. 'Tis as if I went into a gymnasium, and saw youths leap, climb, and swing with a force unapproachable,—though their feats are only continuations of my initial grapplings and jumps."[15]

One of Thoreau's "initial grapplings" with the relationship between work and play came during his 1837 commencement speech. After voicing somewhat commonplace phrases about the "commercial spirit" in America, Thoreau described his ideal version of the weekly calendar: "The order of things should be somewhat reversed,—the seventh should be man's day of toil, wherein to earn his living by the sweat of his brow, and the other six his sabbath of the affections and the soul."[16] Not quite Sabbaths of the body— but just as Thoreau explored metaphors of physical culture in the early 1840s, so too did he begin to cultivate tropes of play. "Like overtasked schoolboys," he wrote in January 1841, "all my members, and nerves and sinews, petition thought for a recess,—and my very thigh bones itch to slip away from under me, and run and join the meleè [sic]—I exult in stark inanity, leering in nature and the soul" (PJ 1: 231). The image here is less childlike (or schoolboyish) than madly (and lasciviously) adolescent. The sly and almost sacrilegious malice of Thoreau's leer, however, yields at year's end to a decidedly less inane but still vigorous observation: "These motions every where in nature must surely [be] the circulations of God. The flowing sail—the running stream—the waving tree—the roving wind—whence else their infinite health and freedom—I can see nothing so holy as unrelaxed play and frolic in this bower God has built for us" (PJ 1: 350). In this last sentence Thoreau specifically challenges Channing's pronouncement in "Self-Culture" that it is "intense, unrelaxing toil" that deserves reward. Through his seeming oxymoron, "unrelaxed play," Thoreau defends unceasing play as infinitely more rewarding—because it is sanctioned by God—than unceasing labor. "The suspicion of sin," Thoreau explains, "never comes to this thought" (*PJ* 1: 350).[17]

In one sense, Thoreau's linking of the physical and ludic dimensions of self-culture recalls the metaphoric thrust of Longfellow's lectures on Goethe to Harvard undergraduates. According to Longfellow, Goethe's pursuit of self-culture made him "like the athlete of ancient story, drawing all his strength from earth. His model was the perfect man, as man; living, moving, laboring upon earth in the sweat of his brow."[18] And yet Thoreau, who even published his own translation of Pindar's *Olympic Odes* in the *Dial* in 1844, would soon challenge Longfellow's tropes—much as he challenged Channing's—as part of *Walden*'s fundamental reconception of the relationship between work and play. "It is not necessary that a man should earn his living by the sweat of his brow," Thoreau will declare in "Economy," "unless he sweats easier than I do" (71).

■

Most Americans probably did sweat more easily than Thoreau, if contemporary reports about the general fitness of the population are reliable. Americans have "spare forms and pallid complexions," Harriet Martineau observed with alarm in *Society in America*, written during her 1834–36 tour of the states. "The feeling of vigorous health is almost unknown. Invalids are remarkably uncomplaining and unalarmed; and their friends talk of their having 'a weak breast,' and 'delicate lungs,' with little more seriousness than the English use in speaking of a common cold." In 1855 Catharine Beecher lamented that American children had become "feeble, sickly, and ugly." She also claimed that of all the married women she knew in America—and she had been to "all portions of the Free States"—only ten could be considered healthy. The "active and industrious" Americans of Jefferson's first administration, as praised by Henry Adams in *History of the United States of America*, had degenerated into consumptive weaklings.[19]

Although both Beecher and Martineau offered more complex analyses of America's ill health, most commentators blamed an increasingly excessive devotion to business as the chief cause. "Americans work too much and play too little," complained *Harper's New Monthly Magazine*, "and would that it were only with the usual effect of making Jonathan a dull boy. The result, however, is worse than this, for it tells very seriously against his health and vigor." Exclaimed *Harper's*, "Look at our young men of fortune. Were there ever such weaklings? An apathetic-brained, a pale pasty-faced, narrow-chested, spindle-shanked, dwarfed race—mere walking manikins to advertise the last cut of the fashionable tailor!" "We are fast becoming," the magazine warned, "a nation of invalids."[20]

Certainly the quickened pace of urbanization after 1830, which brought more and more men and women into the burgeoning cities seeking employment, contributed to what the *Harper's* columnist assailed as the growth-stunting devitalization of American bodies.[21] And although Bruce Laurie usefully reminds us that the monumental shift from rural to urban forms of labor in the mid-nineteenth century did not empty America's farms overnight—as late as 1860 eight out of ten people still lived on the land and "more wage earners worked in farmhouses and small workshops than in factories"—we cannot downplay the effect on American labor of what Daniel Rodgers has rightly called the "startling transformation" between 1815 and 1850 from "an essentially agricultural to a commercial economy." As both Rodgers and Laurie report, the "expansive energy" of the antebellum economy increased production primarily in what Thoreau's contemporaries called the "household factory."[22] Families in country, town, and city spaces became increasingly enmeshed in the world of the market, and often with zeal, not regret. As one immigrant to America concluded in 1837 after ten years in Boston: "Business is the very soul of an American: he pursues it, not as a means of procuring for himself and his family the necessary comforts of life, but as the fountain of all human felicity . . . it is as if all America were but one gigantic workshop, over the entrance of which there is the blazing inscription, '*No admission here, except on business.*'"[23]

Of course American cities *were* growing apace; urban population increased by more than 60 percent in the 1830s and more than 90 percent in the 1840s.[24] And urban workers, particularly in northeastern cities like Boston, were increasingly offered alternative "fountains" of "felicity" to occupy their nonwork hours. Market forces cousin to those revolutionizing American labor nurtured in urban centers "a booming enterprise in commercial amusement," as evidenced not only by "the tremendous growth of the theater, the music hall, the dance hall, [and] the museum, . . . but also by the stunning popularity of amusement apostles such as P. T. Barnum."[25] Mid-century moralists like Channing and Catharine Beecher's younger brother Henry denounced many of the proliferating forms of urban leisure (especially such working-class amusements as cockfights, rat pits, and gambling tables) as desperate dissipations, more harmful to the body and the soul than chronic overwork.[26] Channing, whose original "Self-Culture" lecture was written for and designed to uplift a working-class audience of Boston's manual laborers, particularly inveighed against intemperance, which he felt "prostrate[d]" the drunkard's "rational and moral powers" as thoroughly as it bloated his face and palsied his limbs.[27] Thoreau's pronouncements in *Walden* that the common American was neither "alert" nor "healthy" and that an "unconscious despair is concealed even under what are called the games and amusements of mankind" (8) echoed Channing's concern that play could be as dispiriting an indulgence as work for many Americans.

By contrast, Americans visiting Canada and Europe were surprised by how much more healthy their citizens seemed. "Certainly no one can visit Canada," declared Thomas Wentworth Higginson in his vituperative 1858 essay "Saints, and their Bodies," "without being struck with the spectacle of a more athletic race of people than our own. On every side one sees rosy female faces and noble manly figures." Emerson was similarly struck by the virility of the English. They are "the best stock in the world, broad-fronted, broad-bottomed," he wrote in *English Traits*. "Round, ruddy, and handsome," the men in particular partake of "vigorous health." Emerson remarked, "It was an odd proof of this impressive energy, that in my lectures

I hesitated to read and threw out for its impertinence many a disparaging phrase which I had been accustomed to spin, about poor, thin, unable mortals;—so much had the fine physique and the personal vigor of this robust race worked on my imagination." At times Emerson was almost wistful: "Other countrymen look slight and undersized beside them, and invalids. They are bigger men than the Americans."[28]

At home, personal and national anxiety about the soundness of the "American" body moved in two related yet distinct directions. On the one hand, health and fitness reformers such as Sylvester Graham and William Alcott campaigned broadly to encourage people to eat more healthful foods (more bran bread and less salt pork), get more fresh air (through better ventilation and increased exercise), and drink more pure water. On the other hand, native alarmists sought and found a more human culprit, targeting America's own "foreign" population, particularly the Irish immigrant laborers who came to the United States in record numbers in the 1840s and 1850s, as lazy and sinful breeders of disease and vice that threatened the larger population. If Americans were slow to follow Graham's and Alcott's advice (and evidence suggests that they were),[29] they were even slower to recognize that ill health was as much a labor issue for the working poor, whose abysmally low wages prevented them from moving out of the pestilent slums, as it was for the "young men of fortune" growing pale in the nation's counting houses. Few citizens were ready to acknowledge with Boston census interpreter Lemuel Shattuck that health care was a social and not merely personal responsibility and that as much attention had to be paid to improvements in building construction, street maintenance, sewage systems, cesspools, and privies as to diet and exercise.[30]

■

If one book can be said to have shaped most strongly the course and discourse of health-related reform movements during the period, however, that text would not be Shattuck's *Report to the Committee of the City Coun-*

cil (1846), but Catharine Beecher's *Treatise on Domestic Economy.* The *Treatise* struck a responsive chord in 1840s America, offering a comprehensive program to restore national fitness and—importantly—national pride through both a systematic reorganization of domestic space and a complex of new attitudes toward domestic labor. First published in Boston in 1841, by 1843 the *Treatise* was in its fourth printing, had been adopted by Massachusetts for use in the public schools, and was being distributed nationally by Harper and Brothers. In all, the *Treatise* was issued in three editions and reprinted fifteen times between 1841 and 1856. As Beecher biographer Kathryn Kish Sklar notes, the *Treatise* established Beecher "as a national authority on the psychological state and the physical well-being of the American home."[31] Intended primarily, according to its title page, "for the use of Young Ladies At Home and At School" but articulating concepts that affected both genders, all ages, and all parts of the country, the *Treatise*'s forty chapters constitute an exhaustive reference book on nearly every aspect of domestic life, from food, clothing, and shelter to charitable giving, exercise, and first aid.

The lengthy first four chapters (almost fifty pages) justify to Beecher's audience both the writing and the reading of the book as well as speak to Beecher's recognition of the difficulty and the necessity of her project. The first chapter, "Peculiar Responsibilities of American Women," offers a sustained explanation of women's "exalted privilege of extending over the world those blessed influences, that are to renovate degraded man, and 'clothe all climes with beauty.'" Beecher draws heavily from Tocqueville's *Democracy in America* to support her two main contentions. First, much as Channing had claimed in 1838 that self-culture would mitigate (though not materially alter) the social subordination of the working-class poor, Beecher argues that a strikingly similar process has already mitigated women's social subordination to men. For, she notes (quoting Tocqueville), "while [Americans] have allowed the social inferiority of woman to subsist, they have done all they could to raise her, morally and intellectually, to the level of man; and, in this respect, they appear . . . to have excellently understood the true principle of democratic improvement." In no other country do women occupy "a loftier position."[32]

Second, Beecher claims, in her own words, an exemplary status for America: "for ages, there has been a constant progress, in all civilized nations, towards the democratic equality attained in this country" (10). "Already," she continues, "the light is streaming into the dark prison-house of despotic lands" (12). Thus "no American woman . . . has any occasion for feeling that hers is an humble or insignificant lot," because American women's labor, properly imitated, amounts to no less than the "regeneration of the Earth" (13–14). Beecher closes her exuberant opening chapter by declaring—in metaphoric language echoed in the "Conclusion" to *Walden*—that any woman, working at any labor, aids the greatest work ever committed to human responsibility: "It is the building of a glorious temple, whose base shall be coextensive with the bounds of the earth, whose summit shall pierce the skies, whose splendor shall beam on all lands, and those who hew the lowliest stone, as much as those who carve the highest capital, will be equally honored when its top-stone shall be laid, with new rejoicings of the morning stars, and shoutings of the sons of God" (14).

In chapter 2, "Difficulties Peculiar to American Women," Beecher cites as impediments to the building of this temple both the lack of a ready class of domestic servants (who would not arrive in sufficient numbers until after 1845) and the susceptibility of American women to disease. The first difficulty, Beecher suggests in chapter 3, "Remedy for These Difficulties," is actually a disguised blessing. If American women have to do their own housework, they will eventually—unlike the "frivolous" and dangerously idle ladies of aristocratic countries—come to revalue labor as ladylike, not vulgar (39). This becomes Beecher's chief goal in the *Treatise*: to redefine domestic labor as "refined and genteel" (40). The stakes as she saw them were very high. If American women continued to view housework as drudgery, they would fail to elevate themselves, their husbands, and their families—thus also failing not only their own country but (according to her premises in the first chapter) all the civilized nations of the world. Beecher also works hard to persuade women of the magnitude of both their duties and their capabilities so that they will value their labor as much as men do. She continually figures women's work in the language of American economics. In her preface she refers to women's duties as their "business" (ix); elsewhere these tasks become "domestic employments" (26). In comparison with aristocratic ladies—who do not labor at all—American women have paradoxically both "a loftier position" and "a more elevated object of enterprise" (15). Thus Beecher not only explicitly rehabilitates domestic labor as at once genteel, democratic, and Christian but also implicitly endorses the mid-century, middle-class ethic of enterprise.[33]

It is against Beecher's complicated position that I will consider *Walden,* but first I must detail more carefully the affinities of Thoreau's text with the *Treatise.* "Our lives are domestic in more senses than we think," Thoreau suggests sarcastically in "Economy" (28); yet *Walden* endorses or extends many of Beecher's views, particularly on the proper care of the body. Except for their rhetorical style, several of the *Treatise's* pronouncements on health would not seem out of place in Thoreau's work. "Medical men . . . all agree," Beecher asserts in "On Healthful Food," "that, in America, far too large a portion of the diet consists of animal food. As a nation, the Americans are proverbial for the gross and luxurious diet with which they load their tables" (77).[34] *Walden's* narrator eschews animal food—except for "a very little salt pork" and an occasional woodchuck—and in "Economy" he criticizes men who starve "for want of luxuries" (61), twice punning on the "gross[ness]" of American "groceries" (12, 64). Thoreau would also likely have applauded Beecher's plea for simple cooking; at one point she seems even to yearn for the ultimate in simplicity: "only one article of food, and only water to drink" (71). And he, too, rejects what she termed "stimulating drinks," such as coffee and tea (85).

Like Beecher, Thoreau also saw no more need for clothing than to "cover nakedness" and "retain the vital heat" (21). Beecher warns strongly against overclothing the body, just as *Walden's* speaker derides the "luxuriously rich" who are "not simply kept comfortably warm, but unnaturally hot"

(14). Thoreau's own morning baths and habit of early rising follow Beecher's example, although he attributes his regimen to more distant inspirations: "I have been as sincere a worshipper of Aurora as the Greeks. I got up early and bathed in the pond; that was a religious exercise, and one of the best things which I did" (88). What for Beecher was a prudent matter of cleanliness was in *Walden* ritual and spiritual renewal. Yet a daily full-body bath was something very few Americans took.

Finally, an intriguing connection between *Walden* and the *Treatise* is Thoreau's description of building his shelter and the detailed floor plans Beecher provides in chapter 25, "On the Construction of Houses." In some ways this is an odd chapter in the *Treatise*. In mid-nineteenth-century America, generally speaking, "Young Ladies At Home and At School" did not build houses. But their husbands did. And so Beecher explains to women how to explain to their husbands what kinds of houses best suit American families. She lists "five particulars, to which attention should be given, in building a house" (268). First, strive for "economy of labor": your house should fit your needs. "If a man is uncertain as to his means," Beecher suggests, "it is poor economy to build a large house" (269). For Thoreau, a ten-by-fifteen-foot house of old board sufficed, and if a man were "hard pushed," he could as well take up residence in a railroad laborer's tool box (29). Second, writes Beecher, seek "economy of money": prefer simplicity over ornamentation; avoid what Thoreau called "the gewgaws upon the mantel-piece" (38). Third, attain "economy of health," which to Beecher primarily meant proper "ventilation of sleeping-rooms" (273). Thoreau, too, bragged (like a chanticleer) that the wide chinks in his boards made his house "airy" and "auroral" (85). Fourth, provide for "economy of comfort" by using the biggest rooms for common use. Large kitchens, for Beecher, were especially desirable. Thoreau liked to cook in the biggest room of all—outdoors. Last, show good taste. There is propriety, Beecher noted, in proportion.

■

The foregoing is not meant to suggest that Thoreau threw in his lot with the reformers whose disparate positions Beecher collates and systematizes. On the contrary, he often ridiculed their projects. Though in demonstrable ways *Walden* adopts a reformist posture, particularly in "Economy," Thoreau perceived the lameness that too often afflicts reform. As David Reynolds has shrewdly argued, Thoreau "became the most compelling reform writer of nineteenth-century America" precisely because he "recognized *both* the promise and the perils of contemporary reform movements."[35] I will not reassemble here *Walden*'s invective against "half-witted" reformers (151); instead I return to the implicit question deferred at the beginning of the last section: how does *Walden* challenge Beecher's rehabilitation of American labor?

First, Thoreau would have been highly skeptical of several of Beecher's positions. He would have rejected, for example, her uncritical endorsement of the ethic of enterprise. As Leonard Neufeldt has shown, "the speaker of *Walden* manipulates the language of enterprise so as to acknowledge, parody, and counter the current language and behavior of America, to define his vocation with a logic of opposition, and to justify his art and life with the principle of '*extra-vagance*' (standing outside the circle of extravagant enterprise)." Although one might hesitate to see Catharine Beecher within a "circle of extravagant enterprise," Sklar notes that despite Beecher's emphasis on domestic thriftiness, the *Treatise* actually encourages "the consumption of goods as a means of promoting the national economy."[36] In "On Giving in Charity," for example, Beecher defends the use of "superfluities" in distinctly un-Thoreauvian terms:

> Suppose that two millions of the people in the United States were conscientious persons, and relinquished the use of every thing not absolutely necessary to life and health. It would instantly throw out of employment one half of the whole community. The manufacturers, mechanics, merchants, agriculturists, and all the agencies they employ, would be beggared, and one half of the community not reduced to poverty, would be obliged to spend all their extra means in simply supplying necessaries to the other half. The use

of superfluities, therefore, to a certain extent, is as indispensable to promote industry, virtue, and religion, as any direct giving of money or time. (161)

Walden's speaker, then, who wished "to front only the essential facts of life" (90)—and who charged that "there is another alternative than to obtain the superfluities" (15)—would have been glad to know he was threatening the national enterprise.

Second, Thoreau would likely have ridiculed Beecher's jingoistic designation of America as "the cynosure of nations" (12). *Walden*'s narrator notes with dismay the "popgun" echoes of gala day guns and the "distant hum" of martial music urging Americans to a war with Mexico he does not support (160). In the "Conclusion," Thoreau flatly dismisses such mindless champions of country: "Patriotism," he says, "is a maggot in their heads" (321). To Thoreau, who had used the same image in "Economy" to describe heedless (headless?) followers of fashion, the "ruts of tradition and conformity" were to be avoided at all costs (323). Thus where Thoreau's "essential" narrator threatens the enterprise of the nation, Beecher threatens what Neufeldt has aptly called Thoreau's more individualistic "enterprise of self-culture."

Third, Thoreau would probably have blanched at the dual ideologies of deference and standardization that underlie much of the *Treatise*. As I suggested earlier, Beecher accepts social subordination on the grounds that women are potentially equal to men intellectually and morally. In a sense, however, Beecher urges women to give up their claim to social power as a prerequisite for obtaining it. For not only would each woman, by assuming responsibility for raising her family the proper way, surreptitiously gain social authority within her immediate household; all American women—acting independently but in ideological concert—would exert a massive social influence. Beecher's book became quite literally a textbook, a blueprint for an insistent systemization of American domestic practice. No longer did each housewife need to discover for herself the most expedient, productive, or frugal methods of household management. Transcending region and class, Beecher's rules provided authoritative and programmatic responses to foreseeable events.

In a sense, by turning his back on Concord and heading for the pond, Thoreau, too, divested himself of social authority in order later to claim that authority in *Walden*, which is both an exuberant record of his stay and an urgent wake-up call for his readers. And yet Beecher's goal of subsuming "individual diversity in order to build a commonality of culture"[37]—of forging, that is, an American identity by promoting nationally homogeneous cultural forms—was no doubt a frightening prospect to the Thoreau who hoped that there might be "as many different persons in the world as possible" (71), who insisted that each of his readers pursue *"his own* way" (71), and who reveled in the "myriad" of forms created by the branching streams on the thawing banks of the railroad's deep cut (307).

Finally, where Beecher seeks to transform "vulgar" labor into "noble" work and "aristocratic" leisure into "democratic" industry, Thoreau attempts a fundamentally more radical reconception of the relationship between labor and leisure that anticipates the later theories of turn-of-the-century recreation reformers. Throughout *Walden* he insists that the healthiest approach to life is to make one's work and one's play as alike as possible. To Thoreau this did not mean sacrificing either the rigor of work or the spontaneity of play but rather combining them. This prescription flew in the face of mid-century warnings against idleness; but for Thoreau leisure was anything but idle. "Men labor under a mistake," he asserts at the beginning of "Economy" (5). And the mistake is that they do not take leisure seriously enough. The mid-century laboring man, who toils six days a week to earn his daily salt pork, molasses, and coffee, has neither time for leisure nor "leisure for a true integrity" (6). What Thoreau attempts in *Walden* is to show each of his readers how to turn the waste of "idle work" (57) into the profit of "free labor" (78), how, in other words, to convert life's "hardship" into its "pastime" (70).

These are no mean feats. But there is a significant pattern of just such reconfigurations beneath the surface of *Walden*. Thoreau rehearses over and over in this text a whole series of unexpected transformations of work into play not merely to demonstrate that in his own life labor and leisure were undifferentiated but expressly to counter the standardized, collective model of national "regeneration" offered by popular writers like Catharine Beecher. Consider again, for example, the image of the thawing sandbank in "Spring." The activity Thoreau describes on the bank represents not only a myriad of forms but a process of creation—of work—that is at its heart play: "When I see on the one side the inert bank,—for the sun acts on one side first,—and on the other this luxuriant foliage, the creation of an hour, I am affected as if in a peculiar sense I stood in the laboratory of the Artist who made the world and me,—had come to where he was still at work, sporting on this bank, and with excess of energy strewing his fresh designs about. I feel as if I were nearer to the vitals of the globe" (306). The deliberate juxtaposition of God's "work" and his "sporting," separated by only a tenuous comma, represents Thoreau's narrowing of the semantic gap between the two activities. In the next few paragraphs, in fact, the very word "labor" itself nearly dissolves, much like the famous sandbank. Thoreau deftly (if teasingly) exposes the multiple meanings of "labor," stopping just short of revealing that the word actually conceals its opposite meaning (306). For in Latin the noun *labor, laboris* means "work, labor, toil, effort." But the verb *labor, labi, lapsus sum* means literally "to glide, slide, fall down, slip" and figuratively "to glide by, fall away, decline, make a mistake." Thus "labor" means work, but it also means play or glide—just as Thoreau playfully skates across the pond gathering firewood in "House-Warming."[38] And Thoreau's unmasking of "labor" also makes us see that assertion from "Economy"—"men labor under a mistake"—a little differently. Men have labored under a mistake; men have played under a mistake; men have mistaken both labor and play.

■

But Thoreau's linguistic sleight of hand can conceal neither his desire that his project succeed nor the fact that he is trying to dissolve the distinctions between work and play at precisely the moment in American history when these activities were becoming more, not less, rigidly demarcated. One of the most striking results of the mid-century shift from the more seasonal work rhythms of preindustrial agricultural toil to the day-in, day-out wage-driven shifts of American industrial society was the stricter and stricter separation of "work" and "play" hours. I do not mean to idealize—as Thoreau often did—the preindustrial laborer as a self-sufficient worker entirely in control of his or her own time. As Robert Gross has carefully shown, only the wealthiest of antebellum farmers in Concord (and by extension, most of America) were able to achieve the sort of independence we have come to assume characterized every yeoman landowner.[39] I do mean to suggest that *Walden* betrays its anxiety about the obstacles to its project even more than we have recognized. More specifically, we can locate the source of this anxiety at the very human nexus—in mid-century American culture and in *Walden*—of the troubling issues of labor, leisure, health, and national identity that I have been tracing: the sudden and overwhelming rush of impoverished Irish immigrants to the shores of America.

The period during which Thoreau experienced life at the pond and then re-created that life in *Walden* covers exactly the years that the Irish presence in America triggered national concern. Between 1846 and 1855, the unprecedented era of famine emigration, at least 1.6 million Irish immigrants came to the United States. An overwhelming number settled in Boston; by 1855 between one third and one half of all Bostonians were Irish immigrants. Without adequate means or labor skills, the Irish were routinely exploited by employers. To survive, the new arrivals took backbreaking jobs digging ditches, laying railroad track, running spinning mules in textile mills, and cleaning the homes of Boston's middle and upper classes.[40] Even in Thoreau's Concord, the Irish who were not grading railroad beds were, like John Field in "Baker Farm," spading up boggy meadow land for local native farmers who wanted to grow English hay for the market.[41]

One aspect of this immigration that might have alarmed Thoreau was the defining role played by the Irish in accelerating the separation of work time from play time. The sudden availability of cheap unskilled labor was the crucial goad to Boston's urban and industrial growth. Before the arrival of the Irish, Boston's "rigid labor supply had made industrialization impossible," argues Oscar Handlin. "It was the vital function of the Irish to thaw out the rigidity of the system. Their labor achieved the transition from the earlier commercial to the later industrial organization of the city." The presence of the Irish also helped bring to pass what Gross has called "the revolution in the countryside": the ascendancy in places like Concord of modern agricultural capitalism—the large-scale production of agricultural commodities for city markets—without which "the creation of an urban-industrial society would have been impossible."[42] Each year between Thoreau's departure from the pond to become a "sojourner in civilized life again" (3) and the publication of *Walden*, more and more Irish laborers accepted jobs antithetical to Thoreau's idiosyncratic vision of "free labor."

Thoreau's neighbors, too, were alarmed, if for somewhat less noble reasons. Not only were the Irish believed to be physically unsound—threatening the native population with vice, disease, and ignorance (particularly, Protestants felt, in the form of Catholic doctrine)—they were seen as fiscally unfit as well, an unwelcome drain on the public charities.[43] Anti-Irish sentiment escalated as "prejudice, discrimination, and explosive collisions" became "the order of the day" in mid-nineteenth-century America.[44] In 1851, the peak antebellum year for Irish immigration, the General Court of Massachusetts passed aggressive legislation creating in effect a "frontier guard" against emigrants who might enter the state by land, thereby avoiding the services tax levied at the docks; those who "appeared likely candidates for public support" were denied admission and eventually deported.[45] In the words of Boston mayor Theodore Lyman, the Irish were "a race that will never be infused into our own, but on the contrary will always remain distinct and hostile."[46]

To what degree did Thoreau share the nativist sentiments of his neighbors? Did his desire for "as many different persons in the world as possible" include the mid-century Irish? The few critics who have looked in any detail at Thoreau and the Irish differ in their assessments of his attitude toward them. Frank Buckley concluded some years back that although Thoreau's portrayal of the immigrants in his journal, letters, and published writings is free "from religious and political bias," Thoreau himself could not be considered "a consistent friend and defender of the Irish." But George Ryan has asserted more recently that, despite Thoreau's frequently derisive commentary, "time and increased exposure . . . improved Thoreau's attitude toward the Irish, an ethnic group he could not, at first, quite fully understand." Particularly after 1850, Ryan argues, Thoreau—who not only "performed works of charity among the immigrants" but also wrote letters for them and solicited funds "with which to bring family members out to America"—was, as Walter Harding put it, "one Yankee" that the Irish "could depend on."[47]

Rather than retry Thoreau here in an effort to settle the debate between Ryan and Buckley, I want to focus on the historical and literary circumstances that seem to allow each critic to be, in a sense, correct. Granting Ryan's conclusions about the post-1850 Thoreau (90 percent of all Thoreau's "propitious remarks" about the Irish occur between 1850 and 1857),[48] doesn't *Walden*—taken by itself—support Buckley's position? In other words, if we know that Thoreau's attitude toward the Irish changed significantly for the better after 1850—during the years in which he dramatically revised the text of *Walden*—why does *Walden*'s attitude toward the Irish remain at best inconsistent? If the longest "Irish" entries in Thoreau's journal after 1850 concern young Johnny Riordan, whom Thoreau not only observed with sensitivity and respect but also helped clothe during the chill winter of 1851–52, why doesn't Johnny seem to make any impression on the multiple drafts of *Walden*? Why are James Collins (in his dank shanty), John Field (and his boggy ways), and Hugh Quoil (with his DTs) the text's most prominent Irish figures? Why, to paraphrase Thoreau's famous query near the beginning of "Brute Neighbors," do precisely these objects make *Walden*'s world? Or to put it another way: why does Thoreau make *Walden* say John Field instead of Johnny Riordan?[49]

The answers to these questions take us to the heart of both the larger project of *Walden* and the construction of Thoreau's rhetorical identity within the text. We need first to consider the nature of the additions and revisions that Thoreau made with respect both to the Irish and to relevant questions of labor and leisure during what Robert Sattelmeyer has classified as the second major phase of the composition of *Walden*, namely the four successive drafts written between 1852 and 1854.[50] In general, Thoreau's changes during this period work in two directions at once. To "Economy," whose original Irish references were generally derisive, Thoreau added several passages that more thoughtfully critique the contemporary practices responsible for the conditions his first draft had mocked. For example, as though to mitigate the 1847 manuscript's description of Collins's "uncommonly fine" shanty—which was "dark, . . . dank, clammy, and aguish" and reminded Thoreau of a "compost heap" (43)—and its brief anecdote about the treacherous neighbor and nail thief Seeley, "an Irishman" (44), Thoreau added this lengthy passage in 1852:

> It is a mistake to suppose that, in a country where the usual evidences of civilization exist, the condition of a very large body of the inhabitants may not be as degraded as that of savages. I refer to the degraded poor, not now to the degraded rich. To know this I should not need to look farther than to the shanties which every where border our railroads, that last improvement in civilization; where I see in my daily walks human beings living in sties, and all winter with an open door, for the sake of light, without any visible, often imaginable, wood pile, and the forms of both old and young are permanently contracted by the long habit of shrinking from cold and misery, and the development of all their limbs and faculties is checked. It certainly is fair to look at that class by whose labor the works which distinguish this generation are accomplished. (34–35)

Here Thoreau indicts the exploitative labor practices that create shanties like the one whose boards he had condescendingly purchased from James Collins. Playing somewhat on the false hierarchy of terms like "civilized" and "savage," Thoreau more explicitly puns on the passage's two central descriptive terms. First, the Irish are "degraded," shaved ruthlessly down, just as they themselves grade the slopes for the railroad; second, they are "permanently contracted," not merely shrunken by cold and want but locked into rapacious labor agreements.[51] These are the other "works" that "distinguish" Thoreau's "generation," which, he will remind us in another 1852 addition to "Economy," has witnessed "the fall from the farmer to the operative," a fall as "great and memorable as that from the man to the farmer" (64).

It is fitting that Thoreau's observations of the Irish laborers take place during his daily exercise, for *Walden*'s attitude toward contemporary leisure also comes into focus during these years. For example, 1852 marks the first appearance in *Walden* of Thoreau's indictment of the "unconscious despair" beneath the so-called games of mankind (8). And in 1853 he introduces into "Higher Laws" his preference for "the more primitive but solitary amusements of hunting fishing and the like" (211). But between 1852 and 1854 Thoreau also added to *Walden* some of the more objectionable assertions about immigrants in general and the Irish in particular. In 1852, for example, the same year Thoreau critiqued the degradation inflicted on the poor, he added a fairly uncomplimentary passage about the Irish who had "built their sties" by the pond (192), seeming to blame them along with the railroad instead of distinguishing them from it. And in 1852 and 1853 Thoreau worked into the text his largely unflattering description of Quoil—the prototypical Irish ditchdigger and drunk, with his "carmine" face and his tick-ridden garden (262)—as well as the potentially offensive naturalist/nativist reflections in the opening to "Baker Farm" about the "halo of light" that appears after a rain around the shadows of everyone except "some Irishmen" (202).

"Baker Farm," in fact, is a crucial chapter to decipher in regard to the Irish, for the passages on John Field and his seemingly hopeless family constitute the most detailed and most negative treatment of immigrants in *Walden*. The chapter is also vexing: nearly every leaf on which these specific passages probably appeared is missing from the original 1847 manuscript. Yet we can make some judgments about Thoreau's probable development of and plans for the chapter by consulting the August 23, 1845, journal entry that records his original encounter with the Fields. In that entry, Thoreau's description roughly matches the published text of *Walden*, from his seeking fish and getting caught in a downpour to his taking refuge in the Fields' hut and hearing John's naively cheerful "story" of hard labor for subsistence wages (*PJ* 2: 176). Although the largely negative descriptions of Field as "shiftless," his wife as "greasy," and their infant as "wrinkled" and "sibyl-like" do appear in the journal, one significant addition to that record (which may or may not have been made in the 1847 text) reads: "There we sat together under that part of the roof which leaked the least, while it showered and thundered without. I had sat there many times of old before the ship was built that floated this family to America" (204). This addition is telling because it epitomizes the recurrent tension between proximity and distance that structures the chapter. The first sentence suggests a certain closeness engendered by shared adverse circumstances: Thoreau sits within the hut, huddled "together" with the Fields, trying to stay dry. But the second sentence, its accents falling on "*many* times of old" and "*this* family," seems suspiciously proto-nativist, metaphorically separating Thoreau from the Fields, almost imaginatively returning them to Ireland.

Then, in a long section that also appears in the journal, Thoreau tries to collapse what he perceives as the source of the gap between himself and the Fields by narrating his own "experience." If the Fields could only approach life more like Thoreau himself, they would become his "nearest neighbors" in the most welcome sense (205). But after the lengthy enumeration of what food and drink to exclude from their diet and why—an able critique of the complicity between market economies and political economies that reintroduces an insistent theme from "Economy"—Thoreau snidely despairs of ever communicating the fundamental assumptions of his project to such as John Field: "But alas!" he exclaims. "The culture of an Irishman is an enterprise to be undertaken with a sort of moral bog hoe" (205–6). Even though such a remark effectively stiff-arms Field as a would-be convert to or reader of Thoreau's program—a few pages later Thoreau "trust[s]" that Field "does not read this" (208)—this sentence, like the one about the ship, begins in sympathy ("But alas!") before retreating into sarcastic remoteness. After one more brief run at the family's methods of getting, Thoreau fairly runs from the hut itself back into the woods.

During this retreat from the Fields, Thoreau experiences a brief but intense moment of doubt about the wisdom of his chosen course of life. For an "instant" his own boggy ways appear "trivial" for someone "who had been sent to school and college." But Thoreau, "with the rainbow over [his] shoulder, and some faint tinkling sounds borne to [his] ear through the cleansed air," overcomes this doubt by putting as much distance between himself and John Field as possible. Go "farther and wider," Thoreau's "Good Genius" tells him. "Take shelter under the cloud, while they [presumably people like John Field, or even Thoreau at the beginning of the chapter] flee to carts and sheds. Let not to get a living be thy trade, but thy sport" (207). Even when John Field rematerializes at the end of the chapter, having decided to join Thoreau and fish instead of "bog," Thoreau emphasizes the irreducible gap between them. They angle from the same boat but not the same philosophy; thus Thoreau catches "a fair string" while Field only a "couple of fins"—even when they swap seats—as though they were in separate boats or on separate ponds (208). And that mid-expedition seat-switching, which closes the chapter, mocks in its ineffectiveness not only Field's attempt to get closer to Thoreau but also the very careful, cooperative effort that an exchange of places in a small boat inevitably requires.[52]

Why would the Thoreau whose attitudes toward the Irish were broadening in the 1850s retain passages like these and even intensify them? At a minimum, Field's persistent presence in the text—from the journal to the 1847 manuscript to the final edition—suggests that Thoreau saw the bog farmer from the start as something of an emblematic foil, someone against whom to construct his narrator's identity as, in the words of his Good Genius, a "free" person bound to "seek adventures," not markets (207). The decision to intensify the encounter—to turn a single journal entry into an elaborate set piece in which the narrator invests so much of himself in attempting to aid the Fields that his failure occasions serious self-doubt—was probably made as early as 1847. We know, for example, that Thoreau added to that manuscript the sentences that describe the narrator's doubt and link the Good Genius's instructions explicitly to that sudden sense of failure. We can then surmise that Thoreau simultaneously expanded the encounter with the Fields to include the lengthy (yet vain) account of his own life in order to justify through narrative his subsequent doubt.[53]

What may have prevented Thoreau from modifying his portrayal of the Fields after 1850 was his decision during the second major phase of revision to make "Baker Farm" a more structurally pivotal chapter. The Fields material that appears in the 1847 draft, in which there were no chapter divisions, comes very late in the manuscript, but in the 1854 *Walden* "Baker Farm" is considerably more central: it is the tenth chapter out of eighteen, the first chapter of the second half of the book. In the revised text the Good Genius's urgings represent a renewed call to commitment, resolving whatever doubt the first half of the book may have engendered and moving forthrightly ahead toward "Spring" and the "Conclusion." Thoreau could thus hardly de-intensify the exasperating encounter that crystallized this doubt, which in its turn occasioned the introspective reaffirmation. In the revised version, then, the narrator's identity is even more sharply tied to John Field's and even more strongly requires Field's obtuseness.

And yet while in an odd sense "Baker Farm" holds the two halves of *Walden* together largely by depicting John Field as an Irishman apart, by the 1850s Thoreau seems uncomfortable enough with his characterization of Field to have tried, with mixed results, to soften its edges. In "Spring," for example, when the narrator declares that "in a pleasant spring morning all men's sins are forgiven" and that "through our *own* recovered innocence we discern the innocence of our neighbors" (314, emphasis added), he seems almost to acknowledge Thoreau's guilt over the earlier portrayal of his "nearest neighbor" and figuratively, though at best obscurely, to welcome John Field back into the book.

At about the same time that Thoreau placed this near-apology in "Spring" he also tinkered with the immediate frame of "Baker Farm" itself.

First, although he added the seeming slur about the unworthiness of "some Irishmen" whose shadows "had no halo," he made a point of putting that comment in the mouth of a visitor to Walden ("One who visited me declared that . . . ") and then followed it with a long digression that seems to challenge the whole idea of shadow-election as the "superstition" of "an excitable imagination" (202). Second, after leaving Baker Farm to explore in "Higher Laws" the competing claims of sensuality and purity, Thoreau suddenly introduces the enigmatic figure of John Farmer, who, though not identified as Irish, seems symbolically kin to John Field. Farmer, however, experiences an awakening to—or more accurately, toward—self-culture that is explicitly denied Field:

> John Farmer sat at his door one September evening, after a hard day's work, his mind still running on his labor more or less. Having bathed he sat down to recreate his intellectual man. . . . He had not attended to the train of his thoughts long when he heard some one playing on a flute, and that sound harmonized with his mood. Still he thought of his work. . . . But the notes of the flute came home to his ears out of a different sphere from that he worked in, and suggested work for certain faculties which slumbered in him. They gently did away with the street, and the village, and the state in which he lived. (221–22)

Much like Thoreau washed by the rain before the advent of his Good Genius in "Baker Farm," the cleansed Farmer hears music in the air that prepares him to receive a new message: "Why do you stay here and live this mean moiling life, when a glorious existence is possible for you?" Unlike Thoreau, Farmer is unable "actually [to] migrate thither"; but the chapter ends with the possibility of redemptive self-cultivation still thick in the air, as Farmer "practice[s] some new austerity," letting "his mind descend into his body and redeem it, and treat[ing] himself with ever increasing respect" (222). Through the symbolic redemption of John Farmer, Thoreau may subtly extend the same possibility to John Field—albeit without his wife and children—a possibility that the rhetorical requirements of "Baker Farm" itself refused to allow.

For all its revisions, however, *Walden* still does not welcome little Johnny Riordan into its pages. Even though the longest of Thoreau's several journal entries on Johnny occurs when Thoreau was "engrossed" in the first revisions of the second phase of *Walden* (including the revisions just detailed above),[54] even though Thoreau was pulling considerable material from the journal pages around Johnny into the text, and even though Johnny "dares to live" (*PJ* 4: 216) and his "greater independence" and "closeness to nature" (*PJ* 3: 155) square exactly with Thoreau's larger project, Johnny cannot wedge his way into *Walden* to displace or even comment upon Thoreau's treatment of John Field. If Sattelmeyer is correct in arguing that Thoreau's decision to let stand certain inconsistencies created by his revisions to *Walden* is "a mark of [his] maturity as a writer,"[55] then what do these apparent evasions mark?

To a certain extent they indicate that the same issues of self-identity that so strongly shaped "Baker Farm" are still at work at the end of *Walden*. From one angle the story of Johnny, as Thoreau shaped it in the journal, threatens to undo too much of the crucial rhetorical work accomplished by the treatment of John Field in "Baker Farm." For by emphasizing Johnny's determination to educate himself—he goes to school no matter how cold it is—and in general to meet the world as bravely as possible, Thoreau was in the early 1850s rewriting the pessimistic ending to that chapter, in which the narrator asserts that Field, "with his inherited Irish poverty or poor life, his Adam's grandmother and boggy ways, [will] not . . . rise in this world, he nor his posterity, till their wading webbed bog-trotting feet get *talaria* to their heels" (209). In the journal, Johnny figuratively becomes John Field's posterity; as a four-year-old in 1850, Johnny represents Field's "poor starveling brat" coming of age. And far from wading webfooted through the bogs, Johnny, "lively as a cricket," scampers past the wealthier and more ducklike Concordians who "waddle about cased in furs" (*PJ* 4: 216).

In another sense, the remarkable extent to which Thoreau himself was coming to identify with Johnny in the journal equally threatens to undermine the mature autonomy toward which Thoreau's narrator was struggling. Not only does Johnny receive a winter coat from Thoreau, but the journal records that the "countless patches" on Johnny's other clothes—and perhaps the clothes themselves—"hailed from—claimed descent from were originally identical with pantaloons of mine—" (*PJ* 4: 298). Even in this brief description Thoreau modulates from kinship ("hailed from") toward paternity ("claimed descent from") to an anxious identity. Elsewhere in the journal Thoreau imagines himself *as* Johnny; he even composes a multistanza folk ballad—"I am the little Irish boy / That lives in the shanty / I am four years old today / And shall soon be one and twenty" (*PJ* 3: 155–56)—that purports to sing of life through Johnny's eyes.[56] But while we may be tempted to see in *Walden* traces of Johnny's vivid journal presence,[57] the revised text as a whole moves toward an ethic of self-exploration that—however strong Thoreau's fascination with "the little Irish boy"—could only awkwardly admit a last-minute alter ego, especially an Irish one, to its "private sea" (321). "Let every one mind his own business," Thoreau insists in the "Conclusion," "and endeavor to be what he was made" (326).

Of course by keeping Johnny out of *Walden*, Thoreau willfully disregards one of the key lessons of his Good Genius in "Baker Farm": "We should come home from far, from adventures, and perils, and discoveries every day, with new experience and character" (208). Whatever discoveries Thoreau made about the Irish after 1850, he did not bring all of them "home" to *Walden*. But he did bring them to the journal, and it is literally among those pages that another reason for Johnny's absence suggests itself. For "inclosed between the leaves of one of the journals," remark the editors of the 1906 journal in a footnote to the January 28, 1852, entry on Johnny, lay "some loose sheets of manuscript" containing a "more complete sketch of the little Irish boy, made up, with some revision, from the original entries."[58] If Thoreau had other publication plans for the Riordan material—to issue it as a separate sketch, for example, or as part of some other work—then we might see his decision to exclude Johnny from *Walden* as an attempt to exert some control over both his literary product and the market in which he had to trade it.[59] This would have been a brave attempt in mid-century America, for all around Thoreau the expanding commercial and industrial markets were systematically undermining most forms of autonomous living.[60]

Nonetheless, the public text of *Walden* by and large bars the Irish from the new ideology of work and play that Thoreau was attempting to formulate. If the arrival of cheap (and cheapened) labor gave Thoreau's project a special urgency by accelerating the industrialization of New England, the continued presence of that labor also threatened his project's success. The Irish were paradoxically both unwelcome and essential: in the end, Thoreau can only make his case for "free labor" and "unrelaxed play" by contrasting those ideals to the joyless, wage-bound toil he saw around him. As "the most powerful and articulate critic of agricultural capitalism that America produced in the decades before the Civil War," Thoreau demonstrated an astute understanding of the effect that market forces had on individual Americans.[61] But as the most important mid-century American theorist of the relationship between work and play, he found himself in both a political and a rhetorical bind. Thoreau may have hoped to live outside the "restless, nervous, bustling, trivial Nineteenth Century" (329), but his anxious revisions to *Walden* suggest that he was in it (at least) up to his pantaloons.

CHAPTER TWO

Old Ways, New Ways

Anxiety and Identity in
Roughing It and *Life on the Mississippi*

DURING THE SUMMER OF 1876, while nearly 8 million tourists trooped through Machinery Hall at Philadelphia's Centennial Exposition to behold the amassed marvels of American industry, Mark Twain was closeted away in Elmira, New York, "tearing along on a new book" anchored more firmly in America's preindustrial past.[1] Because *Adventures of Huckleberry Finn* would in due time become a national icon itself, it seems fitting that Twain first eased Huck and Jim into the Mississippi at a time of national celebration. Yet Twain's own progress on the novel was anything but smooth; the text, for example, would require eight years of fitful writing to complete. And the Huck Finn whom Twain was fashioning would be unlikely to embrace the "battery of technology" on display in Philadelphia as enthusiastically as its sightseers.[2] Certainly no one as wary of "sivilisation" as Huck would wait for hours in the pouring rain—as 100,000 eager first-day visitors did in May of 1876—to wander among fourteen acres of mechanical devices.

But Huck's creator (not so much the writer who needed semirural isolation to complete his novel but the inventor-entrepreneur who would eventually sink nearly $200,000 and fifteen frustrating years into the Paige typesetter) might have been intrigued by a "museum to American ingenuity." There is no record that Twain ever attended the exposition; and unlike William Dean Howells (who did attend), he never wrote explicitly of it.[3] But Twain's literary efforts of the 1870s and early 1880s nonetheless reflect his deeply ambivalent responses to the fundamental social, cultural, and economic changes signaled by the fair in Philadelphia. On the one hand, Twain's texts are wary of the depersonalization exemplified by both the rows of machinery and the massed crowds of onlookers. On the other hand, his work—particularly his two texts of American travel, *Roughing It* (1872) and *Life on the Mississippi* (1883)—cannot entirely avoid celebrating the individual genius implicit in the technological regeneration that characterized America in the years that followed Thoreau's mid-century retreat to Walden Pond. As Huck confides to the reader early in *Huckleberry Finn*, "I liked the old ways best, but I was getting so I liked the new ones, too, a little bit."[4]

Taken together, *Roughing It* and *Life on the Mississippi* chronicle an extraordinary forty-year period of economic expansion and social dislocation. Between the 1840s of Twain's Hannibal boyhood and the 1880s of his creative maturity, the United States not only endured a divisive Civil War but also underwent an equally discordant and in some respects more radically transforming shift from a premodern, preindustrial culture—one that emphasized the individual worker and his or her talents for creative productivity—to a modern industrial society that required the anonymous labor of an increasingly undifferentiated mass of workers. Those industrializing decades thus gradually but irrevocably altered not only American forms of labor and leisure, hastening the development of new jobs, new workplaces, new hours, and new recreations, but American social and cultural values as well. If Thoreau's sojourn at Walden marks the anxious beginning of this critical phase, then it is Twain's peripatetic travel texts that look revealingly, and equally anxiously, back over its turbulent course. Mapping Thoreau's zeal for self-exploration onto a national canvas, Twain's texts "vagabond" playfully on the western frontier and nostalgically on the Mississippi River, but they return repeatedly to—and provide an escalating critique of—the conditions of work in a contemporary industrial culture that was already far more advanced (and deadeningly regimented) than that of Thoreau's day. Twain's audiences loved his "leisurely" narratives and playful personas, as would the later recreation theorists.[5] But beneath the surface playfulness of works like *Roughing It* and *Life on the Mississippi* lies a very serious concern with the impact of corporate capitalism on the forms and values of both labor and leisure.

For many Americans that impact was felt most deeply in the tumultuous decade that *Roughing It* and *Life on the Mississippi* even more literally bracket: the early 1870s to the early 1880s. In Twain's career, those years mark an exceptional period of literary productivity that the 1885 publication of *Huckleberry Finn* would culminate.[6] For the country, the span covers a brief but intensely conflicted decade epitomized by the startling juxtaposition of the 1876 Centennial Exposition with the 1877 carnage of nationwide strikes by American laborers against the very industrialists who had made Machinery Hall possible. *Roughing It* stands at one end of this decade as a text willing to explore but ultimately unable to resolve the tensions implicit in a rapidly changing society. Through the tenderfoot narrator Sam, who eagerly flees the "hot" toils of the city for the supposedly leisurely frontier, the book narrates a series of evasions, first of work itself, then eventually of Sam's own critique of contemporary labor relations. A text that begins as a celebration of ex-urban leisure ends in anxious defense of industrial capitalism. *Life on the Mississippi*, however, strenuously resists evasion. Although in significant ways equally anxious—especially when counting the costs to play that the new industrial forms seem to exact—the later narrative more successfully resolves many of the tensions first explored in the "variegated vagabondizing" of *Roughing It*.[7] That it must do so by metaphorically locating the wonders of the Centennial Exposition *after* the bloodshed of the 1877 strikes testifies to the deliberateness, and perhaps even the self-deception, of that resolution.

The crucial goad to this confrontation and resolution lies in Twain's growing identification with the type of American worker most threatened by these convulsive changes: the artisan, or craftsperson. Whereas in *Roughing It* the narrator attempts a halfhearted and unsuccessful empathetic connection with working-class mining operatives, *Life on the Mississippi* records Twain's candid respect for the independent intelligence and mastery of the

American artisan, in whose struggles Twain saw reflected his own efforts to direct both the production and the distribution of his literary texts. If the 1870s brought home to Twain the perils of the "industrialization of literature and the corresponding professionalization of authorship in the late nineteenth century," then it is in the figure of the artisan that Twain saw the creative and economic control he sought in his own life.[8] Although the history of labor in the United States suggests that Twain overestimated the power that American craftspeople would retain after the turbulent 1870s—not to mention the compatibility of individual autonomy (in work or play) with industrial production—*Life on the Mississippi* and *Roughing It* require reevaluation as striking endpoints on a decade that vexed author and nation alike.

■

Before the mid-century, the United States was still very much a preindustrial, premodern society. Even as the rapidly expanding North laced canals and railroads across its waterways and fields, before 1850 manufacturing remained concentrated in the home and the workshop. America was still a country of farmers, artisans, and merchants regulated by seasonal and diurnal rhythms, not (yet) factory supervisors and operatives ruled by the clock. This is not to say that Americans did not work hard or that they took their labors lightly. On the contrary, in the antebellum period work (excepting the compelled labors of African American slaves) remained emphatically the fundamental "core of the moral life." As Daniel Rodgers and other historians have shown, faith in work as the greatest good took root in Puritan New England as the doctrine of the calling, the belief "that God had called everyone to some productive vocation." By the eighteenth century, work for the glory of God had been subtly secularized into work as public usefulness; and by Twain's boyhood in the 1840s work was more anxiously viewed as a necessary means of preventing national economic failure. One worked hard, in the words of Sarah Hale, because there was "so much to be done."[9]

What buttressed this exaltation of work was a complementary Puritan suspicion of idleness (though the Puritans were not as repressive as our myths would have us believe), the belief that doing nothing was tantamount to doing ill—or that doing nothing would lead to doing ill.[10] But after 1850 the ways of earning money in the United States took on a decidedly new character. "In the second half of the nineteenth century," Rodgers reports, "the factory system invaded the antebellum farm and shop economy, overturning . . . the familiar patterns of work." Wage labor replaced self-employment, jobs moved into the factories; and factories thrived on unskilled work. The speed of this transition varied widely, but the overall effect of factory mechanization was "to narrow and consume skills, to create not only new work relations but a new kind of work: specialized, repetitious, machine-paced, and, often, deadeningly simple." Nor was this new kind of work limited to the factory floor. "Slowly, perceptibly, all work grew more and more like factory work."[11]

Changing work rhythms necessarily affected American patterns of leisure as well. New workers in new cities required new diversions, and "commercial pastimes and organized activities, such as the theater, the circus, burlesque, vaudeville, and sports arose to fill this recreational void."[12] The regularization of factory time also drew more clearly the boundaries between work and play. One of the major effects of industrialization, argues sports historian George Kirsch, "was to deprive people of traditional rest periods and compel them to schedule special time for nonwork activities."[13] Where "free" time and "work" time were previously more interfused, workers' leisure hours were gradually compartmentalized into weeknights, Saturday afternoons, and Sundays. In many ways, the industrial boom thus charged into the second half of the nineteenth century tugging a recreation boom behind it. Indeed, by the 1880s, most of the recreational activities we think of as "modern" were firmly in place, including bicycling, tennis, roller skating, ice skating, swimming, baseball, and intercollegiate and professional sports. Not infrequently, industrial developments also influenced American games. During this period, for example, American athletics—following industry's lead—became not only more commercialized but also more systematized, standardized, and specialized. Within a few short decades, recreation "moved from an informal, social pastime still somewhat questioned by the Puritan tradition, to an organized component of American life."[14]

Accompanying this boom was a growing attack on work that mid-century moralists would have found unconscionable. Critics charged that Americans were too devoted to the "industry" championed by Henry Ward Beecher et al. and needed instead to work less and play more. The charges in part grew out of the improved business climate of the country. America clearly was no longer in danger of imminent failure; indeed, signs of surplus abounded. Why not, then, relax (a little) from the physical strain of over-work? Could one not prepare oneself even better for labor by periodically resting? In time, even Beecher joined the rising number of Americans who "learned to take holidays, to play, and, with some effort, to relax." Perhaps coincident with his move in 1847 from the barren Indiana "frontier" to the comfortable, middle-class New York suburb of Brooklyn, Beecher began to sermonize (almost Thoreauvianly) in favor of vacation, not vocation. The Brooklyn Beecher himself began spending six weeks in the countryside each summer, "engaged in what he called 'meditative and imaginative farming.'"[15]

Few of Beecher's urban working-class contemporaries, however, could avail themselves of a weekend in the country, let alone six weeks. And as preachers like Beecher came to praise relaxation, industrial workers began to demand more free time. But their efforts were persistently blocked by capitalist employers, who were not so quick to admit that work might no longer constitute America's moral core and who intoned the old refrains about idleness and vice, even as the employers themselves eagerly booked vacations. One labor historian has even argued that, as a class, industrial workers at mid-century were losing ground. While some skilled groups saw their wages rise as industry flourished, for example, pay for most operatives lagged behind the rewards of capital and was further outstripped by the rising cost of living. Nor did the physical demands of labor diminish in any appreciable way. Although many factory owners claimed that they had reduced daily working hours from fourteen to roughly eleven by 1860 (along with concomitant reductions in pay), "the tendency of the new industrialism was constantly to speed up production and add to the effort and attention required by the worker."[16] Moreover, the drop from fourteen to eleven hours is in many cases intentionally misleading: in 1840 the reckoning of the workday included meals, which were not counted as work time in 1860. The actual length of the laboring day in many industries had really fallen little more than an hour by the Civil War. Not surprisingly, in the postwar period the workplace increasingly became the site of bitter contestation between workers and employers over the disposition of both work time and free time.

■

The bulk of the first half of *Roughing It* would seem to make anybody's case against the moral primacy of work. In the course of the twenty-chapter journey from St. Joseph to Carson City, for example, young Sam exults in his own leisure and almost always mocks the labors that capitalism demands of others. Whisked from stop to stop inside the "great swinging and swaying stage" (33) that resembles not so much a working overland coach as an oversized cradle, Sam is coolly "indifferent" (35) to anything that transpires without. When deep into the first night of travel the stage's thoroughbrace breaks, he takes "no interest in whatever had happened"; indeed, the thought of other people "out there at work in the murky night," as Sam lay "snug in [his] nest with the curtains drawn," only adds to his "comfort" (35). When the subsequent redistribution of cargo eliminates his seat, he is at first dismayed; but he is soon much happier with the newly constructed "lazy bed" (36). At dawn, stretched out and smoking in easy repose, Sam and his fellow passengers "felt that there was only one complete and satisfying happiness in the world, and [they] had found it" (37).

To be sure, the narrator is attentive to the labor of the stage employees, who, he allows, are "hard worked" (37). The "strict discipline" (53) of the company frequently requires sleepless nights for both driver and conductor, for example, and the quick exchange of horse (or mule) teams nearly a dozen times a day was decidedly "lively work" (84) for the stage hostlers. But the narrator makes no pretense of envying any of these men his position—or for a moment projecting himself imaginatively into one of their laborious roles—and takes considerable steps to ridicule the undue adulation that the driver, in particular, receives. Though treated by the "common herd" (54) as "a great and shining dignitary, the world's favorite son" (43), the overland driver is to Sam a mere operative whose labors consist monotonously of driving "backward and forward over the same piece of road all the time" (54). Only the fleet and elite pony express rider, whose exhilarating work permits "no idling time" (63), earns the narrator's admiration; but Sam's chief desire is nonetheless merely to see, not to be one.

The contrast between the narrator's exaltation of leisure and the hard work necessary on the frontier is heightened by the two-day sojourn among the industrious Mormons of Salt Lake City. The "broad, straight, level streets" evince neither "loafers" nor "visible drunkards or noisy people" (92). Twain and company "enjoy"

> a limpid stream rippling and dancing through every street in place of a filthy gutter; block after block of trim dwellings, . . . and a grand general air of neatness, repair, thrift and comfort, around and about and over the whole. And everywhere were workshops, factories, and all manner of industries; and intent faces and busy hands were to be seen wherever one looked; and in one's ears was the ceaseless chink of hammers, the buzz of trade and the contented hum of drums and flywheels. (92)

The Mormon city seems at first glance a modern utopia, boasting every industrial advantage with none of urbanization's taints. Work commands a moral sway that seems right out of Beecher's *Lectures*, and the soothing, almost organic tone of the city (the "rippling" stream, the "buzz of trade," and the "contented hum of drums and flywheels") would pass muster with the Brooklyn Beecher as well. But young Sam offers little praise for the Mormons outside of this paragraph. He even takes steps to undercut its grand effects. In the very next paragraph the comparison of "armorial crest[s]" is both self-mocking (Sam's own crest a pair of "dissolute bears holding up the head of a dead and gone cask") and facetiously laudatory ("But the Mormon crest was easy. . . . It was a representation of a GOLDEN BEEHIVE, with the bees all at work!" [92]). The sojourners, moreover, are not nearly as interested in the labor of the kingdom as they are in its mysterious marital arrangements. The enchanted city, they learn from their Gentile hosts, breeds jealousy and profligate spending—not to mention paternity suits.[17] Even worse, however, is the dulling effect Mormonism and its labors have on the talent Twain will come to prize, the production of literature. The Mormon Bible, for example, is "slow" and "sleepy," "an insipid mess of inspiration. It is chloroform in print" (102). No wonder Sam leaves Salt Lake City disappointed in "fairyland" (91) and feeling he had learned only "two or three trivial things" (111).

Roughing It makes equally well the case against the strain of overwork that was gaining in popularity in the late 1860s and early 1870s. The emphasis in the opening chapters on escaping the toils of "tiresome city life" (37) would make complete sense to an audience already familiar with S. Weir Mitchell's popular 1871 text, *Wear and Tear; or, Hints for the Overworked.* In one sense *Roughing It* reads as a constant search for an escape from such "wear and tear." After a few years of profitless prospecting, for example, Sam moves to San Francisco, the urban center of the West. But only a few months later he is "unspeakably tired" (331) of his daily reporter's work and leaves the "hurry and bustle and noisy confusion of San Francisco" for the "slumberous calm and . . . solitude" (341) of the Sandwich Islands. These tranquil islands seem to be the truer "fairyland," an impression Twain conveys in *Roughing It* and which he reiterated forcefully in the "Sandwich Islands" lecture he delivered nearly one hundred times in America and England between 1866 and 1873, a lecture that typically closed with this description: "It is Sunday land. The land of indolence and dreams,

where the air is drowsy and things tend to repose and peace, and to emancipation from the labor, turmoil, and weariness, and anxiety of life."[18] Of
course, as careful readers of the text that Twain's Hawaiian benediction
most closely resembles—Tennyson's "The Lotus-Eaters"—we know that
too much repose can be deadly.[19] Even in *Roughing It* the "tranced luxury
to sit in the perfumed air and forget that there was any world but these enchanted islands" (341) is quickly punctured by the bite of the scorpion lurking in the grass.

Indeed, *Roughing It*'s suspicion of such drowsy inactivity helps us position Twain within an important debate that is corollary to the attack on
overwork. On the one hand, Beecher and his fellow postbellum "prophets
of repose" identified healthful leisure with a restful passivity that revitalized
body and soul through the careful conservation of energy.[20] Other reformers, however, advocated vigorous activity as the one best path to regeneration. The latter group made (not surprisingly) the louder case, and in the
1870s Americans began to take their recreation as seriously as they once had
their work. Although Twain wrote to his brother Orion in 1880 that overwork is "the bane of Americans"—and insisted at his seventieth birthday
dinner in 1905 that he had "never taken any exercise, except sleeping and
resting," in his life[21]—the narrator of *Roughing It* is at best a conflicted
spokesperson for passivity. A close look at Sam's Lake Tahoe excursion with
his friend Johnny—a four-day trip that Twain strategically expands to two
or three weeks in *Roughing It*[22]—is instructive here. Excepting the exhausting hike to the lake and the chopping down of "three trees" (136) to
mark the boundaries of their wood ranch, Sam appears to do very little. In
fact he consistently insinuates that Johnny does all the work while he himself merely "superintend[s]" (134). And yet the refreshment the lake provides is not nearly as passive as it appears. Sam fishes, bathes, reads, and
plays cards. Championing the "friskiness" that "camp life" engenders, he
pointedly ridicules the pseudo-scientific "water cures" and "movement
cures" that "people will go to" (135).

Although some of Sam's "amusements" (card playing, for instance) would not have met the guidelines prescribed by proponents of better health through greater activity, western travel and the actual practice of "roughing it" were gaining popular (and critical) acceptance as leisure activities in postbellum America. As John Sears explains, the discovery of the Yosemite Valley in the 1850s helped shift the locus of American tourism emphatically west. Glowing reports of the valley as "some stupendous roofless cathedral," a "rolling, upheaving sea of granite mountains," tempted Americans with enough money and leisure to look beyond the customary attractions available in the East. "It was," according to an 1866 visitor, "Niagara, magnified." At first, partly by necessity, tourists seeking the sublime Yosemite experience were forced to camp out because hotel services were scarce until the 1860s. But soon the unavoidable became the desirable, and "the idea that camping out and 'roughing it' might also be a means to better health . . . grew steadily in popularity." By the 1870s—as Sam's Tahoe experience seems to confirm—camping "was regarded as a means of restoring both physical and mental health and of offering a vitalizing change from urban routines."[23]

Twain, however, strategically avoids fanning the flames of the Yosemite craze. He is at best coy, at worst caustic about what nearly everyone had come to call "Yosemite and the Big Trees."[24] Twain did visit the valley—possibly several times—and acknowledges early in *Roughing It* (however sarcastically) that Yosemite was the top tourist attraction in the West (rivaled, he joked, only by the deadly anecdote about Hank Monk and Horace Greeley). He also seems fully aware that his readers expected him to gush over the valley's magnificent scenery. But just as he is on the brink of doing so, Twain declines the office. "Our wanderings were wide and in many directions," he says at the close of chapter 61; "and now I could give the reader a vivid description of the Big Trees and the marvels of the Yosemite—but what has this reader done to me that I should persecute him? I will deliver him into the hands of less conscientious tourists and take his blessing" (330). Twain's demurral on the one hand suggests that by 1872 the travel narrative reader, already deluged with "vivid" descriptions of

Yosemite, might be thankful for one fewer. But at the same time Twain twits both the less discriminating members of his audience and the "less conscientious tourists" whose texts vie with his for dollars in the marketplace.

In 1871 Twain might have had good reason to object, in fact, to the way Yosemite itself was marketed as a commercial attraction. Sears argues that Yosemite (like its later partner, Yellowstone) was "appropriated and produced for an audience hungry for national icons and for places which symbolized the exotic wonder of a region just beginning to be known and accessible to it." Yosemite's natural grandeur did not exempt it from the consumerist culture taking shape in America. "Although Yosemite evoked images of the infinite and the cosmic" in each of its visitors, Sears asserts, the way it was "measured, commodified, and preserved" ensured that the valley and its resources "would not be controlled by individual desires, but by corporate needs and ideals."[25] No other tourist attraction in America had been promoted as systematically, thoroughly, or rapidly. Travel accounts (including Horace Greeley's own 1860 *Overland Journey*) and painting exhibitions played a major part in this promotion; Twain, it seems, would have none of it.[26]

■

Twain's forbearance reminds us that *Roughing It* spends considerably more time investigating the way laborers make money than the way tourists spend it.[27] *Roughing It* takes up this matter explicitly in chapter 26, where Sam announces, "By and by I was smitten with the silver fever" (151). For the next thirty-seven chapters—scarcely interrupted by what most critics term the decisive "turning point" of the narrative, the Blind Lead episode (chapters 40–41)—Twain reports in one form or another on the perils and rewards of frontier mining.[28] His stories, moreover, become increasingly more critical of the industrial relations—and the corporate needs and ideals—that underpin the "flush times."

At first Sam approaches prospecting with the same matchless enthusiasm that some months before had made him leap at his brother's invitation to go west. Despite a "hard, wearing, toilsome journey" (157) lugging provisions for four men (and a pair of recalcitrant horses) two hundred miles to Humboldt County, Sam begins his search for riches "with a feverish excitement that was brimful of expectation—almost of certainty" (160). Overcome with "unmarred ecstasy" when he discovers a glittering deposit of "yellow scales" (160), he is subsequently "stricken and forlorn" (162) to learn not only that his treasures are merely mica, but also that mining silver or gold—as opposed to merely "prospecting" it (163)—is numbingly laborious work. Sam and his "company" try sinking a shaft, then blasting a tunnel. Both experiences sour them on the idea of actually digging for profit. Confused by the paradox of a teeming mining district that seems to have "nothing doing"—"no mining—no milling—no productive effort—no income" (166)—the novice miners judge that "the *real* secret of success in silver mining" was "*not* to mine the silver ourselves by the sweat of our brows and the labor of our hands, but to *sell* the ledges to the dull slaves of toil and let them do the mining!" (168).

Henry Nash Smith is right to correct Vernon Parrington's misreading of this particular revelation. Rather than endorse its overtly cynical attitude, Twain satirizes the idea that interpersonal exploitation is the road to wealth. And yet the passage is also more than just a "burlesque of the clichés which . . . govern the thinking of the deluded speculators."[29] Read in the context of the narrator's growing awareness of industrial rather than personal exploitation, the passage is an early (if inchoate) marker of *Roughing It*'s emerging economic critique. It is, after all, almost exclusively the large and capital-rich mining concerns that actually do the shaft digging and tunnel blasting, although the company owners no more mine by the sweat of their brows than does the labor-chastened Sam. *That* "dull" work is reserved for wage-dependent mining employees, to whom the phrase "slaves of toil" might easily apply.[30]

Although it may be true that in the early 1860s Nevada mine workers earned "the highest industrial wage in the world"—four dollars a shift in the boom summer of 1863—mine owners doggedly "whittled away at the prevailing wage rate" as profits declined after 1864.[31] Grumbling miners threatened union shops and work slowdowns. Twain's later descriptions of people who struck it rich during the "flush times" leave one with the impression that successful individual miner-prospectors were not uncommon in Nevada. Presumably a dissatisfied but diligent company employee could buy up old claims and make them work. But historians have shown that this was not the case. The economic arrangements of Nevada quartz mining had already made profitable independent excavation all but impossible before Twain even arrived in Carson City. What had been true in California (where pioneer mining was the 1850s norm) would never obtain in the Silver Territory.[32]

The corporate presence at which the phrase "dull slaves of toil" hints begins to loom larger in Sam's mining experiences; and as that presence grows so too do the narrative's criticisms of it. Sam himself is soon forced by lack of funds to take a position as a "common laborer" in a quartz mill (191). There he experiences the rigors of post-1850 dawn-to-dusk industrial toil with which an increasing percentage of his fellow Americans were already familiar. "There is nothing so aggravating as silver milling," Sam laments. "There never was any idle time in that mill. There was always something to do" (193). And the doing of it was not particularly diverting. Mill workers either "stood by the battery all day long, breaking up masses of silver-bearing rock with a sledge," or shook quicksilver "through a buckskin sack" into the amalgamating pans, or cleaned "riffles" and blankets, or screened "tailings" (192–93). "Of all the recreations in the world," Sam wryly observes, "screening tailings on a hot day, with a long-handled shovel, is the most undesirable" (193). In Twain's view, industrial labor both degrades work and perverts play.

Four chapters later Sam recounts the "most curious" episode of what he called his "slothful, valueless, heedless career" (209), the blind lead. Already foregrounded in the book's dedication to Higbie, and for years considered a crucial textual moment, in my reading this episode marks not so much the passage of the text from invention and energy to self-plagiarism and narrative fatigue as it does the heightening of Sam's awareness that the Nevada deck is stacked in capital's favor—still a crucial moment, but of a very different sort.[33] At first the discovery of the blind lead casts Sam and Higbie as successful independent challengers to the monopolistic control of the mining concerns. When the "Wide West Company" discovers a rich vein of ore in one of its shafts, only Higbie's pioneering instincts and expert knowledge of Wide West rock (not to mention his sneaky circumvention of watchful Wide West operatives) enable the heretofore luckless pair to outsmart the company and claim the vein for themselves. By taking in a third partner, the Wide West foreman, Sam and Higbie turn the company's remaining strength to their advantage. But the drama Twain places at the center of his narrative does not play out as the three partners hope. Unforeseen circumstances keep each of the men from doing the "work" necessary to hold the claim before the ten-day waiting period expires—and they lose the mine. Though the claim does not revert to Wide West, a new mini-corporation of fourteen "duly armed" (219) men (the "Johnson" company) strong-arms its way into possession. And the original corporate presence—Sam and Higbie's foreman-partner—"buys" his way back into the "lead" at gunpoint. As Twain's page header ironically sums up the episode, the "Third Partner" (and company representative) "Plays to Win" (219). Shortly thereafter, the maverick Johnson company consolidates with Wide West and the corporate victory is complete.

After this suggestive defeat, Sam is both more openly sarcastic about the impossibility of independent claims ever repaying their investors and more covertly critical of large-scale mining operations. Personal labors, it seems, will always lose out to corporate enterprises. In chapter 44, for example, he ridicules the common belief of "every man" that "his little wildcat claim was as good as any on the 'main lead' and would infallibly be worth a thousand dollars a foot when he 'got down where it came in solid'" (230). "Poor fellow," Sam continues, "he was blessedly blind to the fact that he never would see that day" (230). What Twain does not add (but hints at on the next page) is that the expensive mining paraphernalia these independent prospectors buy—wire ropes, dressed-pine windlasses, force pumps (231–32)—are in all likelihood purchased from supply companies controlled by "great mines" (230) such as the Ophir or the Gould & Curry.[34]

In chapter 52—the "instructive" entry that Twain warns readers they may wish to skip (a narrative strategy almost as transparent as the duke's "LADIES AND CHILDREN NOT ADMITTED" flourish on the "Royal Nonesuch" posters in *Huckleberry Finn*)—two lengthy and subversive footnotes subtly critique the "great mines" themselves. The first note reprints a Virginia City *Enterprise* article (possibly written by Twain) detailing a Wells, Fargo agent's estimate of the annual bullion yield on the Comstock for the year 1863, a total he meticulously (and buoyantly) projects at 30 million dollars. A bracketed statement after the note then undermines the effect altogether. It deadpans: "A considerable overestimate.—M.T." (283). The second footnote ends this same chapter. In it Twain reports the actual 1863 yield, which came in at neither the projected 30 million dollars nor the claimed 25 but somewhere south of 20. He then confidently asserts, however, that "the day for large figures is approaching" and proceeds to construct his own hyperbolic estimate of the impact of the soon-to-be-completed "Sutro Tunnel" (286). Mimicking the earlier *Enterprise* footnote, Twain substitutes vague phrases like "millions of dollars" and "astonishing riches" for the precise but equally inflated figures from his paper. And Twain's closing comments on "Mr. Sutro" himself damn where they profess to praise. Sutro is "one of the few men in the world" who is "gifted" enough to "follow up and hound" such a project "to its completion" and has already converted several "obstinate Congresses" to a "deserved friendliness" toward his "important work" (286). Given the controversy surrounding Adolph Sutro at the time, who was widely perceived as vain, money-hungry, and supremely egotistical— Twain's plug for yet another "prodigious enterprise" (286) falls flat.[35]

Part of the "instructive word" about mining provided in the main text of chapter 52 further narrates an instance of spectacular tunnel collapse, which prefigures the dead and decaying mining towns that blight the landscape at the end of *Roughing It*'s mining chapters and cap the stateside phase of Twain's corporate critique. These towns, too, have collapsed, from "thriving and prosperous and promising" young cities into "a lifeless, homeless solitude" (309). As Martha Banta observes, Twain's "backward glance" eulogizes "a period of frontier history already lost forever when *Roughing It* was published in 1872"[36] and laments, in his words, the "stalwart, muscular, dauntless young braves" (309) sacrificed "upon the altar of the golden calf" (310). The miners who remain, still duped by inflated promises of wealth and power, view life from "living grave[s]" (324).

■

In the last section of the book, which takes Sam to the Sandwich Islands, Twain seems curiously to pull away from the mounting critique of the mining chapters. Sensitized to the ways that capital can transfigure both labor and leisure, the narrator notes with sarcasm the combined effect of the missionaries and the sugar industry on the native islanders. The missionaries, besides putting a stop to the human sacrifices of "those old bygone days," show the "luckless" locals "what rapture it is to work all day long for fifty cents to buy food for next day with, as compared with fishing for pastime and lolling in the shade through eternal summer, and eating of the bounty that nobody labored to provide but Nature" (345–46). Other local pastimes suffer equally: the "grand gala" Saturday celebrations, which "interfered too much with labor and the interests of white folks," were gradually broken up; so, too, was the "lascivious hula-hula" dance forbidden to be performed in public (355). Like those of American factory operatives on the mainland, the natives' rhythms of work and play are irretrievably altered by capitalist demands. The hula-hula, for example, is neatly transformed into a private, tightly controlled, commercial venture, performed behind "closed doors, in presence of few spectators, and only by permission duly procured from the authorities and the payment of ten dollars for the same" (355).

But these barbs never quite make a weapon. The Sandwich Islands chapters, even with scattered ironies like these, read more like the proto–public relations documents they in part originally were. Twain's arrangement with the Sacramento *Union* called for entertaining letters that also reported "on prospects for industry and trade."[37] Although *Roughing It* plays down Twain's enthusiasm for sugar production (one original letter provided detailed yield tables) and cheap "coolie labor" (which the same letter urged profit-minded Californians to adopt as soon as possible),[38] the 1872 text nonetheless focuses on Twain's perception of the islands as a tourist's dream. If the natives' activities are curtailed by creeping capitalism, those of the white visitors are augmented. Twain reports a series of excursions that combine sightseeing and frolic; he tours ancient ruins, rides in canoes, explores live volcanoes, and tumbles boulders into dead ones. Along the way he pays out sums insignificant to a tourist, though beyond the means of most laboring islanders. All the while Twain comes and goes as fancy strikes him, enjoying the benefits of what we might rightly call his "well-employed leisure."[39]

Refreshed after this "half a year's luxurious vagrancy" (414), Twain returns to San Francisco to convert his Hawaiian travels into the challenging but profitable labor of lecturing and steers the text toward its "moral," a deceptively simple salute to work. Taken straight, the moral's injunction to persons of "no account" to "go away from home" because then they "will *have* to work" undercuts the narrative's praise of leisure by seeming to endorse "faithful diligence" (422). Taken ironically, however—always a good idea with Twain—the moral resurrects the critique of labor relations initiated in the mining chapters but allowed to fade in Hawaii. Neither reading, however, is particularly satisfying; both seem, at best, weakly supported by the text that precedes it. Twain either simply fails to resolve his narrative's implicit and explicit tensions, or he highlights that failure in order to suggest the impossibility of such a resolution. The latter reading is more charitable to Twain, and I prefer it. But I would prefer it more if *Roughing It* actually ended there, in self-conscious defeat. It does not: Twain tacks on three appendixes, the last of which reopens with a vengeance the issues of

authority, autonomy, labor, and social critique that are nervously (un)re-
solved in the moral. And in the end, *Roughing It* retreats to a shrill defense
of industrial politics.

Briefly, appendix C—which is not even mentioned in the body of
Roughing It—reproduces the lengthy account by Gold Hill journalist Conrad Wiegand of a particularly terrifying experience. Wiegand asserts that
mining executive John Winters, angry over unnamed but "damnably false
charges" levied against his company in Wiegand's paper, had threatened to
kill the editor if he refused to retract them (437). Wiegand refuses, escapes,
and then publishes a "true account" of the "disgraceful affair" to clear his
name, fully suspecting that in so doing he has issued his own death war-
rant (446). Wiegand titles his exposé "A Seeming Plot for Assassination
Miscarried"; Twain's own title, "Concerning a Frightful Assassination That
Was Never Consummated," suggests that he wishes it had been (433). But
Wiegand's report of his defense is fascinating. He first declares that his affronted reader has misinterpreted the editorial itself, claiming that in context the statements about Winters are not actually "preferred *as* charges"
(439). Wiegand next refuses to admit that he even wrote the offending document in the first place: "Of its *authorship* I can say nothing whatever, but
for its *publication* I assume full, sole and personal responsibility" (443).
Sounding, then, much like an embattled author trying to distance himself
from the implications of his material—an anxiety we know Twain sometimes shared[40]—Wiegand nonetheless reaffirms the truthfulness of his original editorial by his repeated references to the "villainy" and "chronic . . .
evils" that he believes characterize "mining management" (446, 433). Wiegand's efforts on behalf of workers are the sort that Twain's narrative has at
least been sympathetic to, but in *his* final word Twain castigates the "weak,
half-witted" editor for maligning the "good name" of a citizen "on hearsay
evidence" (446). And though Wiegand has been no freer with the libel laws
than Twain was himself in his own newspaper days (or would soon be, in
The Gilded Age [1873]), Twain recommends public humiliation for such a
transgression. Thus at the end of the text, and at the outset of the most tur-

bulent decade in American labor history, Twain throws his considerable narrative weight to the industrialists. It was a position he would soon come to reconsider.

■

How much of Twain's appended and anxious support for the industrialist position can be attributed to the tension he felt from having just married the daughter of a northern coal and iron monopolist is difficult to judge. Biographical evidence suggests that Twain chafed more under the strictures of upper-class propriety than he scrupled over the taint of his association by proxy with Gilded Age riches. Certainly, however, "the exploitative rigors of the family coal business" troubled Twain. In 1869, shortly after the publication of *The Innocents Abroad* and his engagement to Livy, he published an "Open Letter to Commodore Vanderbilt," a caustic admonition to the millionaire railroad industrialist to "Go and surprise the whole country by doing something right." Any man who makes wealth a "god . . . instead of a servant," Twain wrote, is "appalling[ly]" impoverished. The following year, as a one-third owner of the Buffalo *Express* (purchased with money loaned by Livy's father), Twain entered into an even more "touchy and vulnerable relationship" with in-lawed plutocracy.[41]

If the impatience with greed that Twain's writings increasingly showed grew in part out of direct personal experience, that impatience was no doubt intensified by the turbulent decade that followed his divestiture of the *Express* in 1871 and the publication of *Roughing It* the next year. Perhaps at no time between Twain's 1840s boyhood and the 1882 completion of *Life* were the conflicts engendered by the shift to the industrial age as violent as they were in the 1870s. In 1873 the Jay Cooke and Company finance house went bankrupt, throwing the country's "entire financial and credit system into panic" and triggering the "Long Depression" of the 1870s.[42] Wage rates and work rates quickly fell; unemployment swiftly rose. Labor met capital's indifference and broken promises with isolated acts of resistance. Angry railroad workers, for example, retaliated with work stoppages, industrial sabotage, and sympathy strikes. The trouble these actions caused for industrialists in the early years of the depression was relatively insignificant in comparison with what followed later in the decade, but they set the tone for an especially tense period.[43]

At the heart of the 1870s Long Depression sat its ironical showpiece, the Philadelphia Centennial Exposition. Major northern cities had begun holding their own industrial expos earlier in the decade. Cincinnati, for example, exhibited its principal manufactures and machinery annually from 1870 to 1888.[44] But the Philadelphia exposition surpassed its regional siblings in both size and ideological importance. Although the fairgrounds also displayed foreign goods and select folk arts and crafts from around the United States, the "nation's pride and the talk of the fair was Machinery Hall."[45] The hall's rattling, whirring machines represented more than just the symbolic power of modern American industry, however. They were also arranged and then interpreted as significant "works of beauty, art, and progress."[46] One machine might put a shop of artisans out of work; but that machine was itself evidence that the spirit of American craftsmanship survived.

Bruce Laurie also shows that a careful reader of the Centennial Exposition would have discerned further evidence of the broad sweep of postwar economic change. First, on their inaugural display were Edison's multiplex telegraph and Bell's telephone, inventions unfamiliar to fairgoers but that would shortly revolutionize the communication industry. Second, Machinery Hall's physical location, on a bluff overlooking the Schuylkill River, "signaled an end to the time when factories were confined to riverbanks in order to take advantage of water power." Improved power sources (such as steam) allowed intra-urban industrial growth and pulled factories "into metropolitan centers and medium-sized cities, reversing the antebellum tendency of industrial development." Finally, Machinery Hall underscored "the transition from the labor-intensive methods of the sweating system to the capital-intensive, machine-paced processes of the factory."[47] Manufacturing, which had initiated the decline in skilled work in the 1840s, was giving way to accelerated forms of industrialization that turned ever-increasing numbers of handworkers into machine tenders.

Only a year later, even Laurie's careful reader might have been shocked by the level of national unrest. Three and a half years of systematic wage reductions, work speedups, and crippling economic depression exploded in 1877 in antimonopolistic labor violence. Across the country, rail workers and other operatives defied owners with strikes more broadly supported and disruptive than those ventured in 1873–74. Embattled industrialists frequently turned to state and federal governments for help to quell the uprisings, and more often than not received it in the form of armed troops. America, which prided itself on escaping the class violence that had plagued Europe at mid-century, quickly became a principal site of labor struggle. As Steven Ross recounts, in the two decades after the Centennial Exposition "there were more strikes and people killed or wounded in labor demonstrations in the United States than in any other country in the world." Industrial laborers were not the only combatants. Herbert Gutman notes that the 1877 strikes "included many [workers] deeply rooted in traditional crafts," people who "worried that the transformation of the American social and economic structure threatened settled ways of work and life and particular visions of a just society." The violence of these workers, who fought to preserve their rapidly disappearing artisan culture, was not merely a reaction to immediate economic woes but "the product of long-standing grievances that accompanied the transformation of Old America into New America."[48]

It is this transformation that Twain's *Life on the Mississippi* interrogates. To do so Twain returns to the river he left in 1861, when he began the travels recounted in *Roughing It*. Where the earlier text is structured in part as a series of evasions, *Life* presents an explicit confrontation with the remembered past in the lived present. (Even Twain's attempts to travel incognito are foiled at every opportunity; he is in 1882 too much the public figure to evade notice.) What we discover through Twain's comparisons, however, is that the present is not quite the clear loser we might at first expect.

Although there are clearly qualities of "Old America" missed in the "New"—particularly when we consider the damage to the spirit of play—*Life* also indicates the limits to the usefulness of nostalgia. As in *Roughing It*, the end of Twain's later book downplays its critique of contemporary industrial relations. But *Life* does so, significantly, with far less anxiety, opting at last to resolve rather than exacerbate the tensions explored in earlier chapters. It remains to us to judge the motives behind, and the textual consequences of, that resolution.

■

Twain was, we know, tentatively conceptualizing the shape and purpose of *Life on the Mississippi* in 1871, and may first have considered writing about his days on the river as early as 1866.[49] When he did put pen to paper in 1874 to begin the seven autobiographical sketches that would see print as "Old Times on the Mississippi" in the *Atlantic Monthly* the following year, he incorporated some of the prominent narrative inflections of *Roughing It*. As in that text, the "Old Times" essays return to Twain's past to narrate a distinctive chapter of American history, mingling fact, fiction, and autobiography in the process. Like the tenderfoot narrator of *Roughing It*, Twain's "Old Times" cub pilot also acts considerably younger than Twain actually was during the period recalled. (The "cub" is even metaphorically kin to the Far West Twain, who in the Mormon chapters of *Roughing It* had playfully figured himself as a dissolute "bear.")

When Twain the experienced author returned to the river in 1882 to collect the material that he would need to complete *Life*, he also literalized the old-timer/tenderfoot dual persona that implicitly controls the point of view in *Roughing It*. Twain then makes that dual perspective the central (and explicit) structuring device of *Life*. But instead of sacrificing *Roughing It's* balanced narrative tension by foregrounding the dichotomy between young and old, Twain masterfully doubles its intensity: in the first third of *Life* the experienced narrator recalls his naive boyhood and piloting days; in the last two thirds that experienced persona narrates his own contemporary experience of a (newly naive) return to the river. This allows the end of *Life*—a portion of the book most critics have dismissed for its hasty composition and flagging energy—to be as morally instructive (and narratively compelling) as its more famous opening.[50]

To complement this doubled intensity, and to show that he recognizes in 1882 that America's pressing concerns are national, not regional, Twain broadens the book's scope as well. While *Roughing It* vagabonds expansively over the plains, the Rockies, and the Pacific, it remains essentially a frontier text; its place is on the boundary of the nation, measuring the costs and rewards of its escape from "the States." *Life*, on the other hand, attempts from the start—before the start, in fact—to embrace the whole country by heading for (and then not straying from) the nation's center.[51] As much is signaled by the book's lengthy epigraph. "But *the basin of the Mississippi is the* BODY OF THE NATION," it announces; and from the heart of that body Twain's text intends to speak. The epigraph itself, as Twain carefully indicates, is imported from an 1863 *Harper's Magazine* "Editor's Table." In its original context, this paragraph (which appears unaltered in *Life*, save Twain's italicizations and capitalization) speaks even more clearly to the question of national unity: it forms the crux of an argument—written at the heart of the Civil War—that America's unique geography guarantees the indivisibility of the nation.

Taking as its starting point Lincoln's December 1862 Annual Message to Congress (in which he asserted that the interior region of the country "is the great body of the republic," and the "other parts . . . but marginal borders to it"),[52] together with his well-remembered warning against a "house divided," the full *Harper's* editorial contends that "organized life is possible only for individuals possessing properly defined external forms." In the United States, it continues, the Mississippi River system comprises America's external (i.e., physical) form, and binds "all the area drained by it into one organic whole." Because the land Americans inhabit is "one organic whole," so too must be its people, or "organized life" is impossible. Therefore, it would be national suicide to divide the country in any permanent way. "To dismember it," *Harper's* editors declare, "is death."[53]

What makes Twain's selection of an epigraph from this editorial so interesting, however, is that in *Life* he challenges the final two crucial conclusions that the editors draw. First, they claim, the organic "unity" of the (North) American people refers to whites only; therefore, the "African element" (who make merely a "forced and unnatural" residence in a land climatically suited to Europeans and their descendants) will have to move to a more suitable region, such as tropical South America. Second, by the phrase "organized life" the editors mean primarily the social and economic structures dictated by contemporary industrial capitalism: "The prosperity which every section of the country . . . has enjoyed under the Union should have taught us wherein lay the secret of our strength."[54] The editorial closes with a recitation of industrial and agricultural profits since 1850, predicting on that basis an economy capable of serving 600 million (presumably white) Americans by the distant year 2000. Twain's later text, however, which figuratively dismembers the *Harper's* editorial by removing it from its original context, critiques both postbellum white racism and the emerging industrial economy.

Life's first gesture, however, is to memory and the past. In the first twenty chapters (of which 4–17 make up the original "Old Times" contribution), Twain reviews the "flushest . . . epoch" of the river, much as he earlier discussed the flush times of mining in *Roughing It*.[55] However, although young Sam never fully identified with the miners whose work practices he tried unsuccessfully to make profitable, on the Mississippi he becomes a full-fledged member of the pilots' "guild" (99). Terminology is important here: Sam the "cub" pilot is not an industrial operative overseen by a foreman; rather he is a type of artisan, a pilot-in-training apprenticed to an experienced craftsperson. The cub then learns an array of skills whose mastery will confer power, status, and freedom. In his steamboat, the pilot answers to no one but the river itself; on shore he recreates as he pleases, bankrolled by substantial wages. In those days, in short, to young Sam the pilot was "the only unfettered and entirely independent human being that lived in the earth" (93).

A pilot makes concessions, of course. Learning the river, Sam quickly discovers, is not entertaining play but "something very real and worklike" (47). Aspects of the natural world that stir romance in the layperson become mere pieces of information that aid or hinder "the safe piloting of a steamboat" (68). Even as a young cub Sam wonders: have he and other artisan-professionals "gained most or lost most by learning [their] trade?" (69). Chapter 15, "The Pilots' Monopoly," suggests that in certain circumstances the benefits considerably outweigh the disadvantages and offers an antebellum example of artisan-class resistance to the control of corporate culture. When owners capitalize on a pilot glut by driving wages down, a small group of determined (and capital-rich) pilots organize the guild into what eventually becomes "the strongest commercial organization ever formed among men" (99). The pilots reassert control over the training and distribution of personnel, as well as the valuable commodity of up-to-date river information. The pilots' success would seem to strike a blow for a preindustrial social structure against the creeping influence of advanced capitalism.

But as Banta and others have shown, *Life* complicates such a reading. First, as the "tightest monopoly in the world," the newly organized union suspiciously resembles the corporate structures it supposedly resists (*Life*, 108). Second, the new association replaces the older, preindustrial apprentice system with an elitist and depersonalized training program. New cubs will have to "pay a thousand dollars in advance" (107) to learn the river and will no longer be attached to one master craftsperson, making Sam a member of an organization whose revised bylaws would have prevented his impoverished former self from ever joining. Third, the pilots' guild already betrays signs of industrial influence in its work rhythms, whose to-the-second four-hour shifts are as structured as any postbellum factory's. The pilots do exemplify control and mastery; but those "old departed steamboating days" weren't quite as "old" as we might think (75).

Twain's lengthy chapter on steamboat racing presents an equally curious blend of the preindustrial and the modern in relation to patterns of leisure. Although the river's "racing days" clearly belong to the past, the community participation Sam describes (immense and partisan crowds in a state of "consuming excitement" [111]) anticipates in form and function the later days of organized spectator sports, right down to the pun on "consuming." As literary critic Christian Messenger points out, the steamboats them- selves, simply in their role as commercial vehicles, had already contributed to the rise of organized sports, first by transporting racing thoroughbreds and their patrons to regional tracks, and then by shuttling race and boxing match results up and down the Mississippi. And the detailed charts of "some famous trips" that Twain provides (114)—the only substantial ma- terial he added to the original "Old Times" chapters—neatly satisfy Allen Guttmann's final two requirements (out of seven) for modern sports: quan- tification and the quest for records. These modern approaches to play, par- ticularly "the almost insatiable tendency to transform *every* athletic feat into one that can be quantified and measured," also saliently correspond to the demands made by Frederick Winslow Taylor and his followers on advanced capitalism beginning in the early 1880s.[56] Thus even within this chapter, the "royal fun" (111) of the crowds and the supreme control of the shrewd and artful pilot yield metaphorically to the regimented factory labor that awaited most American workers in 1883.

■

When Twain in his return to the river casts a "longing glance toward the pi- lothouse" (149), he thus symbolically looks back on an era that was being transformed even in the midst of its "widest-awake epoch" (15). Perhaps in reviewing the "Old Times" chapters while preparing to return to the river and then comparing his memories of 1874–75 with the realities of 1882, Twain felt both a deeper sense of loss and a greater irritation toward the modern economic forms replacing the artisan culture with which he was coming to identify so strongly. Certainly the middle third of *Life*, the trip south from St. Louis to New Orleans (chapters 22–50), supports such a reading. Literal and metaphoric narratives of death and dismemberment dominate this section, in an eerie recognition not just of the "dead" past but of the carnage attending the industrial conflicts increasingly prevalent after 1877. The first significant death in the text—Twain's younger brother Henry's—actually appears in chapter 20, symbolically preparing the way for the ones to follow. But after Henry we are treated to the feuding Darnells and Watsons (chapter 26), the murderer/disemboweler Murel (chapter 29), the grisly corpses that litter Ritter's narrative (chapter 31), and the dismembered Vicksburg handshake (chapter 35), just to name a few. Each of these examples, intriguingly, appears in someone else's narrative; it is almost as though Twain has become a collector (and transmitter) of stories about death.[57]

When not passing along one of these stories, the text takes a series of unflattering looks at contemporary corporate culture. In St. Louis, although Twain professes to admire the "progress, energy, [and] prosperity" of the city (144), he notes that the only business that remained for steamboats is concentrated "in the hands . . . of two or three close corporations well fortified with capital" (146). The implication here is that contemporary prosperity, too, is in the hands of fewer and fewer companies, and thus fewer and fewer people. In the greedy wrangling over how much of Ritter's hidden fortune Twain and his fellow travelers should send to Adam Kruger, the shoemaker whose father Ritter had accidentally killed, the men parrot in escalating severity the typical contemporary capitalist's response to a worker's request for higher wages or more free time. "It would injure him . . . perhaps ruin him," one man declares. He might "take to drinking, maltreat his motherless children, drift into other evil courses, go steadily from bad to worse" (205). Another "fervently" elaborates: "Yes, that's it. . . . I've seen it a hundred times. . . . If it don't pull him down, and take all the usefulness out of him, and all the self-respect and everything, then I don't know human nature" (205). Last, Twain himself cries that even a small amount of money "would rot his principles, paralyze his industry, drag him to the rumshop, thence to the gutter, thence to the almshouse" (206). The three capitalists nearly agree—as an act of "charity" and "high and sacred benevolence"—to send him nothing. But this course seems too mean; they decide to mail him "a chromo" (206).

Twain's mock account of three benevolent capitalists teaming to keep one honest artisan "where he is, and *as* he is" (206)—by stealing his money—takes a more literal shape in chapter 39, "Manufactures and Miscreants." The title forecasts the link the chapter makes: after describing a successful ice factory and a yarn mill (the latter yet another "close corporation" [234]), Twain reports a conversation overheard between two corporate salesmen in which it is revealed that at least one of them is party to industrial fraud. (His firm manufactures a cottonseed oil that it passes off as genuine European olive oil; in the process the company apparently forges, appropriates, or otherwise obtains United States "customhouse marks" [236].) Instead of being offended, the other drummer wants to hear how the thing was done. Thus the chapter suggests that the oleaginous taint of corruption spreads easily from corporation to corporation.

That the deceitful salesman is from New Orleans seems fitting, for *Life*'s cultural and economic critiques deepen as the book moves further south. The "Metropolis of the South" itself, however, is a mass of contradictions: a "progressive" (243) city infatuated with the "inhuman" sport of cockfighting (260); a "driving place commercially" (243) duped by "girly-girly romance" (265). Twain's conflicted interpretations affect his own text as well: on one page he regrets that the city's "troughlike gutters . . . were still half full of reposeful water with a dusty surface" (242); on the next he declares that the gutters are "flushed now, two or three times a day, by powerful machinery" (243).

The emphasis on gutters recalls Twain's appreciative eye for them in *Roughing It*'s Salt Lake City chapters. One advantage New Orleans has over Brigham Young's stronghold is that the river city's residents are as adept at having fun as they are at working. Sports historian Dale Somers reports that by 1860 New Orleans was already "the sporting center of the Old South," and at the time of Twain's visit in 1882 one local newspaper asserted with good cause that "New Orleans is fast becoming one of the most prominent sporting cities of this country."[58] Twain is deeply disturbed, however, by the local pastime of cockfighting. At first glance, in an odd way, the sport seems a Reconstruction success story; Twain reports that there "were men and boys there of all ages and all colors, and of many languages and nationalities" (259). But the bloody contest nonetheless symbolically replicates racial conflict, as the black and white handlers square off with their black and gray cocks. Even though Twain does not actually specify which cock belongs to which man, his descriptions of each animal replay two conspicuous clichés of post-Reconstruction America. The phrase "big black cock," for example, foregrounds white Americans' fear of freedmen's imagined physical and sexual prowess, while the detail that the "little gray one" responds to attack "with spirit" (259) recalls the myth of the valiant, underdog Confederacy. The fact that Twain highlights this particularly violent sport at a time when its popularity was actually in decline further suggests that he found it metaphorically rather than literally instructive for the visitor.

Recreational and sporting events were, after all, conspicuous sites of the failure of Reconstruction ideals in the South after the withdrawal of federal troops in 1877. While contemporary analysts typically praised sport as democratic, in the 1880s color lines appeared in stands and on playing fields throughout the country. As Somers argues, post-Reconstruction leisure all too often "merely reflected the social and political pressures that made rigid racial segregation an established practice in the South and, to an only slightly lesser extent, in the North."[59] The other unusual sports event on which Twain reports, the "picturesque and entertaining" mule race (263), makes visible the multiple caste divisions within southern society in the 1880s. Although the mules (much like the audience at the cockpit) boast "all sorts of complexions, gaits, [and] dispositions" (262), the spectators are all "people of fashion" (263), that is, upper-class southern whites. Even the jockeys are all white—a feature common only after southern racetracks went Jim Crow in the 1880s.[60]

In an equally subtle way, Twain's empathy for and identification with the artisan class is signaled here and in the following chapter, "Enchantments and Enchanters." Twain apportions much of the blame for southern white racial and class nostalgia to the lingering influence of "the Sir Walter disease," a "reverence for . . . and pride and pleasure" in "rank and caste" (266). Scott's "pernicious work" (267) corrupts southern forms of religion, government, and industry, replacing "practical, common-sense, progressive ideas, and progressive works," with "the sillinesses and emptinesses, sham grandeurs, sham gauds, and sham chivalries of a brainless and worthless long-vanished society" (265–66). Twain's contempt for medieval and monarchical social, cultural, and economic relations mirrors the values expressed in the 1870s and early 1880s in the rhetoric of artisans and skilled workers. As Gutman has shown, artisan labor periodicals complained that America had become "an *old* country," run by "capital as rigid as an absolute monarchy." Inquired the *National Labor Tribune* in 1874: "Shall we let the gold barons of the nineteenth century put iron collars of ownership around our necks as did the feudal barons with their serfs in the fourteenth century?"[61]

Absolutely not—no more than Twain wished to let himself be hindered by the "feudal" literary constraints that Scott's immensely popular romantic narratives represented. Twain was equally fearful of the American constraints posed by his contemporaries, symbolized in the aging but revered trio of "littery" men—Longfellow, Emerson, and Holmes—that Twain aggressively lampooned in his infamous 1877 "Whittier Birthday Speech."[62] Whatever anxieties Twain was feeling in 1877 were probably exacerbated by his "humiliating and infuriating" experience with *Tom Sawyer* the year before, when his publisher fell months behind schedule. By 1882, when Twain was writing *Life*, he had essentially become his own publisher, paying his ostensible employer, James Osgood, a small royalty for acting as his sales agent.[63] Thus Twain's attack on Scott in *Life* indicates his affiliation with artisans in two ways: Twain shares not only their economic concerns but, more important, their underlying ethic of independence and control. That Twain's artisan leanings are not themselves innocent of an affection for caste only further signals his identification with actual artisans, who frequently distinguished themselves politically and socially from unskilled workers. Twain's deepening critique, so evident in *Life*'s middle third, is by no means free of internal tension.[64]

■

Nowhere is Twain's attempt to resolve that tension more clear than in the final section of the book (chapters 51–60), in which Twain reboards a steamboat and chuffs back upriver. Chapter 51, which covers in six pages as much geographical territory (New Orleans to St. Louis) as the previous twenty-eight chapters, opens with a tremendously comforting moment for Twain. Seated in the pilothouse of the *City of Baton Rouge*, he watches with "a very great and sincere pleasure" his own past repeat itself (285). An inexperienced cub takes the wheel to guide the steamer out of New Orleans but leaves too much space between it and the other ships. In steps Horace Bixby, who shows the apprentice how to "[crowd] the boat in," exactly as Bixby had done for Twain "about a quarter of a century before, in that same spot" (285). Seemingly reassured that some good values of the past also survive in 1882, Twain reviews more positively signs that had discouraged him on the boat trip down. Watching a pilot successfully run several crossings in deep fog, Twain now sees "great value" in the guidance chart that he had previously criticized for knocking the romance out of the river.[65] As the night clears, moreover, Twain discovers that the romance endures, in the shape of "faint spectral trees, dimly glimpsed through the shredding fog" (285).

The most affecting portions of the trip, however, are the powerful storms that force the steamer to tie up and duck for cover. Twain thrills to the "old-fashioned energy" of the last of these, particularly its spectacular lightning flashes, "which enchanted the eye and sent electric ecstasies of mixed delight and apprehension shivering along every nerve in the body in unintermittent procession" (285–86). When the fury of the storm gets too close for comfort, however, Twain heads below deck. Although we can hardly blame

him for avoiding potential harm, this protected encounter with danger anticipates the dynamics of a strange episode narrated at the end of the chapter. In St. Louis, Twain meets a man whom he had apparently deserted
some "thirty years" (289) earlier in order to avoid a potentially violent situation: namely, a deadly militia confrontation with a rioting mob, in which
Twain and this man had been members of the armed force marching on the
rioters. On the pretense of getting a drink of water, Twain dropped out and
went home. We can't tell why Twain decamped—he is deliberately coy
about his motivations—but he leaves open the possibility that he withdrew
because he objected to the assignment. We also do not know why the rioters were rioting; but labor unrest is another likely possibility. (More con-
temporarily, St. Louis in 1877 had been the site of the first general strike in
an industrial city in the United States.)[66] If these were the circumstances,
then by narrating a personal act of principled (if not particularly vocal) resistance on behalf of working-class rioters, Twain may, once again, be signaling an affinity for the "old-fashioned" energies of American labor.

Even if we accept the anecdote as an indication of such an affinity, however, Twain's conspicuously curtailed retelling of the event limits its contemporary applicability. After the incident rather rudely and unexpectedly
resurfaces (the deserted man, recognizing Twain on the street, gruffly in-
quires, "Look here, *have you got that drink yet?*" [289]), Twain seems satisfied to discover merely that his "friend" had not been killed. The narrative
neatly elides whatever further discussion the two men have when Twain offers to treat to a bottle of champagne; if the recalled incident has any resonance in the present—a time of recurrent, violent, urban riots—Twain
conceals it.

The circumscription that this narrative act (and others like it) entails
seems prerequisite for the last leg of Twain's journey, his 500-mile run north
to the head of the river. For in this final section of the book Twain is noticeably less anxious about the corporate organizations he had disparaged in
Life's middle chapters. "From St. Louis northward," he announces, including in this sweep his childhood home of Hannibal, "there are all the en-

livening signs of the presence of active, energetic, intelligent, prosperous, practical nineteenth-century populations" (321). "The people don't dream," he continues, "they work" (321). Are we back once again to the industrious Salt Lake City of Twain's Far West travels? Not at all: these "substantial" towns also seem to be "happy" ones, full of "wholesome life and comfort," not merely the buzzing and humming of Mormon machinery (321). Twain specifically mentions the presence of both intellectual and recreational leisure activity in several of these cities. Quincy, Illinois, is "brisk, handsome, [and] well-ordered," but also "interested in art, letters, and other high things," and boasts "ample fairgrounds, a well-kept park, and many attractive drives" (321–22); Burlington, Iowa, "belted with busy factories of nearly every imaginable description," also has a new opera house (325); Rock Island has been turned "into a wonderful park" (328).[67]

The motive force for this "amazing region," according to Twain, is its people (327). The northwesterners "compel homage"; like steamboat pilots of old, they are "independent" and "educated and enlightened"; they "keep abreast of the best and newest thought" but also "think for themselves" (326). They are, in short, remarkably like the artisan class with which Twain has come to identify over the course of his book. The success of their achievements is due to the craft they bring to their work and to their ability to turn "old-fashioned" energies to modern advantage. Perhaps the best example of this combination is found in Minneapolis, whose mill power derives from the "art" of tapping the "inestimable value, business-wise," of the eighty-two-foot falls of St. Anthony (342).[68]

Twain's praise is by no means unequivocal. He notes, for example, that the conversion of these falls to industrial power occurs "somewhat to the damage of the falls as a spectacle" (342). And his explicit mockery of the panorama-style narration of an old gentleman passenger as the boat nears St. Paul may be an ironic commentary on Twain's own role as a self-appointed tour guide to the industrial landscape of the Northwest. But none of Twain's equivocations quite dispels the generally optimistic tone of support for corporate culture at the close of the book. One of the potentially

harshest critiques of the impact of industrial labor on the individual operative, for example, is curiously deflected into an anonymous quotation.
When discussing the majesty of Protestant churches, Twain reminds his
readers to reflect "that 'every brick and every stone in this beautiful edifice
represents an ache or a pain, and a handful of sweat, and hours of heavy fatigue, contributed by the back and forehead and bones of poverty'" (340).
Instead of particularizing the labor involved (which is not really industrial
work to begin with), the sentimental rhetoric of Twain's speaker simultaneously dulls the charges and romanticizes the work. The Irish "hired girls"
who "delight" in building such churches are to be pitied, but not necessarily disburdened (340).

A second disruptive moment—the sudden appearance of the "unholy
train" (329)—seems more threatening to the tone of Twain's final chapters.
The demonic locomotive "comes tearing along . . . , ripping the sacred solitude to rags and tatters with its devil's war whoop and the roar and thun-
der of its rushing wheels" and yanking the daydreaming narrator back into
"this world" (329–30). The railroad, after all, is both the chief enemy of the
river (having seduced away its passengers and stolen much of its freight)
and a noisy symbol of industrial production, distribution, and expansion.
"The locomotive," Twain notes ironically, "is in sight from the deck of the
steamboat almost the whole way from St. Louis to St. Paul" (330). But that
does not prevent the narrative from ending with Twain striking for home
from St. Paul via the railroad, which rushes him to New York quickly and
efficiently, not "missing schedule time ten minutes anywhere on the
route"—a pleasant ending to a "most enjoyable" trip (345).[69]

With the benefit of hindsight we might criticize Twain's cheery portrayal
of northwestern (today, midwestern) industry. After all, Twain never really
peeks inside any of the factories his trip north to St. Paul reveals. He certainly never describes actual operatives at work, or even at play. (Indeed,
in many ways Twain's tourist experience in the last ten chapters never pen-
etrates beyond what Dean MacCannell has called the "staged authenticity"
phase; as the product of principally a spectator and not a participant, his

narrative panorama seems potentially as contrived as the old gentleman passenger's.)[70] From another angle, one might even argue that the text, for all its attention to parks and opera houses, still registers the loss of certain freer forms of spontaneous play. Twain notes with apparent regret, for example, the lumber rafts that move downriver in "modern fashion," their men "quiet" and "orderly," where once had floated "leisurely" the "joyous and reckless crews" of "old-fashioned" days (331).

And yet such criticism, however valid, as much overlooks Twain's narrative design as Twain overlooks the real rigors of northwestern industry. For the key to understanding the overall effect of the final chapters is recognizing the crucial inversion that the narrative makes at chapter 51, when Twain turns back upriver. From this point on, the text speaks of itself as moving "deeper and deeper" (326) north, a curiously inverted metaphor signaling that the book still has territory to penetrate and discover. What Twain foregrounds in his strategically guided tour is a new Northwest succeeding where the older South had failed, and the ability of an artisan-led industry (at least as Twain presents matters) to heal the terrible split between labor and capital in the 1880s. In one sense, Twain is historically perceptive: it was ultimately a new breed of worker—the "factory artisan"—who led the major working-class challenges of the 1880s.[71] In another sense, Twain can only achieve the positive vision at the end of *Life* by metaphorically inverting the sequence of American events in the turbulent 1870s that I have argued influence the text itself. For the narrative logic of Twain's optimism requires that his "Centennial Exposition"—which is symbolically what his closing praise of the link between art and industry amounts to—follow, rather than precede, the most violent clashes between owners and workers. In Twain's text the greatest unrest and dissatisfaction appear in the middle section, and the transitional chapter 51 displaces the narrative's one actual riot (which even if not labor-related itself evokes the violence associated with labor riots) into the distant past. And although certain readers may regret Twain's decision to end *Life* with a contemporary historical irony itself ironically reversed, we cannot ignore the calculated structure which that reversal confers on the book. Above all, we need to stop thinking of *Life* as a text that leaves its important work behind somewhere around chapter 20.

The final indication that Twain seriously attempts to craft a structured, healing narrative in *Life* lies in the last appendix. Unlike the wildcat appendix that ends *Roughing It*—the unexpected critical blast Twain ignites beneath Conrad Wiegand's story—the tale "The Undying Head" in *Life* supports rather than undermines the thrust of the main narrative that precedes it. In brief, the Indian legend (for which the text prepares us with a footnote) tells of a powerful supernatural being (a manito) who is accidentally "killed" by his sister. This manito then orders her to sever his head from his dying body and place it in his medicine sack along with his paints and feathers. The head lives on, eventually helping its sister and ten brave warriors defeat another manito. At the end of the tale, the sister and the warriors reattach the undying head to its once-dead body, restoring the manito to "all his former beauty and manliness" (373). Figuratively speaking, then, the appendix heals the split implicitly forecast in *Life*'s opening epigraph on the "Body of the Nation"—a nation split in 1863 by civil war, and split again in the 1870s by labor violence.[72] And Twain's restorative gesture simultaneously reaffirms his faith in the powers and resources of the artist/artisan, for the tale makes clear that the undying manito's strength is concentrated not only in his beautiful paints and skillfully crafted feathers, but also in his ability to control events, even after he is reduced to a mere head. In this way, *Life* comes to a clearer—if not in all ways more satisfying—resolution of the tensions Twain first explored in *Roughing It*.

■

One might be tempted to say by way of conclusion that Twain's resolution of these tensions made his 1886 speech on behalf of the Knights of Labor, titled "The New Dynasty," inevitable; that, as Howells once said of Twain, his "mind and soul were with those who do the hard work in the world." Wasn't his speech, after all, "unquestionably the most eloquent defense of organized labor during the 1880s, and one of the most eloquent in all of American history"?[73] Not if by "eloquent defense of organized labor" one means an unquestioned faith in egalitarian principles. For as Banta has shown, the "cumulative effect" of Twain's metaphorical language in "The New Dynasty" "dampens" any message of total labor-capital equality.[74] Only with difficulty could Twain conceal the limits of his support for industrial democracy.

Nonetheless, *Roughing It* and *Life on the Mississippi* were fascinating texts to put before an industrializing society in 1872 and 1883. In *Roughing It*, Sam's repeated reason for leaving a job or situation is that he is bored by its monotony. "I began to get tired of staying in one place so long," he declares before moving to San Francisco (297). "I wanted—I did not know *what* I wanted. I had the 'spring fever' and wanted a change, principally, no doubt" (297). The ensuing repetitiveness of his work in San Francisco eventually makes him eager to leave again: "I wanted another change" (331). Sam's complaints are no different from those uttered by workers struggling to adapt to the monotonous demands of industrial work in the early 1870s. Where Sam does differ from those laborers—in his ability to leave and take up a new position whenever he wants to—we can measure the imaginative distance between Twain's text and American industrial conditions. This distance accounts for *Roughing It*'s troubled closing retreat from a full endorsement of the American worker's desire for "satisfying variety" (297)—at precisely the time when frustrating repetitiveness was fast becoming the norm.

By 1882, it was (or should have been) more clear to the country and to Twain that the satisfaction an artisan might have received from "his control of each step in the labor process" was an impossibility for all but a few American workers.[75] The precipitate violence that in part characterized the period between *Roughing It* and *Life* helped move Twain from the unsettled ambivalences of his earlier text to a more assured identification with the endangered "factory artisan." As we have seen, Twain's deliberate confrontation with a disappearing past was not itself unagitated. But his closing vision of a future in which satisfying creative and economic control might still be achieved—a vision perhaps influenced by the minirecovery of the early 1880s—indicates the willful resolution of vexing personal and narrative tensions. That the trip to St. Paul was actually a "hideous" one for Twain suggests just how willful that resolution was.[76]

As an anxious witness to the twilight of an entrepreneurial and artisanal economy, Twain looked for ways to hold on to the independence and autonomy that corporate capitalism increasingly threatened. That he could do so in the end only by deliberately rewriting the history of that struggle attests to the deep-seated reservations he ultimately held about the prospects for such retentions. In so doing, as we will see, Twain's works adumbrate the very similar reservations that later American writers would have about play theory, particularly its promises of individual creativity and self-control through a directed play subordinate to the interests of that selfsame corporate capitalism. The principal irony of Twain's position as a prophetic critic of the play theorists is that he became perhaps their favorite American author—the one writer who for play theory best expressed the utopian possibilities for right recreation in an industrializing world.

It was primarily not the troubled texts of *Roughing It* and *Life on the Mississippi*, however, that the soon-to-emerge play reformers, seeking to revive flagging American bodies and spirits, would champion, but instead the one book that Twain actually did publish in that fateful year of 1876: *The Adventures of Tom Sawyer*. Seizing on that novel's apparently idyllic celebration of play—and particularly Tom's brilliant fence-painting con—the reformers optimistically touted Twain's supposed understanding that work is what you make it, and can (in the right light) even be play.[77] As the preceding analysis suggests, Twain's understanding of work and play under industrial conditions was far more ambivalent. And as the following chapters indicate, play theory's own idyllic conception of the purposes and meanings of play could be far more limited (and limiting), particularly for the American immigrants, women, and racial minorities whose bodies and spirits the play reformers hoped especially to regenerate. Whitewash, one might be tempted to say, isn't the half of it.

PART II

ALTERNATIVE
ARTICULATIONS

CHAPTER THREE

Frontier Fairy Tales

Cahan, Rölvaag, and the
Resistance to Play Progressivism

IN 1909, NOTED CITY PLANNER Charles Robinson offered a critique
of the nascent playground reform movement in America:

> To my mind the whole playground conception has heretofore been wrong.
> We have taken as our ideal a bare city lot equipped with paraphernalia for
> children's exercise. The truer ideal would be an acre or so of natural looking
> country, which we should create if necessary and where [there might be] a
> chance for the city child to know the delights of a real outdoors, of a place
> where in the night there might be fairies, as there never would be in the or-
> dinary city playground.[1]

Robinson's evocation of an extraordinary urban play space—conceived virtually at the apex of pre–World War I foreign immigration to the United
States—had much in common with many immigrants' own dreams of
America. Like Robinson, immigrants frequently imagined America as a
place of "natural" freedom, where constraints automatically yielded to "delights," where the very landscape exuded both unlimited promise and re-
juvenating enchantment. The America of their dreams was, moreover, not
simply a bare space for continued "exercise," or work; "the transplanted" (to
use John Bodnar's phrase) believed they would find time and space for play.

Robinson's comments also betray a nostalgia for a lost, magic space of
"real outdoors," an environment to which he believed the city child no
longer had access. In the face of the rapid urbanization that characterized
post–Civil War America, such nostalgia was entirely understandable. As

early as 1893 Frederick Jackson Turner had pronounced the American frontier closed. By the time of Robinson's critique the geographical and psychological gap between "city" and "country" had widened considerably. The "walking city" of the mid- to late-nineteenth century—in which rural space was still "relatively accessible to most urbanites"—had seen nearly all of its open land (both within and without) bought up and then built on.[2] Urban youth, particularly the immigrant children for whom by Robinson's day most playgrounds were being designed, generally had access only to the crowded streets that crisscrossed their industrialized, radial cities.

While not all recreation reformers agreed with Robinson's alternative conception of the urban playground—and although the literal creation of his expansive "country" acreage was made all but impossible by soaring real estate prices—a group of influential turn-of-the-century play practitioners and leisure theorists nonetheless tried to put Robinson's "truer ideal" into metaphorical practice. Alarmed by the loss of contact with nineteenth-century rural values, and confronted by an escalating influx of European immigrants to a country whose quintessentially Americanizing space—the frontier—had recently disappeared, these reformers aggressively reconceived playground space as the culture's most vital space. Properly guided play, they held, would "fit" the city child with the physical, intellectual, and moral skills formerly best developed in the countryside. By accustoming a nation, through its children, to the character-building habits of wholesome play, the reformers hoped to counteract the destructive tendencies of modern industrial labor. And perhaps most important, these largely white, upper-middle-class reformers sought to make their playgrounds, and American leisure in general, a viable substitute for the democratizing, nationalizing crucible that was Turner's frontier. The mass of potentially "unfit" immigrants landing on American shores (and heading straight for the cities) could play their way into becoming productive, law-abiding citizens.

This metaphorical reconception of American leisure (and leisure space) as the new frontier relied in large part on a curious alignment of certain cultural narratives during the first two decades of the twentieth century. On the one hand, by Robinson's day the transformation of the American industrial economy from its craftsperson, entrepreneurial origins to its consolidated corporate maturity had been allegorized as a necessary evolution from competitive individualism to cooperative combination.[3] Never mind that many of these new companies acted as selfishly individualistic as their smaller predecessors; these transgressions (so the story went) were being punished by a vigilant central government looking out for the common good. On the other hand, the new field of child psychology declared that children, too, naturally evolved from anarchic individuals to loyal members of larger social units, such as the gang, the company, or the nation. The recreation theorists' playgrounds were to serve as an appropriate meeting place for these two stories of American development. By training children to see that their ultimate goal was to become self-sacrificing members of a playground team, play reformers could figuratively fit American youth to the demands of the complex, bureaucratic, corporate structure that in all likelihood awaited them. The child could, in a sense, literally grow up with the institutions of the country.

These narratives, of course, lined up particularly well with a popular story of the ideal American immigrant of any age. Arriving in the United States as a cultural and (typically) linguistic outsider, the immigrant could by assiduous application adopt the values and language of the larger culture and become part of the American "team." Turn-of-the-century urban playgrounds offered promising new sites for this refashioning. Even the most stubbornly ethnic outsider, recreation reformers believed, could be magically shaped into a truly assimilated American. But even as the ideologies of play reform and assimilation merged with the story of American capitalism—and even as certain real immigrant narratives applauded the same— other strong voices fought to articulate alternative possibilities.

Abraham Cahan and Ole Rölvaag were two of the strongest of these voices. By showing in their fictions that the play theorists' ideal of teamwork frequently clashed with immigrant notions of communal experience; by exposing how in many cases the supposedly liberating ethic of "American" play promulgated by recreation reformers was (particularly for American immigrants) only the work ethic in disguise; by challenging the Turnerian interpretation of the effects of the frontier on American character; and above all by narrating the often devastating personal costs of assimilating to the American team—of trying to work and play and succeed the American way—Cahan and Rölvaag resist the prevailing logic of corporate capitalism and play progressivism. Much as Mark Twain's two texts of American travel stand as telling endpoints on the highly charged decade of the 1870s while recapitulating forty years of American economic history, Cahan's *The Rise of David Levinsky* (1917) and Rölvaag's *Giants in the Earth* (1927) bracket a crucial period for American immigration policy (the downward spiral from the exploratory 1917 Literacy Test Act to the ultra-restrictive National Origins Act of 1924) as they rehearse and reclaim the twinned histories of labor and leisure that shaped the Russian Jewish transformation of New York City's lower East Side from the 1880s to the 1910s and the Norwegian settlement of the Great Plains beginning in the 1870s. And like Twain, Cahan and Rölvaag endorse to some degree the contemporary assumptions about the very processes their narratives critique. But in the end those critiques stand clear. Cahan demonstrates that David Levinsky's spectacular American rebirth as a thoroughly modern capitalist leaves him a lonely, empty, and (despite his physical strength) unfit man reduced to a bitter society of one amidst the great wealth and promise of the United States. And Rölvaag warns that Turner's valorization of the frontier as a place of "perennial rebirth" masks the way that supposedly "free" lands can exact devastating personal, social, and cultural costs. At the very least, Cahan and Rölvaag remind city dreamer Charles Robinson that not all fairies in the night are friendly.

■

Turn-of-the-century American playground reform developed hand in hand with the spatial reorganization of American cities and grew more specifically out of the mid-century municipal park movement—itself a response to the loss of open space in urban centers. As cities outgrew their walking limits in the 1860s and 1870s, Steven Riess reports, empty lots formerly used for inner-city recreation "were quickly taken up for residential or commercial use, and . . . intensive utilization of all available space overran traditional athletic sites." The drive to create suburban parks, overseen by landscape architects like Frederick Law Olmsted (best known for designing New York City's Central Park in the 1850s), sought to provide alternative open spaces by constructing municipally supported "year-round pleasure grounds" on the outskirts of major cities. These parks were not, however, intended to gird their cities with what Turner would later identify as the boisterous and revitalizing energies of the frontier. Olmsted's parks—whose spirit Charles Robinson's ideal playground of "natural looking country" explicitly evokes—instead encouraged more contemplative, "receptive recreation"; as Riess explains, patrons were to receive "pleasure without conscious exertion" by "looking at tranquil scenes, gentle streams, and grassy meadows."[4] In Central Park, for example, Olmsted deliberately incorporated curved roadways to prevent trotting matches that might disturb the park's repose and supported the prohibition of adult team sports that might attract rowdy crowds and ruin the grass. Above all, Olmsted valued serenity and order. To Thorstein Veblen and others, however, the "make-believe . . . rusticity" that characterized the "accepted ideals" of public grounds marked parks like Olmsted's as conspicuous examples of a strictly upper-class canon of taste.[5] And despite Olmsted's own hope that Central Park would serve as a "working-class refuge," a diversion from (in his words) "unwholesome, vicious, destructive methods and habits of seeking recreation," his parks and their progeny were, in fact, barely accessible to most working-class city residents, who all too often could afford neither the expense nor the time of travel.[6]

Where elite theory failed, working-class politics often succeeded. Eager to secure "breathing spaces" for the inner cities as well as for the suburban fringes, vocal citizens' groups and urban aldermen in cities like Boston and Worcester initiated the push to provide all classes with space to play. Seeing, like Olmsted, the value of open land to an urbanizing and heterogeneous populace, but lacking his anxiety about unseemly lower-class recreation and

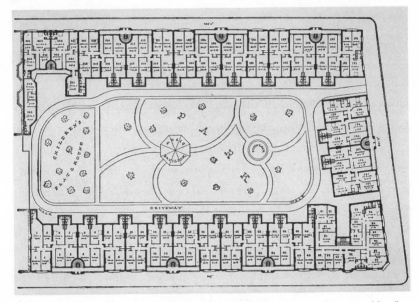

FIGURE 7. "General Plan of the Riverside Buidings (A. T. White's) in Brooklyn."
From Jacob A. Riis, *How the Other Half Lives* (1901 edition).

armed with an almost proto-Turnerian sense of the benefits of buoyant physical interaction, these neighborhood reformers convinced municipal governments to build urban playgrounds as local alternatives to Olmsted's distant
and restrictive parks and to their own increasingly dangerous city streets.[7]

A force that helped unlock even larger city coffers was undoubtedly the
crusading journalism of middle-class reformers like Jacob Riis, himself an
immigrant to the United States and one of the first to publicize the
cramped, unhealthful conditions of the urban slums. Riis's 1890 exposé,
How the Other Half Lives, served up graphic evidence of what he termed the
"slovenliness, discontent, privation, and ignorance" bred in (and by) the
tenement houses of New York's lower East Side.[8] Despite Riis's ethnic and
religious prejudices (he tended, for example, to refer to the racial "instincts"
of each group he examined, sometimes praising in one the very traits he
condemned in another), he showed with painful clarity how the working-
class immigrant slums virtually prohibited "wholesome" human recreation.

This was particularly true for children, he argued, who often "grow up in joyless homes to lives of wearisome toil that claims them at an age when the play of their happier fellows has but just begun" (138).

Because the suburban municipal park system offered poor urban residents little relief from such toil, Riis praised the construction of even small urban parks as a "means of relieving the congested population of tenement districts" (126). Nonetheless, Riis's conception of the role of park space in 1890 was remarkably similar to Olmsted's. In stumping for Brooklyn builder A. T. White's "model tenement" plan in *How the Other Half Lives*, for example, Riis praised White's incorporation of a "great" central park (229), whose curving walkways, shady trees, music pavilion, and fountain explicitly recalled the contours and purposes of Olmsted's New York triumph (see, for example, Figure 7). Indeed, in *How the Other Half Lives*, Riis often emphasized the power of greenery of any kind to bring beauty and order— both physical and moral—to the slums. Noting that "tenement-houses" rarely have "aesthetic resources," for instance, he approved of "the German" and his "strong love for flowers" (124). "His garden goes with him wherever he goes," Riis claimed; "wherever he puts it in a tenement block it does the work of a dozen police clubs" (124).

Despite this Olmstedian politics of shrubbery, Riis at other times praised the virtues of freedom, mobility, and self-supporting democracy in rhetoric that Turner would shortly use to describe the essential qualities of the frontier. In his chapter "The Street Arab," for example, Riis applauds the Children's Aid Society for its progressive dealings with the homeless or "outcast" boy, who "may come and go as he pleases so long as he behaves himself. No restraint of any sort is put on his independence" (156). Another of the aid society's programs that Turner would have appreciated was its sending of thousands of "young emigrants" to homes "in the Far West, to grow up self-supporting men and women safe from the temptations and the vice of the city" (160). "Occasionally one comes back," Riis allows, as though to remind us that the open space of the western frontier—not to mention the claustrophobic embrace of a new family primarily seeking useful labor—

FIGURE 8. Jacob A. Riis, "Shooting Craps (Bootblacks and Newsboys)," 1891.
From the Jacob A. Riis Collection, Museum of the City of New York.
Reprinted with permission.

may not provide the best environment for everyone. But most children, he suggested, thrived.

By contrast, Riis's dramatic photographs suggest that in the absence of the Children's Aid Society or A. T. White's model tenement, an immigrant child of the lower East Side seeking recreation might well end up crouched in an alleyway shooting craps with the bootblacks and newsboys (see Figure 8). This is a fascinating picture, in part because it simultaneously encapsulates late-nineteenth-century attitudes toward unwholesome amusement and foreshadows not only the regenerative strategies of early-twentieth-century organized play reformers (who would try to turn the "gang instinct" to positive use) but also their pervasive ideology of supervision. Like most of Riis's photos, which were far from spontaneous and usually required a certain amount of staging, this picture can be read as a mini-narrative, an economical and interpretable tale of urban life. The framing of the shot, in which the alley's side walls both form the borders of the picture and narrow sharply toward the rear, suggests that the boys' play has led (or will lead) them to a hopelessly urban dead end. Although there is a door of potential escape in the background, it is firmly closed.[9] Each boy's head looks down at the pavement, no face betraying any particular pleasure, suggesting either the joylessness of vice or the earnest attention due even the most junior of economies. The standing boy is a special case. Does he have interest but lack means? At least he has shoes and a hat, unlike the second boy from the left. And what of the odd figure of the standing man? Is he a double for the viewer, expressing mingled concern and disapproval? Or does he represent parental (or social) authority, stepping forward (note the bent right knee) to stop the game? Or is he, with his own hat and hands-in-pocket slouch, perhaps a double for the standing boy, an eerie embodiment of the "child is father to the man" philosophy that had long underwritten American injunctions against youthful idleness?

By any reading, the photo's tale seems grim, except perhaps for the distinct wash of sunlight that surrounds the boys, separating (or possibly protecting) them from not only the deadest end of the alley but also the standing man and even the viewer. And here an early-twentieth-century play reformer, well-versed in the codified theory of the by then national playground movement, might say that Riis's photo succinctly illustrates one of that movement's central tenets: that the "gang instinct" is at heart a healthy one merely awaiting the proper guidance to shape its activities. That same reformer might then point to Figure 9 as, in a sense, what would happen to Figure 8 if one could translate it to the organized inner-city playground. The four solemn shootists become a throng of (apparently) eager ball players, up on their feet, arms raised, exercising their bodies and engaged in a character-building team sport on natural ground instead of cement. The standing man in the left foreground is no longer an idle bystander but the trained play supervisor. *His* double, the young onlooker, stands by his side

FIGURE 9. Bain News Service, Manhattan's Carnegie Playground, 5th Avenue,
New York City (August 1911). Library of Congress, LC-USZ62-71329.

rather than isolated across the busy play space, as in Figure 8. There are
walls, to be sure, but only two (the left one particularly clean and bright),
which together suggest protection and unlimited extension into more open
space rather than menacing enclosure.[10]

There are also signs that all is not rosy on the playground. There appear
to be too many children to make the game of basketball (or any real team
play) very effective; there are actually several onlookers; and at least one
child has turned his back to the game while another walks out of the frame.
Why does the play supervisor need a cane? Or is that a stick? But taken together, the two pictures display enough ideological continuity (the team
game as the maturation of competitive individualism; the genial supervisor as successor to the idle spectator) that it seems fair to let them represent
what our hypothetical early-twentieth-century play reformer has suggested:
"before" and "after" pictures of urban recreation, the "after" achieved by the

play directives of such organizations as the Playground Association of America (PAA).

Founded in 1906 as the country's first national recreation reform agency, the PAA and its play theorists saw latent in leisure almost precisely the same character- and nation-building qualities that Turner identified with America's free lands. For these reformers, leisure was very much America's "new frontier."[11] Much as Turner claimed that the physical demands of the wilderness not only beckoned but created "a fit people," full of "restless, nervous energy" and "that buoyancy and exuberance which comes with freedom," turn-of-the-century play progressives believed that right recreation developed (according to just one prominent play handbook) "strength," "endurance," and "robust health," imparting to the mind "an alertness and vivacity which are essential" and to the spirit a sense of "joyfulness, . . . alertness, . . . [and] optimism which we all love to see." It is only in play, the recreation reformers maintained, that a child "is doing the things that he really wants to do and is acting from the inner law of his own being, and it is hence only in his play that he is a free agent."[12] One could cull similarly Turnerian pronouncements from other play documents almost at random.

If the play theorists did not, for the most part, explicitly invoke the frontier, they did have a keen sense that the virtues they hoped to cultivate were distinctly ex-urban and all too rapidly vanishing. According to G. Stanley Hall, the developmental psychology professor under whom many of the play theorists studied, the city child must be "perpetually incite[d] to visit . . . field, forest, hill, [and] shore, . . . the true homes of childhood in this wild, undomesticated stage from which modern conditions have kidnapped and transported him."[13] Indeed, the most explicit parallels in early-twentieth-century play theory to Turner are found in the striking alignment of Hall's "recapitulation" model of human psychosocial development with Turner's description of the process by which the frontier shaped the American character. According to Turner, the "distinguishing feature of American life" is its recurrent, revitalizing cycle of evolution from its most savage state. "American development has exhibited not merely advance along a single line, but a return to primitive conditions on a continually advancing frontier line."[14] Hall's recapitulation theory—which, despite its dubious standing in the scientific community during the Progressive Era, was the "ideological heart" of the child study movement underlying elite play reform[15]—similarly held that every child rehearsed (or "recapitulated") the evolutionary stages of human life, from the most primitive to the most advanced. It was only this insistent return to the "inborn and more or less savage instincts" that guaranteed the development of civilization's "higher and more completely human traits."[16]

In the hands of the play theorists, Hall's recapitulation model took the form of four distinct childhood stages: the baby age (ages zero to three years); the dramatic age (ages three to six); the "Big Injun" age (six to eleven); and the age of loyalty (eleven to fourteen). All were compelling, but the preadolescent (or Big Injun) age, as in Hall's theory, was crucial. After a babyhood in which the child learns the elemental forms of mastery (via grasping and manipulation), and a brief intervening stage of imitation and empathy, the youth explodes into the lawless (yet formative) rampage that is preadolescence. In the words of Joseph Lee, second president of the PAA and author of *Play in Education* (1915), the Big Injun's is "the anarchistic age, the age of the individual," and his proving ground is the playground.[17] Just as the open frontier supposedly operated as a crucial safety valve for the pent-up energies of the city, so too was the playground regarded as a necessary space for the venting of surplus energies. Without the provision of such space, reformers were fond of arguing, urban children would erupt into what society at large perceived as delinquency, but which was only the natural expression of the Big Injun stage. "Most boys who break laws," claimed an early play handbook, "are usually less to blame than are the authorities who provide no outlet for natural strenuousness but instead attempt to bottle up the energy. As well tie down tight the cover on a coffee tank full of boiling drink and not expect an explosion!"[18] Moreover, if the boy were prevented from exuberant play, he risked failing to evolve smoothly to his "higher heredity," much as the pioneer with no free land, according to Turner, risked being stuck in "a permanent position of social subordination."[19]

Nonetheless, the playground's freedoms differed from those of the frontier. If the play theorists encouraged exuberant play, they also believed that it needed careful direction. Thus where Turner's pioneer "held with passionate devotion the idea that he was building under freedom a new society, based on self government and for the welfare of the average man,"[20] the typical playground curriculum was carefully structured from above. As Dominick Cavallo reports, the PAA hierarchy designed model weekly programs with strict timetables for local play directors to emulate, such as the following after-school schedule for adolescents:

> 1:30–2:00, patriotic songs
> 2:00–2:30, supervised "free play": tugs-of-war, marbles, etc.
> 2:30–3:00, track and field events
> 3:00–5:00, team games, vocational training, and folk dancing.[21]

Here the democratic freedom of the frontier tilts perceptibly toward oligarchy. Even the half hour of "free play" allotted to the children, one notes, is supervised—and further prescribed by the PAA's suggestive delimiting of what that play might look like ("tugs-of-war, marbles, etc."). "There is real freedom on the playground," Luther Gulick explained in one of the central paradoxes of play theory, "because the child must either play by the rules or be shut out by his playmates or those in charge."[22] If you don't like it, Gulick might say, you're entirely free to leave.

What was most important to reformers like Gulick—and what marked their most important modification of Turner's frontier ideology—was that the child learn to see him- or herself as a part of something greater and more enduring than the autonomous self. This is one reason that team games typically superseded timed events on the playground, tending not only to follow them on the schedule (as though each day's play itself recapitulated the evolutionary shift from individual to team) but to be allotted considerably more time and space for their elaboration. "Perhaps the greatest need of every country," argued Henry Curtis, "is that its citizens shall acquire a community sense, that they shall be able to think in terms larger than those of their own individuality, and be willing to work unselfishly for the city, the country, or the organization to which they belong." Lee saw pronounced benefits in this latter possibility. "When the worker can feel that the factory is his team," Lee declared, "and its trade-mark is his flag, that he shares the personality embodied in its product, there will come new life both to him and to the industry, and incidentally a degree of material success of which we have not yet dreamed."[23] In this remarkable process, the play theorists thus redefined individuality as a by-product of corporate membership. Turner, one is tempted to claim, would hardly recognize it.[24] You are only fully an "individual," Lee declared in 1911, when you are "holding down the part assigned to you in the economy of the social whole to which you may belong, as the boy in the school team holds down third base."[25]

Lee's comparison highlights the extent to which recreation reform was always, paradoxically, more concerned about adults than about children. American adults, after all, faced a world in which work no longer provided a reliable sphere for the construction of a self, for the shaping of values that would help one live a productive, meaningful, even happy life. The play reformers thus helped to conceptualize leisure as a new sphere for self-development, as a way to reconnect Americans to the creative, intelligent, and vigorous selves they had formerly developed through work. The new "leisure ethic" was intended to take over the crucial cultural function that Turner claimed the now-closed frontier had always performed: it would help create "new" Americans in a new world.

And what of the newest Americans? Many play reformers regarded the latest immigrants, particularly those from southern and eastern Europe, as potentially violent, anarchistic, and lonely—dangerously stuck, as it were, in the individualistic (and implicitly racialized) Big Injun stage. They would benefit from "patriotic songs," to be sure (the first activity, as we have seen, on many play programs), but they especially needed the social training provided by the team experience, which play theory understood as a specifically

CHART OF ANGLO-SAXON PLAY

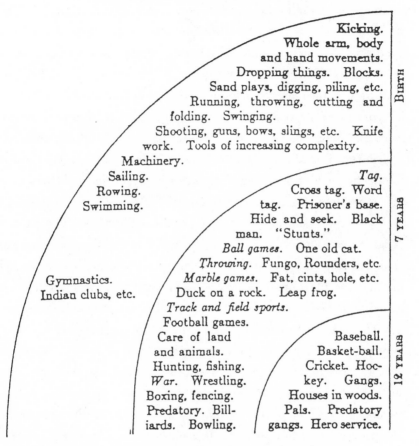

FIGURE 10. Luther Gulick, "Chart of Anglo-Saxon Play" (1899).
From Gulick, *A Philosophy of Play.*

Anglo-Saxon inheritance.[26] Although Gulick, for example, praised the strong "feeling for family unity and group life" that non-northern Europeans seemed to possess (it enabled them, he believed, to accept more willingly than others the cramped conditions of tenement life), he insisted that, with minor exceptions, "the Anglo-Saxons [were] the only peoples who have developed team games."[27] As if to emphasize that the story of child development through play in America was a racial one, Gulick included a

"Chart of Anglo-Saxon Play" (see Figure 10) at the end of the "Play Pro-gression" chapter in his handbook. Thus acculturation to the leisure ethic was for immigrants accommodation not only to the self-forgetfulness of team play, but also to a white, Anglo-Saxon, Protestant model of psycho-political development.[28]

In the end, then, the play reformers even out-Turnered Turner. Although he spoke forcefully of the frontier as the "line of most rapid and effective Americanization," the "crucible" in which "the immigrants were American-ized, liberated, and fused into a mixed race," Turner elsewhere suggests that frontier fusion was perhaps not quite total assimilation. For he also described this "mixed race" as a "composite nationality," reflecting "the map of Europe in [its] variety." Assimilating to America, he would finally say in 1918, was not "a complete fusion in a melting pot."[29] But the story of the new frontier of leisure, as adapted from Turner and popularized by the play reformers, had the unmistakable contours of a classic assimilation narrative, if with an eco-nomic twist: it encouraged Americans (old and new) to construct a self in or-der to forget it, to channel individual desires into team energies, and to play in preparation for work. Much as Turner had declared that "the *true* point of view" in the history of America "is not the Atlantic coast," but "the Great West,"[30] the play reformers hoped to tell *the* story of contemporary Ameri-can development, a similarly romantic narrative of the promise and delights of Americanization through leisure. It would be left to the immigrants them-selves to challenge the assumptions and implications of such a tale.

■

Between Abraham Cahan's early critique of Americanization through lei-sure in his first novel, *Yekl* (whose appearance in 1896 coincided with the origins of the national recreation reform movement), and the more complex reflections of his 1917 masterpiece, *The Rise of David Levinsky* (written at the height of the movement's influence), the immigrant narratives that cap-tured the popular imagination tended to affirm, rather than criticize, the play theorists' Turnerian assumptions. One set of these narratives consisted of the first-generation immigrant autobiographies, drama, and fiction that, beginning around 1900, offered hopeful stories of accommodation with the dominant culture, preaching "optimistic affirmations of immigrant assimilability."[31] These texts include, for example, Jacob Riis's own 1901 autobiography, *The Making of an American*, Mary Antin's enormously popular *Promised Land* (1912), and Elias Tobenkin's *Witte Arrives* (1916), each of which insisted that divesting oneself of old world folkways offered the only sure passage to true Americanization.[32] "I was born, I have lived, and I have been made over," Antin's book begins. "Is it not time to write my life story? I am just as much out of the way as if I were dead, for I am absolutely other than the person whose story I have to tell."[33]

A second set of narratives that reached a wide audience includes the pseudoscientific articles of the day that, under the guise of presenting sociological or historical information, explained to an increasingly anxious and xenophobic American public how "the Jews"—especially East European Jews—were slowly gaining control of most commercial business in the country. One such article appeared in the March 1913 issue of *McClure's*—only a month before the beginning of Cahan's own four-part installment in the same magazine on a fictional clothing manufacturer named David Levinsky.[34] The *McClure's* article, titled "The Jewish Invasion of America," reports the tremendous success of Jewish immigrants in such fields as the garment industry, land speculation, railroads, and banking, and is perhaps most interesting in its half-conscious use of Turnerian rhetoric to justify its critique of this (supposed) Jewish domination. In the railroad industry, for example, writes author Burton Hendrick, Jewish financial houses now have considerable influence in the important Southern Pacific line, "the creation of those hardy and adventurous Anglo-Saxons, the Huntingtons, the Crockers, and the Hopkinses of pioneer California days." And how is this being done? By, it would appear, better pioneering—"those Jews" seem to be beating the "native Americans" (and other earlier immigrant groups) at their own national game. Not that Hendrick quite realizes this. But his language betrays him. In conquering the garment industry, for example, Hendrick reports that "the qualities that stood the Russian Jew particularly in stead are his nervous, restless ambition, his remorselessness as a pace-maker, his ability to work unceasingly day and night, and his willingness to submit himself and his family to all kinds of early privations." He concludes: "No other immigrant people could stand against a steady, inevitable driving power of this kind," transforming a familiar American paradigm of Turnerian restless, nervous energy into a tale of insidious and distinctly foreign domination.[35]

But these, he announces, are merely the facts. It will be left to succeeding articles, Hendrick says—specifically, to Cahan's "Autobiography of an American Jew"—to analyze the "racial traits and training which have made possible this success." Hendrick's inflammatory essay thus not only precedes Cahan's sketches of David Levinsky; it literally previews it. "Mr. Cahan will show, by concrete example," promises Hendrick, "the minute workings of that wonderful machine, the Jewish brain. His articles will make clear why it is that the Jews so easily surpass or crowd out, at least in business and finance, the other great immigrating races."[36] What Cahan makes clear is that Hendrick's article misrepresents its facts and misunderstands America's origins. First, Cahan debunks the notion that the control of parvenu Russian Jews over American business is as complete and tenacious as Hendrick's article might have led readers to believe. His main character, Levinsky, flatly states that "the big men in the department-store field are Hebrews of German-American origin or American Gentiles," not Russian Jews.[37] Second, and more subtly, Cahan turns what Hendrick had presented as negative "Jewish" traits back into honorable "American" pioneer ideals. It is with an "intensity of purpose," and not any racial miserliness or "love of money," that the young Levinsky works in the new world.[38] Levinsky's enumeration of the qualities that account for both his personal success and that of Russian Jewish cloak-makers in general invokes the central characteristics of the westering American: it took "hard work, perseverance, thrift, and ingenuity," "energy, ability, and responsibility."[39] Through technological innovation and massive increases in manufacturing scale, new clothing manufacturers moved almost an entire industry from handwork into machine production. In essence, the Russian Jews simply relocated and revivified an already settled frontier, and in the process they displaced the German Jews, the original "pioneers of the industry." As Levinsky observes, though "foreigners ourselves, and mostly unable to speak English," the newcomers had simply "Americanized the system."[40]

When Cahan turned from this awkward assignment (for as Jules Chametzky notes, given the context in which the *McClure's* article appeared, Cahan risked further encouraging anti-Semitism)[41] to *The Rise of David Levinsky*, he made his narrative's frontier rhetoric even more explicit, although his eventual purpose in the longer work would be in part to critique the competitive and individualistic "American" values that underwrote spectacular capitalist success in the first place. As in the *McClure's* series, the Levinsky of the later novel describes the lure of the United States as chiefly one "of fantastic experiences, of marvelous transformations."[42] But in the novel he adds this telling reflection: "To leave my native place and to seek my fortune in that distant, weird world seemed to be just the kind of sensational adventure my heart was hankering for" (61). "I [am] the hero," he will soon tell himself, "of an adventure" (73). Levinsky is not, however, motivated merely by a desire for excitement. A murdered mother, violent anti-Semitic riots, and "ghastly massacres of Jews" (60) had made his homeland by the early 1880s a place one might readily wish to escape. Thus Levinsky leaves, Turner might say, for both "a new field of opportunity" and freedom "from the bondage of the past."[43] "Those magic shores" of America (Cahan, *Rise*, 87), which Charles Robinson would later claim play reformers needed to re-create in the playground for the newest immigrant generation, were literally and metaphorically Levinsky's new frontier.

Upon his arrival in New York, Levinsky experiences the "perennial rebirth" of the frontier: "Imagine a new-born babe in possession of a fully developed intellect. Would it ever forget its entry into the world?" (86). Amid the bustle of the lower East Side, like the pioneer who sheds his European outfit for the "hunting shirt and . . . moccasin" of the wilderness,[44] Levinsky soon loses not only his Russian clothes but also his side-locks, a symbol in his native country of religious piety. The transformation is immediate and overwhelming. "It was as though the hair-cut and the American clothes had changed my identity" (101), Levinsky recalls, creating almost instantly what Turner called "a new product that is American," not simply a new "development" along old lines.[45] The very streets, for Levinsky, are a revivifying space, "testify[ing] to far more self-confidence and energy, to larger ambitions and wider scopes, than did the appearance of the crowds in my birthplace" (93). "America is a topsy-turvy country" (97), remarks another immigrant to Levinsky. As on the frontier, the new replaces the old with bewildering speed.[46]

This phenomenon is true with respect to more than Levinsky's appearance and his surroundings. It is particularly true in its immediate influence on his relationship to work and to leisure. In Russia, Levinsky had devoted himself to the study of the Talmud, the ancient record of rabbinical law, doctrinal debate, and Jewish tradition. That study was both Levinsky's labor and, in a sense, his leisure—it was, at least, work that gave him intense pleasure and, most important, a clear sense of self. But in America, he quickly discovers, reading Talmud is "no trade" (91). As a result, Levinsky has to cast about not only for something to do but also for a new self to shape. Cahan paces him through a series of unrewarding occupations and activities before Levinsky's spirit fires to a quintessentially pioneer-like American line: entrepreneurial capitalism. His taste for the pleasures of production whetted by his increasing competence as a machine operator in a cloak shop—where, like Turner's practical and inventive frontiersman, he quickly introduces "little improvements" (157) to the process of stitching coats—Levinsky pounces on a chance opportunity to strike out on his own. Abused by one of his managers for spilling a bottle of milk on a pile of silk coats, Levinsky schemes vengeance, plotting to steal the company's top designer, start a rival firm, and become his former employers' "fatal competitor" (189). Though at times, even in the cloak shop, Levinsky has toyed with the idea of returning to more intellectual pursuits, the thought of being a successful entrepreneur now overpowers other motives. "What really hypnotized me," he reflects, "was the venture of the thing. It was a great, daring game of life" (189).[47]

As if to dramatize Levinsky's pioneering spirit, Cahan immediately insinuates Levinsky's new firm into the volatile economy of the frontier. After convincing the ace designer to join him on the sly and mocking up samples to show prospective buyers—and despite having only a skeleton shop and almost no capital—Levinsky finally makes a sale to a "quick, nervous" (209) American purchasing agent from a "big firm out West" (210). "I was American enough," admits Levinsky, "to be alive to the special glamour of the words, 'out West'" (210). Using material he has acquired on credit, Levinsky ships the 500-cloak order on time. Emboldened by this sudden success and confident in his skill as a manufacturer, Levinsky quickly makes another sale, expecting to cover its production costs out of the western firm's payment. But with equal suddenness, the frontier betrays him: the western company fails, leaving Levinsky to seek additional credit with which to pay his first loan. These difficulties are only a temporary setback, but in them Cahan subtly foreshadows the more thorough critique of the uses and misuses of frontier ideology to come. Casting about for a self on the new urban frontier, Levinsky finds one whose successful impersonation will leave him embittered and lonely. It seems only fitting, then, that just before his greatest success in the novel he should be offered (in the failure of the western firm) an ironic rebuke from the very frontier whose values he seeks to inhabit.

That four chapters later this same western firm's recovery provides Levinsky with the capital he needs to put his company back on its feet only underscores the unpredictability of frontier economies while setting the stage for Levinsky's parallel (and, in the end, equally self-absorbed) adventure into adultery. Having brought Levinsky to the new frontier of America and then given him a reasonably secure start in the garment business, Cahan in the middle third of the novel engineers a surprising narrative detour. Rather than simply narrate Levinsky's race to the top of the cloak-making industry,

Cahan simultaneously describes Levinsky's involvement with Dora Margolis, the wife of a former peddling acquaintance. In the process, *The Rise of David Levinsky* explores a second frontier, the new American world of leisure, love, and deception.

For we find that in a novel whose principal narrative task purports to be a description of the rise of its protagonist to financial power, the section that actually sees him develop from an insolvent novice seeking fiscal "rescue" (220) into a secure manufacturer "rapidly advancing on the road to financial triumphs" (289) is titled "Dora," and devotes nearly all of its space and energy to their affair, not to his work. Critics have yet to take this narrative diversion seriously. More than merely an "episode," as one reader has termed it, Levinsky's affair with Dora in Book IX occupies the textual center of the novel and is the major imaginative addition to the original *McClure's* sketches.[48] It is also in this Book and the next (Book X, "On the Road") that Cahan most carefully explores Levinsky's leisure-time attraction to the social theory of Herbert Spencer (the second significant addition to the earlier version of the story) and Levinsky's growing obsession with Americanization. Taken together, these two Books track the business pioneer as he both settles his career and ventures a life outside of his work. At stake is whether Levinsky can do what the play reformers insisted a twentieth-century American immigrant had to do in order to develop into a fully functioning citizen: construct a self through leisure in which his personal desires are unselfishly subordinated to the larger interests of the whole.

At first it appears as though Levinsky's relationship with Dora will simply (if stereotypically) provide a counterbalance to the acquisitive energies that drive his business dealings. In their first meeting she literally distracts him from work. Seeking a loan from Dora's husband, Max, to cover his losses from the failure of the western firm, Levinsky is so intent on his mission that he prays "Heaven to take [Dora] out of the room" (225). Soon, however, he will thank heaven for having brought them together. As Levinsky's affection for Dora grows, business, not leisure, becomes the distraction in his life. ("It was the image of some customer or creditor or of some new style of jacket or cloak that would [now often] interfere with my peace of mind" [256].) Moreover, unlike Levinsky's other female acquaintances in the new world—the prostitutes he visits for recreational sex, the landlady he tries to seduce as a lark, the Yiddish stage actress for whom he develops a fashionable infatuation—Dora encourages Levinsky's sense of himself as an intellectual, someone more concerned with learning than with business.[49] "It's good to have educated people come to the house," Dora remarks. "It's good for the children and for everybody else" (240).

What is most important about Levinsky's relationship with Dora, however, is that she and Max give him a place in the new world where he can feel that he belongs, and where, through familial recreations, he can escape the solipsism of his business concerns. "A great immigrant city like New York or Chicago is full of men and women who are alone amid a welter of human life," Levinsky reflects, thinking of himself. For such people, "nothing has a greater glamour than a family in whose house they might be made to feel at home" (239). Levinsky would come to the Margolises for dinner and conversation, or to play with their children. The three adults "would go to the Jewish theater together," or even "to see an American play" (247). Thus for the first third of Book IX—even though offstage Levinsky is working extraordinarily long hours to solidify his position as a successful manufacturer—onstage he appears overly preoccupied, as it were, with the comforts of recreation. It is almost as though Cahan were suggesting that the play reformers were right: that in the modern world one could develop through leisure a coherent self that also made up part of a larger (and more significant) whole. Soon Levinsky even convinces Max and Dora to accept him as a boarder, virtually as "one of the family" (318).

It is as a near family member, however, that Levinsky turns loyalty to deception. Increasingly attracted to Dora, he schemes to draw her into a flirtation, seeking what he terms "an adventure" with her (263). Though representing himself as an intensely (and selflessly) romantic figure, Levinsky (when he is honest with himself) conceives of their potential affair as simply another frontier on which he can satisfy his own selfish desires, pursue his own continued successes. When Dora finally returns Levinsky's love, for example, he is overcome first and foremost with a sense of his own victory: "'Dora has kissed me! Dora dear is mine!' My heart was dancing with joy over my conquest of her." Even though Levinsky insists that he also felt "almost ready to lay down [his] life for her" (279), Cahan makes clear that the romance appeals primarily to Levinsky's business-honed instinct for acquisition. For almost immediately, Levinsky tallies points: "I was constantly aware of the fact that this was my second love-affair, as if it were something to be proud of," he confesses. "Dora dear! Sweetheart mine!" (279). That it is Max who earlier in the novel convinces Levinsky that love is as much a field of competition as business is an irony Cahan deliberately cultivates. "Every woman can be won, absolutely every one," Max insists, as though in confirmation of Levinsky's play-to-win business philosophy, "provided a fellow knows how to go about it" (116). And yet Cahan also subtly signals that the deepest connection between the self Levinsky creates in business and the one he creates in love-play is not simply his striving to conquer or to acquire in each; it is that he becomes a simultaneously successful cloak manufacturer and lover in this section of the novel through virtually the same specific methods.

As a manufacturer, Levinsky's greatest strength is his ability to cheat the system by posing as a union shopkeeper while paying his workers nonunion wages. From the beginning, cheap, nonunion labor drives his business, making it possible "for a financial midget like [himself] to outbid the lions of the cloak-and-suit industry" (270). He hires "elderly . . . , orthodox and extremely old-fashioned" tailors who prefer his shop's old world dress codes, eating habits, and Saturday holidays (his workers come in on Sunday instead) to the "American" ways of the more "up-to-date" (270) factories, even though they pay better. Thus when the Cloak and Suit Makers' Union forces him to pay union wages and keep union hours, he only feigns compliance. In reality his employees continue to work up to nineteen hours a day (unionized employees worked ten-hour days) and get paid by the piece (as was their preference, and to their advantage, provided they could put in long days) rather than by the hour. Even an industry lockout by the manufacturers poses no problem for Levinsky. He makes "a pretense of joining in" (272), his hands "clandestinely continuing to work" (273). Levinsky even profits; besides filling his own orders, he secretly does work for some of the better-known firms. Eventually his shops are discovered by the union and shut down, but he still does well, getting paid off by the larger companies not to give in to union demands and weaken the lockout.

When with the coming of the profitable winter season the lockout finally crumbles and the manufacturers give in to the union completely, Levinsky ironically achieves his greatest success. The higher the wage scale established by the union agreement, the greater profit advantage Levinsky can obtain by returning to his old ways. Still "able to get men willing to trick the organization," Levinsky pays his employees "official" union wages on Friday only to take an unofficial kickback on Monday. "By thus cheating the union," Levinsky crows, "I could now undersell the bigger manufacturers more easily than I had been able to do previous to the lockout. . . . Money was coming in in floods. The lockout and the absolute triumph of the union was practically the making of me" (285).

In like fashion—and in virtually adjacent chapters to those describing his business deceptions—Levinsky cheats both Max and Dora. To Max he plays not only the loyal friend and chaste boarder but also the neophyte businessperson seeking expert advice. "To flatter [Max's] vanity," Levinsky reports, "I would make him think his suggestions had been acted upon and that they had brought good results." But all was "simply part of my personation" (290). Just as he deceives union officials even under their watchful eyes, Levinsky woos Max's wife in Max's own home. Dora he cheats even more perniciously. Risking her marriage, her sanity, and her soul, Dora opens herself to Levinsky's love because she yearns to experience happiness for what she says is the first time. Matched to Max by her parents, not by her own choice, Dora claims not to care where infidelity might lead. "I can't help it," she tells Levinsky. "At last I know what it means to be happy. I have been dreaming of it all my life. Now I know what it is like, and I am willing to suffer for it" (280). For all Levinsky's apparent joy in their union, however, he seems more intrigued by "the novelty of carrying on a romantic conspiracy with a married woman" (281), as though he regards himself (again) as the hero of a daring tale. Thus Levinsky becomes terrifically "bored" (280, 287) whenever Dora speaks earnestly to him of their love and repeatedly urges her to have sexual intercourse with him. And after "six or seven weeks" of "immaculate" moral conduct, Levinsky renews his "excursions" (288) to the prostitutes he had first frequented soon after his arrival in New York.

Thus it is by sham friendship and sham love that Levinsky vigorously pursues the same self-interest that drives his business dealings. Cahan brings this point tellingly home in the scene where Dora mistakes one of Levinsky's labor agents for a marriage broker. The labor agent, known as a *shadchen*, or matchmaker, is so termed because he brings "employer[s] together with cloak-makers who were willing to cheat the union." In Levinsky's case the *shadchen* is one of his own operatives, whose "gentle disposition" and "gift of expression" give him "power over his shopmates." As Levinsky explains to an enraged Dora—who believes that her lover is trying to arrange a marriage to someone else—this *shadchen*, because of his own invidious charm, is actually the employees' "'shop chairman' and a member of their 'price committee.'" "He was the only man in my employ who actually received the full union price," Levinsky tells Dora. "In addition to this, I paid him his broker's commission for every new man he furnished me, and various sums as bribes pure and simple" (295). Ironically, in order to prove to Dora that he is not deceiving her, he has to explain in detail how he deceives his employees as a matter of regular business practice. Thus Levinsky—who when first pursuing Dora convinced himself that the "telling [of] a complete, unvarnished truth is in itself a pleasure" (263) and who repeatedly assures Dora that he is not feigning his love—regains her trust only by revealing himself as a man who unabashedly manipulates the trust of others. The tactic, oddly enough, works; they even make love for the first time as, in her relief at Levinsky's "honesty," Dora's "usual fortitude melted away" (296). But this coupling does not lead to their permanent union; three days later Dora ends the affair for good, citing her responsibility to her children. Levinsky moves into his own apartment, hurt and alone, with nowhere to turn but his business.

With deliberate irony Cahan suggests that the same philosophy that in part guides Levinsky's behavior toward Dora also consoles him when their relationship ends. For at the same time that Levinsky turns from business to Dora, he also "develop[s] a passion" (282) for the social Darwinist ideology that his own play-to-win doctrine most closely resembles. An avid newspaper reader, Levinsky happens across an antisocialist editorial that "derived its inspiration from the theory of the Struggle for Existence and the Survival of the Fittest." Intrigued, and sensing that these ideas capably articulate his own thoughts, Levinsky goes on to read Herbert Spencer's *Sociology* and *Social Statics*, and Charles Darwin's *Origin of Species* and *Descent of Man.* "I sat up nights reading these books," Levinsky recalls. "Apart from the purely intellectual intoxication they gave me, they flattered my vanity as one of the 'fittest.' It was as though all the wonders of . . . these works had been intended, among other purposes, to establish my title as one of the victors of Existence" (282–83).

It is this self-absorbed Spencerian rapture that helps Levinsky rationalize his behavior toward Dora. As a "victor of Existence," he reasons, he deserves whatever spoils his superior abilities (including his literal physical fitness, his "awfully fine figure" [116]) can garner him. And since life is merely a struggle for survival, in which everyone fights for those spoils as best he can, one need not scruple at such social sins as adultery. Sitting in his bedroom in Max and Dora's apartment, with a copy of Spencer's *Sociology* in his hands, Levinsky justifies his behavior toward Dora once and for all: "everybody was at the bottom of his heart . . . ready to set that rule [against adultery] at defiance," he insists, "provided it could be done with absolute secrecy and safety" (281–82). After Dora has ended their affair, Levinsky laments the loss of her company but still nourishes his sense of himself as one of the "fittest," engaged in ruthless combat with the rest of society.

What fitter doctrine could so ably console a once again lonely, unloved man?

None, the play reformers would in all likelihood have argued: Levinsky doomed himself to loneliness by adopting an all-too-Darwinian (or even Turnerian) sense of his own "fitness." As we might have suspected, many of the play organizers were "reform" Darwinists, "staunchly opposed to the notion that society could be organized around the ideals of rugged individualism and the survival of the fittest."[50] This is not to suggest that they rejected the notion of individual fitness per se. The play reformers certainly sought to create vigorously fit bodies, minds, and souls. But they did so, as we have seen, by ultimately redefining fitness to mean *appropriate* play activities at appropriate ages, banking on "Anglo-Saxon" team games as (in time) the proper vehicles for the development of fully functioning selves. Levinsky seems ferociously stuck in the Big Injun stage of competitive conquest, his enthusiastic recourse to cheating—a reproachful turn for the play theorists—proving just how stuck he is. Not until Levinsky can develop that selfless sense of belonging, they would claim, will he feel himself whole.[51]

■

In the final third of the novel Cahan tests this proposition by examining the consequences of Levinsky's one arguably successful team membership: his ardent sense of belonging to America itself. Levinsky has, of course, tried hard to assimilate to America since his arrival, assiduously shedding his "greenhorn" status along with his old world clothing, manners, and language. But it is only after the end of his temporary union with Dora that the novel fully registers the intensity of Levinsky's desire to belong. It is almost as though the failure of one romance sends him even more urgently toward the delights of another.

The blossoming of Levinsky's love affair with America is at first primarily a result of his desire to advance his standing as a successful businessman. (Wrong from the start, play theory would say; team membership requires self-sacrifice, not self-promotion.) "Forever watching and striving to imitate the dress and the ways of the well-bred American merchants with whom I was, or trying to be, thrown," Levinsky says, "I felt . . . was an essential element in achieving business success" (260). Even when his faithful imitation of American business strategy brings him notoriety, he is secretly delighted. The seal of his membership in the class of American manufacturers, for example, is a defamatory editorial that declares him a traitor to his own former organization, the cloak-makers' union. "I read the paragraph with mixed rage and pain," Levinsky admits, "and yet the sight of my name in print flattered my vanity. . . . For, behold! the same organ assailed the Vanderbilts, the Goulds, the Rothschilds, and by calling me 'a fleecer of labor' it placed me in their class. I felt in good company" (273).[52] Although not especially given to physical recreation, Levinsky is also ready to exploit the economic advantage of learning his way around American sport. After nearly giving up in despair over his struggle to gain entry to the office of an influential department store buyer, Levinsky finds that the buyer is also a bowler—and so teaches himself to bowl in the hope of making his acquaintance when he next comes to the alley. "My labors were not thrown away" (336), Levinsky puns; after insinuating himself into the buyer's bowling party, Levinsky turns the conversation to the cloak business. Impressed, perhaps, by his sporting initiative, the buyer "merrily" (338) agrees to see Levinsky's wares—and eventually places a substantial order, which in turn catapults the newcomer to a position of national prominence in the trade.

In time, Levinsky's infatuation with American ways grows into a full-fledged erotics of national belonging. On one western sales trip, desperate to be accepted into a group of Gentile cloak merchants but anxious lest his "distressingly un-American" "Talmud gesticulations" (327) or rapid speech expose him to ridicule, Levinsky speaks "with exaggerated apathy, [his] hands so strenuously still that they fairly tingled with the effort" (329). Oblivious to what he is actually saying, but acutely aware that he "was in the company of well-dressed American Gentiles, eating and conversing with them, a nobleman among noblemen," he "throbbed with love for

America" (329). Other Jews and other recreations also kindle this intense feeling in Levinsky. During a brief stay at a Jewish resort in the Catskills, he attends a dinner whose social posturing otherwise bores him. But when the dinner band, which has tried unsuccessfully to get the audience's attention with selections from popular ghetto opera, American pop songs, and Yiddish stage music, suddenly strikes up the "Star-Spangled Banner," Levinsky and the other diners rise "like one man, applauding" (424). Burning with enthusiasm, Levinsky recalls, "love for America blazed up in my soul. I shouted to the musicians, 'My Country,' and the cry spread like wildfire. The musicians obeyed and we all sang the anthem from the bottom of our souls" (424).[53]

But in the end Levinsky is betrayed by this passionate embrace of American ways, much as he himself had betrayed Dora. Though enormously wealthy, at times "overwhelmed by a sense of [his] success and ease" (525)—and acutely aware that he has made himself into as thoroughly assimilated an American as he could ever have hoped—Levinsky remains alone, unfulfilled, even impotent.[54] Amid his noisy "triumph" on his American frontier and "the pandemonium of [his] six hundred sewing-machines," he feels "the deadly silence of solitude" (526). Levinsky's loneliness seems at first most attributable to his lack of a spouse, to the absence of an abiding personal love that would bring him the affection and companionship he craves. But Cahan makes clear that Levinsky is more haunted by the failure of his love for America to give him the sense of fulfillment and belonging that he thought assimilation would confer.

As if to stress that Levinsky's brooding sense of emptiness at the end of the novel is less a result of the absence of female companionship than of Levinsky's internalization of what we might call the false team energies of capitalist America, Cahan revises the original *McClure's* version of Levinsky's story in two signal ways. First, in order to emphasize in the novel that Levinsky knowingly exploits a similar sham sense of group belonging as part of his business practice, Cahan has Levinsky create for his workers the "Levinsky Antomir Benefit Society," an organization that helps natives of

Levinsky's Russian birthplace emigrate to the United States and obtain employment. More important, the Antomir Benefit Society nurtures (by design) "something like a family spirit" (378) in the company, of which Levinsky is extremely proud. In this respect Levinsky's creation replicates the effects of the actual welfare capitalism programs growing in popularity at the time of the novel's publication, particularly company-sponsored team recreations.[55] From a company's point of view, however, as from Levinsky's, such programs were truly beneficial only to the extent that they enhanced the bottom line. As Stuart Brandes notes, many firms regarded company-sponsored recreation as a way of staving off other, more harmful desires that might increase absenteeism or lower productivity. Corporate recreation thus operated in a sense almost like Turner's free lands, providing a safety valve or "release in leisure" for the pent-up drives of modern workers. At the same time, companies believed that healthier workers (made more fit through wholesome exercise) would be more productive workers. And companies were not above creating essentially sham teams to promote that feeling of company health or "family spirit" that so touched Levinsky—teams whose better athletes frequently "received preference in hiring, greater job security, travel expenses, and time off for games."[56] Such favoritism undermined the logic of teamwork and family that the sports were intended to fulfill by generating displeasure among non–team members, many of whom resented not only the athletes' perks but also the companies' gradual shunting of general recreational funds into more specialized semipro leagues.[57] Some companies, Harold Seymour reports, even made employees help pay for their equipment or charged admission to "company" games.[58]

Levinsky's Benefit Society does not explicitly involve athletics, but his clear sense of the benefits *he* accrues mirrors that of his real-life counterparts. When the Antomir emigrant being brought to America reaches New York, for example, it is "with the understanding that he was to work off the loan in [Levinsky's] employ" (378). Moreover, despite Levinsky's insistence that he "sincerely cherished that spirit for its own sake" (379), he admits that the society kept his average wages down and "safeguarded [his] shop against labor troubles" (378).[59] That Levinsky thoroughly understands how the manipulative team spirit and false assimilation of the Antomir society might look to a skeptic is made clear late in the novel when a socialist machine operator in his shop—who also happens to be an Antomir native—refuses to join the society. Levinsky interprets the refusal as a "tacit protest against the whole [Antomir] society as an organization of 'slaves.' It means that the society makes meek, obedient servants of my employees and helps me fleece them. As if they did not earn in my shop more than they would anywhere else! As if they could all get steady work outside my place! . . . I felt outraged" (519). Soon thereafter Levinsky abruptly fires this operator, only to see the cloak-makers' union respond with a strike. Anticapitalist feelings run so high that even the Antomir Society members, full of a "family spirit" the socialist Cahan would likely have applauded, join the pickets.[60]

The second major revision that Cahan makes to the original *McClure's* story in order to emphasize in the novel that Levinsky's emptiness results from the embrace of the false energies of American business is to rewrite the tale's melancholy frame. In the final scene of the magazine story, Levinsky contacts Gitelson, a fellow passenger from his trip to America, to commemorate the twenty-fifth anniversary of their arrival with a bottle of champagne in "one of the best hotels in the city." Gitelson is bashful and embarrassed, and his "rather shabby clothes" attract attention in the restaurant. Levinsky realizes that he has "made a mistake," that "the chasm between us seemed to be too much for us to celebrate as 'ship-brothers' in any place." After repaying the ten-dollar loan that Gitelson had given Levinsky to get started in the garment trade, Levinsky returns to "the loneliness of [his] beautiful lodgings," his heart "heavy with self-disgust and sadness," seemingly depressed that his rise in America has left him without a clear path (or companion) back to his past.[61]

The *McClure's* story then ends with the following sentence "echoing through" Levinsky's brain: "Such is the tragedy of my success! Such is the tragedy of my success!" Given the context provided by this final installment, Levinsky's "tragedy" in the *McClure's* story is primarily the gap that exists between himself and his former acquaintances by virtue of his wealth, station, and power. In constructing the later novel, however, Cahan gives Levinsky a very different perspective on his tragedy. Levinsky later sees it as the gap between his Americanized business self and his "real" Antomir self. Where in the opening installment of the original *McClure's* story Levinsky had complained that his present success was "something unreal," in the novel he regards that success as trivial. "My present station, power, the amount of worldly happiness at [my] command, and the rest of it, seem to be devoid of significance" (3)—no longer "unreal," but insignificant. The closing paragraph of *The Rise of David Levinsky* differs from the end of the *McClure's* story as well. Levinsky still longs for "a heart-to-heart talk with some of the people of [his] birthplace" (529) and observes that his wealth sometimes stands between them; but he does not lament that gap as he does in the 1913 tale. Instead, at the end of the novel he regrets his choice of a career in business over something more intellectual. Success in business, he complains, attests to no innate talent: "The business world contains plenty of successful men who have no brains. Why, then, should I ascribe my triumph to special ability?" (529). Levinsky would prefer he had attained success through means that would testify to a more personal ingenuity and integrity, to what Turner called "creative" individualism.[62] Levinsky specifically wishes, for example, that he had chosen "science, music, or art" (529), instead of commerce, to make his mark. He even lists four Russian Jewish immigrants—an architect, a physiologist, a songwriter, and a sculptor—whose pioneering successes he wishes he had emulated. And notably he does not seem to begrudge them the incidental status or wealth acquired through their own scientific or artistic triumphs.[63]

In *McClure's*, when Levinsky says that his inner self impresses him "as being precisely the same as it was" thirty years earlier, he believes that his success has not changed him; it has only changed his relations to others.[64] But in *The Rise of David Levinsky*, when he says in the final paragraph that his past and his present "do not comport well" and that "David, the poor lad swinging over a Talmud volume at the Preacher's Synagogue, seems to have more in common with my inner identity than David Levinsky, the well-known cloak manufacturer," he means more tellingly that he regrets the transformation he has undergone, his assimilation into a successful—yet ultimately insignificant—American businessman. "I feel that if I had my life to live over again," Levinsky sighs, "I should never think of a business career" (530). It is in this disjunction between expectation and outcome, then, that Cahan situates his own critique of a society (America) and an economic system (capitalism) that increasingly enlisted pseudo–team energies in the service of competitive individualism, demanded cultural capitulation as the price of national membership, and offered (un)"fitness" as a rationale for immigrant restriction.[65]

■

The historical irony that shadows Levinsky's list of successful immigrants—the cultural, not financial, pioneers whose paths he wishes he had followed—is the passage of the 1917 Literacy Test Act, the first in a series of severe restrictions on European and Asian immigration to America in the late 1910s and early 1920s. Levinsky's list is thus one way for Cahan to protest the rise of American xenophobia in a novel that (to his dismay) some readers felt perpetuated negative immigrant stereotypes. Much as Turner himself believed that America's new heroes would be pioneers "of the spirit," opening up "new lines of achievement" in arts, letters, science, and politics instead of seeking distinction in "material display," Cahan suggests that immigrants were already filling those vital roles.[66] Even Levinsky, we might say, becomes the very artist he wishes he had been in the act of constructing his compelling narrative out of a lifetime of brooding memories.

By the time Ole Rölvaag sat down to write his saga of the pioneering Norwegian-American immigrants on the western frontier, however, the tentative measures of the Literacy Test Act—for whose passage in even stricter form play theorist Joseph Lee, then president of the PAA, had campaigned hard for over twenty years—were yielding to the explicit quotas of the 1924 Johnson-Reed National Origins Act. Although the harshest restrictions of the 1924 Act targeted southern and eastern Europeans, the xenophobic anxiety that surrounded it affected all non-native Americans, including the supposedly more assimilable Scandinavians about whom Rölvaag had been writing fiction since 1912. The mid-1920s also marked the centennial of the first Norwegian migration to the United States. It was in this political and cultural climate, then, that Rölvaag crafted *Giants in the Earth*. First published as *I De Dage*— ("In Those Days—") in Norway in two volumes (1924 and 1925), the novel was issued in its single-volume English translation in 1927, when it was made a selection of the Book-of-the-Month Club.[67] A popular success, *Giants in the Earth* was also well received by critics, who collectively praised its "simplicity and vigor," its "obvious veracity," and its "heroic" presentation of "man's struggle with the earth."[68]

Rölvaag's novel is perhaps more accurately a re-presentation of an ostensibly closed chapter of the American past: the settling of the frontier. Written in part as a result of Rölvaag's own pioneering ambitions—he began the text upon learning that the famous Norwegian writer John Bojer was planning his own novel on Norwegian immigrants in the United States[69]—*Giants in the Earth* at times seems intended to give fictional form to Turner's pronouncements about the frontier. Its principal male character, for example, looks from most angles like a prototypical Turnerian pioneer, and the fortitude and ingenuity of the tiny Norwegian settlement in the forbidding Dakota Territory of the 1870s could be said to offer synecdochic proof of the very character of the nation. The text's synergistic relationship between work and leisure, moreover, seems almost to suggest that the play reformers were right to look to the frontier for the proper values for contemporary recreation. That all this could be true, and Rölvaag's novel still cogently critique not only the frontier myth itself but also the assimilationist demands of American play reform, attests to the work's complex power. Even more so than Cahan in *The Rise of David Levinsky*, Rölvaag in *Giants in the Earth* calls on the American narratives that would write his tale for him, only, in the end, to resist, reshape, and renounce them.

There is no denying, however, the power that those narratives have in his text and have continued to have on his readers. In 1959, Robert Steensma ventured an influential reading of *Giants in the Earth* as a book whose frontier setting "draw[s] out to the fullest degree the traits of the American pioneer as Turner saw them."[70] Books on frontier history frequently excerpt the more Turnerian passages from Rölvaag's novel as epigraphs or evidence, such as the following quotation John Carter chose in 1985 to accompany Solomon Butcher's late-nineteenth-century photographs of the Nebraska Territory: "This vast stretch of beautiful land was to be his—yes, *his*—and no ghost of a dead Indian would drive him away! . . . His heart began to expand with a mighty exaltation. An emotion he had never felt before filled him and made him walk erect. . . . 'Good God!' he panted. 'This kingdom is going to be *mine!*'"[71] Carter even omitted the clause about the "ghost of a dead Indian" (a moment of grim foreshadowing in the novel) to make Rölvaag's text seem even more exuberantly positive, all the more like Turner's boundlessly confident frontier.

But it requires little editing to demonstrate the Turnerian effect the frontier has, at first, on Per Hansa, the novel's lead male character. Just as Turner hypothesized that it was primarily the presence of free lands that made the settling of the wilderness "a steady movement away from the influence of Europe, a steady growth of independence on American lines,"[72] with equal optimism does Per Hansa associate the open plains with his liberation from the constricting politics of the old world. Almost to his disbelief, in the Dakota Territory he was "really to own . . . this big stretch of fine land that spread here before him"; he was "really to have his friends for neighbours, both to the north and to the south—folks who cared for him and wanted to help him out in every way" (33). "And no old worn-out, thin-shanked, pot-bellied king is going to come around and tell me what I have to do about it, either!" he announces to his wife Beret (43). Where for Turner the continual remove of the frontier to the west signified the "fluidity of American life," its "perennial rebirth,"[73] Per Hansa and his fellow settlers felt as if they had gone back even further—"to the very beginning of things" (32).

As critics like Steensma have noted, Per Hansa of all this group best fits Turner's description of the exuberant, masterful frontiersman. Per Hansa is frequently consumed by an "indomitable, conquering mood which seemed to give him the right of way wherever he went, whatever he did. Outwardly, at such times, he showed only a buoyant recklessness, as if wrapped in a cloak of gay, wanton levity; but down beneath all this lay a stern determination of purpose, a driving force" (41). Nor was this force merely physical. Like Levinsky, who in his early days in the garment industry invented new techniques to make his work more productive, Per Hansa enlists his bodily vigor in the service of his considerable ingenuity, consistently exhibiting what Turner called the pioneer's "practical, inventive turn of mind, quick to find expedients."[74] "Leave it to Per Hansa," the narrator advises: "he was the fellow to have everything figured out beforehand!" (47). It is Per Hansa who decides to plant potatoes before starting on his sod house (and whose early crop gives him food for his family and valuable produce to trade for cash and supplies); it is he who buys a wood lot along the Sioux River for winter fuel, who knits a fisherman's net that is the butt of his comrades' jokes until he uses it to catch a winter's worth of fish, who starts a fur trade with the Indians, and who thinks to whitewash the interior walls of his house. It is Per Hansa, indeed, who in his most confident and dominant moods exudes "bright emanations of creative force" (127).

What is most striking about Per Hansa's pioneering ways is his ability to put into practice the play reformers' own exuberant reformulation of Turner's model of work. From the start, Per Hansa discovers that work on the frontier is actually quite similar to recreation, as his exertions revivify him for yet more (and yet more enjoyable) labor. After his first long day harrowing his quarter-section for planting, for example, Per Hansa begins, that evening, to build his sod house. Beret urges him to take a break: "'You ought to rest, Per Hansa!' Beret pleaded. 'Please use a little common sense!'" "Rest—of course!" her husband replies. "That's just what I propose to do!" For Per Hansa, building the house *is* rest; moreover, it is like a game. "Come along, now, all hands of you," Per Hansa exhorts his family; "you can't imagine what fun this is going to be" (48). Such frontier labors are precisely the sort of work the play reformers insisted they were attempting to cultivate. "It is always the play element in work that is the most important," declared Joseph Lee. "True work is the highest form of play."[75] Work that called out these qualities would prevent the more usual practice among American workers (particularly, the play reformers believed, among immigrants) of stealing time from work for rest or leisure. But because Per Hansa's work is itself liberating instead of constraining, he sees no point in shirking labor. He "was never at rest, except when fatigue had overcome him and sleep had taken him away from toil and care." But fatigue was rare; "he found his tasks too interesting to be a burden; nothing tired him, out here" (107). Imbued with "the elfin, playful spirit of a boy" (109), Per Hansa is alive to what Luther Gulick called life "at its highest and best"—pursuing the work he "wish[es] to pursue," because "it is [his] main desire."[76]

Perhaps because Per Hansa is able to approach even the most grinding toil as though it were at heart play, he seems all the more able to enjoy the actual moments of recreation that do come his way. Far more so, certainly, than his wife Beret—whose much more vexed relation to work and leisure I will take up in a moment—or than Levinsky, whom Cahan pictures on the margins of most of his novel's leisure activity, except when Levinsky can turn play into business profit (as in the case of bowling) or a site of conquest (as with Dora). At the boisterous dance at the neighboring Trönder settlement, for example, Per Hansa is at first surprised to see his married comrades dancing gleefully with Trönder women; but he soon swings himself and a partner into the very "centre of the floor" (274). Indeed, although scenes like these are few, in *Giants in the Earth* leisure for Per Hansa seems not so much an escape from or tool of work, but an exuberantly natural expression of the overflow of energy produced by work.

Leisure is more generally represented in the novel as it appears in the plains photographs of Solomon Butcher, as a small but integral part of the tableau, snuck in at a corner, but snuck in nonetheless. At roughly the same time that Jacob Riis was photographing his way through the lower East

FIGURE 11. Solomon D. Butcher, "J. D. Troyer sod house home, near Callway, Nebraska" (1892). Courtesy Solomon D. Butcher Collection, Nebraska State Historical Society (#B983-1654A).

Side, Butcher crisscrossed the Nebraska Territory, not far from Per Hansa's fictional Dakota settlement, recording the lives of Americans on the frontier. Although his pictures are perhaps best known for their stark presentation of the spare Nebraska landscape, many testify indirectly to the importance of pioneer play. Very few, like the Trönder dance in Rölvaag's novel, make play their explicit subject.[77] More typically, Butcher's photos might include toys, particularly dolls; or a piece of play equipment, such as what appears to be a baseball bat tucked under the leftmost chair in front of the otherwise dour J. D. Troyer homestead (see Figure 11);[78] or even considerably more elaborate apparatuses, such as a swing built into the house itself (see Figure 12). So, too, does Rölvaag fit play into his landscape, from the "prattling laughter" (11) of Per Hansa and Beret's daughter And-Ongen toddling about in the grass to the subtle hint by Tönseten that one reason he does not want the Solum boys to go back to Minnesota for the winter is that he will have no one with whom to play cards.

FIGURE 12. Solomon D. Butcher, "Dugout on the South Loup River, Custer County, Nebraska" (1892). Courtesy Solomon D. Butcher Collection, Nebraska State Historical Society (#B983-1653).

What both the play reformers and Turner would particularly have hailed in the novel is what amounts to the preadolescent play program enjoyed by Per Hansa's two sons. Though only seven and nine, both boys are already fully integrated into what historian Elliott West has called the frontier's "complex economy of mutual dependence."[79] They help Per Hansa plow, plant, and harvest, travel to town with him for supplies, and discover a flock of ducks that provide food during the first winter. They are, in short, pioneers-in-the-making, living the rugged, responsible childhood whose passing, by Rölvaag's day, play reformers loudly lamented and whose values they sought to reconstruct on America's urban playgrounds. Although the boys' fierce loyalty to and worshipful imitation of their father would seem to place them in the play reformers' "dramatic" stage, each boy shows the self-assertive individualism of the Big Injun. (They even meet actual Native Americans and later in the novel chase "one another around the sod hut, playing 'Indian'" [85].) Each competes with the other for attention from Per

Hansa; each prefers the vigorous outdoor chores of the homestead to what they perceive as the unmanly confinement of domestic employments. Like Turner's pioneers, both boys have visions of how they will help transform the land around them, and, like properly progressing preteens, they long to experience what Joseph Lee called "real life, real things, real obstacles."[80] Just as Rölvaag's imaginary frontier energizes Per Hansa, so too, in work and in play, does it invigorate his sons.

■

And yet for all the novel's apparent endorsement of the frontier ideal, whether as formulated by Turner or as reshaped by the early-twentieth-century play theorists, *Giants in the Earth* consistently challenges that ideal's most important assumptions. The open space of the frontier itself, for example, in which Turner claimed that the abundance of free land helped fuse immigrants of widely disparate origin into a "mixed race," is in Rölvaag's text more often than not the site of tension between different immigrant groups.[81] It is true that the Helgelændings of Spring Creek and the Trönders down the road—who had been bitter fishing-ground rivals in Norway—develop an economic and cultural relationship that would have been unthinkable in Europe. But encounters between Per Hansa's people and non-Norwegians can be strained, even violent affairs. When a caravan of Irish immigrants arrives at Spring Creek claiming that Tönseten's and Hans Olsa's quarter-sections belong to them, diplomacy quickly degenerates into threats, then fisticuffs. Only after the immensely strong Hans Olsa knocks one Irishman senseless and then hurls his body against a wagon do the new arrivals give up what the narrative insinuates was a fraudulent claim to begin with. And although the Irish do take up adjacent quarters, the two groups have only tangential contact over the rest of the novel.[82]

Rölvaag's text further suggests that while the frontier did serve, in some ways, as a more specifically Americanizing space, the Norwegian immigrants maintained vital cultural ties to the old world. These ties are perhaps ironically most evident in the kind of new world adjustments that should have hastened their decay. Rölvaag discusses in detail, for example, the Norwegian practice of adopting new names in America. Where the changing of a first name or a surname can produce, in other immigrant narratives, feelings of loss or dislocation, in *Giants in the Earth* such changes affirm, rather than deny, ethnic identification. At first Per Hansa bridles at the notion of any change; "He couldn't understand why [his given name] Peder Hansen would not be good enough even for the United States Constitution" (275). But as Tönseten explains, the intent of the custom is to rechristen immigrants bearing rather common Scandinavian family names with their own original Norwegian place names. Hans Olsa (son of Ole) becomes Hans Vaag, after his hometown; Peder Hansen becomes Peder Holm. Cultural memory, not amnesia, becomes the source for new identities in the new world. This renaming thus represents an Americanization, but not (as frequently happened at Castle Garden or on Ellis Island, for example) a concomitant loss of heritage.

The language school established during the first winter at Spring Creek functions similarly in the novel. The three immigrant families hire one of the native-born Solum boys to teach the children English. In *The Rise of David Levinsky* the American schooling of Dora's daughter Lucy creates violent tensions in the Margolis family because Dora resents Lucy's control over a language (and a culture) that she herself is struggling to absorb. But the Norwegian school ironically brings the families of the settlement together when it is suggested by Tönseten that the classes move from house to house—and that the parents attend as well. Under this arrangement the school quickly becomes "a flexible institution," with a variety of functions:

> It served as primary school and grammar school, as language school—in both Norwegian and English—and religious school; in one sense it was a club; in another it was a debating society, where everything between heaven and earth became fit matter for argument; on other occasions it turned into a singing school, a coffee party, or a social centre; and sometimes, in serious moods, it took on the aspect of a devotional meeting, a solemn confessional. (250)

Instruction is not only bilingual, it is bicultural; lacking books and other educational materials, the Solum boys frequently teach through stories and songs from Norway, enlisting the help of the other adults to supplement their own store of knowledge. Here again memory is the source for advancement in the new world, but with the added twist of communal participation instead of (as in the case of Dora and Lucy) generational separation. Nor does the remarkably "flexible" school resemble the more rigid organizational structures of the play reformers' school programs and playgrounds, where immigrants would have been watched over, not put in charge. "In these ways," the narrator explains—and more important, in its *own* ways—"the school bound subtly and inseparably together the few souls who lived out there in the wilderness" (250). Thus an institution ostensibly founded to Americanize the settlement not only preserves the participants' original heritage but also fosters a group-generated team spirit and collective purpose just when the wilderness itself threatened to dissolve both.

For winters on the frontier, the immigrants soon discover, make the open land seem a deathlike zone of suspended animation, not a site of Turner's "perennial rebirth." Tönseten proposes the school in the first place to dissuade the Solum boys from returning home. "What do you think we're going to do, I'd like to know, when you are gone?" he asks. Per Hansa pleads the case even more strongly: "I'll tell you exactly how we stand—and this is gospel truth. If you . . . leave us now, it'll be so dull and dreary for the rest of us that we might as well hang ourselves" (215). Indeed, when the school itself is not in session, the brutal weather prevents Per Hansa from doing any of the activities that he had found so energizing in the summer and fall. Forced into idleness, he becomes fatiguingly bored. "Time had simply come to a standstill," the narrator observes (198). This first deadening winter grimly foreshadows the literal (and icy) deaths that will later end the novel and that will offer the sharpest rebuke to the frontier ideal by extinguishing the lives of the text's most physically "fit" character (Hans Olsa) and its foremost pioneer, Per Hansa himself. Rölvaag's depiction of the crushing isolation of this western winter also reminds us that however liberating the open spaces of the wilderness may have been, they were also in important senses constraining and "closed," a valuable rejoinder to the play theorists' optimistic pronouncements about the value of "country" ideals.

The principal character through whom Rölvaag explores this alternative conception of the frontier is Beret, who herself becomes increasingly childlike (though unplayful) and increasingly vulnerable to an inarticulable anxiety. From the beginning of their journey west, even as she and her family cross the broad, open plains, Beret has felt oddly menaced. She is uncomfortably aware of a "vague sense of the unknown which bore in on them . . . strongly from all directions" (9). Rölvaag consistently figures Beret's dread of the loneliness of the uninhabited prairie in threatening and confining spatial metaphors—a volatile combination of agoraphobia and claustrophobia. On the first night of Per Hansa's trip to Sioux Falls to register their quarter-section, Beret feels "the purple dimness . . . steadily closing in, [and] a sense of desolation so profound settled upon her that she seemed unable to think at all" (38). When Per Hansa later announces that he must leave on another trip, Beret's sensation of claustrophobic isolation returns: "all at once it had seemed as if the whole desolation of a vast continent were centring there and drawing a magic circle about their home" (56). This "magic circle" is wholly unlike the energizing frontier space that perpetually surrounds Per Hansa, and even farther from Charles Robinson's idyllic, countrified playground.

Rölvaag makes clear that Beret's anxiety about the settlement's isolation is not unique. "Not a soul" in the colony "ever felt wholly at ease," we are told, "though no one referred to the fact or cared to frame the thought in words" (61). (Indeed, only the narrator, recording Beret's thoughts, can "frame" in words the intensity of the settlers' fear.) "All of a sudden, apparently without any cause," the narrator explains, "a vague, nameless dread would seize hold of them." Eventually, the settlers are able to shake these spells off, the men through their work, and the women through "talk" (61). But Beret, who is the least talkative of the Spring Creek women, has a difficult time escaping her dread. Perhaps if she had been more like Hans Olsa's wife, Sörine, "a stout, healthy-looking woman, whose face radiated an air of simple wisdom and kindliness" (23), or the Danish widow whom Per Hansa meets in Worthington, who also has a "ruddy, beaming" face (169), Beret would—by her husband's reckoning, or Turner's, or the play theorists—have coped better on the frontier. But Per Hansa believes that his wife "was not built to wrestle with fortune—she was too fine-grained" (43–44). In fall, rather than even look at the threatening plains, Beret covers up the very windows of their house and stays indoors.

Rölvaag also makes clear that the men of Spring Creek, particularly Per Hansa, can escape this menacing isolation by making trips to other settlements or distant towns. They have access to communities of support from which Beret and the other Spring Creek women are cut off. Per Hansa's increasingly frequent trips, in fact, provide almost an ironic counterstructure to the novel's pioneer narrative, subtly undermining the text's complacent frontier ideology in the process. Each time he leaves the supposedly self-sufficient frontier (where, contrary to Turner's thesis, there never seem to be sufficiently abundant resources to sustain the settlement), Beret's anxiety increases. As Beret grows more and more withdrawn, Per Hansa wants all the more desperately to make a new trip. The only way he can seem to cope with his frontier home is by repeatedly leaving it.

It is not likely, however, that occasional trips to town would have sufficiently reconciled Beret to the loneliness of the plains, for she longs more for the old world communities that she left behind than for any new world substitutes that America, whether through play progressivism or other reforms, might offer its immigrants. Although all of the Spring Creek settlers made significant breaks with their past when they left Norway for the unknown promise of the frontier, Beret seems the most affected by a sense of loss and the least willing to assimilate to the new ways of America. In the dead of the first winter her thoughts wander back to their departure, when "she had been sad with her parents but had rejoiced with Per Hansa" (219), whose "unflinching determination" (218) thrilled her. But from the solitary perspective of the Dakota Territory, her decision now appears to her an act of filial disobedience: they "sold off everything that they had won with so much toil, had left it all like a pair of worn-out shoes—parents, home, fatherland, and people. . . . And she had done it gladly, even rejoicingly! . . . Was there ever a sin like hers?" (219). In the new world Beret's haunting emptiness is compounded by recurring and equally frightening scenes of loss. As the novel opens, for example, the Hansens are themselves lost on the plains, trying to find the tracks of Tönseten's and Hans Olsa's wagons. Soon after their successful arrival, all of the settlement's cows—who provide not only valuable milk but, particularly for the women, a comforting companionship—mysteriously disappear. And later in the text Rölvaag describes a particularly unsettling episode. A Norwegian couple separated from their caravan have had to bury their youngest boy, without a coffin, in a shallow prairie grave. When the family stops at Spring Creek for a night's rest, Per Hansa discovers that the husband has had to tie his wife down so that in the dementia of her grief she won't get out of their wagon to look for their son. Per Hansa and Hans Olsa build a makeshift coffin and take the couple out to the plains to recover the boy's body, but no amount of searching can find the lost grave.

Beret's conviction that the frontier is a desolate "waste" (37), coupled with her longing for the folk (and folkways) of her past, harden her against most of the new customs that her fellow immigrants adopt as they assimilate to the new world. She rebukes Per Hansa for destroying the landmarks of the Irish squatters (a "heinous crime" in Norway [120]) and chafes silently at the changing of Norwegian family names. She so vehemently resists accommodation to the plains that she cannot even hear her own children at play, her ears too oppressed by "the deep silence" to notice their "boisterous" (37) frontier games.

Rölvaag conveys much of the anxiety Beret feels through the very construction of his sentences, particularly his distinctive use of ellipsis and the half-completed phrase. The first paragraph of the novel, for example, actually consists of two sentence fragments; the second paragraph begins with a third—then a fourth. Not until the fifth sentence does Rölvaag offer grammatical closure:

> Bright clear sky over a plain so wide that the rim of the heavens cut down on it around the entire horizon. . . . Bright, clear sky, to-day, to-morrow, and for all time to come.
>   . . . And sun! And still more sun! It set the heavens afire every morning; it grew with the day to quivering golden light—then softened into all the shades of red and purple as evening fell. . . . (3; original ellipsis)

After this opening he relies less on incomplete sentences and more on significant suspensions. At times Rölvaag's elliptical space can prove threatening, as the openness of the plains threatens Beret. Consider the two ellipses in the following description of Beret's recognition of her loneliness:

> It would not do to gaze any longer at the terror out there, where everything was turning to grim and awful darkness. . . . She threw herself back in the grass and looked up into the heavens. But darkness and infinitude lay there, also—the sense of utter desolation still remained. . . . Suddenly, for the first time, she realized the full extent of her loneliness, the dreadful nature of the fate that had overtaken her. (38)

The first ellipsis provides reassuring space for Beret to avert her gaze from "the terror out there" on the plains and to decide to lie down on the grass and look up to "the heavens." But the second is a more terrifying pause, for in it Beret realizes that she cannot escape the grim darkness at all, which lurked even in the first ellipsis that had seemed so safe. Instead of freedom, these ellipses offer enclosure, as in them Beret is "overtaken" by desolation. Thus not even the narrative allows her to escape the dreadful silences of the prairie; the very sentences through which her story is told are composed of them.

In due time these literal and metaphorical silences insinuate themselves into Beret and Per Hansa's once happy romance. Where there had formerly been love, passion, and mutual dreams—where in Beret's eyes her husband "had been life itself to her" (216), "like the gentle breeze of a summer's night" (221), and where she reigned as Per Hansa's "only princess" (217)—there develops distance, mistrust, fitful sleep. In later years, when Beret is overcome by spells of madness, she talks chiefly to the ghost of her dead mother. Per Hansa comes to regard Beret as simply another child in the house, rather than as his wife.

Side by side with the collapse of this romance, Rölvaag narrates the parallel demise of Per Hansa's play reformist dream of American assimilation and success. From almost the beginning of the text, Per Hansa thrills to the notion of himself as the lead figure in a quintessentially American fairy tale, where one can go from being a "newcomer, who owned nothing and knew nothing" (16) to a wealthy American citizen.[83] During their first heady months of kingdom-building, Per Hansa's love for his new country expands with every furrow he etches into "the best land in the world" (107). He is alive to the frontier romance of conquest, of fitness, of riches:

> That summer Per Hansa was transported, was carried farther and ever farther away on the wings of a wondrous fairy tale—a romance in which he was both prince and king, the sole possessor of countless treasures. In this, as in all other fairy tales, the story grew ever more fascinating and dear to the heart, the farther it advanced. Per Hansa drank it in; he was like the child who constantly cries: "More—more!" (107)

The following spring he tries to advance the story yet further—to test this spectacular American romance of the soil—by planting "*wheat*, the king of all grains" (108). As he cleans each kernel lovingly by hand, "playing with the good fairies that had the power to create a new life over this Endless Wilderness," he buoyantly recalls "how the fairy tale started: 'Once upon a time. . . . ' Not much of a beginning, yet the most startling events would unfold as the story went on—strange, incredible things" (286–87).

But at the height of Per Hansa's triumph in the novel—just after he has harvested that first lucrative wheat crop—the good fairies seem to desert him utterly, as though the romance of American immigrant success (at work and play) had never really been his to begin with, as though the romance itself were at heart an empty tale. The men of the settlement are preparing to bring in Per Hansa's oat fields, and joking about how much longer they can wait to reap the bounty of their own burgeoning wheat, when out of the west comes a "weltering turmoil of raging little demons" (332), a dark-brown, ravenous storm of locusts. The pests destroy most of the crops, and although Per Hansa saves his oats he no longer regards his good luck as a fairy's gift. In fact, after this day Per Hansa no longer speaks of fairies or fortune at all, particularly not after he returns home to discover Beret barricaded inside their house, huddling in her father's oversized immigrant chest with And-Ongen and the new baby. Beret has succumbed to the madness that had threatened since her arrival on the plains; Per Hansa finds his former princess unrecognizable. Her "face was that of a stranger, behind which her own face seemed to be hidden. He gazed at her helplessly, imploringly; she returned the gaze in a fixed stare, and whispered hoarsely: 'Hasn't the devil got you yet? He has been all around here to-day'" (338). Out of the promising western sky itself this plague had come, destroying each of Per Hansa's fairy-tale romances in one afternoon.

Over the next five or six years, Per Hansa struggles like the rest of the settlers against successive plagues and recurrent privation. He adapts fairly well—he buys up two more quarter-sections, maintains a reliable potato crop, and runs a profitable fur trade—but his buoyant exuberance has devolved into weary cheerlessness. By the time the preacher who will restore Beret to a measure of sanity arrives, Per Hansa seems a supporting character in a new narrative, a starkly realistic tale of determination and endurance. He has assimilated to a more common, if much less glamorous, American story. His face, like the land itself, is "deeply furrowed, as if by the marks of a ruthless hand; his whole figure seemed fearfully ravaged and broken, like a forest maple shattered by a storm" (372). He and Beret still live in the same sod house, where "all [his] dreams have been crushed in misery" (405). Others still have faith in his magic; at the end of the novel, when Sörine pleads with him to brave the deadly weather to bring a minister to the dying Hans Olsa, she tells Per Hansa that "we all have a feeling that nothing is ever impossible for you—and I thought that perhaps you might find a way out of this, too!" (445–46). Against all of his better judgment— for Per Hansa the realist has shelved his romantic faith in new world fairy tales—he allows himself to be shamed into the life-threatening trip. He leaves hoping that the weather might not be "so dangerous, after all" (451). And yet the next spring his body is found seated on one side of an old haystack, still in winter gear, looking "as though [he] were sitting there resting while he waited for better skiing." But he is dead, his face "ashen and drawn," his eyes "set toward the west" (453) in a fixed stare eerily reminiscent of Beret's earlier dementia.

Per Hansa's dead western gaze is at once both a fittingly ironic conclusion to a text that had opened on those same eyes, eagerly scanning the western prairie for signs of life, and a terse rebuke to the deceptive frontier dream of "opportunity" (5) that had brought them there.[84] By the end of the novel the settlement has suffered devastating losses. Hans Olsa and Per Hansa, twinned embodiments of resolute pioneer strength and buoyant pioneer energy, are dead, leaving six fatherless children and two grieving widows to complete this story of the western frontier—a story, however, that suddenly bears only superficial resemblance to the one that the play reformers were constructing or that Turner himself had been telling for over thirty years. Rölvaag's implicit critique in effect dismantles Turner's popular narrative several years before Turner's own peers were willing even to question "the Holy Writ of American historiography."[85] Had Rölvaag allowed the frontier thesis to tell his tale, he would have had to omit the final chapter—"The Great Plain Drinks the Blood of Christian Men and Is Satisfied"—and end the novel with "The Glory of the Lord," closing on a smiling Beret, recovered from her madness. Many in Rölvaag's contemporary audience apparently preferred such an ending and virtually accused the author in their fan letters of "mayhem" in the book's final chapter. But Rölvaag himself insisted that he wanted to show not just "the wealth and beauty there in the West," but "what it all cost."[86] Who would have known that he meant to revise an entire cultural myth in the process?

■

By explicitly structuring *Giants in the Earth* as a renunciation of cultural make-believe in favor of realistic fiction, Rölvaag rebukes the romantic narratives of immigrant assimilation circulating in the early twentieth century, from the naive optimism of Turner's frontier thesis, to the best-selling autobiographies and novels of actual immigrants, to the unicultural model of psychosocial development of the play reformers. These texts, Rölvaag's novel would seem to say, are at best falsely soothing scenarios for Americans all too worried about the "aliens" in their midst; at worst, they are dangerous fairy tales offering culturally destructive selves for immigrants to emulate. Read these books, Per Hansa's stare seems to say, with your eyes open.

The shift in *Giants in the Earth* from fairy tale to realist novel thus narrates in the space of one text the transformation Cahan achieved in revising "The Autobiography of an American Jew" into *The Rise of David Levinsky*, as he turned Levinsky's original sense of his Americanized business self as "unreal" into the novel's indictment of that self as insignificant. Unfettered by the constraints of the *McClure's* assignment—by whose mandate, in theory, he was to reveal "the minute workings of that wonderful machine, the Jewish brain"—Cahan was freer to critique the minute workings of a far less wonderful machine, American capitalism. The renunciation of romance in *Giants in the Earth* also helps us see more clearly how central the Dora-Levinsky subplot is to the economy of Cahan's text. For by its parallel design that section insists that the story of the rise from immigrant to assimilated businessman is at heart also an antiromance. The failed affair and the unsuccessful attempt to construct a meaningful self through leisure forecast Levinsky's later discovery that his very American career had let him down in similar ways. Cahan, too, critiques and resists the collective fantasies of assimilation.

And yet *Giants in the Earth* does more than provide a narrative telescope through which to bring Cahan's novel into clearer view. It also challenges Cahan's text by offering one specific immigrant story more or less unimaginable in *The Rise of David Levinsky*. If in some respects *Giants in the Earth* is a harsher critique of assimilation than Cahan's novel (Rölvaag's chief frontier enthusiast dies, while Cahan's merely broods), in others it is a more thoughtful exploration of what it takes to survive at work and play in America. For immigrants had never merely been passive victims of scheming hegemaniacs; they fought (and wrote) back. And at the end of a decade of increasingly xenophobic restrictions on the immigrant presence in America, Rölvaag's novel gives us Beret's story, the tale not of an immigrant who cannot "measure up to the challenge of the frontier" (as one critic has read her), but of one whose determined resistance to unquestioned assimilation allows her to endure.[87] For in the end, as Harold Simonson shrewdly observes, it is Beret who survives. It is also Beret who, like Levinsky, looks longingly to the past and who similarly recognizes "the cost incurred when independence, attenuated beyond traditional ties of culture, turns out to be only the autonomous self." But unlike Levinsky, whose recognition of this cost eventuates primarily in impotent melancholy, Beret's gives her a power to resist even in the face of temporary madness. It is Beret's resistance to the frontier that helps make *her*, paradoxically, "the best of Westerners."[88]

It is also, we might say, Beret's resistance to recreation theory that paradoxically makes her the novel's most effective spokesperson for the healing power of play. At the close of the novel, Rölvaag signals Beret's return to physical and mental health in part by showing her in earnest play with her newest child, little Permand. Feeling "released from the bonds of Satan" (400) after a minister absolves her of her sins, Beret is one day overswept by a "sudden surge of playfulness" (406) and throws herself down beside her son. Their subsequent frolic delights the boy and soothes Beret, who eventually dozes off. When she awakens, she is restored to her former self and feels the intensely healing joy of "home-coming" (408). Refreshed by play, she is moreover ready to resume the work of the settlement, and even offers to help get a minister for Hans Olsa when Per Hansa balks at the dangerous trip. To Per Hansa, of course, Beret's "home-coming" is a mixed blessing; her newly rigorous piety, in particular, makes him uncomfortable.

But in Beret's more pronounced devotion she ironically affirms the closing declaration of Joseph Lee's *Play in Education*. "There are certain words written in our hearts," Lee begins his final paragraph, "that are the master words, that contain the possibilities of life for us. These are the ultimate, the things in which our actual life consists, to which all other vital processes are tributary. Play is obedience to these master words."[89] Beret's piety marks her obedience to *her* "master words," the words of God; her devotion is, in Lee's best sense, "play." But by resisting the play reformers' assimilationist plot— of which Lee himself was a principal imaginer—Beret expressly rejects *his* master words, refusing to "fill out the ideal" that Lee saw "waiting for [her]."[90]

Thus both *Giants in the Earth* and *The Rise of David Levinsky*, if to varying degrees, achieve their cultural power through their resistance to the competing narratives that were all too eager to write their stories for them. Where Turner believed that "the true point of view in the history of this nation . . . is the Great West," and that one could actually "read" the United States, "like a huge page in the history of society," "line by line . . . from West to East," Cahan and Rölvaag read against this grain, telling the stories that move, we might say, from East to West, the stories of the Atlantic immigrants who have written their own "true" points of view on the "huge page" of American history.[91] For Cahan and Rölvaag the frontier as region or representation is neither Turner's fluid line of "perennial rebirth" nor the play reformers' countryside of imaginary delights, but a site of ongoing contestation whose meanings for America their texts review, critique, and in the end revise.

CHAPTER FOUR

"Find Their Place and Fall in Line"
The Revisioning of Women's Work in
Herland and *Emma McChesney & Co.*

IN 1910, AT THE OUTSET of the same turbulent decade that shaped the energetic skepticism of *The Rise of David Levinsky* and *Giants in the Earth*, Annie P. Hillis reviewed the liberating social advances being made by women during the Progressive Era. Writing in the *Outlook*, Hillis declared that the days of "idyllic, helpless femininity" were passing. As evidence she adduced the "six-foot captain of the basket-ball team"—who "laughs outright at the slender youth who would protect her"—and the "business woman," who "can earn her own support and would be beholden to no one." In both adult work and children's play, she claimed, American women were achieving "independence and equality with the other sex." But in practically her next breath Hillis makes clear that women's liberation might have reached—or perhaps surpassed—its natural limits. Protesting that it is "too soon to predict the future" even as she reaffirms progressivism's fundamental ideology ("We are in a world where there is a definite purpose running through all events, where there is a definite march forward"), Hillis retreats to a distinctly unliberating position: it is for contemporary women, she insists, to "find their place and fall in line."[1]

The imaginary line into which Hillis pictures women falling leads metaphorically off the basketball court and out of the boardroom back to the more traditional confines of the American home. Rather than "undertake to share the work of man," a woman (particularly a white, middle-class woman) should perform her duty to society, her "real work" in the world, as a "mother and home-maker." Once she has fulfilled these duties, or in the event that she cannot fulfill them, she should turn her attention to the betterment of the homes of other, less fortunate citizens. Thus what all women need is training in "the proper care of a house." Society's role is to "dignify their endeavors with the knowledge that they are doing permanent work, valuable to city and State," thereby making American women feel "that there is before them a definite task for which they must be trained and fitted."[2]

Hillis's retreat epitomizes the strategies of recontainment that women seeking liberation would encounter throughout the 1910s, particularly as the larger culture aggressively redefined the roles of work and play in American society. Increasingly dissatisfied with the soul-deadening routine that had come to characterize the advanced stages of industrial labor, many Americans questioned the once-sacred assumption that work was the primary locus for meaningful human action. In work's place, as we have seen, educators and social theorists proposed play as the one activity that could develop the physical, intellectual, and moral qualities necessary to achieve what Herbert Croly in 1909 had called "the promise of American life." A call for less (destructive) work and more (constructive) play bolstered much progressive legislation in the ensuing decade. But making the "less work, more play" platform appealing to American women, many of whom firmly believed that their liberation lay in the opposite direction—more work and less play—required two additional strategic redefinitions. First, progressives had (much like Annie Hillis) to reimagine home-work as the culture's highest work, essential to the very preservation of the "race." Second, in applying the less-work, more-play dictum to women as well as men, reformers had also to refigure domestic labor as a form of liberating play. The strains that these competing reconceptions produced were evident throughout the decade.

Challenging the imaginative boundaries thrown up by these redefinitions, however, were (in a sense) the very basketball player and businesswoman Hillis so ambivalently heralded in 1910. For almost simultaneously at dead center of this conflicted decade, Charlotte Perkins Gilman (who claimed to enjoy every kind of physical exercise) and Edna Ferber (who created the first enduring businesswoman in American fiction) offered complementary yet competing revisionings of the role of women's work (and, by extension, play) in American culture. In her 1915 novel *Herland*, Gilman imagines women's place as a world apart, simultaneously literalizing and radicalizing the era's prevailing concept of separately gendered spheres. She conceives a "corporate" economy that celebrates the collective, "teamwork" energies of women working and playing together to maintain one State, one corporate Home, in stark contrast to the isolation of individual women within individual homes encouraged by progressive reforms. If Gilman's women fall into Hillis's line it is only to make a circle, a luminous halo of mothers and daughters who find liberation and happiness in a perfect balance of work and play—as part of a utopian vision that rejects "realism" in favor of a sharp sense of how things ought to be. In contrast, Ferber's Emma McChesney finds her place at the head of Hillis's imaginary line, competing (and succeeding) against men in a "man's" world. Emma's corporate vision—particularly in the "realistic" stories that constitute Ferber's immensely popular *Emma McChesney & Co.* (1915)—inverts *Herland*'s by celebrating the satisfying solo of the individual performer over the blended harmony of collected voices. Though repeatedly tempted back into domesticity, Emma insists in the end that her freedom, creativity, and autonomy come from her work outside any "home."

These ideologically polar cultural products share a target—the progressive reformers who pay lip service to women's liberation by discouraging women from undertaking meaningful work of their own choosing—and a strategy: the adoption of popular literary forms through which to convey their differing social critiques. This strategy was not uncommon in the 1910s. It was, in fact, a deliberate tactic of some of the more radical reformers of the decade, the American workers, socialists, and labor organizations who used motion pictures to dramatize their critique of capitalism. Hoping to produce "commercially viable theatrical films that would entertain, not merely preach," these working-class filmmakers wrapped "explicit political messages in the popular garb of romantic melodrama."[3] To a degree, so do Gilman and Ferber. Although only Gilman's political program can fairly be termed radical, both *Herland* and *Emma McChesney & Co.* challenge the dominant culture's assumptions regarding women's work within recognizably conventional frameworks. Both texts, for example, feature a heterosexual love story (culminating in marriage) as an important structural device. Each text is just complicit enough with traditional American progressivism to make its critique palatable.

Such a strategy was particularly crucial in the 1910s, given the wide availability of mainstream progressive thought through the movies, and more important (where Gilman and Ferber were concerned) through mass-circulation American magazines like the *Outlook*. *Herland*, for example, appeared in the teens not as a book but as a twelve-part serial in Gilman's own monthly journal, the *Forerunner*, while the stories collected in *Emma McChesney & Co.* first ran in *Cosmopolitan* magazine. The *Outlook* is a particularly appropriate journal against which to read the critiques of Gilman and Ferber not only because of its wide circulation, its self-proclaimed status as the central weekly document of progressive America, and its typical use of female contributors (like Hillis) to express its positions on the "new woman," but also because it ran in the early teens exactly the sort of fiction to which *Herland* and *Emma McChesney & Co.* seem to have been responding. (In 1912, for example, the *Outlook* offered its readers James Oppenheim's antisocialist short story, "Till To-Morrow," in which a young man discovers and then rejects a utopian cooperative society for the "human world" he left behind. At the same time, the *Outlook* was also running the serial adventures of "Pete Crowther, Salesman," an energetic male businessman.)[4] We will consider the *Outlook*, then, a sort of barometer of the traditional progressivism that both *Herland* and *Emma McChesney & Co.* sought to combat—albeit from strategically different angles. And we will try to judge the extent to which Gilman and Ferber are able to package nontraditional messages in conventional forms and still avoid the cultural co-optation that they inherently risked in the process.[5]

■

The redefinition of play that intensified in the 1910s was prosecuted on two distinct fronts. First, beginning around the turn of the century, local play leaders initiated a push for playground space and organized recreation as part of the larger progressive quest for municipal improvement. Open-air sports and games for urban youth packed into dense city spaces dovetailed neatly with wider efforts, endorsed by journals like the *Outlook*, to promote sounder health, better hygiene, and a reduction in crime. Public, semipublic, and private recreational opportunities multiplied quickly. Between 1900 and 1916, supervised playgrounds skyrocketed from 10 in 10 cities to 3,270 in 414; larger cities constructed independent adult athletic facilities; elementary and high schools developed in-school and after-school programs; and national organizations such as the PAA, the Boy Scouts, and the Girl Scouts established numerous local chapters. By the 1910s the cultural fact of play's expanded role was unmistakable.[6]

The cultural meaning of that role, however, was open to negotiation. Sometime after 1906, with the founding of the PAA and its monthly journal, the *Playground*, genteel play reformers began to construct a more intellectual apparatus for what was fast becoming a movement with national repercussions. Not content merely to supervise play, these reformers theorized it, opening a second front in its redefinition. Almost overnight, play acquired a philosophical as well as a practical history that was then popularized through a series of scholarly and educational texts. These texts varied in execution but not in intention: each championed play over work as the primary arena for individual and civic development. Whether one read Wilbur Bowen's *The Teaching of Play* (1913), Henry Curtis's *Education Through Play* (1915), Joseph Lee's *Play in Education* (1915), or Luther Gulick's *Philosophy of Play* (1920)—or any of the countless other essays, pamphlets, and books published on the subject in the teens—one would finish assured that play had a more powerful effect on "the character and nature of man" than any other possible undertaking.[7]

And what of woman? Although most play theorists included chapters or sections on the changing role of play for girls, the play groups most strenuously targeted in the 1910s were male. There were several reasons for this emphasis. First, the modern industrial system—considered a prime culprit in the crippling of Americans' "native" play "ideals"—still primarily employed men. Second, even given the enormous rise in popularity of recreation for girls and women at the end of the nineteenth century, formal and informal play activities were still dominated by boys, who were seen as most in need of supervision. Third, the model of psychosocial development propounded by the play theorists—G. Stanley Hall's recapitulation theory—gendered the significant human actions as male. According to Hall (as ventriloquized by Joseph Lee), civilized children reenacted through their play what were once the instinctual "work" activities of our savage ancestors, and in so doing anticipated "the becoming of what [they are] to be." Primitive man hunted; the 1910s boy played hide-and-seek and various throwing, running, and chasing games in preparation for the competitive adult male world.[8] "Nearly all of our games have been derived from the activities of savage man," explained Henry Curtis in 1915. "It is to be anticipated, therefore, that they will be somewhat less interesting to girls than to boys."[9]

Girls, to be sure, had their own "primitive" instincts to recapitulate. While men hunted, savage women, the play theorists explained, primarily mothered, overseeing both their children and what Curtis called without irony "the minor activities of the camp," including "the building of the wigwam, the setting of snares, the tanning of skins, the making of clothing, and the pottery and weaving." Contemporary girls' play could include vigorous "boy" games, but the play theorists tended to recommend more domestic and nurturing activities, such as playing house and taking care of dolls. These play forms, it was believed, would develop the essential "feminine virtues" and thus would best prepare young girls for the duties of adult womanhood.[10]

This is not to suggest that women and girls were largely excluded from the boom in sports, exercise, and leisure that accompanied the redefinition of play in the 1910s. Quite the contrary: women not only played in record numbers, sharing a "sense of joyous renewal and regeneration and an underlying conviction of the worth of activity"; they also shaped the development of the activities in which they participated. But play progressivism sought consistently to contain women's liberating experiences within a larger ideology of domestication. In other words, various forms of women's leisure attained cultural legitimacy primarily insofar as they could be shown to contribute to the rebuilding of American society along traditional gender lines. Consider the example of women's sports. Women who rode bicycles, or who swam, or who played tennis, golf, or basketball variously reported that they enjoyed the exhilaration of physical action, the emancipation from the restrictions of the home sphere, the personal control over body shape and weight, and the pleasure of social interaction with their husbands and particularly with other women. The principal concern of physical education specialists, play administrators, and health experts (both male and female), however, was what effect athletic activity would have on women's capacity to bear and raise children. Healthier mothers were clearly a boon to the nation, but there was widespread fear that overexertion or improper exertion could damage a woman's vital reproductive ability. Women's sports received institutional support in the 1910s largely to the extent that they produced women who were "fit and fertile."[11] Men's sports, too, were regulated in a similar fashion; no one seriously proposed activities that would effectively reduce the male capacity for procreation (except, perhaps, the "sport" of war). But whereas men's participation in culturally sanctioned forms of play expressly prepared them for the world outside the home, women's participation (and here sports is just one example) redirected them back inside, reinforcing a domestication of women's play in the teens. Even Progressive Era women reformers, who tended to uphold the general turn-of-the-century belief in separate spheres for men and women in American society—even though they themselves were exposing that split as a cultural fiction— "helped codify a limited public domain for women."[12]

Part and parcel with this domestication of play occurred a process that I call the ludification of women's work. As women's play metaphorically moved indoors, women's domestic work was gradually reconceptualized as a form of play. This is the most striking of a series of redefinitions of women's work during the period. As a facet of the larger cultural project to add purpose and prestige to domestic work (which in the teens was variously reclassified as women's personal "industry," their own "science," and even their "true art"), the ludification of women's work deserves special scrutiny as the natural corollary to the domestication of play. Play prepared women for work; but that work, in itself, could be play. Thus two potentially threatening spheres of liberation for women in the 1910s—women's work and women's play—were carefully contained within familiar bounds.

The pages of high-circulation, middle-class, progressive journals like the *Outlook* were a primary vehicle for the popularization of the ideas and ideals of those with a stake in this project. Writers like Curtis, Lee, and Gulick exerted influence through their own recreational programs and through their books, but a weekly venue like the *Outlook* (whose brief articles and even briefer editorials were considerably easier to digest than four-hundred-page treatises on play) could more quickly and effectively shape a developing national consciousness. The *Outlook* of the 1910s could lay a strong claim to that consciousness. Having begun in 1867 as Henry Childs's *Church Union* (soon to be reconceived as the *Christian Union* under Henry Ward Beecher in 1869), the *Outlook* emerged under Lyman Abbott in 1893 as a powerful and progressive journal of the social gospel in America. By the 1910s, still under Abbott's direction, and with former president Theodore Roosevelt as a contributing editor, the magazine that in 1910 promised to give its readers "the ablest presentation it can secure on both sides of publicly debated questions" enjoyed "days of influence, of respect, of prosperity."[13]

The *Outlook*'s readers were evidently much interested in recent developments in women's health and recreation. (Abbott himself was by 1910 an honorary vice president of the PAA.) The journal reported on female sports champions, particularly in "new" sports such as tennis, swimming, and golf, and ran numerous investigative essays on play in general and specifically on girls' camps, women's exercise routines, and school athletic programs. And each article, at least on the surface, heralded the liberating power of women's play. In May 1911, in "The Girl and the Camp," for example, Elizabeth Fessenden attacks the crippling constraints (and double standard) of social convention—particularly as expressed in women's fashion—in her enthusiastic review of this new outlet for girls' play:

> Why must it be ever he? She needs [camp] even more. He at least has not lived all his days tied up in petticoats and pinched up in corsets, and he hasn't, with pegs under his heels, hobbled through life, stiff, stilted, stylish. He has at least known a little freedom. . . . Actually for girls, a camp! A place where the red gods reign supreme! And for girls! Doesn't it almost seem too good to be true?

For Fessenden, loose-fitting, comfortable clothes mean more activity; more activity means better health. "Oh, the freedom of a camp costume!" she exclaims. Anna Worthington Coale similarly praises the "environment of simplicity and freedom which stimulates [the girls' camps] to activity." And Mary Harrod Northend reminds readers that forming girls' camps was from the start much harder than forming boys', because "mothers had to become accustomed to allowing their daughters the freedom of life away from home."[14]

But what did that life away from home consist of? Over the decade, activities varied from camp to camp, but from the beginning all included camp work as well as play. What a close reading of the *Outlook* reveals, however, is that for girls the role of domestic work at camp grew in importance as the teens progressed. Fessenden reports at the beginning of the camp movement in 1911 that while a "few camps" devote time each day to "domestic science, art, or to one form of handicraft or another," every camp requires "a share in the daily work" from each girl. The expressed goal of the camp experience is "to make every girl stronger and happier" and "more useful," although Fessenden does not restrict that usefulness to one particular sphere. Just one year later, however, an *Outlook* editorial notes with approval the significantly increased emphasis given to domestic labor in the newest camp movement, the Camp Fire Girls. Because girls have an "instinctive desire in them for those experiences that develop" their "natural"

traits—and because those traits center on the home—all girls should be especially attracted to "the interesting Adventure of Home-Making" offered
by the Camp Fire Girls. By 1914, in an article about girls' camps in general,
Anna Coale emphasizes that the result of camp training should be to provide young women "with a reserve of strength and steady nerve as a preparation for living." That living, however, is quite clearly domestic; Coale rejects any programs of play or study (in the camps or in the schools) that are
"wholly unrelated to the life of the girl who is preparing to make a home."
And in *every* camp, Coale notes with satisfaction, "a *definite* part of each
camp day is sacredly devoted to work."[15]

This figurative recontainment of otherwise liberating experiences for
girls and women was often "brought home" more literally (and, in an odd
way, more symbolically) to readers of the *Outlook* in the pictorial representations within each issue. The *Outlook* prided itself on its photographs,
which appeared at first primarily in its end-of-the-month "magazine" issue
but soon in other weeks as well and, beginning in 1913, every week in the
journal's "Current Events Pictorially Treated" section. In many cases the
pictures accompanying the girls' camp articles underscored the subtext of
domestication described above. In Mary Harrod Northend's 1915 article
"How to Choose a Summer Camp for Boys or Girls," for example, the text
stresses the role of vigorous sports in giving a girl a "confidence in her own
power which otherwise she would never have had," but the only picture of
girls at all—directly facing the paragraph that refers to this power—shows
half a dozen girls cleaning out their tent and is captioned "Active Little
Housekeepers in a Girls' Camp." The vivid "power" of the picture (combined with the diminutizing "Little" of the caption) effectively undermines
the message of the accompanying text.[16]

Other pictures in the *Outlook* work hand in hand with their text to channel liberating energies into safer streams. One mid-decade advertisement
that appeared frequently, for example, offered to teach young women how
to double their typewriting speed through "Simple Gymnastic Finger Training" (see Figure 13). Here the potential power of an activity like gymnas-

Typewriting Speed Doubled by Simple Gymnastic Finger Training

In Europe, and in America, for many years it has been a regular part of every musician's training to take special gymnastic finger exercises. Teachers would no more expect their pupils to become good pianists without special finger training, than they would expect them to play without first learning to read notes.

Now, for the first time, has this principle of gymnastic finger training been applied to typewriting. Its necessity is proved by the fact that the one great difficulty which handicaps ninety-nine out of every hundred stenographers is their inability to gain full control of their *finger movements*.

The average stenographer typewrites thirty to forty words a minute. A "trained finger" operator can typewrite eighty to one hundred words a minute, without errors and with amazing ease. There you have the reason for the difference in salaries paid to stenographers.

It remained for Mr. R. E. Tulloss, who is known the country over as among the greatest typewriting authorities of the present day, to invent a marvelous system of finger exercises especially designed for typewriting, which can be learned *away from the machine*, in only ten remarkably easy lessons, and which with amazing quickness brings this wonderful flexibility, speed and control of the fingers.

Already thousands have adopted the new method with results bordering almost on the miraculous. Many of them were so-called "touch writers," others, after years of fruitless effort, had practically given up hope of ever attaining more than merely average typewriting ability, many had taken other courses, with no marked increase in speed—yet, by the New Way, practically without exception, they all have developed the remarkable speed of eighty to one hundred words a minute.

Every stenographer can secure an interesting book about this New Way in Typewriting, free. It is brimful of eye-opening ideas and valuable information. It explains how this unique new method will quickly make your fingers *strong and dextrous*, bring them under *perfect control*, make them extremely rapid in their movements—how in a few short weeks you can transform your typewriting and make it *easy, accurate* and *amazingly speedy*.

If you are ambitious to get ahead—if you want to make your work easier—if you want to get more money in your pay envelope—don't wait a single moment before sending for this book of information and proof.

This new method is bringing such marvelous results to others—is proving itself to be so sure a means of quickly increasing salaries—that you will be doing yourself a big injustice if you fail to write for it *at once*. Just send a letter or postal card request *now* to The Tulloss School, 2923 College Hill, Springfield, Ohio, and your copy will be sent by return mail without cost or obligation. Do this now, before you turn this page.

FIGURE 13. "Typewriting Speed Doubled by Simple Gymnastic Finger Training." From the *Outlook*, Mar. 14, 1917.

tics (a term that in the 1910s tended to denote exercises to build general strength rather than the more specific routines involved today) is not only transferred into the domestic sphere (the woman appears to be practicing in her home), but is concentrated into a very small portion of the body. Indeed, the picture itself focuses on only one finger, an emphasis intensified by that finger's appearance in three places, once on the hopeful typist herself and twice in the pages of the book spread out in front of her. The goals of the exercises, the ad copy tells us, are to make the fingers "*strong and dextrous*" and to "bring them under *perfect control*."

This ad is also in some ways an anomaly in the *Outlook*, for the simple reason that it focuses approvingly on a young working woman who will deploy her new skills *outside* the home, even encouraging her "to get ahead" in her job and "to get more money in [her] pay envelope." More typically, the *Outlook*'s advertisements and editorial pages addressed themselves to the middle-class homemaker, not the working-class typist. Its only consistent endorsement of freedom for women was in the domestic sphere. Indeed, the *Outlook* initiated an aggressive campaign from the start of the decade to convince women that the housework they lamented as drudgery really contained all the possibilities of life for them. After a pair of 1910 essays on domestic issues ("Some Failures of American Women," on the effects of divorce on homemaking, and "Our House in Order," on household management and the servant question) generated "considerable comment" from *Outlook* readers, in 1911 the journal launched an exhaustive serial inquiry into "the problems of the home." Titled "Home Making the Woman's Profession," the series offered a "valuable" reinterpretation of the management of the home "as one of the most complex, intellectual, and difficult of professions." Presenting the perspective of "women of wide practical experience," the series explicitly sought to counter progressive feminist rhetoric—which suggested that women needed, above all, release from menial home labor—by arguing instead that women need look no further than their own kitchens for empowerment and satisfaction. The "Editorial Introduction" to the series announced that the

common view expressed by many leaders of the so-called women's movement is that the housewife's work is drudgery and the housewife is a drudge,
and that the way to liberate women is to give them opportunities for escaping from such drudgery and for relief from the position of drudge.

This series of articles will point out the fact that there is a better way. The
articles will show from one point of view after another that there is no more
drudgery in the work of the housewife than there is in the work of the lawyer
or the editor or the physician or the politician or any other profession which
women are these days being urged to enter.[17]

Rather than demonstrate this proposition by examining each of the
"male" professions and showing women how equally drudging those occupations really are (an interesting possibility), the series promises to argue
in precisely the opposite direction, offering to show that the talented housewife actually combines the very best skills of a broad variety of compelling
professions. A properly educated homemaker, according to the series introduction, will be part factory manager, chemist (the kitchen as culinary
laboratory is a favorite metaphor), teacher, captain of industry, architect,
landscape gardener, and artist. The ensuing articles will then in theory
"cover" these "different topics." What each article tends to cover, however,
are the principles of scientific management as applied to the home, effectively subsuming the rhetoric of liberation within one of efficiency.[18] What
was promised as "a better way" to "liberate" women quickly became the
study of budgets, task charts, and time and motion studies: do your household chores more efficiently, the articles seemed to say, and free time will
follow. The clear message of this early series was that if the woman's profession was not drudgery, it was nonetheless hard work.

Over time, however, the dedrudgification of work as expressed in the
Outlook began to put on a cheerier face. After the first series on homemaking ended in 1912, the journal continued to publish regularly on domestic
reform; but by mid-decade it was suggesting that one's work would improve
if work were more fun. In a four-part 1916 series titled "How to Make Play
out of Work," for example, Ellen Chattle explains that simply making one's
work hours more efficient (in order to liberate time for play) is not enough.

Truly to "help people to become good and happy" we need to "get the spirit of play into the work hours" themselves. Although Chattle's series is not limited to women's domestic work, her most specific examples are. In the second article, "Competition," for example, she suggests that the best way "to save our work from the slough of drudgery" is to convert it to "glorious sport," and offers for emulation "the housewife of more primitive days who forgot the weariness of the family washing in her ambition to be the first to get it on the line in the morning." In the fourth and final installment, "Joy of Self-Activity," Chattle encourages women to reimagine their work as play in order to release the "hidden spring" of "joy" that can "freshen monotonous tasks." Since the proper dusting of a room requires "a great many poses of the body" rehearsed quickly, the "whole exercise"—pun probably intended—"may be conceived of as a gymnastic performance." Even a broom "may be made to move rhythmically with as fine a swing as a conjurer's wand." The magic of this liberation was not only that it was neatly contained within one's own home, but that it required no lengthy study of the latest theory of domestic science. One merely had to decide that housework was fun and one would be "good and happy," just as when one was "a very little child."[19] Any woman could do it.

This philosophy seems also to be the subtext of a series of advertisements running in the *Outlook* at mid-decade for none other than the Arco Wand vacuum cleaner system. An elaborate home-installed device, the Arco Wand was figured as a tool for the imagination as well as the hands. The American Radiator Company would set a pump machine in the basement and run suction pipes to each floor of the house; the housewife would then plug her wand in and suck up dirt instead of sweeping it with a broom. "Merely point or stroke the fairy like hollow wand over carpets, rugs, curtains, upholstery, mattresses, floors, walls, clothes, furniture, etc.," the ad copy directs, "and the cleaning is done!"[20] In several of the advertisements, moreover, the power gained by the woman who uses the wand—at least as expressed in the copy—is accompanied by her curious infantilization in the ad pictures. One can see in both Figure 14 and Figure 15 that, to a degree,

A worker with giant strength may give the whole house a heavy, thorough sweeping—but this doesn't mean thorough *cleaning*—there is a difference.

The secret of the ARCO WAND is its lightness and its strong, steady suction which draws all the dirt away without wasting your strength or raising a dust.

Clean house—no labor

The ARCO WAND way saves woman's strength and cleans house better than a powerful workman could do. In ten minutes you can do an immense amount of cleaning without fatigue or waste of strength.

ARCO WAND
VACUUM CLEANER

Merely point or stroke the fairy like hollow wand over carpets, rugs, curtains, upholstery, mattresses, floors, walls, clothes, furniture, etc., and the cleaning is done!

The ARCO WAND suction is steady and strong, going into the very fabric of rugs and carpets, instantly drawing out the dust, dirt and grit into the sealed dust bucket.

The ARCO WAND is built for a lifetime of good, steady service. It is not put on the market as a *temporary* selling proposition, but will do vastly better work and outlast many of the portable types of machines. We believe that equipment for vacuum cleaning should be as substantial as radiator heating. If you are building a new house tell your architect you want the ARCO WAND and insist that your contractor furnishes it.

Lasts a lifetime and guaranteed

ARCO WAND machines have been in successful use for over six years in all kinds of buildings—residences, apartments, schools, hotels, churches, clubs, office buildings, factories, etc. Costs about a penny a day to run. No other up-keep expense; also made for gasoline engine power. As easily installed in *old* buildings as in new ones.

Send at once for copy of our book "Arco Wand." It will help you to make the right choice and really informs you on the great advantages of vacuum cleaning.

Write to
Department
C-5

AMERICAN RADIATOR COMPANY

816-822
S. Michigan Ave.
Chicago

Machine is set in basement or side-room. A suction pipe runs to each floor. ARCO WAND Vacuum Cleaners, hose and tools are sold by all Heating and Plumbing Trade.

Makers of the world-famous IDEAL Boilers and AMERICAN Radiators

FIGURE 14. American Radiator Company, "Clean house—no labor."
From the *Outlook*, Jan. 24, 1917.

Household help becomes discouraged and dissatisfied by the heavy labor of cleaning

There is no worry about cleaning in the home where the Arco Wand does the work

Lighten Household Work!

The cleaning of the house is a heavy physical strain and expense for help (if you can get it) as long as you cling to the old, tiresome broom and duster methods of cleaning.

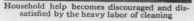

ARCO WAND
VACUUM CLEANER

The Arco Wand Vacuum Cleaner changes weary household cleaning into a few moments of light, quick use of the suction-wand, with no labor and without extra help.

Use the Arco Wand on your floor, carpets, rugs, upholstered furniture, hangings, curtains, mattresses, clothes, furs, shelves, drawers, books, picture frames and mouldings, etc. All will be cleaned instantly, and dust, dirt, and lint piped away into the sealed dust bucket of the machine.

Easily and quickly installed in *old* or *new* residences, apartments, hotels, clubs, theatres, schools, and public and private buildings. Also made mounted on truck for use in factories, and large business buildings. May be purchased on easy payments, if desired, from dealers everywhere.

Send at once for catalog, The ARCO WAND, which gives full descriptions, and illustrates many of its labor and money saving uses.

Department CS — AMERICAN RADIATOR COMPANY — 816-822 S. Michigan Ave. Chicago

Makers of the world-famous IDEAL Boilers & AMERICAN Radiators

Machine is set in basement or side room. A suction pipe runs to each floor. ARCO WAND Vacuum Cleaners, hose, and tools are sold by all Heating and Plumbing Trade.

FIGURE 15. American Radiator Company, "Lighten Household Work!" From the *Outlook*, Jan. 8, 1919.

the woman's diminution is meant to convey that the wand does not require special strength; and yet in each of these ads the woman (as she is clearly denoted in the copy) appears much more like a child. In Figure 14 the wand itself appears several feet longer than the woman is high. And in Figure 15 the wand wielder appears as an oddly proportioned woman-child, with a young girl's body (and clothing) but with what seems to be a woman's head (though topped by a girlish bow).[21]

What these ads so vividly illustrate are the merging trajectories of the originally parallel movements to reform girls' play and women's work. Where girlhood recreation was refigured as preparation for domestic work—recall the "Active Little Housekeepers in a Girls' Camp"—here women's work is pictured as a recovery of childhood play. The collapsing of generational distance involved in this merger—as the daughter acts like her mother and vice versa—serves in some senses to contain the American "female" within a more restricted sphere than she had previously occupied. (Many other advertisements in the teens conspicuously linked a daughter's play behavior to her mother's work. See, for example, the Ivory Soap and Valentine's Valspar ads in Figures 16 and 17.) This recontainment becomes particularly strategic in the 1910s, given the strident attacks being made against what Theodore Roosevelt deplored as "race suicide," the supposed failure of "old stock" Americans to bear children at the same rate as "alien" Americans. Indeed, as cultural leaders like Roosevelt and the *Outlook* repeatedly expressed it, the ultimate purpose for guiding women back happily into their homes—especially those women contemplating careers outside the traditional "home" and postponing marriage—was to reinstill in women their pride in motherhood. If the "real work" of American women, then, was what one essayist in the *Outlook* termed "mother work"—that is, the conservation of the home through the bearing and raising of children—then the real goal of this home conservation was to preserve the "race," or what we might perhaps more accurately call America's conception of itself.[22]

■

FIGURE 16. Ivory Soap advertisement. From the *Outlook*, Dec. 24, 1919. Courtesy of Procter & Gamble.

The famous Valspar Varnish test brought home—

" Oh, no, mother won't mind. She did this herself the other day just to show Mrs. Bates how perfectly wonderful the floor is since we had it varnished.

" You see, Josephine, it doesn't hurt the varnish a single bit. 'Cause this isn't just the ordinary varnish like the kind that turns all white when you leave the soap dish setting on it. This is *Valspar* varnish.

" You can pour the boilingest water in the world on Valspar, and it won't turn white.

" We have it in the bathroom, too, and it doesn't matter how much spatter you make, it won't show any spots.

" Papa says he's going to have all our floors and window sills varnished with Valspar—and our front door and vestibule too."

Why not have this wonderful waterproof varnish on the floors, the linoleum, the woodwork, and the furniture in *your* home ?

It is easy to apply ; it dries over night ; and once on, it wears and *wears* and *WEARS*. And it will never spot or turn white, no matter *what* happens !

VALSPAR ENAMELS These Enamels are composed of pigments, finely ground in Valspar and have all the desirable qualities of Valspar itself for outdoor or indoor work of all kinds. They are made in 12 rich colors, and in black and white. Like Valspar Varnish they are absolutely waterproof and very durable.

VALENTINE & COMPANY
456 Fourth Avenue, New York
Largest Manufacturers of High-grade Varnishes in the World

ESTABLISHED 1832

New York   Chicago   Toronto   London
Boston   **VALENTINE'S** (Trade Mark)   Amsterdam

W. P. FULLER & Co., San Francisco and Principal Pacific Coast Cities

Copyright 1919 Valentine & Company

FIGURE 17. "The famous Valspar Varnish test brought home."
From the *Outlook*, Oct. 1, 1919.

Reimagining America's self-conception was, in several ways, precisely Charlotte Perkins Gilman's project in her writings, even many years before she serialized *Herland*. As early as 1892, in her short story "The Yellow Wall-Paper," for example, Gilman forcefully critiqued the then dominant American belief that nothing short of intellectual inactivity and domestic isolation—as embodied in S. Weir Mitchell's late-nineteenth-century "rest cure"—could restore a woman's physical, mental, and emotional health. Based in part on her own experiences with Dr. Mitchell, Gilman's harrowing story vividly imagines the physical and psychological destruction that such a restrictive "cure" might have on women. Central to the fiction is a tension between liberation and recontainment whose resolution is thwarted by restrictive cultural definitions of appropriate women's work.

The story consists of a dozen journal entries made by a young woman on vacation for the summer with her husband and child. The vacation, however, is a forced one; the couple has rented "ancestral halls" in the country in order for the female narrator to recover from what her husband-physician has diagnosed as "temporary nervous depression—a slight hysterical tendency." John, the husband, is not on vacation. He continues to practice medicine and "is away all day, and even some nights when his cases are serious." John's freedom of movement and his involvement in meaningful work contrast starkly with the narrator's own daily routine. As part of her treatment, she is virtually restricted to the upstairs master bedroom (whose many windows offer the freshest air of any room in the house) and is "absolutely forbidden to 'work' until [she is] well again." "Perfect rest" and "proper self-control" are crucial to her recovery, John insists.[23]

Rather than heal the narrator, however, such restrictions merely turn vacation into vacuity, as each supposedly restful day offers only an intellectual and social void that she is prevented from filling. Whereas Mitchell's infamous cure prescribed domestic work and child care but forbade all mental activity, John even forbids housework, enlisting his sister ("a perfect and enthusiastic housekeeper" [765]) to cover the daily chores and another woman to care for their infant son. The narrator's human contact—even of the strictly domestic sort—is severely limited. The other "work" that she is specifically enjoined from doing is her writing, which her husband believes will only aggravate her "excited fancies," given her "imaginative power and habit of story-making" (764). Much skillful commentary, which I will not rehearse here, has delineated the complex relationship between gender, imagination, and art in the story.[24] But what critics have not emphasized is the value the narrator attaches to the social nature of her desired work. Rather than perceive writing as John does—an isolated activity indicative of unhealthful "fancy"—the narrator sees it as a form of communication and interaction, a social process in which meaning is negotiated through discussion with others. John himself sees no value in such exchange; he "scoffs openly at any talk of things not to be felt and seen and put down in figures" (762). But the narrator longs for "congenial work, with excitement and change," and finds it "so discouraging not to have any advice and companionship" about her writing (762, 764). She would very much like "cousin Henry and Julia" to come down "for a long visit," but John refuses to expose her to such "stimulating people" (764).

The people John does bring down only reinforce the narrator's dependence and isolation. Rather than surround her with the company she desires, John invites "Mother and Nellie and the children" for a week, creating an intensely domestic tableau in which the narrator, however, has no functional role. Although John insists that she get well "for his sake" and their child's (767), there is no evidence that anyone in the house needs her. "Of course I [don't] do a thing," she says of the week the guests are visiting. "Jennie sees to everything now" (765). Rather than perform any meaningful work, even in the house, the narrator, like just another child, is totally dependent on others. (John even refers to her as his "blessed little goose" [764] and "little girl" [768].) Gilman heightens the irony of this visit (in which the narrator desires adult excitement and change but gets an infantilizing domestic pattern pressed back upon her with a vengeance) by having it culminate on the Fourth of July—a day of independence that the narrator has little personal reason to celebrate.[25]

As the journal entries progress, the narrator's perception of her loss of freedom becomes at once more acute and more unstable. She spends less and less time walking in the garden or sitting on the porch, and more and more time upstairs in her bedroom trying to decode the grotesque pattern of the yellow wallpaper, an activity that she decides is "as good as gymnastics" (766). The room itself gradually contributes to her infantilization (it was first a nursery, then a playroom, she speculates) and also to her imprisonment, through the bars on the windows and in the moonlit wallpaper. Soon the only "admirable exercise" she can imagine is jumping out the window to the ground below (773). The narrator begins to strip the wallpaper from the walls—much as, in her view, little boys from a "boys' school" might have done (763)—at first in patches, to reveal the subpattern she believes lurks beneath, but eventually all around the room, in order to free the woman she sees trapped within the paper itself. By the close of the tale she believes *herself* to have escaped from "behind the pattern" but refuses to leave the room, preferring to "creep smoothly on the floor" (773) on her hands and knees, a startling (if not "admirable") exercise of self-control (however atavistic, her crawling is, after all, "smooth") that causes John to faint dead away when he finally sees what she has become—or, as Janice Haney-Peritz suggests, what his own restrictive "demands and desires" have turned her into.[26]

■

In Gilman's imaginary 1915 world of *Herland,* however, men pass out not in horror at a woman's madness but in submission to the anesthetic of powerful women in total control of their own country, freedom, and identity. The land that explorers Vandyck Jennings, Terry O. Nicholson, and Jeff Margrave force their way into, they soon discover, bears little resemblance to the United States they left behind. Not only is Herland inhabited only by women, it is clean, spacious, and free of the disease, crime, and poverty that progressive America fought so earnestly to eliminate. Much of what the trio sees is literally unrecognizable, a point that the narrator, Van, emphasizes when he laments in his introductory remarks the unavailability of his "books full of notes, carefully copied records, firsthand descriptions, and the pictures—that's the worst loss," he says, for without photographs nobody "will ever believe" how everything (particularly the women) looked.[27] And yet Herland should have been perfectly recognizable to Progressive Era play reformers; it was in many ways the very utopia of which they had been dreaming.

For excepting the absence of men, Herland is a model version of the recreational, educational, and social changes play reformers sought to make in a modernizing American society. Although the male explorers will not discover the extent to which this is true until they have been in the country for some time, Gilman's narrative signals from the beginning Herland's harmonious synthesis of contemporary play ideals with the two most influential late-nineteenth-century models of recreation reform: New York City's Central Park and Chicago's Columbian Exposition. The principal feature of Herland that the men notice in their initial reconnoiter is the remarkable order of the land. In sharp contrast to the "desperate tangle of wood and water" that characterizes the terrain at the base of Herland's mountain hideaway, Herland (as the "well-woven fabric, with a pattern" found by the men a year earlier distinctly foreshadows) is "a land in a state of perfect cultivation, where even the forests looked as if they were cared for; a land that looked like an enormous park" (3, 4, 11). "We'd better import some of these ladies and set 'em to parking the United States," Van declares (18).

In both form and function, Herland's carefully cultivated landscape most closely resembles New York's Central Park, the famous recreational experiment of environmental designer Frederick Law Olmsted. Like Central Park, which Olmsted sought in the 1850s to isolate from the city itself "by planting a row of trees completely surrounding the park,"[28] Herland is "well forested about the edges" while possessed of "wide plains, and everywhere parklike meadows and open places" in the interior (10). Olmsted's design was intended to create a "rural retreat" within an "artfully natural landscape," whose "primary recreational value . . . consisted in [the] contemplation of natural scenery";[29] Herland, too, offers "broad green fields," with "good roads winding pleasantly here and there, and narrower paths besides" (17). Much as Olmsted hoped his park would have a contemplative and restorative effect on its visitors—particularly boisterous young urban males (not entirely unlike Van, Terry, and even the more subdued Jeff)—Herland impresses the enthusiastic explorers with its "placid silence" and "quiet potency" (18).

And yet, as Van and the others are quick to point out, Herland is not all park; the first town they come to offers them another familiar, yet different experience. "It's like an exposition," one of them suggests, and the comparison is apt. Like the 1893 Chicago exposition, for example, which was conceived as "an embodiment of public order, cultural unity, and civic virtue"— and which displaced the "urban pastoralism" of Olmsted's parks[30]—Herland's towns bespeak "beauty, order, [and] perfect cleanness" (19). All the buildings look like "palaces," particularly the "big white ones" (19) that explicitly recall the gleaming white (though fake) marble facades of Chicago's White City. Herland improves on these complementary yet competing visions of alternative urban order, however, by merging them. Rather than isolate park from city (and vice versa), Herland's city planners weave them together, with "rambling palaces grouped among parks and open squares, something as college buildings stand in their quiet greens" (19). And as we learn through the rest of the story, this combination represents in *Herland* precisely the "common effort" of the reform impulses behind such diverse projects as Central Park and the Chicago exposition, which sought "not simply to amuse but to instruct their users in lessons of aesthetic taste and social responsibility and to inspire them with a respect for cultural standards."[31]

Gilman's mixed-use landscape has a streak of the contemporary as well, perhaps best represented by the "three bright-hued figures" (the young Herland foresters Celis, Alima, and Ellador) who dash swiftly across the open country like "wild antelopes" (17). For into this nostalgically progressive setting Gilman has placed an exuberant population of 3 million tremendously fit women and girls. Physical culture, the explorers discover, is also integrated into Herland society precisely as play and health reformers were urging. Infants in Herland, for example, are raised in what Van calls "a babies' paradise," in which they are taught "as rapidly as feasible, to use and control their own bodies" (107). Simple developmental tasks like walking are turned into physical education games, producing "sure-footed, steady-handed, clear-headed" and distinctly happy youngsters (107).[32] Van marvels that Americans had not thought to train children this way—letting them learn to walk on a raised rail as well as a level floor, for example—although play reformers like Joseph Lee were prescribing just such activities in their handbooks.[33]

Physical culture in Herland is not restricted to the young, however. Van, Terry, and Jeff are particularly impressed by the abilities of the older women who detain them (the "Colonels," in Terry's mocking yet admiring phrase [27]). Though all somewhere between the ages of forty and fifty, these women are "light and powerful," fully capable of restraining three strong young men (22). The women can also run and leap like deer, using "a quick folding motion of the legs" that the men find quite difficult to mimic (32). Gilman herself (in her mid-fifties in 1915) would later claim in her autobiography to have had a "life-long interest in physical culture." As a young woman living in 1881 Providence, Rhode Island, she reports, she persuaded the superintendent of the local men's gym to open one for women, too; attending it soon became an athletic and also "social pleasure" (much as exercise is in *Herland*) for Gilman. Going to this gym twice a week, Gilman ran a mile each visit and enjoyed a number of activities that later became part of the imagined regimen in *Herland*. "I could vault and jump, go up a knotted rope, walk on my hands under a ladder, kick as high as my head, and revel in the flying rings," she notes. "But best of all were those traveling rings, those wide-spaced single ones, stirrup-handled, that dangle in a line the length of the hall." Gilman reports that in her youth she could travel back and forth on the rings four times without stopping, and that as a more mature woman—including once in her fifties and again at age sixty-five—she could still complete one full circuit. "I was never vain of my looks, nor of any professional achievements," she claims, "but am absurdly vain of my physical strength and agility."[34]

One does not find the same enthusiasm for older women in either the play reformers' handbooks, which focus almost exclusively on children, or the *Outlook*. Indeed the closest the latter comes to addressing mature women's health in the teens is William J. Cromie's 1914 essay "Eight Minutes' Common-Sense Exercise for the Nervous Woman." Cromie's piece is the second of a three-article series that first offered "Eight Minutes' Common-Sense Exercise for the Busy Man" (a nice contrast to the "Nervous Woman"); the third installment mapped out "Eight Minutes' Common-Sense Play for the Growing Child." Patronizing though Cromie is in his article for women (he insists on referring to the reader as "you, Mrs. Nervous Woman"), he offers, as promised, fairly sensible advice: one should try walking, swimming, and basic calisthenics, including his centerpiece—a daily eight-minute "Turkish towel" stretching routine.[35] And yet his whole article is prefaced by a rather traditional appeal to beauty, in which he reverses a formula implicitly central to *Herland*. For Cromie, outer beauty is a sign of inner health; for Gilman, outer health reflects one's inner beauty.

Despite this difference, however, Herland's overall project of recreational reform—with its ultimate goal of "education for citizenship" (108)—matches quite closely the proposals being made in America in the 1910s. Central to both is the idea of growth. Herlanders saw fit to cultivate their youth just as vigorously and carefully as they did their forests and gardens. "Life to them was growth," Van reports; "their pleasure was in growing, and their duty also" (102). Both body and mind need nourishment and stimulation, which in Herland are provided through "a properly graduated series of exercises which will best develop [them]" (105). So too did play reformers formulate the relationship between play and development. "Growth through play is an example of growth through action," Lee argued in the opening chapter of *Play in Education*. "Play is, in sober truth, the very act and throe of growth."[36] Even the editors of the *Outlook*—who in 1915 still believed in Lyman Abbott's 1895 declaration that progress is the "divine law of life"[37]—could find no fault with Ellador's list of Herland's cultural goals: "Peace and Beauty, and Comfort and Love—with God! And Progress too, remember; Growth, always and always. That is what our religion teaches us to want and to work for, and we do!" (117). Abbott himself might object to some of the *details* implicit here (a female god-spirit, for example, or the denial of personal spiritual immortality), but as Van concludes, the Herlanders "are more Christian than any people I ever saw" (115).

Another way in which *Herland* signals its complicity with the play spirit of its age is in its use of pageantry. As David Glassberg reports, between the turn of the century and World War I, America experienced a "pervasive" (though ephemeral) pageantry "craze." In the early teens, at the "height of the craze, thousands of Americans in hundreds of towns from Portland, Maine, to San Gabriel, California, joined in civic celebrations by acting out dramatic episodes from their town's history." Such public historical imagery, Glassberg argues, contributes to a culture's "sense of identity and direction. It locates us in time, as we learn about our place in a succession of past and future generations, as well as in space, as we learn the story of our locale. Images of a 'common' history provide a focus for group loyalties, as well as plots to structure our individual memories and a larger context within which to interpret our new experiences. Ultimately, historical imagery supplies an orientation toward our future action." Progressive play reformers, Glassberg reports, were particularly interested in the new historical pageantry. "Public reenactments of local history on holidays" were seen as a way not only to promote safe public celebrations (especially in the face of what were perceived by reformers as increasingly dangerous Fourth of July festivities) but at the same time to encourage local residents to embrace "a common civic identity and thus a common interest in undertaking needed reforms." Historical pageantry was for play reformers thus both a dynamic expressive form and "an instrument for the reconstruction of American society and culture using progressive ideals."[38]

Van, Terry, and Jeff first encounter a form of pageantry during their early imprisonment when watching the "Colonels" take their recreation, which included "a good deal of music, . . . posture dancing and, sometimes, gravely beautiful processional performances" (32). Van remarks that the men "did not know then how small a part of [the Herlanders'] physical culture methods this really was," but later in their stay he and the others discover just how essential a component of Herland's general culture pageantry is. In the chapter "Our Relations and Theirs," for example, Van describes in more detail what he terms their "drama":

> There was a most impressive array of pageantry, of processions, a sort of grand ritual, with their arts and their religion broadly blended. The very babies joined in it. To see one of their great annual festivals, with the massed and marching stateliness of those great mothers; the young women brave and noble, beautiful and strong; and then the children, taking part as naturally as ours would frolic round a Christmas tree—it was overpowering in the impression of joyous, triumphant life. (99)

Play reformers would have been delighted to witness such a pageant in the United States, especially the "natural," childlike joy of the participants, for the reformers believed that native-born Americans sorely needed more free emotional expression. Immigrants in particular were thought to offer a "native" source of "communal gaiety" through their folk rituals and games, and American pageants of the early-twentieth century tended on the one hand to incorporate ethnic ritual liberally, while on the other strongly to encourage Americanization.[39]

Although Herland, as Gilman makes clear, consists of a "pure stock" (122) of women and is thus exempt from the specific pressures play reformers brought to bear on American immigrants and their folk customs, Herland's massive public rituals nonetheless fulfill the discrete cultural functions that Glassberg sees operating in historical pageantry.[40] The Herland pageants definitely confer a "sense of identity and direction" on their participants and are the single most important cultural "focus for growing loyalties." How explicitly historical these pageants are may properly be questioned; after all, as Ellador makes clear to Van, the women of Herland quite consciously "[ignore] their past and [build] daringly for the future" (111). But as Van later notes, the pageants were "as much educational as religious, and as much social as either" (114). They are "triumphant group demonstrations" of how the Herlanders "should live—and why" (115)— and as such they are quintessentially historical, for however much the Herlanders profess to ignore their past, their central cultural experience of "Motherhood" depends entirely on their miraculous history of parthenogenesis. Each Herland girl is raised to anticipate "her time," an expectation that can only make sense in the context of a shared history and a commonly imagined future. And even though the novel does not make entirely clear that these pageants are structured historically, they certainly function so, for the "revivifying combination of great multitudes" moving in a rhythmic "union of all the arts" enacts the very ritual of the historico-religious "Loving Power" without which Herland would not exist (115, 114).

The form and function of the play pageants taking place in the United States as Gilman was writing her novel also bear a demonstrable relationship to Gilman's conception of her text and, to a lesser extent, its own construction. Chapter 5, "A Unique History," in effect offers a literary pageant of Herland, a history pieced together by Van over his year's stay and then retold (as he likely received it) as a series of simple, emblematic episodes. One could easily imagine an actual historical pageant of the stirring tale: the decimation by war; the volcanic outburst; the slave revolt; the infuriated virgin counterrevolt; the hard years of work; and finally the miracle of self-willed birth, followed by the generational quintupling that founded the new race (or perhaps finally—though this is given in the next chapter—the population explosion and subsequent voluntary birth control). But while the very genre of utopian fiction virtually requires some historical narration of the "how we got here" variety, Gilman signals her affiliation with the specific American pageants that Glassberg so carefully describes by the type of utopia she constructs. For at the very center of the decade in which, one could argue, modern American industrialization (as epitomized by assembly-line mass production) cemented its hold on the public psyche as well as the national economy, Gilman casts her utopian eye at once *back* to a nineteenth-century model of preindustrial America (Herland does have industry, but it apparently has no ill effects on the country) and *forward* to a society that has survived a cataclysmic upheaval (something like World War I, perhaps) to reconstruct itself as a triumphant, genderless modern civilization. Thus, to the extent that it places "nostalgic imagery in a dynamic, future-oriented reform context," *Herland* flourishes at the same cultural crossroads as historical play pageantry: "the intersection of progressivism and antimodernism."[41] Just as historical images, then, provide "plots to structure our individual memories," Gilman, we might say, borrows a plot from "her land" and the play reformers to construct her own reformist text.

■

However complicitous (or congruous) Gilman's plot is with certain goals of the historical pageantry of the teens—and however traditional the overall trajectory of *Herland*'s narrative appears (particularly its triple love story)—Gilman's reformist aims nonetheless strike at the heart of other crucial cultural assumptions behind play progressivism. Perhaps the most obvious assumption Gilman undermines is the belief that recreational training for young girls should have as its goal the development of the home "instincts." As already outlined, this dominant view of the play theorists found expression both in their manuals and in the widely circulating pages of journals like the *Outlook*. Even historical pageants tended to reinforce this stereotypical view by portraying women's work as domestic work and only rarely depicting women "in economic or political roles outside the home."[42] (For an illustration from the *Outlook*, see Figure 18. In this "Pageant with a Purpose" the artists are represented by both genders, but the scientists are represented only by boys and the cooks only by girls.)[43] But there were other models for organized female play development in the 1910s, and Gilman carefully signals in *Herland* her preference for the cultural alternatives less ballyhooed.

More specifically, *Herland* gives us a nation of Girl Scouts, not Camp Fire

FIGURE 18. New York City school pageant. From the *Outlook*, June 23, 1915.

Girls. The distinction between these two organizations, perhaps not so obvious today, was telling in the teens. They were founded at virtually the same
moment (March 1912) in response to the enormous success of the Boy
Scouts, which had begun in 1908 in England and came stateside in 1910.[44]
Both also saw themselves as the logical counterpart to the boys' program.
But each had a strikingly different conception of the goals and means of
girls' play training. The Camp Fire Girls, as indicated earlier, imagined
themselves as the "women" who took care of the hearth to which the "men"
would return after a hard day's scouting. Originally intended to be called the
"Hearth Fire Girls" (but changed to "Camp Fire" to suggest a wider sphere
of influence), the group still placed its highest value on what it called
"Home Craft." As Hartley Davis and Mrs. Luther Halsey Gulick explained
in the *Outlook* in a lengthy article published just two months after the Camp
Fire Girls were founded, the emphasis on domestic skills was an attempt to
put Hall's recapitulation theory into gendered practice by offering the girls
a "sort of prevision" of the "duties and . . . fundamental virtues which will
be useful" in their adult lives. "Complete womanhood," according to Davis
and Gulick, is impossible without proper training in housework.[45]

Although this virtually total emphasis on homemaking skills would have
been incomprehensible to the girls of Herland—who shared neither the
1915 American conception of home nor the "housekeeping duties" of, as
Van calls it, "wifehood" (123, 124)—some features of the Camp Fire Girls
do seem to reflect certain Herland values. One might, for example, imagine the Herlanders singing these lines from the poem "A Credo for Camp
Fire Girls" at one of their massive pageants:

> I believe in the future;
> I believe, therefore, in the To-day.
>
> I feel my responsibility as a citizen of a great nation;
> I feel my glory as one of the mothers of the new generation
> Which with new eyes and with steadier steps
> Will reach the new places that now
> Are but a purple haze on the horizon.[46]

Indeed, in the elaborate ceremonies of the Camp Fire Girls one might see a source for the ritualistic group celebrations in Herland. But only in general: the Herlanders would take little interest in the primarily decorative attention Camp Fire Girls were supposed to spend on their ceremonial gowns, for instance, or on their Indian headbands. Nor would a necklace of colorful beads—where each bead represents a separate honor won for completing Camp Fire tasks—appeal to the unornamented Herland girls. Gilman even indirectly mocks the sexist implication of this practice when she has the young forester Alima—whose "interest was more that of an intent boy playing a fascinating game than of a girl lured by an ornament"—deftly snatch Terry's glittering necklace (or "bait") before he can seize her (16).

The Girl Scouts, to be sure, also awarded symbolic badges to its members to commemorate group and individual achievements. But the badges were conceived as akin to military decorations, not women's jewelry. The Girl Scouts also included domestic crafts in their program, but training in such skills was regarded as necessary for well-roundedness (much as it is in *Herland*), not as an end in itself. Even the *Outlook* specifically warned its readers that the Girl Scouts' goals were insufficiently domestic, perhaps dangerously so. Noting in a 1912 editorial that it would be "disastrous" for the United States if American women "were to turn their backs upon the household and the family" and that there was therefore an urgent need to "render the girls of the country a service similar to that rendered to the boys by the Scout movement," the *Outlook* declared that the "suggestion of the Girl Scouts did not meet [this] need," because it "did not sufficiently recognize that first grand division of labor which arose when the man went forth while the woman guarded the fire of the household." Only the Camp Fire Girls, the editorial concluded—who embraced rather than resisted the domestication of play taking place in the teens—provides for both "the future welfare of the country" and "the best development of American girls" by making "the preservation of the home" its goal.[47]

In the 1910s, then, the Girl Scouts were popularly perceived (and denounced) as more "masculine"—what Gilman would have called more "human"—than their Camp Fire rivals, a perception likely confirmed when the Girl Guides of America (the officially chartered title of the group in 1912) changed their name to the Girl Scouts in 1915.[48] (The *Outlook* probably used the phrase the "suggestion of the Girl *Scouts*" in its 1912 editorial both to accentuate the male connection [the British sister organization had always been the Guides, not the Scouts] and to deny the American Guides organizational [and therefore cultural] legitimacy.) The Girl Scouts even adopted most of the Boy Scouts' procedures and structure, including their arrangement by military rank (perhaps suggestively recalled in *Herland*'s "Colonels"). Like their male counterparts—like, indeed, their female counterparts in *Herland*—the Girl Scouts perceived themselves primarily as handy, hardy explorer-pioneers, not traditional homemakers.[49] Gilman's books (including *Women and Economics, In This Our World, A Man Made World,* and *Concerning Children*) were even recommended as general background reading for Girl Scout officers.[50]

Though *Herland* challenges the domestication of girls' play, the novel is far more accepting of the ludification of women's work, if for reasons different from those of the play reformers. Gilman had pointed out as early as 1899 in *Women and Economics* that women's employment outside the home involved far more than mere financial gain, even if economic independence was the crucial first step in improving women's position in society. Having one's own socially useful work also satisfies a deep human need for "personal expression"; opponents of women's extradomestic work should remember, Gilman had argued, that "human labor is an exercise of faculty, without which we should cease to be human; that to do and to make not only gives deep pleasure, but is indispensable to healthy growth."[51] In *Herland* girls are encouraged to find the work for which they are "most fit" and in which they can feel the "deep pleasure" of contributing to the "healthy growth" of both themselves and the State, particularly through their children (83). Herlanders might actually become "mothers"— that is, women specially trained to guide the education and upbringing of children—if they are so inclined and if they are deemed "the most highly competent" (83). The play reformers would want nothing less; but they would want each biological mother to be the industrial mother as well, raising her own children in her own home, buttressed by the training provided her through the work and play of her own girlhood. In Herland, many, perhaps most, women select other equally satisfying and productive careers.[52]

Gilman offers Ellador, arguably the most representative Herlander, as an example of a woman who finds real pleasure in her work. As Ellador explains, women of Herland grow up in an environment that they enjoy as "frankly and utterly" as "young fawns," eventually selecting a profession from the "endless range of common interests" that this environment produces (100). "It was a butterfly that made me a forester," she explains. Discovering and then catching the large, colorful insect one day when she was "about eleven years old" (100), Ellador was informed that she had actually found a moth that was quite dangerous to an important food supply and had done a very important deed by capturing it. "Everybody congratulated me," Ellador tells Van. "The children all over the country were told to watch for that moth, if there were any more. I was shown the history of the creature, and an account of the damage it used to do and of how long and hard our foremothers had worked to save that tree for us. I grew a foot, it seemed to me, and determined then and there to be a forester" (101). As Ellador reports, she was motivated both by her personal satisfaction ("Everybody congratulated me") and by the contributions she felt she could continue to make to the country. A young girl, at play outdoors, finds the work that is to be her calling—though that work will keep her, as it were, permanently outdoors. Thus Van can with accuracy say that the Herlanders "loved their country because it was their nursery, playground, *and workshop*" (94, emphasis added).[53] Instead of suffering the infantilization perpetuated by the reformers trying to turn women's domestic work into play, the Herlanders gain maturity ("I grew a foot, it seemed to me") by approaching all work with commingled curiosity and joy.

■

One obvious irony in Ellador's celebratory experience with the moth is the way in which that creature is so easily sacrificed for the good of the whole. When Van concludes from Ellador's story that the Herlanders obviously "grew up in a wide, friendly world" (101), we have to add: but not for obernut moths. We could perhaps draw out the implications of this irony by showing the beautiful but dangerous moth's symbolic connection to those Herlanders who display "atavistic" "sex-feeling" and who are thereby "denied motherhood" (92). But rather than review Gilman's complicity with the questionable ethics of early-twentieth-century eugenicists, I want to take a new look at Gilman's lifelong exaltation of the group over the individual, particularly as it undermines the superficially collective rhetoric of play progressivism.

The play theorists claimed repeatedly that their reforms aimed at creating what Luther Gulick called in an 1911 essay for the *Outlook* a "corporate morality" in the United States. As children develop through proper play, the reformers argued, they learn to regard themselves as part of a "corporate personality" in which their individuality is merged "in the common consciousness." The theorists' favorite examples of this successful merger were found on the athletic field, where a "participant in team play feels . . . to the marrow of his bones how each loyal member contributes to the salvation of the rest by holding the conception of the whole so firmly in his mind as to enable them to hold it also, and how the team in turn builds up their spirit."[54]

Although Lee's formulation sounds uncannily like a description of the self-willed parthenogenesis that saved Herland—a country that figuratively and literally conceived itself—the play theorists doubted that women had any real sense of team spirit. Gulick announces flat out in *A Philosophy of Play* that the "women of the world have never played team-games." Any self-sacrificing virtues women possess, he claimed, were acquired within the home, which was therefore the best place to nurture them. Somewhat more circumspect, Lee says that women might have a team sense but that they are far less likely than men to combine instinctively "in the achievement of a common enterprise." Women's loyalty is "apt to be narrow, rigid," he argues; it "needs training in the art of holding to the ideal image of a social body while remaining open-minded as to the means of realizing it, in seeing the . . . essence as more enduring than the form." On the off-chance that women could develop the team sense, Lee encourages team play for girls during the "team play age" (about eleven to fourteen); after age fourteen (when "young-ladyhood" begins) the girl should resume her apprenticeship in household affairs and motherhood.[55]

Lee's play priorities for women—group recreation as preliminary training for individual homemaking—are mirrored implicitly in the wider cultural response to the New Woman's extradomestic aspirations in the 1910s. Journals like the *Outlook* repeatedly proclaimed the decade an age of collectivism, of organization. "We cannot go back," the *Outlook* insisted in 1916, "to the old free-lance, individualistic economic order."[56] But women who tried to change that order by organizing themselves to fight for suffrage, or to strike for better working conditions, shorter hours, and higher wages, were told either that they were not team spirited enough for the new order (women, a writer in the *Outlook* reported, "are looked on as the sluggish and inert members of the labor body")[57] or that they should worry about their domestic affairs first. In an otherwise fairly progressive *Outlook* article, Juliet Everts Robb made the latter case: "Before we force ourselves into the wider field of full citizenship, let us show our fitness by putting our [own] house in order." Two years later Martha Bensley Bruere told women reading the *Outlook*'s "Home Making the Woman's Profession" series that the best route to social reform was to get the individual household running smoothly—and then go about "harmonizing" women's "individual plans with a programme of social welfare."[58] For all the age's talk about collectivism, the real goal where women were concerned—as we have seen over and over—was to guide them back to their own homes, much as Lee saw any group training merely as preparation for the individual housewife raising her individual family.

Herland sets all these expectations firmly on their heads. Women in Gilman's novel are entirely capable of collective organization and need no training whatsoever in seeing the "essence" of their society as "more enduring than the form," as Lee would insist. The male visitors, in fact, who largely share the play theorists' assumption that a civilization of women will inevitably "fight among themselves" in a tense and jealous sisterhood, are astonished to discover that the Herlanders, despite the complete absence of more "naturally" team-minded men, think only "in terms of the community" and share "a broad sisterly affection" (8, 79, 81). This is particularly true in the sphere of work. Ellador, Celis, and Alima, for example, though each is a forester in her own right, function as a sort of team. After Van, Jeff, and Terry have been in Herland for some time, they join the three women (soon to be their "wives") as "assistants" (125), and all six apparently work together.

The explorers, moreover, find that Herland's enduring collective sensibility is developed through play forms strategically different from those that play reformers recommended to American children in the 1910s. As Van explains, the Herlanders "had games, . . . a good many of them, but we found them rather uninteresting at first. It was like two people playing solitaire to see who would get it first; more like a race or a—a competitive examination, than a real game with some fight in it" (32). Van's stutter is doubly revealing: on the one hand, American play theorists would have found a competitive exam more appropriate for the classroom than the playroom (the Herlanders, as Gilman imagines them, refuse to draw the distinction); and on the other hand, the very presence of a competitive game in the otherwise cooperative utopia surprises the observant scientist. But as Somel, Van's special tutor, later explains, a secure individual identity—consisting of "individual judgment and will" (106)—precedes a sound collective identity. The solitaire-like games—not team sports—are thus believed to lay "the foundation for that close beautiful group feeling into which [the children grow] so firmly with the years" (108). Unlike the play reformers and progressives who promise liberating collectivism for all but send women home alone to find it, Gilman fulfills (at least fictionally) her prescriptions for cooperative human development.

■

A cynic might sneer that Gilman—who wrote every page of every issue of the *Forerunner*, which amounted to roughly four full books a year for seven years—was at best an equivocal spokesperson for collectivism. Wasn't Gilman after all something of a loner, writing and often speaking by herself "on the margin of mainstream American culture and intellectual life," on the margin even of the feminist movement?[59] Gilman herself recognized the oddity of her position in 1909, the year she launched the *Forerunner*. As she notes in her autobiography, between 1900 and the beginning of the 1910s, though both her reputation and her "importance" grew, her "market value" proportionately shrank. "Social philosophy, however ingeniously presented," she observes wryly, "does not command wide popular interest." Gilman found herself forced to bring out her own journal primarily because no one else would take her new work. Editorial rejection, then, not ego, fueled the "literary *tour de force*" that was the *Forerunner*. Consumer indifference, unfortunately, brought it to a halt. Despite a modest subscription rate of $1.00 per year, Gilman's unpopular ideas and her self-proclaimed lack of "business sense" made the venture a money-losing one from the start.[60]

Virtually the opposite qualities define the title character of Edna Ferber's *Emma McChesney & Co.* As copartner and creative genius behind the Buck Featherloom Petticoat Company, Emma McChesney depends on both her uncanny ability to supply (and even shape) popular taste and her extraordinary business acumen. Although Ferber critiques traditional progressivism with a perspective markedly different from *Herland*'s (largely because Emma's social philosophy tends toward an ideology of individualism that Gilman decried), Emma is in many senses sister to the energetic, work- and play-loving inhabitants of Herland. From the beginning of the text, Emma is a model of mental and physical agility, snapping off business decisions and moving swiftly to and fro like a much younger woman—or even like a man. In the words of her partner, T. A. Buck, Emma has "imagination, and foresight, and nerve, and daring." She is, at least in the opening chapters, not only the "real head" of the company but also its "pace-maker," and it is Emma's "erect, brisk, alert, vibrating energy" that jump-starts her coworkers: "Every day of her life she figuratively pressed the electric button that set the wheels to whirring."[61]

The opening scene of the book foregrounds Emma's "lightning mind," which, like the Herlanders', is always "leaping ahead to a goal unguessed by the slower thinking" (5). Quickly surmising from a casual remark by T.A. that a rival company is plotting to expand its line into South America, Emma confirms her hunch with a clever phone trick and hustles off to prepare, in two days, for a four-month business trip. To do so she performs "a series of mental and physical calisthenics that would have landed an ordinary woman in a sanatorium," setting her apartment and the factory in order like a combination "housewife," "general," and "the business woman she was" (13, 14). Her energy and foresight abate not a whit on the ship: Emma maneuvers her deck chair next to the owner of the finest clothes shop in Buenos Aires, shuffleboards her way into his family's confidence, and goes right to work scheming for future orders. Once in South America, she practically sprints through the continent, displaying skirts and gathering customers, all the time one vigorous step ahead of the rival company's salesman, the grossly overweight and physically unfit Fat Ed Meyers.

Emma's South American exertions leave her flushed with excitement and good health, much like a contestant in an athletic event. Indeed, Ferber repeatedly signals that Emma approaches her work as though she were involved in a competitive game—and is satisfied only with winning. Besides getting the jump on Fat Ed, she tricks Señor Pages, the Buenos Aires shop owner, into receiving her and looking at her line, smoothly buys off the Brazilian policeman who threatens to detain her for ignoring customs to make a sale, and in general handily wins all of the psychological games that are part of each transaction. This is not to suggest that Emma or her tactics are in any way disreputable or underhanded. She is simply very good at what she does—at being, in her words, "the most experienced *salesman* on [the company's] staff" (11, emphasis added). In trying to explain her business instincts to T.A., she relies on a gaming metaphor that recurs throughout the text. Imagining herself as T.A.'s deceased father, the former head of the company, she tries "to see a situation as he'd see it if he were alive. It's like having an expert stand back of you in a game of cards, showing you the next move. That's the way I'm playing this hand" (11). As Michael Oriard has suggested, Ferber's whole McChesney series celebrates "the joyful competition of honest business on a small scale [small, that is, in comparison with the titanic deals chronicled in "male" business novels], particularly as played by a woman in a 'man's game.'"[62]

Clearly working against gender role expectations, Emma's gamesmanship is often perceived as masculine, even combative. T.A. calls her an "admiral" (12); the narrator likens her South American tour to an invasion and then later compares her to Napoleon at Waterloo when she realizes that she has surrendered some of her influence in the office to T.A. during her otherwise successful absence. The military imagery can have an edge to it as well, much like Terry's derisive labeling of the athletic older women in *Herland* as "Colonels." When Emma is trying to talk business with Señor Pages on the ship to South America, he assures her that a "woman cannot be really charming and also capable in business." "Business," he declares, "is for your militant sisters" (25). But Emma's unusual success depends on her ability to bring "womanly" charm into business transactions, a powerful combination of appearance and intelligence that routinely outperforms the exertions of her male rivals. As Fat Ed Meyers moans upon learning that Emma has already "clean[ed] up" Buenos Aires as she did Rio (perhaps hoping to bring her down to his level, or wishing merely to punch her out): "Oh, if only you were a man for just ten minutes!" (40, 41).

Frustrated by and defensive about his South American failure, Meyers declares that Emma is "the Maude Adams of the business world." He whines, "It's her personality, not her petticoats. She's got a following that swears by her. If Maude Adams was to open on Broadway in 'East Lynne,' they'd flock to see her, wouldn't they?" (42). Though on one level complimentary—Adams was a famous contemporary stage actress—Meyers's comparison subtly replicates a strategy of containment typically used in journals like the *Outlook* for women who were perhaps too successful at men's games. Although the professional woman only rarely appears in the pages of the *Outlook* in the teens, when she does, a predictable effort is made to recontain her threatening "male" energies in some stereotypical (usually aestheticized) female context. At the end of a biographical sketch of Maria Montessori (the first woman doctor in Italy and the developer of an innovative method of children's education widely praised and copied in the 1910s), for example—a sketch that has generally praised Montessori's courage, her feminism, and her work—the writer declares that Montessori's "subtility of gesture," combined with "her noble beauty, her poetic fire, her tempest of moods, could have made [her] a great actress," as though that were somehow preferable to her chosen field.[63] On another occasion the *Outlook* designed a two-page picture spread to illustrate "A Professional Woman of Yesterday and a Group of Professional Women of To-Day—As Seen by a Famous Painter and by the Camera." On the right-hand page in separate boxes are pictured four leading women doctors from around the world, all delegates to the First International Conference of Women Physicians in New York City; on the entire facing page the professional woman of yesterday—striking a tragic pose (her eyes curiously averted from the four women seated on her right)—is early-nineteenth-century actress Sarah Siddons, as painted by Sir Joshua Reynolds. While these overt comparisons may intend no more than to offer readers a familiar (if stereotypical) context for interpreting contemporary women's success, they covertly imply not only that women should be judged in their physical and emotive (as opposed to more strictly intellectual) capacities, but that successful professional women are in a sense only playing a role, acting a part scripted and directed (and watched and approved) by someone else.[64]

Meyers's specific comparison of Emma to Maude Adams—a comparison, the narrator tells us, that "stuck" (42)—threatens to contain Emma within a potentially even more restrictive sphere. Adams's most famous stage role in the early 1910s, after all, was Peter Pan, as whom she starred in more than 1,500 performances between 1907 and 1918.[65] On one level the

194 • ALTERNATIVE ARTICULATIONS

link to Peter Pan is, again, complimentary: Emma's seemingly inex-
haustible, almost magical energy makes her a spectacular salesperson. But
Meyers's nickname for Emma also strategically diminishes her, even infan-
tilizes and desexualizes her, by comparing her to the perpetually childlike,
androgynous Peter. This aggressive male containment (where, figuratively,
"if only you were a man for just ten minutes!" becomes instead "I'll make
you into Peter Pan forever!") recalls the simultaneous containment and
diminution apparent in the movement to ludify work, particularly in the
Arco Wand ads. Here Emma's tremendous business insight and marketing
skill—not to mention her years of hard work selling on the road—are collapsed into some sort of magic wand of female "personality" that she need
merely flourish to move her product.

Ferber signals the impotence of Meyers's attempt to refigure Emma as a
woman-child who plays rather than a woman who works, however, by drop-
ping both Meyers and the Maude Adams sobriquet (even though it supposedly "stuck") after the beginning of chapter 2. Ferber also makes clear
that although Emma, somewhat like the women in the Arco Wand ads, is
redefined by others as both mother and daughter, she nevertheless resists the
containment that the collapsing of the two roles might imply. The young
women who work in the Featherloom factory, for example, clearly regard
Emma as a surrogate mother, seeking her advice on their relationships and
viewing her as a "source of love and sympathetic understanding" (179). Ferber underscores Emma's role as the company's mother figure by killing off
the firm's former matron—the elder Mrs. Buck, T.A.'s mother—in chapter 2. T.A. even tells Emma that she has, in a sense, raised (or, more accurately, *produced*) him, just as she did her own son Jock—"actually made,
molded, shaped, and turned out two men," he says (92). And at the same
time the novel emphasizes how young Emma looks, repeatedly suggesting
that, as a woman who "dimple[s] like fourteen instead of forty" (18), she
more closely resembles Jock's "younger sister" than his mother (222). But
rather than find her business identity threatened by these more traditional
roles, Emma uses them to make herself an even better businesswoman. Her

counseling of the shop girls, for example, turns unproductive workers (distracted by personal problems) back into productive ones, their "pay-envelope[s] bulging" (183). And although Emma by no means exploits her youthful appearance for financial gain, she does know "the value of a smartly tailored suit [or a well-timed dimple] in a business argument" (14). Her roles may conflate, but they don't confine. Unlike the women in the Arco Wand ads, Emma controls the different uses to which her energies are put.

■

Of course Emma figuratively stepped out of the Arco Wand ad twenty years earlier when she divorced her first husband and left the strictly domestic sphere for the business world, eventually reaching the point she occupies at the opening of the text, where she can hire a housekeeper to "circle around" her apartment with a "carpet-sweeper" (71). Once T. A. Buck proposes marriage, however, the whole question of Emma's identity is radically reopened, and *Emma McChesney & Co.* takes up its central issue: what defines the contemporary American woman? In what sphere—business or domestic, work or play—is Emma most herself?

T.A.'s proposal has an immediate physical and mental effect on Emma. At work, where her brisk manner formerly set the pace for the entire office, Emma becomes "a floundering, hesitating, absent-minded Mrs. McChesney—a Mrs. McChesney strangely starry as to eyes, strangely dreamy as to mood" (78). Even Emma's language is adversely affected: her usual "rapid-fire-gun method" of dictation, "each word sharp, well timed, efficient," stalls in convoluted periphrasis (78). As the wedding approaches, Emma's enervation passes but is replaced by a nervous tension—an equally unusual mood for the typically "poised, sane, composed" Emma (93)—that adversely affects her work. When, for example, on the eve of T.A.'s and Emma's ceremony a letter arrives from a long-sought mail-order buyer promising record-breaking purchases the following week (when both Emma and T.A. will be away), Emma is uncharacteristically unable to frame a reply. But when T.A. takes the letter from her and tells her to disregard it, Emma relaxes in "relief and acquiescence" (97). "I've been a ramrod so long it's going to be hard to learn to be a clinging vine," she says. "I've been my own support for so many years, I don't use a trellis very gracefully—yet. But I think I'll get the hang of it very soon" (97).

In the context of this chapter ("A Closer Corporation"), Emma's refiguring as a "vine" in need of "support" still takes place within the business world. That is, she sees herself benefiting from T.A.'s assistance at the office, sharing some of the burdens she's borne for so many years—years in which, the text makes clear, T.A. was by and large a lackadaisical employee. But in the next chapter ("Blue Serge"), Emma agrees to try clinging as her full-time occupation, deciding to leave the office for three months of enforced leisure. The beginning of "Blue Serge" (which, as the fourth chapter out of seven, occupies the novel's center) reveals that Emma has fantasized about being a woman of leisure for some time. In her many years on the road as a traveling salesperson it "had been her habit" to climb early into her train bunk, snap off the light, "raise the shade, and, propped up on one elbow, watch the little towns go by":

> They had a wonderful fascination for her, those Middle Western towns, whose very names had a comfortable, home-like sound—Sandusky, Galesburg, Crawfordsville, Appleton—very real towns, with very real people in them. Peering wistfully out through the dusk, she could get little intimate glimpses of the home life of these people as the night came on. . . . As the train slowed down, there could be had a glimpse of a matronly housewife moving deftly about in the kitchen's warm-yellow glow, a man reading a paper in slippered, shirt-sleeved comfort, a pig-tailed girl at the piano, a woman with a baby in her arms, or a family group, perhaps, seated about the table, deep in an after-supper conclave. It had made her homeless as she was homesick. (109–10)

This fast-frame domestic tableau, Emma's nightly equivalent of a moving-picture show, offers her a "glimpse" of family life she has not lived but can only imagine. What she imagines is fairly traditional: a world where mothers bustle (however deftly) in kitchens, tend children, and say things like "Well, folks [i.e., men and boys], go on into the sitting-room. Me and Nellie've got to clear away" (111). And even though Emma's glimpses show women at work, she longs for what she perceives as their relatively greater freedom from busy-ness, their opportunity "to loll in leisure. . . . to luxuriate" (112).

When T.A. officially proposes the three-month, no-work trial, Emma eagerly accepts. Because she has no family to raise (and has a housekeeper to do her menial work), Emma envisions herself becoming a leisured woman in the extreme, "what the yellow novels used to call a doll-wife," "blossom[ing] out into a beauty" and shopping for "pink things with lace ruffles on 'em" or "evening dresses with only bead shoulder-straps" (114, 115). In short, she says, invoking both Thorstein Veblen and the South African feminist Olive Schreiner, "I will now . . . mingle with the predatory" (115). Emma's pledged devotion to her clothing and appearance will make her not only a "doll wife" (a toy fit to by played with by her husband, played with and learned from by children), but also a "fine lady," the type Schreiner excoriated in *Woman and Labor* (1911) as "the human female parasite—the most deadly microbe which can make its appearance on the surface of any social organism."[66] Emma, "never . . . a woman to do things by halves," takes to her new role with enthusiasm (117). She buys fashionable dresses, goes walking or driving in the daytime, and positively shines at dinner parties, where T.A. is "very proud of her popularity" (124). Emma's "conspicuous leisure," to use Veblen's phrase, succinctly communicates her exemption from productive labor as well as T.A.'s ability to support a non-working wife.

But just as Veblen shrewdly observed in 1899, the leisure of the exempted worker is not her own but is "in some sort a performance exacted from [her], and is not normally or primarily directed to [her] own comfort."[67] This is entirely the case with Emma. After the initial "novelty" (117) of being able to spend her time as she wishes, she finds herself practically "bored to extinction" (124), particularly by the dinners at which T.A. is so proud to observe her. Even before the three months is up, Emma has entirely lost her admiration for the leisured class of women to which she had thought she so aspired to belong. As Hortense, the former Featherloom stenographer whom Emma meets in a downtown department store, explains, these women look "aimless as a lot of chickens in a barnyard. . . . They don't seem to have anything to do. Nothing to occupy their—their heads" (127). Even when they do "go in" for some sort of community work, Emma discovers, they all seem "so amateurish, so untrained, so unprepared" (124). Rather than keep at bay the "ravages" of daily existence, as Emma once thought a life of leisure would do, that life exacerbates them (112). "I've never been so tired in my life," Emma complains to T.A. at the end of her forced hiatus from business. "Another month of this, and I'd be an old, old woman. I understand, now, what it is that brings that hard, tired, stony look into the faces of the idle women. They have to work so hard to try to keep happy" (137). Thus the life of the "home-body" (136–37), which from her train compartment window for all those years had seemed so enviable—which had indeed become a "minor but fixed ambition in her heart" (112)—is exposed as a more dully laborious mode of living than she could have ever imagined.

But wait, we say. Isn't Emma conflating two rather dissimilar lives of leisure by calling both idle New York women (who "shop and dress and drive and play" [137]) and matronly midwestern housewives "home"-bodies? Doesn't she actually reject the latter having only tried the former? Yes—but for Emma this is not necessarily a contradiction. For Emma, what she believes she saw out of the train windows and what she attempts in New York are merely two different designs on the same side of the coin: the side on which one isn't "in the harness," as she puts it, the side on which one doesn't have to go "to" work (112). Emma is being somewhat willfully naive here, particularly in believing that midwestern housewives live lives of leisure. Indeed, she will get her chance later in the text to test that specific proposition more directly. At this point, however, Emma is more generally discovering that being a businesswoman is more satisfying for her than being unemployed.

Two opportune encounters during her leave confirm for Emma that it is in work, not leisure, that she is most youthful, energetic, and creative— in other words, most herself. In the first, Emma's dress-fitter, Miss Smalley (who is, like Emma, a "successful woman in business"), urges Emma not to give up her occupation (120). "I've found out that work is a kind of self-oiler," Miss Smalley reflects. "If you're used to it, the minute you stop you begin to get rusty, and your hinges creak and you clog up. . . . Work that you like to do is a blessing. It keeps you young" (121).[68] In the second encounter, Emma's chance meeting with Hortense described above, Hortense laments her own housewifely inactivity and suggests to Emma that their true selves are maddeningly unfulfilled if they do not seek work through which they can produce something. "Some people," Hortense asserts, "are just bound to—to give, to build up things, to—well, to manufacture, because they just can't help it. It's in 'em, and it's got to come out. Dynamos— that's what [my husband] Henry's technical books would call them. You're one—a great big one. I'm one. Just a little tiny one" (134). Emma, still committed to finishing her three-month trial, is reluctant to encourage Hortense to go back to productive work. "Just forget to be ambitious and remember to be happy," Emma advises. "That's much the better way" (135). But even Hortense can see that Emma is only mouthing convention, not speaking from the heart, and predicts that her former employer will return to the office—a prophecy Emma cannot deny.

The next chapter makes clear that Emma's work (to which she does speedily return) also offers her a measure of independence and control that enforced idleness could not supply. In "'Hoops, My Dear!'" Emma's usual office bustle once again subsides into dreamy reflection, but for entirely different reasons. Where in "A Closer Corporation" Emma dithered because she couldn't keep her mind on work, in this chapter she can't keep her mind off it. She suffers an "attack of imagination," brooding over a new skirt design (143). During her "attack" she refuses to discuss her ideas with anyone, not even T.A. When she finally reveals her invention—a "wildly" bouffant number that completely revises the constricting hobble skirt then in vogue

(152)—Emma persists against all objection (and even a conspicuous sales failure) to see her vision through. T.A. and the creative staff of the firm defer to Emma both because of her previous success and because they respect her, not merely as an expert saleswoman and marketer but specifically as a craftsperson. Emma has a knack, it seems, for designing clothes "before the trade knew such a thing could be" (147), and it is as an "American designer" (161) that she gets her greatest satisfaction. True to form, by the end of the chapter Emma has launched her latest creation in spectacular style, modeling it in Madison Square Garden at the "first annual exhibition of the Society for the Promotion of American Styles for American Women" (161). Emma thus not only escapes the trap posed by leisure, but also seizes dramatic control of her own work at a time when very few women in America had the managerial power to do so.[69]

Moreover, Ferber may unintentionally reveal the stakes involved in such a radical act of self-definition in a series of depictions of African American work and play that form a troubling subtext to the book's opening chapters. What appear at first to be unconnected references to minstrel show humor culminate in a vivid representation of the ways that black Americans in the 1910s were contained within cripplingly restrictive social (and literary) roles.[70] In chapter 1, Ferber has Emma, just for a moment—and presumably, just for a cheap if unsettling laugh—play minstrel show interlocutor to T.A.'s end man:

> "Oh, say [announces T.A.], that's what I came in to tell you! Guess whom I saw at the tailors?"
> "Well, Mr. Bones, whom did you see, and so forth?" (4)

When T.A. reveals that he saw Fat Ed Meyers, Emma snaps out of minstrel mode and back to business. In chapter 3, more explicit references appear. (Hortense's fiance, Henry, is described as "singing like a whole minstrel troupe all day long" [82], and Emma's response to the discovery that both she and T.A. are ordering brown suits for their trousseaux is "Good heavens, T.A., we'll look like a minstrel troupe!" [86].) At the end of that chapter, however, Sam appears—"Sam of the rolling eye, the genial grin, the deft hand" (101). Sam is a professional man—a train porter—but Ferber represents his work as though he were performing in a minstrel show. He talks in exaggerated black dialect, laughs "his infectious negro chuckle," and saves T.A. and Emma's honeymoon by sweeping Emma off the platform and onto the moving train after she gets off to talk to a customer. This acrobatic stunt is climaxed by said customer tossing a "round, silver Western dollar" to "the toothy Sam. That peerless porter caught it, twirled it, kissed it, bowed, and grinned afresh as the train glided out of the shed" (105). Sam's antic pantomime of devotion and subservience mocks whatever dignity and autonomy a "peerless porter" might have hoped to claim for himself in 1915. And although the text does not seem entirely in control of this scene, it is hard not to read it as a metaphor for the containment Emma will face as a leisured woman in the next chapter. Not only will she be figuratively snatched away from business; she, too, will play the role of the contented servant (just as for Veblen, the leisured "lady of the house" is its "chief menial"), thankful for the master's largesse.[71] But as we have seen, Emma can only grin contentedly for so long.

■

Indeed, Ferber figures Emma in the closing chapters not just as a woman who escapes her own containment, but as a liberator of all women, the self-proclaimed "Lincoln of the Skirt trade" (157). By reversing the trend of tighter and tighter skirts in one extravagant flourish, Emma sees herself as "literally freeing [her] sisters from the shackles that have bound their ankles for five years" (157–58). This seems on one level a logical narrative gesture, allowing Emma the newly confirmed craftsperson to use her individual talent to extend her own liberation metaphorically to other women. The invidious connection between women's constrictive clothing and their subjection had already been forcefully made by Veblen—who probably would have attacked the hobble skirt (as he did the corset) as a symbol for women's incapacity for "useful effort" had it been in vogue in 1899.[72] Gilman herself, we recall, also made dress reform an important component of *Herland*—and published *The Dress of Women* serially in the *Forerunner* right alongside it. But both Veblen and Gilman would likely have also pointed out that Emma's immediate reward, if not her motive, was industrial profit. The potentially liberating chapter "'Hoops, My Dear!',", after all, closes on Emma's smug reckoning of the economic value of her new design.

And yet Emma frustrates the easy charge that she is a capitalist exploiter in the very next chapter, "Sisters Under Their Skin," where she advocates women's control over their own dress, and by extension their own money, their own bodies, and their own freedom. In this chapter Ferber dramatizes one facet of the complex cultural negotiation of women's leisure taking place in the 1910s by showing the resistance of working-class women to uplift programs imposed from above. As Kathy Peiss has demonstrated, such programs were common in the Progressive Era, when middle- and upper-class reformers "believe[d] that the primary purpose of recreation reform for working women was to inculcate standards of respectable behavior." Seeking particularly to curb the "expressive sexuality enjoyed by working-class youth," these reformers pushed for more "wholesome" and sensible clothing and amusements. Working women, however, pushed back, and reformers had grudgingly to accommodate the heterosocial commercial culture, in which female laborers found their best opportunities for "choice, autonomy, and pleasure."[73]

When "the Movement" (184) hits the Featherloom Petticoat Company in Ferber's novel, this process of negotiation is reenacted in capsule and comic form. "We are launching a campaign against the extravagant, ridiculous, and oftentimes indecent dress of the working girl, with special reference to the girl who works in garment factories," announces the haughty Mrs. Orton-Wells, one of the movement representatives. "Our plan is to influence them in the direction of neatness, modesty, and economy in dress" (193). Emma, who generally approves of "movements" but not "Movers," whom she sees as rich outsiders "striving to peer in" at the working lives (including her own) that they themselves have never experienced, argues against Mrs. Orton-Wells's proposal of "a fixed idea in cut, color, and style" and in favor of autonomous commercial consumption (185, 194). "Our girls are very young—eighteen, twenty, twenty-two," Emma explains. "At eighteen, or thereabouts, practical garments haven't the strong appeal that you might think they have" (195). Undaunted, Mrs. Orton-Wells insists that her daughter Gladys address the factory girls. But the sallow-complexioned and poorly dressed Gladys, already chafing against parental restriction in her own life, is quickly convinced that she could learn a thing or two about dress reform from Emma's employees rather than the other way around. Instead of delivering a speech on propriety, Gladys fields advice on her own clothes and then runs off to marry the man of whom her mother disapproves, much to Emma's delight.

Emma's solidarity with her factory hands does have its limits. She tends, for example, to treat her female employees (regardless of their age) as if they were her children, not her sisters. And feeling united with her workers does not necessarily lead Emma to advocate collective action; her narrative much more strongly endorses individual autonomy and personal choice.[74] We might even say that the advice that shop girl Lily Bernstein gives Gladys Orton-Wells stands in for Emma's own independent philosophy: "If I was you, I'd go right ahead and do what I wanted to" (204).

But in the last chapter of the text, Ferber makes her protagonist answer one more time the nagging questions, "What is it that I want to do? Who do I want to be?" As a parallel chapter to the fourth ("Blue Serge"), in which Emma is offered the choice between work and leisure, "An Etude for Emma" springs yet again the domesticity trap, though with a difference. This time Emma is offered the chance to play midwestern grandmother to her son Jock's new baby, to step off the train of business and into the warm domestic spaces she had spent so many years envying. For the previous few years Emma had been living the life she chose at the end of chapter 4, a life in which she "worked and played and constructed, and helped others to work and play and construct" with her usual electric vitality (215). But her "perspective on life itself" has changed somewhat, shifting subtly from a belief in personal will to a feeling closer to fatalism: "She saw [life], not as a series of incidents, pleasant and unpleasant, but as a great universal scheme too mighty to comprehend—a scheme that always worked itself out in some miraculous way" (208–9). Emma, too, has begun to conceive her position in life in a less individualistic way. "I used to see life in its relation to me and mine," she explains to T.A. "Now I see it in terms of my relation to it. Do you get me? I was the soloist, and the world my orchestral accompaniment. Lately, I've been content just to step back with the other instruments and let my little share go to make up a more perfect whole" (214).

It is with this new collectivist philosophy that Emma makes her way to Chicago to visit her granddaughter. What begins as a short stay, during which Emma is delighted to see the baby but also finds her mind wandering back to T.A. ("to the big, busy factory with its humming machinery" and "to all the vital absorbing, fascinating and constructive interests with which her busy New York life was filled to overflowing"), soon lengthens "to four weeks, five weeks, six" (227, 228). Emma even manages, "little by little, to take the place of a second mother in the household" (228). As a substitute mother—but this time without the compulsion to work in the business world, as had been the case when she bore Jock—Emma begins to take on the characteristics that the *Outlook* and the play reformers were urging mothers to adopt. She becomes "the humblest of the satellites revolving about [the little] sun of the household" (225). She learns "to efface her own personality that others might shine who had a better right" (228).[75] Emma is both remade as a domesticated mother and figuratively reborn as the little baby herself, who is christened, after her grandmother, Emma McChesney. And this newborn Emma, the older Emma insists, will not be a "militant" woman like her grandmother, but "a throwback. . . . a clinging vine. . . . a reversion to type" (217). Thus suddenly at the end of a text that had energetically resisted women's containment within conventional roles we find Emma's identity triply collapsed into traditional mother, grandmother, and daughter. The "triumphant example of Woman in Business"

(184), we might say, takes up what Ida Tarbell approvingly called "The Business of Being a Woman."[76]

But not for long. In the sixth week of her stay Emma discovers, much as she had when she was purely a lady of leisure, that her entirely domestic role drains rather than reinvigorates her vitality. She begins to lose "her own bright color, a measure of her own buoyancy," and finds herself, once again, aging before her eyes (228). With the alacrity and self-possession of the old Emma, she immediately decides to return home, to New York, to her work. As she explains to T.A. on her arrival, "I feel a million years old. One more day of being a grandmother and I should have died!" (230–31). And just as she had discovered for herself in chapter 4 that the life of leisure she thought she craved was in reality a trap, so too does Emma revise the self-effacing, collectivist philosophy she espoused at the beginning of the final chapter. "Oh, T.A., my dear," she says, in the very last words of the text, "it's all very well to drown your identity in the music of the orchestra, but there's nothing equal to the soul-filling satisfaction that you get in solo work" (231).

■

Emma's valedictory declaration may also gloss Ferber's own decision to discontinue the McChesney series itself after the publication of *Emma McChesney & Co.* in 1915. After more than thirty McChesney stories, Ferber found herself in danger of having her identity as a writer swallowed up by Emma. "One day I picked up a review of the third McChesney volume entitled Emma McChesney & Co.," she reports in her autobiography, *A Peculiar Treasure* (1939). "'Edna Ferber,' the review said sagely, 'in her latest volume of the saga of the traveling saleswoman is evidently keeping Emma McChesney alive with injections of black ink.'" Ferber was stunned. "I stared at that line for a long time. It had brought me to my senses like a blow to one half asleep. I had been sliding to oblivion on a path greased by Emma McChesney." When *Cosmopolitan* offered her an unprecedented blank contract for more McChesney stories—Ferber was to set not only the number of stories but also her price—she knew the time had come to strike out in a new direction. "The truth was—though I hadn't realized it—that I didn't really enjoy writing the McChesney stories any more. I could do them with my eyes shut and one hand tied behind me." "I know now," she declared in 1939, "that if I had signed that contract I never should have advanced as a writer and probably never would have written a fresh line again in all my life."[77]

Ferber may also have recognized that her stories were in equal danger of tying Emma's hands, so to speak, behind her back. For despite Emma's decision to return to the soul-satisfying world of creative, autonomous work, there are signs in the text that her radical energies are slowly being contained in more mainstream postures. Her marriage to T.A., for example, a step that the first collection, *Roast Beef Medium* (1913), strenuously resisted, is hardly unconventional.[78] Even so traditionally "progressive" a reader as Theodore Roosevelt—whose first remark upon meeting Ferber in 1912 was supposedly "What are you going to do about Emma McChesney?"—lobbied her to steer Emma's plot in such a direction.[79] And despite the title of the final collection, which seems to suggest that Emma is really the corporate head in (and of) the text and all the rest of the characters mere employees in *her* company, the stories themselves hint that Emma yields corporate (though not literary) control to T.A. after their marriage. At the end of chapter 2, for example, Emma tells T.A.: "You're not only president of the T. A. Buck Company in name. You're its actual head. And that's as it should be" (73). Later, at the beginning of chapter 6, the narrator describes Emma as "wife of the head of the firm" instead of as cohead herself (179). Over the course of the text the corporate name even changes subtly from the "Buck Featherloom Petticoat Company" (1) to the "T. A. Buck Company" (207). Perhaps, then, Ferber's resolution "never to write another McChesney story as long as [she] lived" was based on a sudden (and double) awareness of the cultural co-optation she faced as an extremely popular writer of stories about an unconventional woman who by degrees was becoming more and more conventional.[80]

In January 1916 Ferber "settled down" for a "long pull of novel-writing," shelving Emma and the short-story genre to develop an entirely different sort of project, "the story of a Jewish family in a small Wisconsin town." The partly autobiographical result, *Fanny Herself* (1917), was thematically new and culturally risky, and Ferber might have seen her career wilt out of the sunlight (and profit) that Emma had provided. The novel did not sell particularly well, and Ferber continued for some time to be known best as the creator of Emma McChesney.[81] And yet, ironically, Ferber would go on to have a highly productive, popular (and arguably mainstream) career, returning to the best-seller lists in 1924 with *So Big* (which also won her a Pulitzer Prize) and conquering the musical stage with the 1929 adaptation of her novel *Show Boat* (1926).

Gilman, too, resists the cultural co-optation that she risked in *Herland*, but only to move into a phase of relative silence, not revitalized productivity. Despite the trappings of the conventional love story in *Herland*—each explorer marries one of the three young foresters who had first discovered them—Gilman creates a text that frustrates conventional expectations to the end. As Christopher Wilson has argued, for example, even the triple marriage plot satirizes popular formula and "undermines the rhetoric of romance" by subverting contemporary assumptions about gender.[82] The three women are by no means "tamed" by their suitors, and the weddings do not represent the privatization of three previously communal women; the Herlanders resist husband-wife cohabitation even after the ceremonies. (Moreover, only two of the unions proceed happily; Alima ends her marriage to Terry after he attempts to rape her.) And yet to some degree the cost of Gilman's resistance was indifference. As she well knew, very few subscribers read *Herland* as it was serialized in the *Forerunner*. Gilman was therefore not so much culturally co-opted as she was culturally ignored. After 1916, when she ended the *Forerunner*'s seven-year run (believing that it was "sociologically incorrect to maintain an insufficiently desired publication"), Gilman wrote little and influenced few.[83] What she did write immediately after *Herland*, ironically, were stridently mainstream attacks on

Germany during World War I. Gilman, ever unconventional, was then herself attacked by her own former supporters on the left as a reactionary and
became a social (and literary) outcast, even, in Gary Scharnhorst's view, an
"anachronism"—a truly odd position for the author of so radically progressive a text as *Herland*.[84]

What the experiences of Gilman and Ferber illustrate is the difficulty for
American women writers in the 1910s—a decade of ostensible progress and
influence for women in general—to create satisfying literary selves that
were both marketable (and that might therefore have some broader cultural
influence) and truly liberating. And while it might seem that the only solution to this dilemma is either to end one's literary project when its radical energies become recontained (as in *Emma McChesney & Co.*) or to continue writing into a readerly void (as in *Herland*), Gilman and Ferber at
least demonstrate that women writers did not necessarily have to surren-
der either their literary texts or their literary careers to the demands of the
market. Each of these women willfully sacrificed popularity in order to
maintain control over the words she felt needed to be spoken. Each in her
own way challenged the strategies of recontainment faced by her female
readers both at work and in play. Each, that is, was able to "find her
place"—without having, as the larger culture seemed to require, to "fall in
line."

PART III

WHOSE GOLDEN AGE?

CHAPTER FIVE

"An Ideal Body to Be Lived Up To"

Play, Display, and the Self in *The Autobiography of an Ex-Coloured Man* and *The Great Gatsby*

ON THE MID-NOVEL OCEAN VOYAGE that carries the "miserable" and exhausted narrator of *The Autobiography of an Ex-Coloured Man* (1912) from the violent clubs of New York City to the pleasant port of Havre, France, only one event, the sighting of "a large iceberg," revives his spirits. "I was curious enough to get up and look at it," he recalls, "and I was fully repaid for my pains. The sun was shining full upon it, and it glistened like a mammoth diamond, cut with a million facets. As we passed, it constantly changed its shape; at each different angle of vision it assumed new and astonishing forms of beauty." In a novel that James Weldon Johnson almost titled *Chameleon*, the iceberg's virtuoso shape-changing neatly foreshadows the contortions of identity that Johnson's narrator will soon himself undergo en route to his final incarnation as an upper-class mulatto businessman passing for white back in America. Even the choice of language ("As we passed") anticipates this final step. Equally emblematic of the novel's central concerns is the narrator's next observation. Watching the dazzling ice through a pair of binoculars, he hopes "to verify [his] early conception of an iceberg," which in his grammar-school days had "always included a stranded polar bear, standing desolately upon one of the snowy crags." "I looked for the bear," the narrator reports, "but if he was there, he refused to put himself on exhibition."[1]

The unlikelihood of spotting a polar bear on a mid-Atlantic iceberg and the narrator's imaginative need to discover one are each less revealing than his explanation for the hypothetical bear's invisibility. As narrated, the bear's act amounts to a deliberate concealment, a purposeful decision not to display himself to the passing ship. On one level, we can see latent in this refusal the narrator's subsequent decision to conceal his own racial identity in the white world. A "stranded," desolate creature is almost literally what the narrator becomes, as he cuts himself off from his family and his past. And yet the unseen polar bear also functions more complexly. For the image of the bear deliberately choosing not to "put himself on exhibition" also mirrors a cultural advance made by African Americans in the world of leisure during the 1920s, in moving from at times complicit roles in the minstrelization of commercial amusement to the achievement of more autonomous cultural selves. In fact it is along precisely the lines of the polar bear's imagined assertion—I will decide how, when, and where to exhibit myself—that these black figures gained a long-sought measure of cultural and performative control.

Johnson's novel is often regarded as an important pre-text for the 1920s Harlem Renaissance, an almost uncannily prophetic unveiling of that era's racial and recreational politics. The influence of *The Autobiography* on black fiction of the twenties, particularly the passing novels of Jessie Fauset and Nella Larsen, has been well charted, as has Johnson's long friendship with Carl Van Vechten, a man who perhaps unwittingly came to embody the manipulative aesthetic values of the white "benefactor" in *The Autobiography*. One important writer of the 1920s with whom Johnson is not typically linked, however, is the putative "Jazz Age" spokesperson himself, F. Scott Fitzgerald. Reasons for this lack of connection are not hard to find. Unlike many of his "lost generation" contemporaries, whom David Levering Lewis claims were especially "drawn to Harlem on [their] way to Paris," Fitzgerald often seems more anxious about than appreciative of African American culture.[2] Nor did the white author appear to have had much contact with black writers or texts. (For his part, by Fitzgerald's heyday Johnson's literary interests lay chiefly in poetry, not fiction.) At least one black reviewer of Fitzgerald's popular short-story collection, *Tales of the Jazz Age* (1922), hastened to point out that his "jazz" had "nothing in common with music by

Colored dance orchestras."[3] Thus Fitzgerald's and Johnson's cultural and literary disjunction seems unsurprising.

And yet *The Great Gatsby* (1925) is in many ways the first major text of the postwar period to revisit the issues of display and desire, of autonomy and control—even of the psychology of passing—that are so central both to Johnson's novel and to the decade that enthusiastically republished *The Autobiography* in 1927. In fact if we look at the 1920s as an age attempting a very public renegotiation of the values and limits of American leisure, an effort underwritten in part by play theory's vision of what reformer Joseph Lee called the "ideal" American body, then *The Great Gatsby* makes an intriguing companion text for *The Autobiography*. Fitzgerald's characters inhabit a world of conspicuously white, upper-class leisure not far removed from the racial and cultural environment into which the narrator of Johnson's text finally insinuates himself. In the ex-colored man's peripatetic journey toward whiteness he struggles to shape a satisfying self through his work and his play in ways that anticipate Gatsby's insistent attempt to imagine and then inhabit a social (and racial) position that will allow him to recover Daisy, the trophy of the white leisure class. Both texts bring their protagonists—two men on the outside of their cultures looking in—to the brink of success, only to see their dreams and their ideals, in the end, betrayed.

At the same time it is not my intention to collapse these two works into uncomplicated replicas of each other. Certainly the concerns of *The Great Gatsby* are not entirely the same as those of *The Autobiography*. Johnson's text, after all, is not literally about the 1920s. Nor does Fitzgerald's novel directly acknowledge the cultural conditions of the Harlem Renaissance. But taken together, in collision as much as comparison, these works explore the complex dialectics of exhibition and concealment, energy and exhaustion, and performance and punishment that lay at the heart of the racial politics of leisure of the 1920s. Johnson's novel both predicts and regrets those politics, praising the multiple public identities being constructed by blacks in the world of leisure at the turn of the century but also foreseeing their later control by the whims of "benevolent" white capital. In *The Great*

Gatsby, the main white capitalist turns out to have less control over his own constructed identity than his race and class would have been assumed to provide. Needless to say, in these two novels appearances are not always what they seem. Which is exactly what they tell us about play theory: both texts cogently critique the play reformers' own notion of the "ideal body"— and its implicit whiteness—first by exposing the dependence of that ideal on the laboring bodies of black workers, and then by imagining the sorry fate of those bodies closest to the envisioned ideal. What such critiques give us is an excellent introduction to the cultural, racial, and socioeconomic contradictions of the supposed golden age of American leisure, the subject of these final three chapters.

■

No era, of course, is as carefree or prosperous as our collective cultural memory insists, and the "Roaring Twenties" is no exception. Beneath the glitter of good fortune all too frequently lay the gloom of depression.[4] But prominent signs of prosperity and abundance were very much in evidence during the decade, and perhaps nowhere more so than in what had truly become the industry of leisure, in all its manifestations. Americans coast to coast, finding themselves with more and more free time, flocked to parks, tennis courts, movie theaters, baseball diamonds, and even churches for evening and weekend play. By the end of the decade Americans were spending hundreds of millions of dollars a year on sporting goods and equipment. In 1929 alone, consumers laid out nearly a billion dollars to purchase radios for their homes. Play, in the 1920s, was a national growth market.[5]

What in part underwrote this massive expansion and commodification of leisure was the growing acceptance of the play reformers' turn-of-the-century reconception of recreation as a life-affirming activity. This is not to suggest that the simultaneous explosion and consolidation of leisure during the decade (the latter in the form of increasingly oligopolistic control) required the inspiration of theory.[6] But certainly by the age of Tilden, Dempsey, and Ruth, Pickford, Fairbanks, and Valentino, not to mention the car, the radio, and the paid vacation, the urgings of reformers to give more scope to leisure were met with fewer and fewer blanket objections in the dominant culture. Moralists still warned of the "threat" that unsavory amusements posed to body and soul and cautioned against the character-stunting effects of passive spectatorship. But they found themselves well matched by the new purveyors of leisure, who cheerfully promoted the healthful benefits of their wares. By the 1920s, the debates over play's social role indicated its arrival, not its vulnerability.

In the world of commercial leisure, that arrival depended on and in many cases exploited the energies and accomplishments of black Americans. Music and dance were perhaps the most conspicuous fields of appropriation in what might be called the pop cultural fascination with blackness in the 1920s. As David Ewen reports, white-produced songs that drew their "rhythmic momentum and kinesthetic force" from the "blues harmonies and jazz colorations" of black music were immensely successful during the decade, especially with white audiences. White composers and conductors such as George Gershwin and Paul Whiteman incorporated the "beat and pulse" of the improvisational jazz of small black combos into the more formal arrangements of what would become much larger jazz bands and orchestras.[7] Many African American performers followed suit, forming their own orchestras and "emulating the instrumentation" of Whiteman while simultaneously incorporating the spontaneity of classic jazz. Jazz orchestras were soon headlining vaudeville shows and starring in movie house stage shows.[8]

The majority of popular dance styles in the 1920s, including the shimmy, the Charleston, and the black bottom, were also of African American origin, though most white Americans who stepped out to them did so without actually encountering black performers or black consumers.[9] One increasingly conspicuous site of such interaction, however, was the nightclub scene of cities with large African American populations, such as Chicago and New York. In Harlem, for example, curious white thrill-seekers experienced "authentic" black entertainment by slumming to New York's "Black Broad-way," the concentration of restaurants, theaters, cabarets, and speakeasies along Seventh Avenue between 127th and 134th Streets.[10] Part of what attracted white Americans to black-inspired cultural forms and, in particular, historians have argued, to streets like Black Broadway, was a longing to experience the freedom from social constraint supposedly typified by African Americans. During an age perceived as one of ever-increasing industrialization and mechanization—when work for most Americans had lost much of its potential for personal creativity, autonomy, and enjoy-ment—many whites regarded blacks as desirably primitive and romantic, offering through their purportedly less inhibited dances and music a route back to a more carefree self to which overcivilized white Americans no longer had access. African Americans were seen as "that essential self one somehow lost on the way to civility," Nathan Huggins suggests, "ghosts of one's primal nature whose very nearness could spark electric race-memory of pure sensation untouched by self-consciousness and doubt."[11]

Although many Americans viewed certain aspects of black popular cul-ture with alarm—church figures in particular objected to the "savage" de-bauchery of jazz and the "jungle standards" it represented[12]—progressive recreation reformers had urged a consonant return to more "primitive" ori-gins since the turn of the century. As we have seen, G. Stanley Hall's influ-ential recapitulation theory posited a necessary and insistent return to the "inborn and more or less savage instincts" of primitive humans.[13] Play the-orists analogously welcomed certain forms of adult play as necessary erup-tions of the spontaneous, active life absent from the deadening routine of specialized modern work. For "unless some remedy [to modern labor] be supplied," Wilbur Bowen and Elmer Mitchell warned in *The Theory of Or-ganized Play* (1923), "it is safe to say that the decay of modern civilization has already set in, and that there is a grain of truth in the assertions of the present-day anthropologists who predict that the future race of human be-ings will have abnormally large heads, but spindlelegs, the latter having dwindled away to mere appendages from disuse."[14]

When play theorists talked about the need for twentieth-century Americans to rediscover their primitive side they did so (usually) without explicitly linking "primitive" to "African American"; they more typically, we recall, racialized primitive energies as "Injun." But the theorists frequently did trade on the same jungle stereotypes invoked by jazz detractors in the 1920s. "Among the lowest types of savages," claimed Bowen and Mitchell in their discussion of the evolution of play forms, "the only pleasures are almost purely animal ones, such as are found in appeasing the cravings of hunger, thirst, and sex." These peoples are "peculiarly susceptible to music. . . . Their bodies react somewhat as sounding boards, and different vibrations produce different excitements. Passions of anger, love, sorrow, etc., can easily be aroused and then continued almost indefinitely."[15] At other moments the play theorists praised certain qualities stereotypically associated with African Americans. Joseph Lee, for example, argued that "the rhythmic instinct" was of "inestimable service to mankind" in its capacity for generating "social fusion." "Rhythm is the great get-together agent of the world," he claimed, "the mightiest ally of the belonging instinct"; it is "the social alchemist," able to "fuse individual minds and temperaments into one substance." For Lee, rhythm is thus a crucial constituent of the team identity so essential to the psychosocial development that recreation reformers were hoping to foster through play. Lee specifically praises black American soldiers for their team spirit, as they rose up in battles "from Fort Wagner to San Juan" very much like "Zulus," who "come against any odds like a great wave, in a single, fused, tribal determination to sweep over and submerge all obstacles."[16]

On the infrequent other occasions that play theorists addressed African Americans, however, they tended to interpret what they understood as black behavior as a telltale marker of deficiency. In their 1923–26 interracial study of the psychology of play activities, for example, Harvey Lehman and Paul Witty concluded that black children were indeed "more social in their play than white children." But rather than interpret this difference positively—especially given play theory's preference for the team sensibility—Lehman and Witty link blacks' "high index of sociability" to their "inferior scholarship." Forms of strong African American social behavior such as going to church, they argued, may in fact be "compensatory mechanism[s]" for the otherwise inferior "social, intellectual, educational, and economic" status of American blacks.[17] Other theorists who found traits to admire in blacks frequently allowed racist stereotypes to have the final say. Elmer Mitchell, for example, writing a series of articles entitled "Racial Traits in Athletics" for the *American Physical Education Review* in 1922, praised blacks for their clean play, sportsmanship, and skill. But he closed his section on African Americans by reminding readers that the black athlete is nonetheless "temperamentally . . . inclined to be lazy" and carries himself with "a shuffling gait."[18]

These examples do not simply demonstrate the predictable observation that recreation reformers shared many of the racist assumptions of their time. Rather they show more precisely how on the rare occasions that actual black bodies emerge in the play literature of the period those bodies are carefully recontained within certain prescribed boundaries. For in their imaginings of the selves that right recreation would help construct, the play theorists severely limited the roles that African Americans and black culture might play. Recreation theory tended, that is, to imagine the playing American body as an implicitly white body to which African Americans and newly arriving immigrants should aspire. What is unique in the case of African Americans, however, is that their bodies were also viewed, as we have seen, as potential sources of energy for the revitalization of white subjectivity. In the face of the debilitating effects of modern labor, reclaiming one's primitive side was thought to reinvigorate the dwindling body and reanimate the suffocating soul. But one did so, play theory assumed, in order to evolve from selfish primitivism to other-directed civilization; primitivism was a stage one inhabited on the way to what Joseph Lee called the ideal "corporate" self. In important respects, early-twentieth-century play theory thus looks suspiciously like a sort of psychobiological minstrelsy. One took on primitive energies, in other words, primarily as a way to contain and control them for one's own use, not to grant them a subjectivity of their own.[19]

We can see evidence of such containment even in texts that claim for play the power to bridge rather than accentuate racial difference. In *Education Through Play*, for example, Henry Curtis suggests that recreation can help create the interracial friendships that hasten "human brotherhood." He offers as testimony his experience on New York's East Side, where "for a long time . . . there was a [bitter] faction between the Jews and the Italians." After an unsuccessful attempt to "correct this state of affairs" by organizing integrated baseball teams, Curtis and the other play leaders began to arrange larger games involving more children and found that after six weeks those children "did not know whether they were Jews or Italians. They had entirely forgotten in the intimacy of play the racial prejudice that went before." And yet Curtis's call for "racial solidarity" is already seriously undermined by one of the central anecdotes of his very first chapter, an unexpected outcropping of the minstrel tradition that implicitly denies blacks an active role in the creation of an American self through play. Discussing Hall's theory that in their play humans recapitulate the "pleasurable emotions" connected with the struggles of the earliest humans for survival, Curtis argues that the more closely today's civilization can reproduce the "original conditions," the "more intense is the pleasure." It is, for example, he says, "more pleasant to throw at a mark than it is merely to throw aimlessly; but it is far more pleasant to throw at a living mark, and especially one that is moving, than to throw at a dead one." To illustrate this point, Curtis then asks that we recall "the various devices that are used at county fairs. One of the commonest of these," he says, "is a darky who sticks his head through a screen as a target for a baseball. I always find it difficult myself to keep my hands off the baseball at such times, although I have no desire to injure the person in question." Curtis's illustration represents the black body as a source of "darky" entertainment rather than as an agent of play, a disembodied target (or "living mark") on exhibit through which the passing play theorist may rediscover the pleasure of his "highest values."[20]

By implication, Lee's theory of the "ideal body" to which individuals and societies aspire works similarly to contain rather than empower blacks. Near the end of *Play in Education,* Lee claims that "for each of us there is an ideal body to be lived up to, a flower which the seed was dreaming of, not yet fulfilled." Each society, moreover, like each individual, "has an invisible body toward which it tends," and when "any person so places himself as to fill out that form, he is received into it," somewhat as a block of stone, in its proper place, is "received" into the larger form of a cathedral. Then "the life of the whole passes through him and sustains him, as the law of the cathedral thrills down through each detail, bursts out in the gargoyle here, restrains the pinnacle there, vibrates upward in the spire, and holds every stone in place."[21]

An exciting prospect this, if one's own ideal body turns out to be a bursting gargoyle or a vibrating spire. But Lee's analysis of these ideal and invisible bodies is offered in the context of a discussion of finding a proper place for "invalids" in society—those individuals believed by many to be incapable of providing "useful work." What "we" need to do, Lee says, "is to help enlarge the general conception of what constitutes useful work, so as to include the service that [invalids] can render." This enlarged conception will in turn change the form of the ideal social body, since that form "exists in the minds of the people, and changes with their thought." But Lee also suggests that it is "*only* the places that the public conception calls for that exist and in filling which a man partakes of the common life"—itself a rather narrow conception of the possible roles one may play in a given society, "invalid" or otherwise. If it is truly the "voice of the *corporate ideal*" that calls up "from the mass" the "individuals [who] will arise to fill out the unseen body that the city has projected at its heart," one can scarcely wonder what places a determinedly segregationist society like early-twentieth-century America would call its citizens to fill.[22] No matter how Lee's "we" might enlarge the public conception, such enlargement comes to look much like recontainment—or like holding "every stone in place." For by Lee's formula it would seem that "society" will always insist that its members serve its majority (or "corporate") interest. "No drop of blood" in the "social organism," Lee will shortly conclude in metaphorical language that (perhaps innocently) recalls the worst of antiblack stereotypes, "can go singing on its way content and happy, unless the man is himself a servant" to the social whole. "Our physical life depends upon our loyalty."[23]

■

But what if your conception of your own ideal body conflicts with the demands of that loyalty—or if the part in the "unseen body" that you are called to "fill out" does not, in the end, make you "content and happy"? What if, in other words, the body that you dreamt you were meant to "live up to" isn't what the social whole had in mind at all? These are questions, of course, with which minority America has long contended. What gives them special significance in relation to play theory and the interracial inflections of the growth of leisure in the early twentieth century is that during this period African Americans in particular were having some success projecting their own ideal bodies onto the American "scene" without necessarily seeing them reduced to minstrel caricatures. I am not referring (yet) to the chiastic cultural relationships of the 1920s. Indeed, before the 1920s—even at the turn of the century, a time generally considered the nadir of American race relations—many black Americans were wresting a personal and artistic autonomy from a caste system hoping to keep them loyal and invisible. The most conspicuous of these successes took place in the growing fields of popular entertainment and athletics, and it is precisely this dynamic that Johnson's *Autobiography of an Ex-Coloured Man* both represents and critiques. Though often read as a text penned before its time— as a work more attuned to the artistic milieu of the 1920s than to the turn-of-the-century details it actually describes—*The Autobiography* is very much a product of its own day, interrogating cultural relationships that in some cases no longer obtained in the later decade. It will be important to consider the ways in which Johnson's brief yet complex novel simultaneously predicts and laments the racial politics of leisure in the Harlem Renaissance, a movement to which the text's narrator himself seems so dearly to want to contribute; but first we need to inspect the roots of that yearning in their own soil.

At its historical core, *The Autobiography* chronicles a period of very public black achievement in the newly emerging sphere of commercial leisure. Despite the political, social, and economic repressions that pervaded Jim Crow America, black entertainers and athletes took artistic control of the formerly all-white minstrel show, competed on relatively equal terms with whites in such individual contests as boxing and horse-racing, and began to integrate professional team sports, including baseball. Johnson thought these developments significant enough to place an extended portrait of them at the center of his novel. In an unusually long set piece, offered to the reader at what the narrator suddenly announces is a "pause in [his] narrative" of which he "shall take advantage," Johnson's unnamed speaker describes the activities of "the 'Club,'" a gathering spot for black artists and sportsmen, "at that time the most famous place of its kind in New York" (103). "It was, in short," he declares, "a centre of coloured Bohemians and sports. Here the great prize-fighters were wont to come, the famous jockeys, the noted minstrels, whose names and faces were familiar on every billboard in the country; and these drew a multitude of those who love to dwell in the shadow of greatness" (105). The narrator himself is one of those shadow-dwellers, until he eventually graduates from a fawning "habitué" into one of the leading lights of the Club (103).

In the process of making that transition, what the narrator observes are black athletes and entertainers crossing the color line—and ironically with greater success in many areas than their later counterparts would have in the 1920s. The "three great professional sports" of "horse-racing, baseball, and prize-fighting," for example, as Johnson himself would later note in his history of Harlem, *Black Manhattan* (1930), were all more fully integrated before the turn of the century than they were during the Harlem Renaissance.[24] Throughout the 1880s and 1890s, black jockeys such as Isaac Murphy (who won the Kentucky Derby three times) were extremely successful competing against whites nationwide. As Harold Seymour reports, at least fifty-five African Americans played in organized baseball between 1883 and 1898, including Moses Fleetwood Walker, who in 1884 became the first to break the major-league color barrier.[25] And there were five different black world champion prize-fighters between 1890 and 1908.

The profit motive trumped racism in the opening of these and other sports to African Americans. Benjamin Rader reports that efforts by white cyclists to exclude Marshall "Major" Taylor from the nation's white tracks, for example, failed largely because of "the influence of the bicycle manufacturers and racing promoters," who "had a stake in keeping Taylor [the U.S. sprint champion from 1898 through 1900] on the tracks." In the earlier days of boxing, too, "if pitting a black against a white could be profitable, the sporting fraternity was not averse to promoting such a battle."[26] But economics could also fan racist flames. The number of black jockeys declined after 1900 in part because of white resentment over the large sums black riders were winning.[27] Black baseball players were finally barred from the white professional leagues in 1898. And in boxing, the riots that followed Jack Johnson's victorious July 4, 1910, title defense against white challenger Jim Jeffries made it virtually impossible for other black fighters in the teens and twenties to compete for the championship once Johnson finally lost in 1915. Thus at almost the very moment that Johnson was composing *The Autobiography*, the cultural conditions that made his novel possible were slowly disappearing. By its publication in 1912, *The Autobiography* in many ways recorded an era already dangerously in decline.

Some might argue that the narrator's only real interest in the "celebrities" of the Club is a superficial one. One could point, for example, to his seemingly crass commentary on the "photographs or lithographs of every coloured man in America who had ever 'done anything,'" which "literally covered" the walls of the Club. After noting the comprehensiveness of the portraits, which range from "Frederick Douglass and . . . [nineteenth-century prize-fighter] Peter Jackson . . . down to the newest song and dance team," the narrator observes that "most of these photographs were auto-graphed and, in a sense, made a really valuable collection" (104). Although here the narrator appears to evaluate the pictures more from the perspec-tive of a dealer in memorabilia than an admirer of black achievement, the text nonetheless encourages a reading of the photographs' cultural value that the narrator himself may miss. The specific inclusion of Frederick Doug-lass among the sport and entertainment figures (particularly in a text that scrupulously avoids naming names), for instance, is one sign that the novel endorses that value. So may be the fact that some years later, when John-son described the same professional milieu in *Black Manhattan*, he selected lengthy excerpts from *The Autobiography* to do so, including, verbatim, his narrator's comments about the photographs. If in *Black Manhattan* John-son could offer those observations as reliable history—as a piece of writing that he hoped would "furnish, perhaps, a fresher picture of [those] places and the times than anything I might now write"—and specifically not as the musings of a self-centered and unreliable narrator, then perhaps the original text not only accommodates but invites a double reading.[28] Even the nar-rator may signal his recognition of the photographs' cultural, as opposed to monetary, value. When he describes the pictures as being of "every coloured man in America who had ever 'done anything,'" his placement of "done anything" in quotation marks seems deliberately to evoke more than a "Club" phrase; it also signifies the ways that that expression (and others like it) have served to constrain African Americans in a society that generally moved more quickly to punish than to praise a black person who has "done something." The text itself later visits the scene of just such a punishment.

But the most important reason to recover and then reconsider the rep-resentational power of the wall of photographs is that through it the novel concisely epitomizes the expanding (if still limited) range of public black identities available to the narrator at the turn of the century. In fact, al-though the text does not name them, I would argue that in this scene *The Autobiography* invokes for its 1912 readers the two most prominent African American leisure figures of the early 1900s, Jack Johnson and Bert Williams.

Given their contemporary fame, these are the men to whom the explicitly historical trajectory of the photographs (which range from Douglass "down to" the latest entertainers) symbolically points.[29] They are also the men whose contradictory personas the novel most insistently examines. Both Johnson and Williams were successful entertainers who had a hand in integrating their particular fields; both achieved a national reputation (if not notoriety) in their day. But they differed signally in their own performative representations of blackness, and *The Autobiography* shows how both influence the narrator's shaping of his own identity.

Jack Johnson, for example, offered America the image of a strong and proud black man who could not only beat the best white boxers in the world but who also displayed theretofore exclusively white trappings of success, including "fast cars," "fancy clothes," and "white women." He stood tall in the ring, often taunting his opponents, and became a "powerful symbol" of resistance to white supremacy for the "increasingly militant urban black masses."[30] Although many black elites of the period objected to Johnson's "reckless, independent, [and] bold" style, James Weldon Johnson, who had met Jack three years before his first championship bout in 1908, found him immensely likable. The boxer, Johnson felt, had a "huge but perfect form" and "supreme ease and grace"; "even after the reckoning of his big and little failings," Johnson later said, the prize-fighter had still done "his share" to help solve "the Negro question."[31]

In Johnson's novel the figure of the Jack Johnson–like militant black body continually resurfaces. The narrator, for example, "never an admirer of Uncle Tom, nor of his type of goodness" (41), recalls the time that one of his black classmates, angry at the merciless teasing about his skin color, "turned suddenly on his tormentors and hurled a slate" (15), striking a white boy and splitting his lip. Another classmate, the narrator's friend Shiny, delivers a graduation speech in "tones of appealing defiance." "What were his thoughts when he stepped forward and looked into that crowd of faces, all white with the exception of a score or so that were lost to view?" the narrator asks, setting the scene much as one might a Jack Johnson bout. "I think there must have rushed over him a feeling akin to that of a gladiator tossed into the arena and bade to fight for his life" (44). Other striking figures include the angry black man with whose female companion (the white "widow" [109]) the narrator flirts at the Club and the "gigantic" black doctor who pounds his "great fist" on a table to emphasize that he will not allow race prejudice to move him "one foot, one inch, out of the place where [he is] comfortably located" (149, 150).

These figures, however, are not presented unanxiously. In the narrator's search for his own ideal body, he is alternately fascinated and repelled by such defiant blackness. The narrator admires Shiny and the doctor, for example, but attacks the boy who throws the slate (albeit before he realizes that he himself is considered black) and flees from the murderous vengeance of the widow's companion. Later in the novel the body of a black man accused of defying social custom will be literally burned from the text. And of course the narrator will ultimately decide to become "ex"-colored, repudiating his own connections with the visibly (let alone the defiantly) black body. Indeed, the contemporary black body closer in both color and temperament to the narrator himself, and even more explicitly evoked in the Club scenes, is Bert Williams, the West Indian musical comedy performer whose success depended in part on a stage role conspicuously different from Jack Johnson's boldly black persona. From his earliest years in vaudeville, the light-complexioned Williams played the comic foil to his partner George Walker's black "dandy," Williams's part requiring not only blackface makeup but also a "kinky wig" and a "shuffling" gait.[32]

It is precisely men like Williams that the narrator describes among the talented but frustrated stage professionals at the Club who discuss "the time when they would compel the public to recognize that they could do something more than grin and cut pigeon-wings" (105).[33] At the turn of the century Williams and Walker were already trying to stretch the boundaries of black stage performance beyond the constricting roles originated by antebellum white minstrels. By the time Williams moved to the Ziegfeld Follies in 1910, he was impersonating characters reflecting the broadened range of contemporary African American identities, from prominent leisure-class figures (including, ironically, Jack Johnson) to the gardeners, porters, and taxi drivers of the new black working class.[34] Thus Williams was to some extent already accomplishing the cultural work that the narrator of *The Autobiography* yearns to attempt, the transmutation of black experience into art. The narrator's designs may be grander—he wants to "voice all the joys and sorrows, the hopes and ambitions, of the American Negro, in classic musical form" (147–48)—but his professional goals are not categorically different from Williams's own. (Throw in the narrator's personal detachment from the very blacks whose experiences he hoped to represent—a self-distancing Williams shared—and the influence of Williams on Johnson's characterization of the ex-colored man is even more clear.)[35] Thus although *The Autobiography* is most often read as the story of one man's failure to embrace a public black identity, by invoking the presence of such prominent figures as Johnson and Williams the novel both narrates and admires the very public color-line successes of pre–Harlem Renaissance blacks in the emerging world of American leisure.

■

And yet by the early 1920s, as the largely elite-driven Renaissance began to hit its stride, the cultural meanings of these two figures were under serious revision. Speaking to the Playground Association of America's 1924 Recreation Congress about the need for organized play for African Americans, for example, Emmett Scott, secretary-treasurer of Howard University, turned his topic to, of all people, Jack Johnson. Given the "desire [of black citizens] for healthy recreation and also [their] desire and ambition to achieve some physical prominence," Scott told the largely white audience, "we think we have somewhat diverted the children from the perverted ideal which all the boys had when Jack Johnson won the heavyweight championship of the world, and they all wanted to be pugilists. . . . We are now trying to hold up at Howard . . . a new type to be emulated"—the amateur college athlete—"rather than to have the boys, as I have said, seek the lower ideal which for so long had a hold upon their imagination." Scott's primary objection to Johnson appears to be to his milieu; boxing had long been considered barbaric (and gambling-tainted) by middle-class Americans, black and white. But a second subtext may well be Johnson's notorious disregard for interracial sexual taboos, particularly given Scott's choice of the phrase "perverted ideal" and also his closing call for the establishment of "those happy, *wholesome* relationships" brought about by "the *proper* utilization of leisure time."[36]

Williams's legacy was also under revision in the 1920s. Well chronicled is the black middle- and upper-class suspicion of African American folk culture, and although Williams himself was a wealthy man, his characterizations perhaps carried too much of the taint of "lower-class" vulgarity. Even the radical black monthly the *Messenger*, which generally assailed the snobbishness of elite black leaders who presumed to speak for the race, critiqued Williams as an accomplice in the white-controlled entertainment world's exhibition of clownish black inferiority at the expense of—or, I should say, by the necessary concealment of—black genius. And it is in part this dialectic of the exhibition and concealment of black bodies that *The Autobiography* itself critiques if we read it anew from its publication date in 1927. For by being republished—and then by achieving a far greater circulation and influence than it had in 1912[37]—Johnson's text gains a second critical life as well, yielding meanings less available in the earlier period. This is not to say that this particular dialectic was not in operation before the 1920s (because it certainly was), but instead to claim that the issues it represents became more contested in that decade as black artists tried more aggressively to claim the cultural autonomy so long denied them.

The *Messenger* offered its assessment of Williams's career upon his death in 1922. "As we see it," the obituary/editorial declared, "Bert Williams as he was, rendered a disservice to black people. He was heralded throughout the country as a great comedian; but he left in his train the fallen gods of Negro culture-urgings." Performing in theaters from whose galleries blacks were typically "barred or Jim-Crowed, . . . Williams himself was a facile instrument of this insidious cult," displaying his comic talent for an audience willing only to receive an African American as a "*half-man.*"[38] Virtually echoing *The Autobiography*, whose narrator argued that "no matter how well" a black performer plays tragedy, for example, "the public is loath to give him up" as a comedian (168), the *Messenger* complained that Broadway "will not countenance the Negro in a serious, dignified, classical drama"; indeed, the only black faces to which "theatre-going white America" will "respond favorably" bob comically above the bodies of "Negro clowns, buffoons, [and] funny-men." "Modern capitalist America," the editorial contended, "won't have it otherwise." Here the *Messenger* turns what has been primarily a bio-theatrical critique into a more vigorously socioeconomic one, eulogizing Williams as an oppressed minority first acquiescing to and then defending his own oppression. Regardless of how much Williams "smart[ed] under the cork" or "struggled to rend the veil" to reveal his "pulsing, rebel genius," to Williams, the *Messenger* claimed, remained

> the ignoble lot of dragging his people through the flotsam and jetsam of art to the derisive and vulgar hand-clapping of race prejudiced America. His funmaking, of course, was what they wanted, the lowest form of intellection. They delight in visualizing a race of court-jesters. . . . It is also expressive of a certain contentment and docility that sap every drop of *red, vital radicalism and revolt* out of the wide working masses and render them helpless, anaemic creatures to the most unspeakable exploitation. Such is the reason for white capitalist America's flattering Bert Williams.[39]

Although we would be hard-pressed to impute to Johnson, the experienced musical comedy songwriter, so extreme a disdain for mass culture, the critique of capital's hegemonic influence over contemporary leisure is by no means absent from *The Autobiography*. We are meant, I think, to find ironic—and perhaps a little appalling—the narrator's decision to make Coney Island virtually the first stop on his flight from the horror of a southern lynching into the safety of a white identity. Confused, lost, and lonely—but determined to have "a couple of weeks' good time before worrying seriously about the future" (193)—the ex-colored man's symbolic entry into whiteness takes place on the public grounds of the early century's most famous commercialized amusement park.[40] *The Autobiography* also gestures critically toward a material object that brought into a provocative nexus late-nineteenth- and early-twentieth-century attitudes toward race, capital, and play: the black-themed mechanical toy bank. After the Civil War, mechanical banks designed to encourage children to save money flourished in the United States; in order to see "the fascinating movements of the bank," one had to insert a coin.[41] Many of these banks featured African Americans, whose "fascinating" movements traded profitably (and often politically) on minstrel stereotypes. These included one bank known as "Always Did Spise a Mule" and another—depicting a watermelon-eating black man driving a mule-pulled cart—called "Bad Accident" (see Figure 19).[42] In *The Autobiography* we are told that in the narrator's youth, whenever his white father came to visit, one of the little boy's "appointed" duties was to "bring him a pair of slippers," a "service" that brought the narrator a "bright coin"—which his mother taught him "to promptly drop in a little tin bank" (5). We don't know, of course, if the bank is composed of black figures, or even if it is mechanized; but in the text the middle-class lessons of service and thrift play out against a potentially ironic background of commercialized racism, accentuated by the "ten-dollar gold piece" the narrator's father ties around the narrator's neck.

But it is primarily through the narrator's relations with his white "benefactor" (135) that Johnson's novel most deeply explores the dialectic of exhibition and concealment attacked by the *Messenger* and symptomatic of the 1920s racial politics of leisure. At the Club, the narrator develops into a "remarkable" pianist who specializes in "rag-time transcriptions of familiar classic selections" (115). His talents attract the attention of a "clean-cut, slender, but athletic-looking" (116) white slummer who hires the narrator to play at his home, initiating a patron-performer relationship that will ultimately change the narrator's life. At this first engagement, an elegant dinner party, the narrator begins by playing "classic music" for the respectful

FIGURE 19. "Bad Accident" cast-iron mechanical bank (1887). Courtesy of Sotheby's, New York.

but "decidedly blasé" guests (118). Much later in the evening, "at a word from the host," he "struck up one of [his] liveliest rag-time pieces" (119). The unusual music has its desired effect: filled with "astonishment and delight," the guests keep the narrator playing rags until his arms ache (120).

This episode, which we are told is repeated in kind over and over for many months, epitomizes the semipublic negotiations of racial identity into which the narrator has already repeatedly entered in the novel. In his school days, for example, it is only when the narrator rises to be counted with the white children in his class that he is told, publicly and much to his confusion, that he is black. It is by a more willful public exhibition that he proclaims his blackness at the Club, gradually turning himself from a wide-eyed visitor (and thus by virtue of his skin color someone visually indistinguishable from the other white slummers) into a full-fledged (and "black") performer of rag. In the scene at his patron's dinner party—and by extension in all the subsequent, identical command performances—the narrator figuratively reenacts this public emergence into blackness, transforming himself from an apparently white player of "classic music" into the "black" musician who lay concealed just beneath the surface. We might almost say that he comes to the patron's parties in whiteface, acting the part of the cultured but unremarkable white performer until given the signal to reveal his "truer" emotional and artistic colors. Or to read his figure somewhat differently, perhaps just as he turns classic music into ragtime, so too does he metaphorically transcribe his white body into a black soul.

Johnson never lets us forget, however, that all of these performative negotiations of racial identity are controlled by the wealthy white benefactor. Only at the patron's cue, after all—literally at his giving of the "word"— does the narrator shift musical modes. The narrator inhabits a racially coded musical identity only, that is, at the whim of the white capital that brokers his engagement—even when that engagement means being "loaned" out to some of the patron's friends (120). This is not quite the same critique of white capital as the *Messenger*'s; in the person of the narrator the patron exhibits a serious (if playful) musical talent, not a clownish buffoon. But it is nonetheless a prescient critique of the white control of black performance that will later constrain many of the central figures of the Harlem Renaissance. For his part, the narrator believes that his exclusive contract (the patron asks only that he accept no other engagements) gives him a measure of personal and professional autonomy. His new income does free him from having to play nightly at the Club, where he now gives only special exhibitions. But even those performances, of course, are indirectly controlled by his patron; the narrator can be called at almost any time to perform almost anywhere.[43]

What this relationship (proleptically) helps illustrate is the degree to which the racial politics of leisure in the 1920s recapitulated certain structures of mid-nineteenth-century minstrelsy, particularly the ways in which white American subjectivity was partially constructed through the culturally sanctioned mimicry of (supposedly) uninhibited black leisure. When minstrelsy emerged in the 1840s as an autonomous form of entertainment, companies such as the Virginia Minstrels advertised their shows as faithful representations of the "sports and pastimes" of American slaves, whose black bodies they depicted in ludicrous simulations of endless play.[44] But what these poses disguised—and, as Eric Lott argues, were in fact meant to repress—was the absolute necessity of African American work to the economy of slavery. Indeed, the stage performances themselves often revealed what they had hoped to hide; for by mimicking the words and movements of actual slaves, what the "minstrel songs and dances conjured up," to cite and extend Lott's argument, was "not only the black body [at play] but its labor; not only its sexuality [and other forms of imagined leisure] but its place and function in a particular economy."[45] Thus *The Autobiography* suggests that much as nineteenth-century white Americans constructed more uninhibited selves on, as it were, the bodies of laboring black slaves, so too did contemporary whites—like the benefactor's restless guests—attempt to revitalize themselves through the medium and energies of working black bodies like the narrator's.[46]

It is only in Europe that the narrator is able to break out of the restrictive economy set in place by his patron. Encountering other musicians who reawaken in him the improvisational genius of his earlier, more creative days, the narrator decides to attempt a truer cultural autonomy, returning to America to create original music out of African American themes. The narrator does not himself articulate what would be the *Messenger*'s critique of his employer—that by restricting the narrator's art to the narrow but well-compensated channel of white-defined exoticism the patron had safely contained the rebellious energies of ragtime and at the same time made the narrator content with his own exploitation—but he does suddenly suspect that he has wasted his "gifts" and is eager "to get to work, to begin to do something" (142). At least for the moment, the narrator envisions himself in personal and artistic control, ready to renegotiate the racial and cultural identity he has let his white patron shape. It seems particularly fitting in this regard that he chooses to become a "composer," intending to form his music out of constitutive African American elements much as he will try to form (or reform) a self. We may be duly critical of the narrator's approach to his new artistic career; he not only seems motivated by thoughts of financial reward but also regards much of his folk material with an ill-disguised condescension. But the work he undertakes does offer more autonomy and creativity—and more of a chance for self-discovery—than any other he has attempted or, indeed, will attempt.

■

What ultimately prevents the narrator from successfully negotiating an identity as a black American, let alone a black composer, is the horrific burning scene he witnesses in a small southern town. Visiting the area for the purpose of collecting black "themes" to use in his compositions, the narrator has just finished gathering "a mine of material" (173) from a countywide religious meeting. While sitting up late reviewing his notes, he becomes aware of a commotion outside and soon discovers that a black man, accused of "some terrible crime," is being sought for punishment (185). Because the town has no reason to suspect that the light-colored narrator is black, he can venture outside without being apprehended himself and is thus able to watch the scene of brutality as it unfolds. The captured man is dragged to the railroad station, where a large crowd has assembled. He is about to be lynched when someone in the mob cries "'Burn him!'" (186). They do, to the narrator's stunned silence. "Before I could make myself believe that what I saw was really happening," he recalls, "I was looking at a scorched post, a smouldering fire, blackened bones, charred fragments sifting down through cells of chain; and the smell of burnt flesh—human flesh—was in my nostrils" (187).

For all its narrative simplicity this is a scene of tremendous complexity in the novel. It serves as a structural and symbolic counterpoint, for example, to the earlier episode at the Club where the black companion of the white widow guns her down in front of the narrator. Both are scenes of extreme violence that abruptly conclude the narrator's involvement with a particular facet of black leisure culture (New York's cabarets, southern folk religion), and propel him into predominantly nonblack worlds (first Europe, then the American North). Both scenes, moreover, involve a murderous reply to a perceived sexual transgression. In the first episode, the black man kills the white widow for her supposed infidelity. The second encounter, after a fashion, inverts the first: a white mob kills a black man on suspicion of an interracial sexual crime.[47] We might even say that the burning metaphorically punishes the first black man, both for the murder of the white woman and for the miscegenation to which their original love affair gave sanction. It is then also, ironically, a punishment that the narrator himself—a "black" man who later marries a white woman—will avoid.

In its portrayal as an intensely public event, the burning is also explicit counterpoint to the "big meeting" in the black community that the narrator has just attended. The big meeting, for example, where congregations from around the state "unite at some centrally located church for a series of meetings," carries a "social as well as a religious function" (173). Here people gather to hear "famous preachers" like "John Brown" electrify their audiences with pyrotechnic oratory filtered through the "intuition of a born theatrical manager" (174, 175). Also an attraction, especially for the narrator, are the talented hymn leaders like "Singing Johnson," whose strong voices and improvisational skills turn "people from different communities" into vocally and spiritually united congregations (178). The performances of Brown and Johnson in particular leave the narrator in a state of energizing "inspiration" (182).

But at the burning he encounters an eerily similar performative economy that proves more powerful, ultimately, than the big meeting. There, too, though it is around midnight, "gathered . . . a crowd of men, . . . [while] others were steadily arriving, seemingly from all the surrounding country" (185). The men say very little, but the assembly is clearly, like the big meeting, a social function, in the sense that it both draws the immediate community together and attracts additional spectators eager to share the experience.[48] By sunrise the presence of "a great many women and children" makes the burning a family-style leisure event. Once the black man is brought to the station, the white men offer up their own shrill hymn, "that terror-instilling sound known as the 'rebel yell,'" and their own pyrotechnic oratory ("Burn him!") runs "like an electric current" through an equally unified congregation (186). As at any powerful performance, "some of the crowd yelled and cheered," some "seemed appalled," others "turned away"; but all witness, and none stop, the exemplary event (187).[49] The big meeting had left the narrator inspired to create; the burning shames him into re-creating himself.

For what the narrator encounters is not just a performative economy more powerful than the big meeting, or indeed more powerful than his own creative self. He encounters an emblematic display in which virtually all of the text's African American identities—including his own—are simultaneously represented and destroyed. In the killing of a black man in front of a crowd, for example, he sees the metaphorical assassination of men like John Brown and Singing Johnson, who just pages earlier had each inhabited a similar role. This is at the same time a dumb black man who is exhibited and killed—his mind without "a single ray of thought," his body "too stunned and stupefied even to tremble" (187)—and thus a mockingly silenced version of both the gigantic doctor whom the narrator meets on his return voyage to America and the narrator's eloquent childhood friend, now professor, Shiny. (Even the burned man's eyes are "dull" [186]; that is, they do not "shine.") It is also a symbolically minstrelized black body that is killed ("his eyes, bulging from their sockets, rolled from side to side" [187]) and thus by extension a strategically inverted representation of the narrator himself, who has nearly completed the successful renegotiation of his autonomous black artistic self.[50] As Johnson crafts the scene, the narrator even appears as a spectatorial double for the man at the stake, experiencing the victim's physical and emotional responses in almost identical sequence. Like the black victim, the narrator is first "fixed to the spot," then "dazed," and finally unable to stand (187). "I was as weak," the narrator recognizes, "as a man who had lost blood" (190).

And, in a sense, he does "lose" blood, for this metaphorical elimination of the text's available black identities drives him headlong into the white world. Ashamed by his connection to a race that could be so murderously mistreated—and so spectacularly controlled—the narrator retreats, choosing the security of self-concealment over the potential dangers of self-exhibition. Though the novel is critical of oppressive white control, this is not a retreat that the book particularly admires. After all, once the narrator's shame subsides, he treats passing as a kind of recreation. As a black man pretending to be white, the narrator regards himself as someone merely playing a role, the success of which he finds so amusing that it amounts to a "practical joke" (or a "capital joke," as he says later) on society (3, 197). Even the white world of "money-making," into which the narrator feverishly throws himself, is only an "interesting and absorbing game" whose little victories give him "a great deal of pleasure" (195).

Although the ex-colored man soon attains considerable wealth and "a grade of society of no small degree of culture" (197), his description of how he reaches the latter is tellingly ironic. While most of the narrator's sense of coming into whiteness is rendered in metaphors of accumulation—he gets better jobs, acquires more money, buys New York real estate—finding the people with whom he wishes to spend time occurs instead, he says, by "a process of elimination" (197). In literal terms, of course, he means that over time he has maintained only those acquaintances who share his regard for culture. But to say (as he does) "*I* reached [that] grade" by "a process of elimination" suggests that some of the eliminating must also have been self-inflicted. This sense of the phrase is borne out by the acuteness of the regret that the ex-colored man expresses at the close of his narrative, when he makes clear that his passage into the white economic and social world has effectively stripped him of much that had gone into the making of his self. He is "glad" to be white, in the end, because his whiteness ensures his children's position in American society. But he sees himself as a distinctly diminished man, "small and selfish," the cost of whose whiteness, ultimately, is steep: "a vanished dream, a dead ambition, a sacrificed talent"— a steady paring away of the self, as it were, until even the "tangible remnants" of his past signify absence, not presence (211). After the death of his wife, the ex-colored man "gradually drop[s] out of social life" altogether (210), choosing to protect his children's secret at what is surely the expense of his own identity.

Thus the final result of the ex-colored man's attempt to gain control over the construction of his identity—chiefly by deciding when, where, and how his body will be exhibited—is the deconstruction of any identity. By only "playing" at being white, he forfeits the possibility of achieving anything like a coherent "white" selfhood. And by feeling that he has "never really been" one of his "mother's people" but has "been only a privileged spectator of their inner life" (210), he is ironically still further from being "black." In the end, neither agent nor actor (nor player), the ex-colored man as passive "spectator" can only withdraw into his wholesale business and watch. Resembling nothing so much as that imaginary polar bear in the Atlantic—white, hidden, and alone, refusing to put himself on exhibition— the narrator would seem, finally, to have played a practical joke on no one but himself.

■

Of course in telling his story the ex-colored man is attempting to reconstitute and then exhibit that hidden self to the reader. A further irony occasioned by the novel's republication in the 1920s concerns the ex-colored man's assumption that in passing into whiteness he must forfeit his dream of creating new American music out of African American materials. This sacrifice is presented in *The Autobiography* as a necessary result of the decision to pass; certainly no white man at the turn of the century, particularly one yearning for the upper reaches of white leisure society, could nurture such an ambition. But in the more freely cross-cultural artistic climate of the Harlem Renaissance such forfeiture need not have been automatic. This, at least, was the position taken by Alice Dunbar Nelson in her review of Johnson's republished novel for *Opportunity*. Praising *The Autobiography*'s "bold prophecy" that (in the narrator's words) "the day will come . . . when this slave music will be the most treasured heritage of the American Negro," Nelson reminds her readers that "that day has come, and more than that, for this slave music is the biggest thing in the modern musical world." But she also notes that the narrator's "dismay when he [finds] he must throw over his chosen career if he were to be white" would be inappropriate in 1920s America. "Had he lived now," she avers, "it would only have served as a whet to his ambition, whether white or black, to write of the music of the Negro."[51] Thus in 1927, in an age newly warming to the black-themed music of such American composers as George Gershwin, the ex-colored man could perhaps have passed for white and still "voice[d] all the joys and sorrows" of the black race.[52] In 1912, however, Johnson's text stops well short of imagining that possibility. How could one pass for something one was not and still make one's dream come true?

In an important sense this is precisely the dilemma that Fitzgerald sets for Jay Gatsby. How could "James Gatz of North Dakota," the son of "shiftless and unsuccessful farm people," pass for "a person from much the same stratum" as Daisy Fay Buchanan—that is, the cream of the white leisure class—and still "win" her? If he did attain the upper reaches of that class, but did so under "false pretenses," could that dream survive?[53] Perhaps by the 1920s, when amidst the unpredictable postwar economy the very categories of wealth, status, work, and leisure were increasingly in flux, it had become easier than in the ex-colored man's day for certain American outsiders (even "racial" ones) to construct new and satisfying identities for themselves.[54] Certainly one such impulse initiates the action of *The Great Gatsby*: Nick Carraway, "restless" in the Middle West isolation of his family's wholesale hardware concern, comes East "in the spring of twenty-two" to "learn the bond business" instead (2). (In so doing, Nick's tale also starts virtually where the ex-colored man's ends, as he figuratively emerges from the latter's isolating retreat into the white world of his wholesale house.) And it is Gatsby's own desire to refashion himself as, in the logic of the text's racial categories, a "white" man of means that drives much of the rest of the narrative. Indeed, Gatsby's passage into the world of upper-class white leisure and the subsequent effect of that passage on his (and others') notions of his identity constitute some of the text's main fascinations, and constitute mine in the rest of this chapter. Gatsby's passage—or, more accurately, his "passing"—is not to him, however, a joke, as it is at first to the ex-colored man; Gatsby inhabits his chosen self with complete seriousness. And Gatsby does not inhabit that self surreptitiously, but with a bold and public flourish commensurate with his sense of his own promise, even of his own destiny. It will be due in part to the uncontrollability of that self-exhibition that Gatsby's attempt to build a self equal to his dreams will fail. But before we consider Gatsby's failure, both on its own and in collation with the ex-colored man's, we need a clearer sense of the contours and the constitutive energies of the world in which he is trying to play a part.

This is Tom and Daisy's world, the 1920s Anglo-Saxon leisure domain of those who, as H. L. Mencken put it in a review of the novel for the Baltimore *Evening Sun*, "have too much money to spend and too much time to spend it."[55] Critics have already helpfully adumbrated, for instance, the ways in which Daisy exemplifies the conspicuously consumptive class practices outlined by Thorstein Veblen in 1899 and brought spectacularly to life in the 1920s. As Richard Godden explains, Daisy is "the 'badge,' 'prize,' or 'trophy'" of her class, noticeably disengaged from any productive activity in order best to signify what Veblen would have called the "pecuniary reputability" of her husband Tom, the prototypically Veblenesque ruling-class predator.[56] Performing his duty as a leisure elite, Tom not only "disembodies" his wife Daisy "for purposes of display,"[57] but he also acquires and exhibits horses, one of the domesticated animals Veblen singled out as an example of wasteful display. It was Tom's ostentatious transporting of "a string of polo ponies [down] from Lake Forest" at the decidedly young age of thirty that turned the Buchanans' move East (in Nick's eyes) into something "that rather took your breath away" (4). Once in place in East Egg, the horses indeed seem primarily to attest to Tom's own domineering personality. The very first time we see him in the novel he is packed into "glistening" riding clothes, "standing with his legs apart on the front porch" of his Long Island mansion (5). His dress and defiant carriage suggest not so much that he is, in Nick's famous assessment, "drift[ing] on forever seeking . . . the dramatic turbulence of some irrecoverable football game" (4), but rather saddled up and ready to "ride" whatever is at hand—horse, house, wife, or guest.

Tom's role in the maintenance of canons of "honorific waste" is evident even when he is away from East Egg, slumming in New York City with his lower-middle-class mistress, Myrtle Wilson. On their way from the train station to their 158th Street apartment, Tom and Myrtle buy a dog—another of Veblen's conspicuously useless domestic animals. In its industrial purposelessness, the dog functions effectively, according to Veblen, as "an item of expense," thereby holding "a well-assured place in men's regard as a thing of good repute."[58] Myrtle exhibits an inchoate sense of these functions when she sees the dogs on the sidewalk: "I want to get one for the apartment. They're nice to have—a dog" (18). The dog is "for the apartment" in much the same way that any other "nice" object "to have" would be: it is brought there, set out for show, and then largely ignored. Through the afternoon and into the evening the dog sits pathetically on a table, "looking with blind eyes through the smoke, and from time to time groaning faintly" (24), as though aware of its purposeless role but powerless—much like the reluctant guest Nick himself—to get up and leave.

It is through an analogous draining of purposeful energy, according to Veblen, that the white leisure class conserves the economic, political, and social arrangements that make its position possible. True cultural innovation—any real "learning [or] adoption of new habits of thought"—requires strenuous effort, which in turn requires "surplus energy." But in a class system of conspicuous emulation like Tom and Daisy's world, any potential surplus energy at the top (or in the aspiring middle) is generally expended in the acquisition of yet more goods for consumption or waste, while at the bottom one struggles simply to provide "the bare physical necessities of life." As a result, Veblen explains, "the requirements of pecuniary reputability tend . . . to absorb any surplus energy which may be available"—an endlessly entropic cycle that only accentuates the inertia already present in the system.[59] Thus even when characters in *The Great Gatsby* seem to disrupt society's static arrangements—as at the 158th Street party, where Tom and Myrtle aggressively merge their disparate classes—the more things stay bleakly the same. In the end, Tom and Myrtle's gathering disintegrates into a miasma of blood and ash (Myrtle's broken nose, the endless cigarettes) that renders its energies figuratively indistinguishable from those of the swarming gray men who repeatedly stir up "impenetrable" clouds of "bleak dust" (15) in the desolate valley of ashes beside the railroad. This will not bode well for Gatsby's attempt at racial self-reinvention.

■

One might analogously claim that Gatsby's parties, too, though of decidedly different cast (and caste) from Tom and Myrtle's, contribute to the novel's systematic absorption of surplus energy. Gatsby's affairs, after all, do seem to cycle endlessly, almost interchangeably, through the weekends of summer, each party picking up not where the last left off but where they all begin. Nick's first description of a Gatsby fete is offered with exactly this iterative quality, as though every gathering progresses from the afternoon swimming, to the opening of the bar, to the first notes of the orchestra, to the sudden emergence of one of the "confident girls" who glides out onto the dance floor to get things started. Then the party, Nick explains, "has begun" (26, 27). For all of the subsequent mingling and carnivalesque atmosphere, no more comes of these parties, it seems, than of Tom and Myrtle's, or of the daily ash-stirring along the railroad. On Monday mornings Gatsby even has his own little swarm of servants and gardeners who bustle about the house, "repairing the ravages of the night before" and preparing for the ravages of the nights to come (26). And yet this charge of purposelessness seems off the mark, for despite the apparent role of Gatsby's parties as mere providers of a conspicuous outlet for surplus social energy, they do serve a distinct function for their host. Gatsby, after all, hopes that one of his glittering affairs may by chance draw Daisy into its orbit. When Nick himself finally understands the point of Gatsby's seemingly pointless parties, he sees his neighbor for the first time as a distinct and vital person, energy-driven instead of energy-draining. "He came alive to me," Nick says, "delivered suddenly from the womb of his purposeless splendor" (52).

Nick's figuring of Gatsby as a newborn child is also particularly appropriate, because in Nick's reconstruction of the story of that tragic summer Gatsby brings to the tale a freshness and vigor altogether lacking in the other principals and altogether unanticipated by Veblen's model of enervative emulation. Gatsby's energy is instead better explained through the quite different theories of the self offered by early-twentieth-century play reformers such as Henry Curtis and Joseph Lee, who were far more willing than Veblen to posit the existence of genuinely constructive forms of personal and social energy in capitalist America. What strikes Nick most about Gatsby, he realizes one morning when he sees the latter skillfully "balancing himself on the dashboard of his car," is his "resourcefulness of movement," a "peculiarly American" posture that comes, Nick supposes, "with the absence of lifting work or rigid sitting in youth and, even more, with the formless grace of our nervous, sporadic games." Observes Nick: "This quality was continually breaking through [Gatsby's] punctilious manner in the shape of restlessness. He was never quite still; there was always a tapping foot somewhere or the impatient opening and closing of a hand" (42). Gatsby's restlessness thus differs signally from Tom's, Jordan's, even Nick's own. Tom's eyes flash about "restlessly" as he surveys his East Egg estate (5); Jordan develops a "restless" knee during her visit to the same (13); and Nick finds his "restless eye" satisfied by "the constant flicker of men and women and machines" that pass him on the streets of New York (38). These instances of impatience seem physical expressions of what Curtis described as "the high nervous pressure that comes from motor energy unused."[60] But Gatsby's restlessness is more than a mere symptom of available energy; it is closer to the outward sign of the very forces that have shaped and sustained him.

For although play theorists agreed that properly directed leisure played an important role in self-development, they disagreed on the precise relationship between play activities and the structures of the body itself. Proponents of what was commonly known as the "surplus energy theory" diagnosed play as (in the words of German philosopher and proto–play theorist Friedrich Schiller) "the aimless expenditure of exuberant energy." Bodies are generally so "overcharged" with muscular vitality, these theorists held, "that they cannot keep still."[61] Supporters of the "recreation theory" approached play from the opposite direction: as an activity intended to restore vitality to an already exhausted body. Lee, drawing on yet a third school of thought, "instinct theory," argued that one did need a surplus before one could play (indeed, before one could act), but that the surplus one required was not of energy, but "intention," or "desire." Lee, too, regarded play as an activity that builds one up, rather than as a discharge of one's surplus. But by the same token, he held, play does not simply restore the body's vitality. Play instead virtually directs the body's growth, making possible its realization of what it is to be. "The play of children, as actually observed, always aims beyond existing powers," insisted Lee. "Desire invariably outruns performance." The child at play is "reaching for something beyond himself—not pushed from behind by a surplus of power and talent, but drawn on from in front by an inspiring goal."[62]

But because that "inspiring goal" is in some sense a product of one's own intention, play for Lee is not merely the process of a self-in-the-making, but a potentially radical site of willful self-creation, a virtual field of desire-in-motion. Thus physical restlessness for Lee is not so much a problem as it is a sign of the healthy body yearning to fulfill its sense of its own potential, its own ideal. To Lee, Gatsby's impatiently tapping foot—and particularly his opening and closing hand—would be expressions of the instinctive "struggle onward" to create oneself. "Play is ever the reclamation of new territory," Lee averred; "it is the child's nature reaching out for fresh worlds to conquer."[63] The deliberate self-fashioning of Gatsby's young adulthood is Lee's theory come to fictional life, as the "quick and extravagantly ambitious" James Gatz, "searching for something to do"—or more accurately, for something to be—"invents" himself out of the "pattern of . . . fancies" taking shape in his restless imagination (65–66). Mingling the nightly labor of his urgent, half-waking musings with the "half-fierce, half-lazy work of [his] bracing days" along "the south shore of Lake Superior," Gatz is ready with his tanned, hardened body and his new name when his "destiny," millionaire Dan Cody, drops anchor in Little Girl Bay (65, 66).[64]

Nick's description of Gatsby's self-imagining further echoes Lee's explication of what he called "the need to dream." The young adult is "obsessed," Lee claimed, "to set forth in imagination the demands of his own soul. . . . Such dreaming is a part of the life process, a necessary step in the translation from instinct through achievement into growth." In Gatsby's case, a whole "universe of ineffable gaudiness spun itself out in his brain" each night (65). But "the dream, if it remains a dream," Lee counseled, "may not be a step in successful action, but a dereliction from it." In Nick's estimation this is exactly what happens to Gatsby once Daisy—whom he has wooed but lost—becomes his dream. His "illusion," Nick explains, "had gone beyond her, beyond everything. He had thrown himself into it with a creative passion, adding to it all the time, decking it out with every bright feather that drifted his way" (63–64). Gatsby is paradoxically also guilty of what Lee poses as the second pitfall of illusions: "the danger . . . that we become governed not by our dream but by the exigencies and limitations of our material and of practical life, [that we] find some smart and easy way that succeeds, but involves a forgetting of what we started out to do."[65] In Gatsby's headlong sprint for wealth and respectability he chooses Meyer Wolfsheim's inside lane of bootlegged prosperity and gambled profits, an easy but disreputable path whose later discovery hardens Daisy against Gatsby's continuing advances.

Gatsby's vulnerability to the "colossal vitality" (63) of his illusion is figured tellingly by Nick as a failure of Gatsby's defining restlessness, a loss of the motive power of the self. Nick senses this shift in momentum even at the height of Gatsby's apparent success—his teatime meeting with Daisy at Nick's house. At one moment, Gatsby "literally glowed; without a word or a gesture of exultation a new well-being radiated from him and filled the little room" (59). But only a short time later, during the triumphant tour of Gatsby's mansion, Nick notices that Gatsby

> had passed visibly through two states and was entering upon a third. After his embarrassment and his unreasoning joy he was consumed with wonder at her presence. He had been full of the idea so long, dreamed it right through to the end, waited with his teeth set, so to speak, at an inconceivable pitch of intensity. Now, in the reaction, he was running down like an over-wound clock. (61)

After this point in the narrative, Gatsby seems more and more susceptible to the static energies that lay in wait for the unsuspecting dreamer. When he holds a protective vigil outside Daisy's house the night of the fateful drive back from New York, for example, he stands anxiously but quietly, waiting and watching ("over nothing," Nick says), "his hands in his coat pockets" (98)—a much less energized pose than the one he struck the first night Nick saw him, when Gatsby stood on his lawn looking across the bay to-ward Daisy's dock and suddenly "stretched out his arms toward the dark water," trembling (15). And the closing image of Gatsby awaiting death in his bathing trunks seems strategically to rewrite the formative scene of Gatsby's youth. In place of Dan Cody's magnificent yacht bobbing on Lake Superior, Jay Gatsby floats disconsolately on an inflatable mattress in the di-minished sea of a backyard pool. And instead of Nick Carraway coming to warn Gatsby that a certain ill wind (i.e., George Wilson) "might catch him and break him up in half an hour"—as Gatsby himself had warned Cody (65)—Wilson (guided by Tom) glides fantastically toward the pool to stop Gatsby's tapping foot once and for all.

■

These images serve a vital corollary function as well: they accentuate the novel's own dialectic of visibility and concealment, a dialectic that helps structure Nick's tale much as it does the ex-colored man's. Gatsby's protective vigil over Daisy, for example, is not merely a more static version of his earlier, grasping gesture; it is also a more hidden one: he shifts from a semi-public display of desire to a stealthy lurking in the bushes. But sprawled on the pool float, Gatsby (who by his reticence had formerly nurtured the welter of misinformation about his past, shrouding his well-known figure in a paradoxical anonymity) suddenly puts himself on display, even dangerously so, becoming a vulnerable target for a willful foe. Like *The Autobiography of an Ex-Coloured Man*, *The Great Gatsby*'s plot turns on the whens, wheres, and hows of its protagonist's self-exhibition. But unlike the ex-colored man—who gradually gains control over his self-presentation (paradoxically and concomitantly losing his identity, however)—Gatsby, who had virtually willed himself into energetic being, slowly loses that control, as the "babbled slander of his garden" (90) crystallizes in Tom's menacing accusations about his "affairs" (89). Gatsby's final self-exhibition on the raft is only a literalization of the figurative (if ultimately, for Gatsby, more fatal) scene of exposure played out at the Plaza Hotel. There, Daisy's pained admission that she loved Gatsby "too" (88) strips away his illusion that she had never loved Tom, and Tom's determined unmasking of Gatsby's illegitimate wealth reveals the tangle of untruths—particularly about his identity—that Gatsby had hoped to hide from Daisy.[66]

Gatsby's literal and textual fortunes are only the most prominently affected by this particular dialectic. Virtually every other character is in some way defined by a similar interplay between exhibition and concealment. Tom virtually flaunts the fact of his adulterous affair to Nick, while trying (ineffectively) to hide it from Daisy. Behind Jordan Baker's public position as a sportswoman and her "bored haughty face" (38), she conceals an "incurably dishonest" (39) alter ego. Even Nick, whose story of his friend Gatsby is as much a public unveiling of its narrator as of its eponymous protagonist, depicts himself not as an exhibitionist but as a secret and silent watcher, irresistibly attracted to the "shadow[y]" forms of others, particularly women (71). Nick's tale itself is constructed to reveal crucial information about Gatsby's past in widely spaced flashbacks, giving the text its own narrative economy of concealment and display.

There is a series of related representations in the novel, however, of which Nick seems only partly in control. These are perhaps most dramatically illustrated by the half-hidden corpse of George Wilson, which lies near Gatsby's pool "a little way off in the grass" (108). Wilson's only partially obscured body is symptomatic of *The Great Gatsby*'s inability (or perhaps unwillingness) to conceal a host of otherwise unnamed and largely unvoiced working-class bodies circulating through the text. These are the bodies whose labors underwrite the leisure-class identities of the more prominent characters in the novel; these are, in other words, the caddies, the chauffeurs, the butlers, the chambermaids, the taxi drivers, the gardeners, the grocery boys, the cooks, and so on—figures who collectively command a surprising amount of narrative attention.[67] And Nick's frequent mention of these figures is not merely incidental or ornamental. He often brings them into close proximity with more visible characters, or notes the potentially symbolic actions of a few. To illustrate Jordan's streak of moral carelessness, for example, Nick recalls the time in her car that she "passed so close to some workmen that our fender flicked a button on one man's coat" (39). In another instance an affronted "elevator boy" responds to a perceived indignity from one of the guests leaving Tom and Myrtle's party by "snap[ping]" at him to "keep [his] hands off the lever" (25). After leaving Gatsby and Daisy alone in his house during their first reunion—that interlude for Gatsby of maximal joy but also gnawing disillusion—Nick observes a maid in an upper window of Gatsby's house spitting "meditatively" into Gatsby's garden (59).[68]

My purpose here is not simply to generate a new context in which to review Fitzgerald's critique of class relations, but more specifically to consider the text's insistent intertwining of labor, leisure, class, and race—and then to look more closely at the relationship between Gatsby's passage into the white world of leisure and the ex-colored man's. For it seems clear that these working-class bodies are potentially, if not implicitly, racialized bodies, not only because of the rising percentage of African Americans and foreign-born immigrants being employed in such positions in the 1910s and 1920s,[69] but particularly given the text's more general anxiety about race, best exemplified in (but not limited to) Tom's impatient rantings about the rise of "other races" (9). Although people of color are explicitly identified only infrequently in *The Great Gatsby*, their more general presence can be strongly inferred. When Nick goes out of his way to notice that the chauffeur of a limousine is white, for example—as he does when he sees one driving three African Americans across Blackwell Island—then Fitzgerald seems to imply that the unremarked chauffeurs (and, by extension, the unremarked servants, elevator operators, and so on) may well be some "other" color. Their textual unremarkableness should not be construed, that is, as absence. Indeed, their unremitting presence—the way those potentially racialized bodies keep popping up in the narrative—allows the novel to keep Gatsby's own concealed past in view, right down to the "janitor's work" he had tried but despised during his abortive stay at St. Olaf's College (65). In the end, even Gatsby's funeral is attended by more servants than members of any other class.

Recent criticism has begun to explore some of these issues. Walter Benn Michaels reminds us that in the novel's racial logic, Gatsby—born James Gatz—is not himself "entirely white." Recalling that the racist discourse paraphrased in the novel by Tom not only distinguished whites from "browns, blacks, reds, and yellows" but also Nordic whites from non-Nordic Alpine and Mediterranean immigrant stock like (presumably) Gatsby, Michaels argues that "Gatsby's love for Daisy seems to Tom the expression of something like an impulse to miscegenation."[70] Mitchell Breitwieser weaves together three "very small loose strand[s]" of blackness in the novel—the black witness to the aftermath of the accident; the blacks in the limousine crossing Blackwell's Island; and particularly the music of black jazz—to show how Fitzgerald "*perceived*," though not necessarily affirmed, the cultural subjectivity of African Americans.[71]

Here I want to weave Michaels's and Breitwieser's arguments together, taking seriously not only the proposition that the text is more concerned with racial subjectivity than we have heretofore allowed but also the notion that Gatsby, as a sort of racial outsider himself (and almost an alter ego for the text's unnamed working-class bodies), is implicated in that subjectivity. In such a reading, one becomes aware of an abundance of racial signifiers in the novel. Tom and Daisy's home, for example, is a "cheerful . . . Georgian Colonial mansion" (4), perhaps an ironic nod to the conventional all's-happy-in-the-South settings of plantation school fiction, if not a mocking symbol of Tom's view of himself as a member of the dominant race. Daisy's own racial identity is at one point subtly and suggestively destabilized. When Tom launches into his theory of racial solidarity ("This idea is that we're Nordics. I am, and you are, and you are, and—"), it is only "after an infinitesimal hesitation" that he includes Daisy "with a slight nod" (9). What gives Tom pause? Is it simply the fact that he and Daisy, their marital relations quite strained, tend to talk past each other rather than to each other? Or is it because when Tom looks at Daisy he may instead be thinking of Myrtle—a woman who by Michaels's argument is, like Gatsby, not "entirely white"? Or is there something not "entirely white" about Daisy that Tom cannot bring himself to speak? Fitzgerald codes Tom with a racial ambiguousness as well. On one hand he presents him as the panicky defender of the white race; but on another he makes him a "brute of a man, a great, big, hulking physical specimen" (one who has already bruised Daisy's knuckle [8]), calling into play a cluster of signifiers not entirely separable from racist depictions of "black brutes" who supposedly threatened the safety of white women.[72]

Similar signs also underwrite key scenes in the novel, particularly in ways that comment on the racial politics of leisure in 1920s America. This is a text, after all, that conspicuously avoids face-to-face encounters with contemporary Harlem. When Tom, Nick, and Myrtle take their taxi from the train station to the apartment on 158th Street, for example, their journey literally skirts the black community. Driving uptown on Fifth Avenue, which in the 1920s was the eastern boundary of Harlem, they cut "over the Park toward the West Hundreds" (18)—presumably to go north on Eighth Avenue, Harlem's western border. When a more direct racial encounter does occur, Nick reveals the limits to his own perception of black subjectivity by turning the three African Americans he sees in the limousine into minstrel caricatures.[73] In its representation of the white spectator looking peremptorily on "modish" (45) black bodies, this encounter metaphorically reproduces the socioeconomic and even sociogeographic dynamic of the white leisure slumming increasingly in vogue when Fitzgerald's novel was published at mid-decade.

Even more important in terms of Gatsby's character are Fitzgerald's representations of the explicitly racialized leisure world of jazz, the more extensive appearance of which in the original manuscript leads Breitwieser to conclude that Fitzgerald at least recognized the potentially disruptive heterogeneity of authentic black music. Breitwieser rightly focuses on the scene at the Gatsby party in which the orchestra plays "Vladimir Tostoff's *Jazz History of the World*," a piece that had supposedly "attracted so much attention at Carnegie Hall" the previous year (33).[74] But there is a second interlude, more crucial to the plot, that Breitwieser does not discuss, in which jazz functions as musical commentary on the action itself. At the Plaza Hotel, where the novel's principals have temporarily taken a room to escape the city's heat, the music from a downstairs wedding plays beneath the bristling confrontation scene between Tom, Gatsby, and Daisy. First are heard "the portentous chords of Mendelssohn's Wedding March" (84), an ironic detail given the pending battle upstairs over who is really "married" to Daisy. But soon, as the wedding reception begins—and almost at the same time that Gatsby's spirited defense against Tom's insinuations begins—the band lets out a "burst of jazz," which then serves, as it were, as the musical accompaniment to the rest of the scene, led by the "short, restless tattoo" of Gatsby's foot (85). By the time of Daisy's fatal hesitation in her resolve to leave Tom, however—"as though she had never, all along, intended doing anything"—the burst of jazz has devolved into what Nick describes as a series of "muffled and suffocating chords . . . drifting up on hot waves of air" (88). The literal smothering of the music quite fittingly underscores the metaphorical asphyxiation of Gatsby's dream.

At least this is one way to read the role of jazz in this episode. But if we are trying to make sense of what I have called the novel's dialectic of exhibition and concealment in relation to the foregoing discussion of leisure, race, and culture, then the appearance of jazz in this crucial scene of exposure offers an even more complex and ironic commentary on Gatsby's own urgently self-willed identity. For the jazz filtering up from the ballroom, as Breitwieser would remind us, is in all likelihood (given the white, upperclass venue of the Plaza) "white" or "covered" jazz, a culturally "neutralizing" appropriation by nonblack performers of the "force or power of jazz" to "ornament" otherwise "homogenized performances with episodes of jazz effect."[75] What Gatsby and the others hear at the Plaza is thus white music passing for black, white music playing at blackness. But is this not—especially if we recall Michaels's argument about *The Great Gatsby* and nativist constructions of race in the 1920s—an ironic inversion of the way Fitzgerald has constructed Gatsby in the novel, as a not "entirely white" man passing for one? In other words, if Tom's exposure of Gatsby is, according to the logic of the text and the time, an unmasking of both his class and racial (or more broadly, as Michaels would suggest, his *cultural*) identity, then this is the point at which the novel most closely explores the psychology of passing central to *The Autobiography.* For Gatsby is not just posing as someone with impressively reputable (and visible) income; he is passing as a white man with a legitimate claim to the intrinsically racialized leisure class. Such a reading of *The Great Gatsby*—as an intriguing if by no means fully realized novel of cultural line-crossing—certainly raises the stakes of an interpretation of Gatsby's insistent imposture in the text.[76] Passing, for Gatsby, after all, is anything but play.

Indeed, had Gatsby approached his entry into the white world of upperclass leisure more as though he were playing a role than inhabiting a self, he might have fared better in the novel's economy of performance and punishment. The ex-colored man, fully aware that he is impersonating a white man when he falls in love with the "fragile . . . body" and "passionate" voice of a cultured white woman ("the most dazzlingly white thing" that he "had ever seen" [198]), has a much better sense than Gatsby of when to disclose the truth about his position. Believing that this white woman's independent discovery of his identity would likely end their relationship, the ex-colored man instead reveals his secret to her, orchestrating the disclosure and thereby maintaining control over the self he has constructed. Gatsby, however, blinded by the intensity of his own dream, withholds the entire truth from Daisy. As a result, in the scene at the Plaza, instead of the coolly confident Gatsby who shrugs off inquisitive reporters trying to entangle him in some scandal, we have the flustered Gatsby backpedaling to recuperate Daisy's faith. After Tom discloses the real nature of Gatsby's "drug-stores" (which retail illegal grain alcohol) and suggests that Gatsby is also involved in gambling, Gatsby begins "to talk excitedly to Daisy, denying everything, defending his name against accusations that had not been made" (90). But these words come too late, and protest too much; Gatsby is unable to regain control of the self that is suddenly, starkly on exhibition, and with "every word" Daisy draws "further and further into herself." Gatsby's energetically imagined future deflates into nothing more than a "dead dream" (90). The accidental death of Myrtle Wilson and his own sorry slaying at the hands of her husband are all that await him in the narrative, two more events in which Gatsby plays a principal part but over which he is equally unable to exert control.

Ironically, then, the price of passage into leisured whiteness for Gatsby is strikingly similar to the ex-colored man's, despite the differences in performative control outlined above. The ruthlessly exposed Gatsby yields up his dream and his self, while Wilson's misguided bullet drains the last of his energy from the text. So, too, Johnson's narrator: secure but ultimately trapped in his static whiteness, the carefully concealed ex-colored man recalls his own dead dream, mourns his own vanished self. This is the fate, these texts would seem to say, of the outsider who seeks a way in, of any recalcitrant subjectivity not already a part of society's (implicitly white) ideal body, or indeed not content to conserve its structural laws. Gatsby, in the end, after all, is "lynched" as surely as the anonymous black man (and his double, the narrator) in *The Autobiography*—and on the same suspicion of interracial sexual misconduct. But both texts also say more than this. They challenge the very notion of play theory's ideal white body through their representations of the fate of exemplary whiteness itself. This is especially clear in *The Autobiography*, where the narrator's patron—"about all a man could wish to be" (121)—eventually takes his own life rather than continue his parasitic relationship with the energies of the world. But it is also evident, if less dramatically so, in *The Great Gatsby*, where leisure-class icons Tom and Daisy amount to little more than predatory particles of "foul dust" floating "in the wake" of Gatsby's dreams (2).

What neither text seems able to imagine, either literally or metaphorically, is an interracial work or leisure encounter that is not somehow manipulative or destructive.[77] Neither, that is, can in the end instantiate the hypothesis of a March 1911 editorial cartoon that appeared in the still fledgling NAACP journal, the *Crisis* (see Figure 20). Titled "Social Equality," John Henry Adams's drawing seems to argue that when African Americans and white Americans can meet in a moment of mutual repose and relaxation—instead of on opposing ends of a command performance—then blacks will have attained some measure of the social respect so long denied them. Adams pictures two older men, one white and one black, seated comfortably at a table sharing a drink and a smoke. They seem to be enjoying each other's company and may even be gently laughing together. The cartoon is not entirely uninflected by latent power relations, and indeed one might point to the white man's more generally proprietary air (he sits somewhat more comfortably in a nicer chair and appears to control the decanter from which they drink) to suggest that Adams intends a more skeptical

FIGURE 20. John Henry Adams, "Social Equality." From the *Crisis* (Mar. 1911).

reading of the relation between his drawing and its title.[78] One might even interpret the central box of matches as a small but potent marker of the ritualized burnings of black citizens that had not abated by the 1910s. And yet the black man here pictured does not appear to have come to the table in fear or subservience, or even defiance. His open mouth acknowledges that he is a speaking presence, a far cry from the dumb black body burned in *The Autobiography*. Above all, he sits with ease and meets the eyes of his white partner-in-repose on a level plane.

Yet however one reads Adams's stance toward his picture, this is precisely the type of face-to-face encounter between races that *The Great Gatsby* skirts and *The Autobiography* deflects into either a patron-performer or performer-audience relationship. The only time in Johnson's novel that this dynamic veers even metaphorically toward the one depicted in Adams's drawing occurs when the narrator tells his patron of his decision to return to the United States and they talk "for some time on music and the race question" (145). In *The Great Gatsby*, as we have seen, Nick turns the text's closest racial encounter into minstrel mockery. But this is only the most panicky of Nick's meetings with those different from himself. He condescends almost equally to immigrants (and their "foreign clamor" [91]) and to women. When Nick looks at the world he seems to encounter little more than reflections of his own stereotypes: eye-rolling blacks, obstreperous foreigners, dissembling women.

Closer to the mark of Nick's mode of perception may be another cartoon drawn not for the *Crisis* but for what was in many ways its cultural opposite: the *Princeton Tiger*. The 1917 sketch, captioned "True Democracy"—and apparently worked up from an idea by Fitzgerald himself—revisits the scene of Adams's cartoon (see Figure 21).[79] At first it appears to do so in simple parody: once again two men (one black, one white) join for drink, but in this scene they have passed out in their seats, intoxicated. Spilt beer pools on the table. Perhaps "true" democracy (or even social "equality"), the cartoon seems to smirk, involves not just sitting down at the same table but getting sloppy drunk there together—letting go of *all* one's inhibitions, as it were. The more closely one looks at the drawing, however, the more one is struck by the complexly chiastic relationship it bears to the earlier cartoon. Instead of elderly, the men are young, perhaps college students. Their mouths are not open in talk but shut in inebriate silence. In their stupor, they do not even face each other. Finally, they have switched positions: the white man is on the right, the black on the left, the latter in almost perfect mimicry of the white man's posture in Adams's drawing. But is the black man in the later cartoon, we should ask, really black? Or do his grossly stereotyped features—his giant white mouth and white eyes, his kinky hair—make him more of a caricature of imaginary blackness? Indeed, upon closer inspection this cartoon begins to resemble a drawing of one drunken white man sharing a booth with another, with the second in blackface. It comes to look, that is, like a representation of one white man's simultaneous confrontation with and denial of his own "idea" (or ideal) of blackness.[80]

The ironies here may be well beyond the artist's (or Fitzgerald's) control. And yet what this drawing may suggest is that the first step toward a "true

FIGURE 21. "True Democracy." From the *Princeton Tiger*, Mar. 17, 1917.

democracy" of social relations—*before* one sits down directly with the Other—requires confronting one's *own* "blackface" self, the self that simultaneously projects and protects one's racial prejudices. Nick has opportunities to do this in *The Great Gatsby* but never recognizes them, making the novel as much about his own failure to confront his illusions as about Gatsby's. The ex-colored man, on the other hand, attempts something like the reverse: he confronts himself in *white*face (that is the motive power of his confessional "autobiography") only to discover that whiteness has not brought him the better self that he had hoped for. What the Fitzgerald cartoon also finally suggests is that genuine "social equality" (at least between men) may ultimately need to test its energies in the public realm of exhibition and display; for in revisiting the *Crisis* drawing it signally moves the encounter from the private space of one man's dining room to the more public environment of the restaurant or pub. As the Harlem Renaissance itself would soon testify, even the most public displays may be frightfully open to misappropriation, or may hide as much as they reveal. But as Johnson's and Fitzgerald's novels attest, the penalty for the willful (or delusional) concealment of the self—whatever that self may be—is regrettably steeper than one ever imagines.

CHAPTER SIX

Public Space, Private Lives

Recreation and Re-Creation in
An American Tragedy and *Native Son*

I simply want to tell about life as it is. Every human life is intensely interesting . . . even where there are no ideals, where
there is only the personal desire to survive, the fight to win, the
stretching out of the fingers to grasp—these are the things I
want to write about—life as it is, the facts as they
exist, the game as it is played!

THEODORE DREISER, June 1907

Goddammit, look! We live here and they live there. We black
and they white. They got things and we ain't. They do things
and we can't. It's just like living in jail. Half the time I feel like
I'm on the outside of the world peeping in through
a knot-hole in the fence.

BIGGER THOMAS, *Native Son*

ONE OF THE KEENEST RISKS of writing a novel that focuses its attention on the often thwarted lives of the so-called American underclass, instead of on the trials and glories of the "higher" levels of society, is neatly allegorized near the end of Richard Wright's *Native Son* (1940). As Bigger
Thomas sits in jail reading a newspaper account of his inquest, another
man is thrust, screaming and kicking, into Bigger's cell. "Give me my papers!" he shouts at the disappearing guards. "I'll report you to the President,
you hear?" An angry novelist? No: a sociologist, determined to "publish . . .

to the whole world" his investigations into the treatment of blacks in American society. In a frenzy to tell his story, he shouts his way through the list of deliberate injustices he has uncovered, from residential redlining, to supermarket price-fixing, to discriminatory hiring. And the response of his auditors to this urgent sketch of his stolen text? The "men in other cells," Bigger observes, "began to holler":

> "Pipe down, you nut!"
> "Take 'im away!"
> "Throw 'im out!"
> "The hell with you!"[1]

Not exactly a ringing endorsement. But the fact that the shouting man actually voices many of *Native Son*'s own trenchant observations about black life in America testifies to Wright's awareness that the social novel may be met by readers with indifference, even scorn. What if no one wants to hear your story?

When Theodore Dreiser expressed in 1907 his desire to "tell about life as it is, the facts as they exist, the game as it is played," the memory of *Sister Carrie*'s near rejection by Doubleday, Page (whose editors found it "hard to believe" that the "kind of people" Dreiser wrote about would "interest the great majority of readers") was still fresh in his mind.[2] He may also already have begun to plot out his next major novel of the aspiring working class, *An American Tragedy*, since one of the murders whose details would help order its plot had just occurred the previous summer. Clyde Griffiths, of course, veritably embodies what Dreiser called "the personal desire to survive, the fight to win, the stretching out of the fingers to grasp," and it is ultimately the leisure "game" of upper-class American society that Clyde aches to play.[3] One of Dreiser's strategies for making *An American Tragedy* a compelling text is to show, with a sociologist's thoroughness, how the tragedy of Clyde's tale is in fact shaped by powerful forces at the heart of that leisure world. To do so, Dreiser's novel inserts itself into the debate percolating briskly in the 1920s over the disposition of Americans' ever-increasing surpluses of spare time, money, and energy. On the surface of this debate—in which play theorists and their collateral supporters (particularly organized religion) squared off against entertainment entrepreneurs—lay the reiterated question, What are you going to do with your leisure? But at its core were more urgent concerns; all sides were implicitly (and impatiently) asking, What kind of person are you going to be? What kind of "self" are you going to create? These are questions that Dreiser lays across Clyde's path on every step of his tragic journey, from his playless boyhood, to the eager freedoms of his teenage years, to the anxious (and lethal) fumblings of his recreational maturity.

But as Bigger Thomas's frustrated exclamation in *Native Son* ("Goddammit, look! . . . They got things and we ain't. They do things and we can't") succinctly points out, such questions assume that one has a sufficient amount of control over the shaping of that self—that one can, in other words, actually get into the "game" about which Dreiser, for example, so longed to write. All too frequently, however, black Americans were denied meaningful access to either participation or power, finding themselves, like Bigger, "on the outside of the world peeping in" (23). Thus when Wright appropriated the contours of *An American Tragedy* in crafting *Native Son*, he strategically revised Dreiser's plot to confront the racial dynamics of American leisure deemphasized, if not ignored, by his predecessor. *Native Son* argues powerfully that Dreiser's tale must be retold if we are to understand more fully the multiple lines of force that shape American character. How else to explain why one person's "game" can be another's "jail"?[4]

And yet the closer one looks at *An American Tragedy* the more one recognizes a similar critique of the assumptions underlying the play debate. Although at times Dreiser's novel appears to side with the recreation reformers—who claimed that only "wholesome" play and "right" recreation nourished the self and soul—*An American Tragedy* finds due fault with play theory's unwillingness to challenge the economic conditions that put such play out of reach for many citizens. Clyde is drawn to the "wrong" recreations in part because of his inadequate play training, but also because such recreations are the only ones widely available to him in a capitalist society that (even in boom times) keeps working wages low in the service of rising corporate profits. Thus even when Clyde does try to fit himself for more healthful leisure, he finds his opportunities sharply constrained by class boundaries. Play theory might have bemoaned the soul-crushing conditions of modern industrial labor, but it tacitly accepted the caste hierarchies of corporate capitalism. After all, as we have seen, "corporate" loyalty was play theory's highest goal. The reformers may have sought to create happier laborers, but they weren't after a worker's paradise.[5]

Thus *Native Son*'s critique of the racial segregation of leisure will in many ways second—if necessarily complicate—the class critique already mounted by Dreiser in *An American Tragedy*. Clyde kills his pregnant working-class girlfriend in a desperate attempt to free himself for the upper-class delights that seem suddenly within his grasp. Bigger kills two women—one wealthy, one poor—and in the process discovers a meaning in his life that neither his work nor his play had ever delivered. If Wright's novel is a calculated rebuke to Dreiser's, both texts nonetheless bring into sharp relief the failure of play theory to reimagine the class and race relations produced by capitalist ideology. Perhaps not surprisingly, then, both texts also make *remaking*, in all its multiple manifestations, their central imaginative concern. After all, by the 1920s, participants on all sides of the play debate recognized the recreative powers of leisure—its capacity not only to relieve stress but actually to renew and revivify. By focusing on that trope of remaking in these two texts—from Clyde's and Bigger's repeated efforts to reconstruct their lives, to Dreiser's and Wright's own imaginative reshaping of historical and sociological information into powerfully expressive forms, to Wright's urgent rewriting of *An American Tragedy*—we can clarify not only the ways in which these texts participate in the play debate but also the ways they playfully (yet in all seriousness) refashion the naturalist novel itself, particularly its range of narrative techniques.

The play debate of the 1920s—at its heart a struggle to control the very energies of the decade itself—pitted backers of the newly emerging and rapidly nationalizing leisure forms against play theorists and their followers. The motion picture and stage industries, for example, plus professional and collegiate sports concerns, spent a great deal of money urging consumers to watch their movies, plays, and athletic contests. At the same time, however, other influential groups, including recreation reformers, religious leaders, psychologists, and criminologists, denounced these events precisely because they *were* spectacles. Insisting—publicly and strenuously—that Americans participate, not spectate, these voices championed constructive play as the crucial element in proper physical, mental, and moral development. This was not an entirely new concern in the 1920s; fifty years earlier, J. E. Frobisher's *Blood and Breath* had criticized those who "gaze wearily on" while others play.[6] But in the age of consolidated corporate capitalism more was at stake. Americans spent more than 30 million dollars to attend sporting events in 1921, for example, and ten times that to see motion pictures. The entertainment industry was understandably eager that its postwar profits continue to escalate in the new decade. Watchdogs from the other side of the recreation debate viewed the rising numbers with trepidation—and no little envy. They repeatedly cautioned against the misuse of leisure, stressing in particular the presumed link between harmful amusement and juvenile delinquency. But those institutions that felt most adversely affected by the growth of popular entertainment, such as organized religion, also sought ways to gather the profits to themselves. "Leisure is the church's great undeveloped resource," declared a popular religious recreation handbook in 1922. "How can the church capture and use for Christ the spare time, money, and energy of America?"[7]

Not everyone sympathetic to the goals of the play reform movement objected so strenuously to the rise of public entertainment. Jane Addams, for example, had expressed high hopes for professional athletics as early as 1909, in *The Spirit of Youth and the City Streets*. At their best, she ventured, sporting events might encourage fellow-feeling; at the least they provided a common topic of conversation in an otherwise divisive urban environment. Intrigued by the "overwhelming outburst of kindly feeling when the favorite player makes a home run," Addams wondered, "Does not this contain a suggestion of the undoubted powers of public recreation to bring together all classes of a community in the modern city unhappily so full of devices for keeping men apart?"[8] Popular essayist H. Addington Bruce, writing in the *Outlook* in 1913, went so far as to argue that watching athletic contests could supply many of the same benefits as playing them. Baseball, for instance, was "from the spectator's standpoint" not only a safety valve for pent-up urban emotions but also a democratizing force (as classes mingled in the bleachers) and even a source of vicarious exercise—since laughing, shouting, and cheering, Bruce held, were "muscle-expanding noises."[9]

But by the 1920s such optimism appeared to many as willfully naive. Many old-stock religious groups, for example, though increasingly tolerant of both public and private recreation, deplored the proliferation of commercial amusements. The religious press in the late 1910s and early 1920s spoke with a fairly consistent voice against the terrible "sex slush" of the movies, the moral degeneracy of jazz dancing, and the professionalization of athletics. To these critics, moreover, most "modern" recreations were too passive to provide any physical benefit via spectatorship. "Two or three hours in a ball park do not take anything off the waistline or add anything to chest measurements," chastised the *Presbyterian Banner* in 1921.[10]

These attitudes were by no means inconsistent with the direction taken by the secular play reform movement in the 1920s. Prominent play theorists, educators, and sociologists provided their own data (sometimes scientific, often anecdotal) linking the improper use of leisure to immorality and delinquency: "90 per cent of the people," claimed Wilbur Bowen and Elmer Mitchell in *The Theory of Organized Play*, "need guidance of some sort for their leisure time."[11] The lack of recreation was perceived to be as dangerous as its misuse. "The dull, brutish men of today," observed George Cutten in *The Threat of Leisure* (1926), "usually look back upon a playless childhood." Confirming testimony—in the words of the Chicago Crime

Commission—will prove prophetic for Chicagoans Clyde Griffiths and Bigger Thomas: "In retracing the tortuous path of the youthful criminal it is seldom found that the trail leads back to the playground, the diamond, the athletic field, or the community center."[12] More likely, it dead-ends at a gang, the criminal manifestation of the otherwise valuable team instinct—though Clyde and Bigger, as we shall see, don't even have these support systems.

Many churches and community centers decided to do more than merely complain about the dissipating influence of contemporary amusement; they began to organize their own recreational programs. By the 1920s a number of religious denominations were devoting time and funds to the supervision of physical education classes, the outfitting of athletic teams, and even the design and construction of playgrounds. To combat the "plethora" of new leisure activities outside the church, congregations in cities like Muncie, Indiana, threw up "new batteries of clubs within."[13] They also put their stamp on more worldly recreations, such as the Boy Scout movement, whose troops were overwhelmingly church-sponsored in the 1910s and 1920s.[14] Religious organizations were thus both the most vocal and among the most active supporters of the core beliefs of play reform during the 1920s. In fact, it is in the contrast between their schemes for the decade and those of the entertainment industry, particularly the motion picture business—each competing for the same bodies at rest—that the contours of the play debate emerged most clearly.

For accompanying the financial and physical involvement of religious groups, and in most cases spurring it on, was a substantial body of church-generated literature on play that rivaled in volume and scope the secular productions of the Playground Association of America and its associates. Two of the most influential texts were William La Porte's *Handbook of Games and Programs for Church, School, and Home* and Norman Richardson's *Church at Play: A Manual for Directors of Social and Recreational Life*, both published in 1922 and reprinted throughout the decade. Together these books describe hundreds of games, point readers to additional resources (La Porte's sixty-item bibliography suggests the already heavy involvement of clergy in organizing children's play), and, most important, spell out "the principles and methods of social and recreational leadership *that are consistent with the ideals of the church.*" Richardson, professor of religious education at Northwestern University, pulls no punches in describing the importance of right recreation. "The task of training the present generation how to use its leisure," he declares at the end of his introductory chapter,

> is an undertaking, the magnitude of which cannot readily be encompassed even by the most active imagination. No generation in the history of the race . . . has had as much money, time, and energy to place at the service of the church. Resting down upon a system of mechanical, labor-saving devices, the human race is now enjoying the greatest amount of leisure that the world has yet seen. *Multitudes of people are now set aside either to make permanent contributions to this nominally Christian civilization or to lay the foundations for the most tragic and gigantic moral catastrophe that history has yet recorded.*[15]

Richardson's flair for the dramatic is matched by an eye for detail. He reports that on one Sunday morning, called to preach to a congregation whose church was "situated on a main thoroughfare," he watched (approximately) 4,300 automobiles pass by in two and a half hours, shuttling an estimated 16,000 passengers (inside, the congregation numbered only 94 souls) to unknown, and presumably ungodly, sites of leisure. And taking with them— "on that one day"—enough money to fund that church's budget for four years, and enough time and energy to carry on its program for five. Richardson may exaggerate only slightly; automobile sales indeed skyrocketed in the 1920s, and with them leisure driving.[16] Robert and Helen Lynd's *Middletown* reports a similar irritation on the part of ministers in Muncie. After all, automobile advertisements like the full-page 1924 notice for the "easy-riding" "Jewett Six" in the *Saturday Evening Post* (see Figure 22) were ever more graphically urging Americans to increase their "Week-End Touring Radius"—which typically meant skipping Sunday services altogether.[17]

In All The World No
Car Like This

Where's the fun in just driving around town?

Increase Your Week-End Touring Radius

ARE you a boulevard tourist? Do you stick to the same old familiar routes within smooth, easy distance from home? If you do, you're losing the big "kick" in motoring. For the real joys lie in the open spaces—reached in the same driving time if you have a powerful, easy-riding car.

Look at the map above. What delights await you weekly if you had a car that would make such trips as surely and as comfortably as the powerful Jewett. Perhaps you hesitate, with good reason, to attempt such longer trips with a lighter, less able car than Jewett, although it cost about what Jewett costs. But Jewett, remember, is built for hard service, high mileage, recreation without vexation.

Why Be a Concrete Crawler?

If you're going to have any fun on your week-end trips you've got to have a car that can get away from the army of concrete crawlers—take side roads comfortably.

Jewett increases your touring radius because it has big six power and performance. Think of the thrill of handling full 50 horsepower in a Paige-built motor! Sustained speed is yours, easily, quietly, safely, indefinitely!

"Big-League" Power—That's Why

You will notice Jewett's amazing power countless times daily in its quick getaway. You run around the "crawlers." Accelerate from 4 to 25 miles an hour in 7 seconds in high. You will notice Jewett's power in marvelous pulling over poor roads—in scampering up hard hills in high where most cars shift or stall. Whatever your route you breeze steadily along in Jewett, conscious always of "big-league" power.

Whatever your speed or route, comfort is yours in Jewett—comfort you never dreamed possible. Jewett weighs 2805 pounds—200 to 400 pounds more than "light" sixes. There's a 6-inch-deep frame; Paige-Timken axles, front

and rear; all-steel universal joints. Jewett is husky. Its substantial weight makes it hug the road, even at the higher speeds Jewett owners enjoy. You go farther and finish fresher because of Jewett's club-chair comfort.

All Jewett bodies are loungy. Seats are comfortable, tilted just right. Lots of legroom for the tallest. No cramped positions.

Master of Miles—$1065

Increase your touring radius. Get the real fun out of motoring—cover new ground—reach strange places. You can do it with a Jewett! Sample the open roads and the byways. Leave the city tourists behind. Thrill to the delights of rolling country. Visit that camp or lodge. Have a real demonstration in a Jewett. You'll find that, for $1065, you can be in company with splendid cars costing much more than Jewett, which are known for their easy mastery of miles. There's a Jewett dealer waiting to show you.   [404]

Touring $1065
Brougham $1325
Sedan $1495
Prices at Detroit. Tax Extra

JEWETT SIX
—PAIGE BUILT—

Coupe $1250
De Luxe Touring $1220
De Luxe Sedan $1695
Prices at Detroit. Tax Extra

FIGURE 22. "Increase Your Week-End Touring Radius."
From the *Saturday Evening Post*, July 5, 1924.

One resource of which the church took increasing advantage was the editorial space in the national monthly of the PAA, the *Playground*. That the clergy's involvement with the PAA was still something of a novelty in the early 1920s is signaled by the Rev. Charles Gillkey's insistence in his speech to the secular Recreation Congress in 1923 that a "bold committee" must have arranged his appearance.[18] But the next year church-related recreation articles appeared in the *Playground* fairly regularly. Of course the PAA's connection to "Christian" recreations extended back through cofounder Luther Gulick's years as director of the Springfield, Massachusetts, YMCA, where in 1891 he had challenged instructor James Naismith to create an indoor winter ball game for men. (The result: modern basketball.) Thus in the PAA religious leaders found an extremely compatible ally in the fight against the "spectacular" nature of movie houses and professional sports. When Jay Nash, professor of education at New York University, declared that much of commercial recreation "might better be called dissipation or wreck-reation," heads in the pulpit and on the playground nodded in assent.[19]

The faces grinning out of the film industry ad pages in magazines like the *Saturday Evening Post*, however, begged to differ. Despite a 1915 Supreme Court ruling that movies were "spectacles" (like circuses) and therefore subject to review by state boards, the popularity and profitability of the medium continued to grow.[20] By the 1920s the motion picture studios had adopted a number of effective strategies to counter the insistence that their films were a dissipative force in American life. Prominent among these was the formation in 1922 of the self-regulating Motion Picture Producers and Distributors of America (MPPDA), headed by Will Hays, who steered the industry toward "cleaner" films that turned higher profits and kept the reformers at bay. Motion picture print advertisements communicated other strategies. "Letting Yourself in for a Good Time!" proclaims the text of a 1920 Paramount Pictures ad beneath a half-page illustration of an eager family striding into a movie house (see Figure 23).

The artwork subtly stresses the active nature of movie-going: the family, drawn leaning slightly forward, is indeed "letting itself in," while other

FIGURE 23. Paramount Pictures, "Letting yourself in for a good time!"
From the *Saturday Evening Post*, Dec. 11, 1920.

patrons bustle smilingly in the background. The ad copy (rather unsubtly) emphasizes the movies' broad appeal: rather than a disruptive force, motion pictures keep families "happy" and *undivided*," even forging larger and more powerful groups ("five million strong"), much as the play reformers were trying to do. Flanking the center copy are two columns of titles of new Paramount releases, including several—such as *Sins of Rosanne*, *Her Husband's Friend*, and *The Frisky Mrs. Johnson*—that do suggest risqué subject matter. Of course, as *Middletown* points out, movie titles often "overplay[ed] the element of 'sex adventure' in a picture."[21] Nonetheless, after 1922 distributors insisted ever more loudly that their movies were "clean." "One thing you can be sure of," promised a 1924 Universal Pictures "Watch This Column" advertisement above the signature of its president, Carl Laemmle, "when you start out to see a Universal picture, you will *know* it is clean—and good. . . . You will *know* that you can take your children without fear that they will be shocked or made familiar with the world's follies before their time." And yet Universal didn't want to be perceived as too clean—or worse, too self-righteous. "Don't get the idea from what I have been writing about clean pictures, that I am a 'reformer,'" implored Laemmle in another column. "Heaven forbid! What I am really trying to do is to please the most people and to make pictures that *the whole family can see* without a single blush. So, I have instructed our directors to make clean pictures, because I am sure that's what the people really want."[22] But even industry censor Hays recognized that what many people "really wanted" to see was sex. In a letter to Laemmle in 1922 he instructed the filmmaker to produce pictures that were "passionate but pure," giving the public "all the sex it wants with compensating values for all those church and women groups." Indeed, film historians point out that despite the MPPDA's insistence that it had gone "clean," the industry still produced extremely profitable films that "visualized more sex . . . than any previous photoplays."[23]

All those "church and women groups" were probably discouraged by the steady increases in profits and patronage that the movie industry enjoyed

"Come on to the movies, Dad, you're not going to back out again, are you?"

Good eyes for good pictures

HARD to withstand those pleading, ardent eyes, the wheedling touch of that impulsive hand! You almost hate yourself for once more refusing your son's appeal to go to the movies. You have a good excuse, for the pictures make your head ache. But your family's beginning to suspect that excuse as a shabby pretext to stay home and doze.

Do you want to know the truth about your "movie head ache"? The effort required in focusing your eyes on a brilliantly lighted, ever-changing surface and the closeness with which you watch the action produce a constant nervous tension. Your enjoyment of moving pictures depends largely on your eyes. And yours are the bread-winning eyes, working all day. If any eyes in the family should not be overtaxed, they are yours.

Yet those evenings in the motion picture theatre would mean a lot to you—relaxation, freedom from worry, wholesome enjoyment. To work well, you must play well; and to play well, you must see well. Who can measure the bracing influence two hours given over to the movies has on the working hours of your life?

Make the most of your leisure hours

If you are too tired after dinner to do anything but doze in your chair, if using your eyes in the evening means dullness and depression next day, if two hours at the movies ends in a headache or eyeache, you are missing half the joy of living. Look to your eyes! The chances are that the trouble begins there.

Although you may think you see well, there is only one way to make sure. Have your eyes examined immediately.

American Optical Company Southbridge Mass U S A

for Better Eyesight
WELLSWORTH
PRODUCTS

FIGURE 24. American Optical Company, "Good eyes for good pictures." From the *Saturday Evening Post*, July 5, 1924.

after 1922. One source estimates that by the end of the decade weekly attendance had reached 90 million, with yearly receipts approaching three quarters of a billion dollars.[24] Reformers may also have been discouraged by the increasing interpenetration of the movies with other "spectacular" American industries. Professional sports figures, for example, such as Christy Mathewson and Jack Dempsey, began to appear in films, which themselves featured athletic actors like Fairbanks. In the same *Post* issue as Laemmle's antireformer statement one even finds an ad for Wellsworth Products, makers of their own "spectacles"—namely, eyeglasses. The large photograph features a smiling boy trying to pull his tired father away from the evening newspaper and out to the movies (see Figure 24). Mom stands next to her son, dressed and ready to go. Dad, the copy tells us, is backing out because he gets "movie headache." The problem is not the movies, however; more likely it's Dad's eyes, which the ad encourages him to have examined "immediately." And all because, it tells Dad, "those evenings in the motion picture theatre would mean a lot to you—relaxation, freedom from worry, wholesome enjoyment. To work well, you must play well; and to play well, you must see well. Who can measure the bracing influence two hours given over to the movies has on the working hours of your life?"

■

To Clyde Griffiths's street-missionary parents in *An American Tragedy*, the movies were far from "bracing"—"motion pictures," Asa and Elvira felt, were "not only worldly, but sinful."[25] Clyde's first premeditated "rebellion"—and essentially his first assertion of self—is to sneak off to the theater or the picture shows with his younger brother Frank. One senses that their parents' religious beliefs have prevented Clyde and his siblings from any sort of recreation, even the type that playground reformers (and increasingly, as we have seen, religious leaders) would classify as beneficial. The itinerant Griffithses are of course "always 'hard up'" (9) and thus unable to provide even rudimentary play equipment for their children. Yet in its travels through the country the family has stopped at enough major cities—"Detroit, Milwaukee, Chicago, lastly Kansas City" (14)—to have encountered the play movement's burgeoning facilities, so it is likely parental disapproval, not merely lack of funds, that makes the twelve-year-old Clyde feel "deprived of many comforts and pleasures which seemed common enough to others" (9). Even adults remark that Clyde seems "outa place" (11)—no doubt he belongs elsewhere, doing what "other boys" in the city do: namely, play. The first time we notice Clyde in the novel he is in fact demonstrably restless, moving "from one foot to the other" (9), a sure sign, the social psychologists would say, that he yearns to fulfill his play needs. And yet Clyde's parents—Asa the weak father in particular—are "in no way sufficiently equipped" to help him (19).[26]

Asa and Elvira do not even recognize the value of keeping the children in school and thus limit Clyde's exposure to another important source of supervised play. Under the influence of the "new psychology" of William James, G. Stanley Hall, and particularly John Dewey, American schools after the turn of the century had begun to emphasize physical education and organized play "for teaching intellectual awareness and moral and social behavior."[27] And Clyde's informal play does not make up for these lacks. Ashamed to bring others to the family's rooms in the mission, Clyde "had always avoided boy friends," preferring to play "very much alone—or with his brother and sisters" (30). To social behaviorist George Herbert Mead, Clyde's infrequent and typically solitary play, coupled with the discomfort he feels toward his family's "mission," would seriously affect the young boy's ability to shape a coherent identity. "One has to be a member of a community to be a self," Mead insisted in his lectures at the University of Chicago in the 1920s. "Only in so far as he takes the attitudes of the organized social group to which he belongs . . . does he develop a complete self or possess the sort of complete self he has developed."[28] In the terminology of the play theorists, Clyde's avoidance of group play stifles the "wholesome" development of his "gang instinct," necessary for both social adaptation and "social morality."[29] Betwixt and between his family and peers (but connected to neither), Clyde has perhaps willfully joined only one group: the community of movie patrons—a community, ironically, of individuals who largely avoid interaction.

It is only when Clyde becomes a bellboy in a Kansas City hotel that he joins a bona fide community in Mead's sense, though the self he eventually shapes in that community would have met with the play reformers' grave disapproval. After his initial distaste for the "libertinism and vice" (54) of the other bellboys shades "by degrees" (55) into "the delight of personal freedom," Clyde can finally "sniff the air of personal and delicious romance" (57). He carves out an increasingly guilt-free "play" sphere by lying to his mother about his hours and pay, and in his free time dives enthusiastically not just into the world of recreation but into a project of self re-creation through play. What Clyde fails to realize is how unprepared he is to face the challenges of his new recreational life and how constrained his actual choices are. Moreover, the reformers would say, his poor play background practically guarantees that he will choose unwisely.

He does. Clyde's recreational desires quickly focus neither on wholesome group play nor on communal entertainment but on the costly "adventure" of sex: "He must find a free pagan girl of his own somewhere . . . and spend his money on her," Clyde resolves (70). That girl materializes as Hortense Briggs, the pretty yet manipulative shop clerk who turns out to be free in virtually no sense of the word. In addition to exciting (but also frustrating) Clyde's sexual desire, Hortense also makes him angrily aware that he lacks certain rudimentary leisure skills. When Clyde first meets Hortense she is on her way to a "mostly dancing" party; because Clyde doesn't dance, however, she treats him with indifference. "Why hadn't he gone to a dancing school before this?" Clyde asks himself. "To think that this girl, to whom of all those here he was most drawn, could dismiss him and his dreams and desires thus easily, and all because he couldn't dance. And his accursed home training was responsible for all this. He felt broken and cheated" (76).

Determined to make up for this intense feeling of "deprivation" (79),

Clyde spends more and more time, money, and energy pursuing Hortense and having "a good time" (96)—all at the expense of family, as he ignores his mother's pleas for money to help his sister Esta through her pregnancy. These misplaced priorities come to a disastrous head in the winter automobile excursion that closes Book One. Ten young adults, Clyde among them, motor out of Kansas City to "the Wigwam," where they dance to "The Grizzly Bear" and slide energetically about on the frozen river. Though angered by Hortense's flirting with someone else, Clyde enjoys the heterosocial horseplay out on the ice. But he soon fears—as though Hortense had all along been only a prize in a game he was playing—that "he was not to win her after all" (136). Only artful attentions from Hortense (still hoping that Clyde will buy her a $125 coat) and the "very agreeable illusion" (136) that she will soon offer Clyde the "ultimate condescension on her part" (107) soothe his anxiety. But that illusion is both literally and figuratively wrecked when on their return to the city the partygoers run over a little girl and flip the car; Clyde is forced to flee the scene in fear, ironically, for his freedom.

Dreiser's staging of the last scenes of Book One suggest a writer aware of both the dynamics of urban play and the rough contours of the play debate. Consider the elements he brings grimly together. On the one hand he offers a "gang" (145) of dissolute youth who, by driving at "break-neck speed" (137) after a day of dancing, drinking, and "spooning" in what is essentially a stolen car, resemble the delinquents that reformers were warning America about. One of the "gang" (not surprisingly, Hortense) is made up "in imitation of some picture beauty she had seen," indicating the influence of the movies on her appearance and, suggestively, her values (125). When the accident occurs, Hortense, in a "selfish panic" about her bleeding face (142), leaves without bothering to help anyone else. On the other hand, Dreiser offers a nine-year-old girl who, "running toward the [street] crossing, jump[s] directly in front of the moving machine" (138)—a death that dramatically reenacts a type of violent collision common enough in the 1910s and 1920s to prompt newspaper editorials against careless drivers and

FIGURE 25. Cyclone Fence Company, "The Safe Playground."
From the *Playground* (Nov. 1923).

anguished calls from playground reformers for fenced play spaces in the urban environment.[30] Indeed, one 1923 advertisement for chain link fence in the *Playground* could serve as an illustration for this very scene: it pictures a little girl dashing into the street, about to be struck by a large, dark, speeding car (see Figure 25). Dreiser also seems well aware of the ways that these events frustrate Clyde's first serious attempt to remake himself. The accident forces Clyde to leave Kansas City, where he has tried to rise in the world primarily on the strength of new clothes and new modes of play. But, as Dreiser implies, Clyde's new recreations have not proved particularly satisfying; he has still never truly experienced the power of leisure to renew, re-vivify, or re-create. And that lack, the novel seems to suggest, leaves Clyde critically ill-equipped for the struggles that lie ahead. Clyde's failure in Book One, then, is a prophetic one. For when the young man who is crawling away from Kansas City on his hands and knees—"to lose himself," we are told (145)—attempts to re-create himself through leisure once again in Book Two, he will seek essentially the same paths as before, and meet an even harsher fate.

■

For a while, at least, Clyde tries to make better choices. Meeting up in Chicago with another of the Kansas City refugees, he lands a job as a bell-hop at the Union League Club. Clyde is fascinated by the club, an all-male, upper-class leisure preserve where the members "came and went, singly as a rule, and with the noiseless vigor and reserve that characterizes the ultra successful" (169). This is Clyde's first intimate look at how the top of society recreates, and it is instructive. In stark contrast to Clyde, these men are not only "quick, alert, incisive" (171) but "self-integrated and self-centered" (168). They seem, moreover, to be wholly unaffected by "passion." Clyde feels different when he is in the club: "more subdued, less romantic, more practical." And he senses an opportunity to remake himself. By working "very steadily" and making "only the right sort of contacts," Clyde hopes he might turn careful observation into purposeful action. But this seems unlikely, we are quickly told. Clyde is the type "not destined to grow up"; he lacks both "mental clarity" and the "inner directing application" that permits others "to sort out from the facts and avenues of life the particular thing or things that make for their direct advancement" (169).

Play theorists of Dreiser's day would have found the narrator's analysis of Clyde's lacks entirely compatible with their view of the importance of childhood play and particularly team sports. "It is the ability to make . . . judgments rapidly and accurately which makes the successful person both in society and in business," asserted Henry Curtis in *Education Through Play*, "and it is just this type of judgment which play everywhere trains." Curtis's central example (like Mead's in his Chicago lectures) is baseball, where over and over a participant must make a decision "in a quarter of a second and act upon that decision instantly or he will never make a successful ball player"—or, by extension, a successful businessperson.[31] Bowen and Mitchell's analysis of "Play Experience as the Basis of the Higher Mental Processes," to take another example, glosses Clyde's "immature mind" and his lack of "mental clarity" particularly well:

> The play life, which is the natural life in the tender years of childhood, is the way to acquire plentiful experiences. . . . The wider the range of concrete experiences in the developing manhood or womanhood, the greater the power for *clear image making*, for judgment making, and for building up an individual philosophy; and, in consequence, the richer the intellect in *maturity*.[32]

Clyde won't grow up, then, not because he can't stop "playing" but because he never learned how to play—and thus to image himself "clearly"—in the first place.

A chance encounter with his uncle Samuel Griffiths pulls Clyde from Chicago to upstate New York, where he takes an entry-level job in the uncle's collar factory. The combination of a new job, a new location, and new family connections gives Clyde hope that he might at last be in a position to lift himself "up" both in his work and in his play. But his work is bor-ing; the town is dull; and what play there is, Clyde soon discovers, is rigidly segregated by class. "There are a lot of cheap dance halls around here," explains Dillard, Clyde's more experienced boardinghouse companion, "but I never go to any of those. You can't do it and keep in with the nice people. This is an awfully close town that way. . . . You have to 'belong' or you can't go out anywhere at all" (197–98). Clyde hopes that the dinner invitation he finally receives from the Griffithses will grant him the very highest insider status; but his relatives—who believe firmly that "one had to have castes," at work and in play (176)—do not "take him up"; they leave him instead to face his first small-town summer on his own.

Cut off from leisure-class enjoyments and unwilling to continue his association with the likes of Dillard, Clyde is further restricted by his new position in the factory as the head of the stamping room. Although his new job brings Clyde into contact with a number of women his own age, company policy forbids social interaction between a foreman and his charges. No play—particularly of the sexual sort—may be allowed to interfere with the business at hand. As Clyde's cousin Gilbert coldly informs him: "If a young man, or an old one for that matter, comes in here at any time and imagines that because there are women here he's going to be allowed to play about and neglect his work and flirt or cut up, that fellow is doomed to a short stay here." These prohibitions extend outside the factory as well. "We hear anything about it," Gilbert warns, and "that man or woman is done for so far as we are concerned" (232). Accepting the arrangement, Clyde finds himself lonelier than ever. His leisure time is largely given to solitary, passive activities, such as movie watching, or obscuring himself "as an ordinary spectator" to watch town beauty Sondra Finchley and the rest of the leisured upper-class youth participate in the city's annual "automobile floral parade and contest" (236).

Although on the one hand Dreiser here seems (once again) to criticize Clyde for his passive play, on the other he has little patience for those who preach the gospel of right recreation while simultaneously reinforcing class exclusions. Dreiser's depiction of Clyde's eventual summer romance with

Roberta Alden, for example—who, as one of Clyde's employees in the stamping room, is just as forbidden to him by class as someone like Sondra—dramatizes the stifling effects of small-town snobbery and particularly "middle class religious" (195) mores on working-class leisure. Roberta's recreational options are even more circumscribed than Clyde's. As an unmarried female boarder with a "religious and narrow" family (271), Roberta discovers that "dancing or local adventurous gayety, such as walking the streets or going to a moving picture theater—was . . . taboo" (250). Even at the local church socials—the only acceptable recreations for someone like Roberta—she finds herself ignored (she is not, after all, of the right social station) and thereby cut off from the "entertainment and diversion which was normally reaching those who were of [her] same church but better placed" (250). Roberta's lack of opportunity for satisfying leisure makes her a well-matched double for Clyde. Dreiser seems acutely aware of this connection, not only in bringing the two together at Crum Lake (where each has gone seeking diversion) but also in guiding their relationship to its final tragedy. As Dreiser himself explained in a 1925 essay written a few months before the release of the novel, even in a country as successful as America, tragedy is "always at hand. For while a nation, of which the individual is a part, may be and often is a huge success, it does not follow that he is so. Amid the plenty of the nation the individual may well starve. Amid the seemingly unbounded resources for the entertainment for the many he still may be wretchedly unhappy, alone, and devoid of that which entertains him."[33]

To this end, Book Two verifies *Middletown's* observation that despite a general increase in leisure opportunities in small-town America, conservative forces were striving to restrict these new forms through both social and civic regulation. In Lycurgus, for example, as in Muncie, there is little approved public space to which a young unmarried couple like Clyde and Roberta can repair. Youths of more means, of course, were not equally affected; access to an automobile, in particular, enabled couples to create private space within the public environment. Clyde and Roberta meet, by accident, in the acceptable public space of Crum Lake, although both worry about the potential impropriety of being alone in a canoe together. When they try to maintain a relationship in Lycurgus—a desire complicated by their need for secrecy—they are stymied from the beginning. They cannot meet at either boardinghouse and must settle for a stolen hour or two in which they walk out past the end of Roberta's street where there are "no houses" (269). The tenuousness (and uselessness) of their one memorable escape to a "pleasure park" in another town, where Clyde feels that "at last he had her all to himself unseen, and she him," is underscored by Dreiser's depiction of the park as a "fragile, gimcrack scene" (278, 279). Indeed, one might argue that Dreiser re-creates for Clyde and Roberta only in the narrative's rich landscape of internal monologue the private space that Lycurgus denies them. The intensive interiority, or "private" expanse, of Book Two is perhaps best read as Dreiser's way of supplying what "real life" did not.

What the "real life" of Lycurgus does provide is a collision of social and recreational economies that will crush both Clyde and Roberta, whose relationship changes dramatically when the summer ends. Once the "out-of-door resorts which . . . had provided diversion" close (288), Clyde and Roberta's play necessarily (if riskily) shifts indoors to more private, and increasingly sexual, recreation. At the same time, however, Clyde is suddenly swept into the very public club activities of Lycurgus's upper-class youth when Sondra Finchley, mistaking Clyde for his cousin Gilbert, invites him into her automobile one evening. Intrigued by Clyde's good looks and his obvious desire, Sondra initially "take[s] him up" as a "prank" (310, 311). But Clyde, as thrilled by his new social status as though he had won "the bays of victory" (354), finally sees an opportunity to re-create himself as a "Lycurgus Griffiths" (205). He pours himself into the hard work of social climbing, attending with Sondra the dinners, dances, and automobile excursions that the local society pages then chronicle in every detail. Clyde tries in particular to "fit himself athletically" for Sondra's world once he realizes that "the one subject that not only fascinated, but even excited" her is "everything out-of-doors" (328, 327). But just as Clyde begins to inch away from Roberta, with whom he has continued to "play" in private, her pregnancy—the inevitable outcome of their circumscribed pleasures let loose—makes their separation (for Clyde) at once more urgent and more difficult.

Clyde's fumbling attempts to solve the problem of Roberta's pregnancy are made more tragic by his own precariously constructed social position. Cut off by design from potentially knowledgeable but socially undesirable individuals like Dillard and by embarrassment from the well-connected young men in his new circle, Clyde has absolutely no idea how to arrange the abortion that might have been had, Dreiser hints, for the right price. Struggling on their own, Clyde and Roberta are fittingly thwarted by the same "solemn, cautious, moral, semi-religious" (397) people whose conservatism regarding public leisure in some ways precipitated Roberta's pregnancy. By the following summer, once the abortion appears out of the question, Clyde's poorly trained imagination (which seems capable of conceptualizing routes of action only in a debased language of play) takes over. First he considers staging "some possible fake or mock marriage such as he had seen in some melodramatic movie" so that by pretending to marry Roberta he might leave himself "free" for Sondra, who has also come to love him (423). Finally he decides to re-create a boating accident that he reads about in the paper, thinking to drown either Roberta *or* Sondra in the act. Here the ironies of the class segregation of leisure multiply: first, Clyde quickly picks Roberta, because she "could not swim," while "Sondra could swim so well" (440); next, Clyde's own ability to perform the "work" of murder will depend on his opportune practice the previous summer of swimming, diving, and canoeing; and finally, the event that at last pushes him over the "border-line . . . between reason and unreason" (450) is the weekend of endless play that he spends with Sondra, reveling in the upperclass games that betokened "Summertime—leisure—warmth—color—ease—beauty—love—all that he had dreamed of the summer before, when he was so very much alone" (445). In the end, Clyde is driven to murder to preserve the new leisure-class identity he believes is in his reach: with his "poorly balanced" (463) thoughts on Sondra and the recreations of her caste, Clyde lures Roberta to the private expanse of a public lake, where the clumsy job of killing may be done.

■

Unable in either Book One or Book Two to shape a self wholly commensurate with his desires, in Book Three—on trial for Roberta's murder—Clyde faces a bewildering array of identities, personalities, and histories that are shaped for him by others. In the process, the novel shifts attention from recreations to re-creations, and from the tennis court to the criminal court. Class assumptions, appropriately, underlie many of these reconstructed identities. Newspapers around the country, for example, characterize Clyde as "a respected member of Lycurgus smart society" (620), an inaccurate assessment of his social standing but a fair reflection of opinion in Cataraqui County—if not also ironically close to Clyde's own class fantasy. Prosecuting attorney Mason also depicts Clyde misleadingly as a "bearded man" with an "important position" and "more social and educational advantages" than any of the jurors (641–42), yet at the same time as a preying "wolf" and a cold-blooded killer (646). Clyde's own lawyers sift through a series of possible Clydes and matching defenses before settling on one: the "mental and moral" coward who kills Roberta accidentally (669).

If this sudden surfeit of identities is not in Clyde's control, it is nonetheless firmly in Dreiser's, as are the seemingly endless repetitions of Book Three. Far from tedious recapitulation, as critics have charged, these insistent reenactments—from the replotting of Clyde and Roberta's actions at Big Bittern Lake, to the rereading of Roberta's letters, to the retelling of "the short but straitened story of [Clyde's] youth" (673)—suggest a writer shrewdly aware, for example, that a murder trial in a backwoods county is in its own way a form of public entertainment, its onlookers thirsty for every re-created detail. To this end, Dreiser imbues the trial with the at-

mosphere of a play or motion picture. "We're going to have quite an audience," one of Clyde's lawyers remarks. "A lot of country people come to
town to see a show" (632). In court, Mason delivers his preliminary arguments "as if some one had suddenly exclaimed: 'Lights! Camera!'" (639),
and throughout the trial each attorney strives for "striking and dramatic
presentation" (665). Like an actor, Clyde gives answers that he has memo-
rized; Mason comments in whispered asides on the excellent "stage play" of
the defense (680). And the sensation-starved locals—who can buy (along
with "'Peanuts!' 'Popcorn!' 'Hot dogs!'") "the great plot" of Clyde's story
outside the courtroom for a quarter (630)—hang on every word. Dreiser's
own presentation of the proceedings verges on absolute dramatization, as
the narrative voice is squeezed to the margins by the testimony itself.

In borrowing that testimony from sensational reports of the trial in the
New York World rather than verbatim accounts from the courtroom, Dreiser
further signals his interest in giving Book Three not just a dramatic presentation but an entertaining, even playful one. By working from the intentionally melodramatic *World*, in other words, Dreiser seems less concerned with turning fact into fiction (or into more grist for his naturalist
mill) than in engineering a narrative spectacle of class relations—a spectacle, moreover, not simply imbued with the atmosphere of a play or a movie
but conveying the very energy and movement of such productions.[34] This
desire for filmic intensity infiltrates the very language of the novel. In particular, Dreiser's deliberate and unusual use of present participles in place
of main verbs gives his text what film historian Terry Ramsaye called in
1926 the "present progressive" feel of "kinetic, motion pictorial journalism"—and also helps us reappraise Dreiser's long-standing reputation as the
stylistic oaf of American letters.[35] The essence of this kind of writing, as of
the movies themselves, according to Ramsaye, is "this same principle: a picture of movement, always on and on."[36] By shifting from the perfect tense
to the present participle, Dreiser can play with sentence forms to emphasize
the cinematic energy and immediacy of certain actions, as in this description of Clyde's paradisiacal weekend of athletics with Sondra:

The next morning, true to her promise, there was the canter to Inspiration Point, and that before seven—Bertine and Sondra in bright red riding coats and white breeches and black boots, their hair unbound and loose to the wind, and riding briskly on before for the most part; then racing back to where he was. Or Sondra halloing gayly for him to come on, or the two of them laughing and chatting a hundred yards ahead in some concealed chapel of the aisled trees where he could not see them. (447)

The first sentence gradually accelerates (as if to keep pace with the horses) toward "riding briskly" and "racing back," pauses for a moment at the period, then canters on again through "halloing" to "laughing" and "chatting." Later in the paragraph, when the participles shift to Clyde, they convey both urgent activity and an ironic and frustrating suspension—as though Clyde, trapped between Sondra and Roberta, were mentally running in place: "And Clyde thrilling, and yet brooding too—by turns—occasionally—and in spite of himself drifting back to the thought that the item in the paper had inspired—and yet fighting it—trying to shut it out entirely" (447). Here the participial strategy deftly conveys Clyde's central trap in the novel: caught between an intense desire to act and an equally powerful indecisiveness, he is broodingly incapable of choosing how to act—and thus, in an important sense, who to be.[37]

During the trial scenes Dreiser relies on this participial technique more and more frequently, often structuring a series of events to read as though the narrative observer is himself describing what a motion picture camera might have recorded. Consider, for example, the account of the close of the prosecution's case:

And at points in the reading, Mason himself crying, and at their conclusion turning, weary and yet triumphant, a most complete and indestructible case, as he saw it, having been presented, and exclaiming: "The People rest." And at that moment, Mrs. Alden, in court with her husband and Emily, and overwrought, not only by the long strain of the trial but this particular evidence, uttering a whimpering yet clear cry and then falling forward in a faint. And Clyde, in his own overwrought condition, hearing her cry and seeing her fall, jumping up—the restraining hand of Jephson instantly upon him. . . . (663)

The sequence is both a cinematic rendering in prose of an emotional moment in the trial and—particularly in the movements of Mrs. Alden and Clyde (she falls forward; he, "hearing her cry and seeing her fall," jumps up)—a symbolic restaging of the climactic scene between Clyde and Roberta in the boat. And the effect on the "audience" of this kinetic tableau—this doubly moving picture—is telling: the courtroom onlookers are "as moved and incensed against Clyde . . . as though, then and there, he had committed some additional crime" (663). Thus in a real sense Dreiser creates for both readers and characters the dramatic and entertaining spectacle of Clyde on trial. Even where the text is most serious, then, it is also "at play."

Movies are not the only popular form whose playfully spectacular energies Dreiser appropriates to express Clyde's tale. The genre of the boys' book, which sold in the millions through the early century, is another such form. Critics have in fact long suggested that *An American Tragedy* is structured as an ironic inversion of the Horatio Alger myth: like an Alger hero, Clyde struggles by dint of honesty and hard work to rise from poverty to wealth, only to fail bitterly. The argument seems sensible; Dreiser himself was a boy during Alger's heyday. But *Clyde's* boyhood is distinctly not in the Alger period—the best-selling boys' tales at the turn of the century were Gilbert Patten's stories of Frank Merriwell, the morally and athletically virtuous Yalie. And while Clyde certainly seeks to rise from rags to riches, his deepest desire is to approximate the social standing of his cousin Gilbert Griffiths, the Merriwellian icon of Dreiser's novel. It is not the money Clyde wants, one might say, but the leisure it makes possible. Like Merriwell, Gilbert is the product of elite schooling and exudes "gentility, manliness, athletic proficiency, and financial success."[38] Both could be poster boys for the recreation reform movement, ideal play leaders in their own right. "Think of being such a youth, having so much power at one's command!" marvels Clyde (218).

Gilbert's power, the narrative makes clear, is a result of his active, "innate" "force" (216). Clyde is "neat, alert, [and] good-looking" (172), but in comparison with Gilbert is also more passive, "more soft and vague and fumbling," "undoubtedly lacking" the very qualities of "force and energy" needed to get ahead in the world (216). As others have noted, Clyde is also "less athletic and physically effectual" than his real-life models Chester Gillette and Roland Molineux.[39] Thus one irony of Clyde's attempt to emulate the Merriwell hero (and not the Alger protagonist) is Clyde's physical incapacity for the role, since Merriwell's power—his seemingly inborn ability to lead other young men—is derived from "his total mastery on the athletic field."[40] As the narrator of *Frank Merriwell at Yale* (1903) puts it, "there was not the least suggestion of anything soft or effeminate about him."[41] A further irony, deliberately cultivated by Dreiser, is that Gilbert himself fails in other crucial respects to meet the standards of Patten's ideal. Gilbert's vigor and force, for example, are undercut by a snide condescension and a nasty streak of jealousy more befitting a Merriwell foe than a Merriwell hero. If the novel in part faults Clyde for his misspent recreations, it turns out to have few kind words for the character in the novel that play theory would largely have admired. Clyde thus aspires, in the end, to a debased model, as perhaps emphasized by how far he falls. For instead of evolving through his play into a "Lycurgus Griffiths," Clyde—whom Mason melodramatically denounces as a "quadruple-dyed villain" (665)—comes finally to inhabit not the Merriwell ideal but the same lowly space as the "ruffian" or "scapegrace" that the leisure-class hero typically duels.

■

In Richard Wright's powerful rewriting of Clyde's story in *Native Son*, Bigger Thomas comes to represent an even darker-hued villain, a black "fiend" (346) whose own crimes of murder, prosecuting attorney Buckley proclaims, are "steeped and dyed with repellent contagion!" (373). But Bigger, unlike Clyde, is decidedly not perceived as "soft and vague and fumbling" by his captors. He is instead, in their eyes, the very incarnation of a violent, almost bestial force, his five-foot, nine-inch body giving "the impression of . . . abnormal physical strength" (260). This perception, of course, makes Bigger's tale no more susceptible to a Merriwellian reading than Clyde's. Despite his physical vigor, as a member of the urban black "underclass" Bigger has even less of a chance of playing the role of boys' book hero than his fictional white predecessor does. More to the point, despite Bigger's own urgent if inchoate yearnings to shape a meaningful self through both his work and his free time, Wright's protagonist faces an even more noxiously constricted world of choices than Dreiser's fumbling lead.

This is not to argue that Wright's novel is necessarily a more deterministic text than Dreiser's. It is rather to emphasize that the play debate within whose contours we have been situating Clyde had additional implications for African Americans. When play reformers encouraged people to visit parks and playgrounds instead of vaudeville and motion picture houses, for example, there were very few such "wholesome" public facilities to which black Americans could go, because lines of race were drawn even more tightly around leisure than lines of class. Although "public recreation facilities are needed by all," complained an *Opportunity* editorial in 1924, "they are especially needed by Negroes, who as a rule can get no recreation except the expensive and often degrading commercialized kind." At mid-decade— some forty years after the first sand-garden playground had been opened in Boston—the PAA's *Normal Course in Play* could honestly admit that it was "only comparatively recently that communities have felt any large degree of responsibility for organizing for the leisure of colored children and adults."[42]

Indeed, the PAA was exceedingly slow in recognizing the recreational needs of blacks. Before the 1920s African Americans appeared only infrequently, for example, in issues of the *Playground*. When an article did purport to address meaningful black play, such as T. S. Settle's 1916 "Recreation for Negroes in Memphis," it not infrequently betrayed a deeper interest in productive black labor. Though offered as a profile of William Jones, a successful black administrator of African American play facilities, in its final paragraphs the article makes a telling shift from recreation to domestic labor. Settle concludes by praising the social service department founded by Jones at a local black college, where he helps train young men and women to "earn a living by working for the white people of the city." It is this work, not Jones's play efforts, that most impresses Settle, because Jones is not only "helping to fit [these young people] for practical service in life," but also providing "a number of excellent servants for the community." With this training, "every negro child . . . can grow to adult age with a physical and mental equipment which will enable it to take its place in the struggle for existence with a fighting chance." Besides the depersonalizing pronoun "it" that Settle chooses to represent every black child, the implication that domestic service is the appropriate "place" for blacks to "take"—and that this is the real value of "Recreation for Negroes in Memphis"—indicates both the limits of the play movement's racial progressivism and the ideological consonance of play theory's vision of leisure with capitalist configurations of race and class.[43]

When the PAA finally began to pay more sustained attention to black play needs in the mid-1920s, the organization's ideological focus shifted perceptibly from service to segregation. Judging from the "Program Planning" chapter of *The Normal Course in Play*, for example, if blacks were to be encouraged to play, it would be at "colored social centers with trained colored leaders and . . . other facilities made possible by the initiative of the colored citizens"—effectively isolating black playing bodies from white ones.[44] T. S. Settle, addressing the 1924 Recreation Congress in Atlantic City, argued that the segregated public school system offered "a very fine analogy" for the development of American playgrounds. Play practitioners in particular, he felt, needed to keep in mind that they cannot fight "all the battles of the colored race." Advised Settle: "Now if you want to start recreation, start recreation—that is an awfully big job." But "we are not talking about social life and segregation and the legal rights and everything else," he warned. "We are talking about the recreation of the colored people."[45]

And yet as any black member of Settle's audience would have known, recreation already inextricably involved the "social life and segregation and the legal rights" of African Americans. As Elliott Rudwick has noted, the tremendous migration of blacks to the North beginning in the 1910s exacerbated existing inadequacies not only in jobs, housing, and transportation, but in recreation as well. Indeed, disputes over black access to "public parks, playgrounds, or bathing beaches . . . controlled by whites" often ignited more widespread, violent conflict.[46] The "red summer" of 1919 offered a vivid case in point. On a hot Chicago Sunday in July, a race riot erupted after an argument over the use of a white beach resulted in the drowning of an African American boy whose raft had drifted too close to rock-throwing whites. In the nearly full week of rioting that followed, approximately twenty-three blacks and fifteen whites were killed, and more than 500 people were injured. According to St. Clair Drake and Horace Cayton's 1945 study, *Black Metropolis*—for which Richard Wright himself wrote the introduction—youthful white gangs from "so-called athletic clubs" raided the black community "with the tacit approval of the ward politicians who sponsored them."[47] It would indeed be hard not to see embodied in such a conflict—particularly the belligerent perversion of the age's interest in recreation expressed by the race-baiting "athletic clubs"—what T. S. Settle had dismissively called "all the battles of the colored race." For African Americans at least, recreation was never as socially innocent a pastime as some wanted to imagine it.

■

Wright himself had already imagined the deadly seriousness of African American recreation in "Big Boy Leaves Home," an important precursor text for *Native Son*. The first story in Wright's 1938 collection, *Uncle Tom's Children*, "Big Boy Leaves Home" explicitly recalls the underlying tensions of the 1919 Chicago riot. Four African American teenagers in an unnamed southern town decide to go for a swim in a local creek. Although they are aware that the site is off limits to blacks—"Yuh know ol man Harvey don erllow no niggers t swim in this hole," says one of the boys—after looking "carefully in all directions," they strip off their clothes and dive in. Enjoying the water, the boys wish that they didn't have to steal such pleasures. "The white folks got plenty swimmin pools," observes one, "n we ain got none." After tiring of their swim, they lie drying in the sun and talk bravely of what they would do if "ol man Harveyd come erlong right now." Old man Harvey doesn't show, but to the teenagers' confusion his son's fiancée suddenly does. Not quite knowing what to do—and lacking their clothes, beside which the white woman stands—the four boys decide to retrieve their belongings and leave. But their running toward the white woman frightens her, and her panicked screams bring Harvey's son Jim, who shoots two of the boys dead before Big Boy wrestles the rifle away and kills Jim himself. Thus what had begun as a playful summer episode quickly turns, on the imputed threat posed by naked black bodies to a southern white woman, into a murderous rampage. Big Boy and his surviving friend Bobo flee the scene, but the white townspeople eventually catch Bobo and tar, feather, and burn him while Big Boy looks on in horror. The next morning Big Boy escapes the mob by sneaking out of town in another friend's delivery truck and heading north to Chicago.[48]

In some ways *Native Son*'s Bigger Thomas is an older version of Big Boy, grown yet bigger. Having come to Chicago himself after experiencing a parallel instance of race violence (Bigger tells Jan Erlone and Mary Dalton that his father "got killed in a riot when I was a kid—in the South" [74]), Bigger shares Big Boy's acute sense of the unequal distribution of American resources. Whites "got things and we ain't," Bigger complains to his friend Gus (23). "They own the world" (25).[49] After five years in Depression-era Chicago, however—where (as in the rest of the country) economic hard times landed hardest on African Americans, in play as in work—Bigger feels this imbalance more deeply and more broadly than young Big Boy lamenting the lack of black swimming holes. Twenty-year-old Bigger knows that white "ownership" restricts his options for both leisure and labor, denying him not merely more opportunities to recreate (or even just a decent chance to earn a living) but more perniciously, the very possibility of doing something—*anything*—that would give him a fuller sense of what it means actually to live. "Goddammit!" Bigger shouts aloud in frustration. "They don't let us do *nothing*" (22). With only a fleeting awareness of what it is he might do in the absence of a color line ("I could fly one of them things if I had a chance," he tells Gus, pointing to a passing airplane [20]), Bigger's days oscillate between "indifference and violence; periods of abstract brooding and periods of intense desire; moments of silence and moments of anger—like water ebbing and flowing from the tug of a far-away, invisible force" (31).

The play reformers would have tried to reroute these almost schizophrenic energies into the soothing orbit of a supervised recreational experience or indeed the character-building circuit of a full-time job. But Wright firmly forecloses either possibility for Bigger even before the accidental death of Mary Dalton. Although there is, for example, a "South Side Boys' Club," its meager ping-pong tables (provided by none other than Mary's philanthropist father) fail to keep Bigger out of trouble.[50] Indeed, the club is where he and his friends "planned most of [their robbery] jobs" (329). These "jobs," moreover, are considerably more satisfying to Bigger than the scraps offered him by the state welfare agency. "He could take the job at Dalton's and be miserable," Bigger reflects, "or he could refuse it and starve. It maddened him to think that he did not have a wider choice of action" (16). The so-called "relief job" (32), Wright suggests, will do nothing to relieve the intense pressures of Bigger's internal desires.

Longing "for a stimulus powerful enough to focus his attention and drain off his energies" (30), Bigger turns not to relief work or ping-pong but to the only resources left: commercialized leisure and his own imagination. He and Gus, for example, like to "play 'white'" (21). Their mockingly serious impersonations of investment bankers, the president of the United States, and his Cabinet ("I bet that's *just* the way they talk," declares Gus) do provide moments of relief, as the two young men "[bend] double, laughing" (22). But Bigger is also bent double in pain at the distance between himself and the white figures he mocks. "I just can't get used to it," Bigger says. "I swear to God I can't. I know I oughtn't think about it, but I can't help it" (22–23). Bigger's other place of temporary refuge is the movie theater, where he "could dream without effort; all he had to do was lean back in a seat and keep his eyes open" (17). Like Clyde, cut off from other "wholesome" recreations, Bigger seeks through commodified leisure a sense of the world beyond the constricting limits of his own vision, a sense, indeed, of the very possibility of a self beyond the one granted him in the "real world."[51]

Early in the novel, Bigger attends a movie that has precisely this effect. At a neighborhood theater to see *Trader Horn*, Bigger first watches a fictional film called *The Gay Woman*, whose depiction of white upper-class leisure fascinates him. Watching the scenes of "cocktail drinking, dancing, golfing, swimming, and spinning roulette wheels" (33), Bigger wonders if his new position will offer similar sights. At the end of the movie he is so "full of the sense of a life he had never seen" (35) that he can barely pay attention to *Trader Horn*. He replaces the African scenes of "whirling" black figures with "images in his own mind of white men and women dressed in black and white clothes, laughing, talking, drinking and dancing" (35–36). His thoughts turn to money, and he remembers "hearing somebody tell a story of a Negro chauffeur who had married a rich white girl" (36). "Yes," Bigger decides, his brain spinning out scenarios, "his going to work for the Daltons was something big. Maybe Mr. Dalton was a millionaire. Maybe he had a daughter who was a hot kind of girl; maybe she spent lots of money; maybe she'd like to come to the South Side and see the sights sometimes. Or maybe she had a secret sweetheart and only he would know about it because he would have to drive her around; maybe she would give him money not to tell" (36). Seeing "practically nothing" of *Trader Horn*—a film that Wright ironically suggests featured black "men and women who were adjusted to their soil and at home in their world, secure [as Bigger assuredly was not] from fear and hysteria" (36)—Bigger dreams himself into a warm world that finds happiness for black chauffeurs on relief jobs, instead of degradation and misery. It will be a painful dream from which to awake.

■

Although much of what Bigger imagines does come true—Mr. Dalton *is* rich; his daughter *does* want to see the South Side; she *does* have a secret sweetheart—Bigger's actual encounter with the Daltons proves more disastrous than he could have conjured up in his worst nightmare. Indeed, the "pull and mystery" of the upper-class white leisure world fade almost the moment Bigger enters the Daltons' "quiet and spacious white neighborhood." "This was a cold and distant world," Bigger senses, "a world of white secrets carefully guarded," not confidingly shared (45). "He had been foolish in thinking that he would have liked it" (46). And yet as Wright makes clear, the events that do take place as a result of Bigger's hiring, horrifying as they are, confer on him an unexpectedly intense and ultimately satisfying sense of self-discovery and even self-creation. Bigger does not have to wait for his lawyer to explicate these feelings to the judge late in Book Three in order to understand them. They first emerge the morning after he has killed Mary Dalton, while he sits at his family's kitchen table awaiting breakfast. The "thought of what he had done, the awful horror of it, the daring associated with such actions" give him "a certain confidence," a "barrier of protection between him and a world he feared" (101). Unlike Bigger's earlier "curtain" of indifference (14), this barrier fortifies an emerging self instead of concealing a disengaged one. For Bigger believes that in killing Mary—and then in accepting responsibility for her death—"he had murdered and had created a new life for himself. It was something that was all his own, and it was the first time in his life he had had anything that others could not take from him" (101). This sudden apprehension of the "hidden meaning of his life" (101), coupled with Bigger's acceptance of it, makes it all the easier for him to kill Bessie, later in the novel, when he believes that his safety requires her death. "In all of his life these two murders were the most meaningful things that had ever happened to him. He was living, truly and deeply, no matter what others might think" (225). Unlike Clyde, we might say, who kills in order to preserve his newfound leisure-class identity, Bigger kills in order to create the self that neither work nor play, in their constricted orbits, could ever have made possible.

The sense of self that Bigger creates thus hungers for a new relationship to work, leisure, and self-control. Unlike earlier in the text, when Bigger curses his lack of any meaningful "choice of action"—either accept the miserable Dalton job or starve—after killing Mary he remains in that job because he chooses to. He does so not simply to cover his tracks, but "to take his life into his own hands and dispose of it as he pleased," to move "toward that sense of fulness he had so often but inadequately felt in magazines and movies" (141). Bigger thus temporarily experiences a feeling of control that distances him from other black characters in the novel who feel they have no choice but to work, like Bessie. Laboring "long hours, hard and hot hours seven days a week" (131), Bessie represents every black laborer who lives someone else's life instead of her own. When she tries to convince Bigger to leave her out of the ransom scheme, she appeals for sympathy on these very grounds: "Bigger, please! Don't do this to me! *Please!* All I do is work, work like a dog! From morning till night. I ain't got no happiness. I ain't never had none. . . . I just work! . . . I just work" (169–70). In fact in killing Bessie, Bigger may act less out of concern for his safety than in eagerness to blot out the sign of the perpetually working black body. "I'm black and I work and don't bother nobody," Bessie explains. "Go on," replies Bigger; "Go on and see what that gets you" (170).

What murder "gets" Bigger, in addition to this sense of control, is a clearer understanding of the relationship between urban space and the space of the self. After buying the materials necessary to prepare his ransom note, Bigger walks through the streets of a black neighborhood looking for a deserted apartment house through whose "black gaping windows" Bessie can watch the money being delivered (164). Having selected one of the "many empty buildings" that stand "like skeletons . . . in the winter winds"

(163), he sees a realtor's sign that makes explicit a link he had only dimly suspected: Mary's father, head of the South Side Real Estate Company, owns the very building in which Bigger and his family live. Bigger is now "sullen[ly] . . . conscious" that men like Dalton not only profited from the crowding of entire families into single rooms like theirs but by residential redlining also kept blacks "in this prescribed area, this corner of the city tumbling down from rot" (164). For his own part, Bigger feels free from such entrapment. Having found the "hidden meaning" of his life, he discovers that "the feeling of being always enclosed in the stifling embrace of an invisible force had gone from him" (142). But he will send the "kidnap note," he avers, in order to "jar" the Daltons of this world "out of their senses" (164).

It is thus especially ironic that after the discovery of Mary's bones spoils Bigger's ransom plan, Bigger seeks his safety and freedom in the selfsame kitchenette flats whose overcrowding symbolizes for Bigger the inability of working-class black citizens to escape the stifling "forces" of Jim Crow America.[52] Alerted by the newspapers that the police are searching black homes and abandoned buildings, Bigger decides to look for something in between—an empty flat "in a building where many people lived" (230). Such a space, however, is extremely difficult to find, since "empty flats were scarce in the Black Belt" (233). Bigger finds a vacant kitchenette. But as the rapidly shrinking maps in the newspapers make clear, the authorities' methodical search will soon collapse dead center on his hiding place. Clarity of perception, it turns out, will not prevent recapture. His sense of confidence and control similarly collapsing, Bigger climbs through a trapdoor to the roof of the building, a futile move that inversely recalls Bigger's origins as Big Boy, who had concealed himself under a trapdoor on his way to Chicago and liberty. Forced into a corner on the roof of the city, on the very top, ironically, of precisely the sort of building whose pernicious influence he had temporarily transcended, Bigger yields to the police, though not before resurrecting his "wall" of indifference.[53] After his capture, Bigger refuses to allow even an "image of what he had done" into his mind, resembling a person "not so much in a stupor, as in the grip of a deep physiological resolution not to react to anything" (255).

■

At the beginning of Book Three, Bigger's will to participate in the world revives when he senses himself being exploited as entertainment. He lets himself, in other words, be dragged lifelessly down the stairs of the apartment building after his capture ("his head bumping along the steps" [253]); but when led by his manacled wrists to the coroner's inquest past popping flashbulbs and mocking crowds—realizing on the way that his captors intend to make him "a helpless spectacle of sport for others"—Bigger springs "back into action, alive, contending" (257). He fights in part against the petty blindnesses of the mob and the newspaper hacks who tell them how to read him: as a "missing link," a jungle "beast," and a "Negro sex-slayer" (260) who should either be displayed as a freak or be publicly lynched. But Bigger also fights mightily against himself, struggling to recover that sense of self he had nurtured in Book Two, struggling to defeat the urge to give up.

Wright's depiction of the destructive power of a murder trial conducted as spectacular entertainment over and against the re-creative urgings of Bigger's dormant self vividly recalls Dreiser's patterning of the final book of *An American Tragedy*. The similarities are perhaps most apparent in the courtroom theatrics of the prosecuting attorneys, particularly as they attempt to re-create the events of the crimes. Just as Mason brings to court the actual boat that Clyde and Roberta rented at Big Bittern, Bigger's prosecutor Buckley rebuilds the Daltons' actual furnace and then has a proxy for Mary crawl dramatically inside. As in Dreiser's text, physical evidence is not so much introduced as rewielded, including the Daltons' hatchet, Bigger's gun, the brick he used to kill Bessie, and the kidnap note. Most excitably damning are the remains of Bigger's victims themselves. Where Mason had brought in what he claimed to be strands of Roberta's hair, Buckley displays

Mary's bones. At the inquest, the coroner even wheels in Bessie's battered body to parade it before the hysterical white crowd.

As in Dreiser's novel, these theatrics prop up competing interpretations of Bigger's life and its meaning. But even more so than for Clyde, the contest to define Bigger pivots crucially on contemporary debates over work and play. Almost immediately, for example, the Chicago papers lay part of the blame for Bigger's deeds on the supposed sanction of interracial recreation. Argues the *Tribune*: "Crimes such as the Bigger Thomas murders could be lessened by segregating all Negroes in *parks, playgrounds,* cafés, theatres, and street cars" (261, emphasis added)—though as we have seen, play theorists frowned on such contact anyway. In making his own case for putting Bigger to death, Buckley insists that Bigger is a walking affront to the "industrious people" of Chicago (378). Notified by the welfare agency that he must "report for work" to help his family off the relief rolls, for example, Bigger balks, according to Buckley. "What was the reaction of this sly thug when he learned that he had an opportunity to support himself, his mother, his little sister and his little brother?" Buckley asks.

> "Was he grateful? Was he glad that he was having something offered to him that ten million men in America would have fallen on their knees and thanked God for?
>
> "No! He cursed his mother! He said that he did not want to work! He wanted to loaf about the streets, steal from newsstands, rob stores, meddle with women, frequent dives, attend cheap movies, and chase prostitutes."
> (374)

Bigger—who kills in order to create the self that the lack of meaningful work and play denied him—must be killed, Buckley claims, in order to protect the American work ethic itself.

Bigger's attorney, Boris Max, also locates Bigger's crime at the volatile nexus of work, leisure, and the shaping of selves. "We know that happiness comes to men," Max explains, sounding just like the play theorists, "when they are caught up, absorbed in a meaningful task or duty to be done, a task or duty which in turn sheds justification and sanction back down upon their humble labors" (365). These labors "may take many forms" and are not limited to literal instances of work (365). But as a poor black man in a racist society, Max argues, Bigger has virtually no access to such activities in either work or play, and thus no opportunity "to be, to live, [or] to act"—to feel in himself, in other words, a fully realized personality (366). Moreover—and here Max mounts the very critique of capitalism that play theory could never quite bring itself to speak—instead of being an exploiter *of* leisure, someone who merely wants to "loaf about the streets," Bigger, Max maintains, is exploited *by* leisure. This is true, he holds, in a doubly constricting sense. First, as a member of the underclass, Bigger is someone from whose laboring body upper-class whites "have bled *their* leisure and *their* luxury" (357, emphasis added). Second, as a black member of that class Bigger is mocked by the very "tokens" of white American leisure civilization, "the advertisements, radios, newspapers and movies" whose "bright colors . . . fill [the] hearts" of most Americans "with elation" (363). Instead of picturing Bigger as an insolent loafer, Max suggests that the audience "imagine a man walking amid such a scene, a part of it, and yet knowing that it is *not* for him!" (363).[54]

In fact it is in the very nature of Max's defense plea that the final book of *Native Son*, for all its like-minded impulses, signals its most telling divergence from *An American Tragedy*.[55] Where Clyde's defense amounts to a welter of extenuating circumstances that together suggest that his acts toward Roberta were "innocent and unintentional" (665), Bigger's defense permits no such evasion. And though Bigger's guilt does have its own extenuating circumstances, the factors that lessen Bigger's crime give him a fuller, not more fragmentary sense of who he is.[56] In gaining that sense, Bigger also attains a fate far different from Clyde's. In his last moments Clyde becomes virtually a stranger to himself, a weak, shuffling automaton whose own voice sounds "so far distant as though it emanated from another being walking alongside of him" (810). As Clyde approaches the electric chair, passive verb constructions replace Dreiser's kinetic participles: "Now it was here; now it was being opened. There it was—at last—the chair . . . that he so dreaded—to which he was now compelled to go. He was being pushed toward that—into that—on—on" (810). Bigger is analogously driven at the end of *Native Son*, but to self-revelation, not destruction. His final movements, moreover, are active, not passive, as he "grasp[s]" his bars and "smile[s] a faint, wry, bitter smile" (392). Rather than feel distant from himself, he is, as it were, securely inside, beginning to understand, he tells Max, "what I wanted, what I am" (391). "I'm all right," Bigger says over and over in his final scene; "For real, I am" (392).

■

In grasping not just his bars but a sense of his life, Bigger also wrests control of his own story from the other voices in the text that have until then told it for him. Foremost among these are the newspaper reporters, the spirit of whose inflammatory columns Buckley appropriates for his courtroom speeches. Bigger is himself a voracious reader of the papers, in part to follow the developments in the Dalton case but also to see how they explain his life to their readers. He is first conscious of this need after Mary's bones are discovered. "The papers ought to be full of [me] now," he thinks to himself. "It did not seem strange that they should be, for all his life he had felt that things had been happening to him that should have gone into them. But only after he had acted upon feelings which he had had for years would the papers carry the story, *his* story" (208). But they do not carry his story; they carry their own. They endorse the mistaken belief of the police officers, for example, that the murder and kidnapping plan is "too elaborate to be the work of a Negro mind" (229), reducing Bigger to a supporting role in his own tale. After he is caught, the press condemns him as "shiftless and immoral" (261), "a beast utterly untouched by the softening influences of modern civilization" (260). At this point Bigger's urge to read his story becomes "an impulse to try to tell [it]" (286), but he is unable to satisfy that desire until his final talk with Max, when out of the echo of Max's plea for mercy Bigger crafts his own competing narrative. The power of that tale, resting as it does on Bigger's belated understanding that he "didn't want to kill! . . . [But] what [he] killed for must've been good!" (391–92), shocks even its auditor and enabler, Max. Terrified by Bigger's raised voice and his heightened self-awareness, Max leaves the jail—and the tale—to Bigger.

Bigger's successful shaping of a counterstory also neatly glosses Wright's own re-creative efforts in *Native Son*. The novel itself, for example, revises the literal newspaper accounts of accused black criminals on which Wright actually based much of the fictional reportage in *Native Son*.[57] As Wright suggests in "How 'Bigger' Was Born," *Native Son* also functions as a counternarrative to *Uncle Tom's Children*, over whose sad stories "even bankers' daughters," Wright had discovered in dismay, could "weep . . . and feel good about." Wright swore that if he ever wrote another book "it would be so hard and deep that [his readers] would have to face it without the consolation of tears."[58] But *Native Son* is also an explicit counterstory to *An American Tragedy*. For Wright's novel revisits Dreiser's plot to argue that the constricting public circumstances that shaped the private lives of Depression-era black Americans require a grimmer tale of youthful crime and punishment. Where Dreiser's novel can end with a figurative gift to the reader, a "souvenir" in which Clyde's nephew Russell skips off for ice cream under the now "more liberal," less restraining hand of Clyde's mother (814), *Native Son*'s final paragraph rings with the sound of "steel against steel as a far door clang[s] shut" (392).

By ending this way, *Native Son* further suggests that Dreiser's sympathetic reading of play theory is misguided as well. There is no Russell in *Native Son*—no reincarnated version of Bigger who may be saved from Bigger's fate through more wholesome recreation. There is Buddy, of course, but by the logic of the text he will turn out just like Bigger, ping-pong tables at the Boys' Club or no. And yet as we have seen, Dreiser's sympathy with certain aspects of play reform does not prevent his critique of the "religious and narrow" mores that (like play theory) were quick to praise "right recreation" but slow to challenge the economic inequalities that limited working people's leisure. After all, who is to say that Russell, "this fresh and unsoiled and unspoiled and uncomprehending boy" (813), will not soon knock up against the same class barriers that Clyde encountered, no matter how much ice cream he is allowed to eat? Nor is this Dreiser's only critique of the early-twentieth-century play debate. Consider again the novel's insistent foregrounding of the active-passive conflict so central to the debate. Clyde, suspended within this conflict, strains to attain a level of activity that even the novel's own language urges, energized as it is by Dreiser's unusual use of the present participle. Clyde's failure, in a sense, marks Dreiser's success. The novel creates for us the fascinating spectacle of Clyde's fall; in turn we are made into spectators, particularly as we watch Clyde's trial. For while the novel seems to side with the reformers' notion that the inability to recreate properly contributes to Clyde's doom, Dreiser nonetheless makes his audience do exactly what the reformers counseled most strenuously against: passively watch a melodramatic spectacle. Of course I exaggerate here somewhat. Reading is certainly an active, not a passive, encounter.[59] But Dreiser, rather than blindly follow the play reformers, constructs in *An American Tragedy* a new and instructive spectacle, writing in a space of his own creation between the reformer and the moviemaker, between the clergyman and the sociologist—even, we might say, between the naturalist and the modernist.[60]

Native Son, of course, is if anything more sensational than *An American Tragedy*. But that quality of Wright's text—which in part made it an immediate and enthralling best-seller—only serves, in the end, to make its paradoxical status as a double counternarrative to Dreiser's novel all the more ironic. On the one hand, *Native Son* limns its "American" tragedy in racial as well as class terms, making it not just a more grim version of Dreiser's plot but a sharper critique of play theory's uncritical acceptance of much of capitalist ideology. But on the other hand, by granting Bigger the sense of fullness (however fledgling) that Dreiser denies Clyde, *Native Son* is at the same time a more hopeful recuperation of *An American Tragedy*'s imaginative terrain. When we consider that Wright accomplishes this feat in part through melodrama—the stylistic mode by means of which texts such as the newspapers attempted to deny Americans like Bigger and Clyde a fully rounded sense of self—we can better appreciate *Native Son*'s deeper irony. For within a resolutely self-denying mode—itself deployed within the self-constricting genre of naturalism—Wright brings Bigger to an empowering, and unpredictable, self-realization. And thus in addition to appropriating the energies of such countertexts for himself and his characters, Wright finally, like Dreiser, also challenges the play reformers' notion of the spectacular. There can indeed be value, *Native Son* seems to say, in being made to look at a spectacle; though not, as it were, through the knothole in the fence, but from the front row, up close and decidedly personal.

CHAPTER SEVEN

Southern Counterpoint

Bodily Control and the "Problem" of Leisure in *Sanctuary* and *Their Eyes Were Watching God*

IN A SCENE THAT WILLIAM FAULKNER eventually excised from *Sanctuary* (1931), Horace Benbow and his nephew Bory Sartoris join Bory's great-great-aunt Miss Jenny Du Pre in her room one night after dinner. Bory is lounging against the fireplace mantel; Horace examines a series of portraits on the wall by Miss Jenny's bed. Miss Jenny, ninety years old and confined to a wheelchair, relaxes in front of her evening fire: "Her head lay back, her hands lay on the arms of the chair, the firelight rosy upon her." After a period of quiet, Miss Jenny suddenly confronts the house servant seated on the footstool next to her:

> "Saddie. What are you doing?"
> "Aint doin nothin, Miss Jenny."
> "What does the devil find for idle hands?"
> "Mischuf, Miss Jenny."
> "Then what are you going to do about it?"

As Saddie stoops to the sewing box to claim some "work" for her idle hands, Miss Jenny reiterates her stand against unproductive leisure. "Yes, sir," she says, "I can't have any idle folks around me."[1]

Miss Jenny's declaration, of course, is both locally ironic (neither she, Bory, nor Horace works at anything), as well as interracially revealing (only idle *black* folks are open to this southern white woman's charge).[2] Given the novel's positioning by Faulkner at "a point of passing from the Roaring

Twenties to the Depression Thirties," moreover, Miss Jenny's attitude expresses a national moral crisis.[3] At that significant historical moment, many Americans began seriously to question whether the hedonistic values that helped energize the postwar "Golden Age" were themselves part of a morally bankrupt code. Perhaps the gospel of play masked an insidious "problem" of leisure—and needed once again to be subordinated to a more sober ethic of work. An attentive reading of *Sanctuary* (in either the original or the revised version) would do well to take these general tensions over labor and leisure into account. Yet even in the scene recalled above, Faulkner suggests that we look further—behind Miss Jenny, as it were—to the potent forces of history and tradition whose supervisory ethos she channels. We need to look, that is, at the portraits on the wall. For in the nearly twenty faces, all male, that watch over the scene (and specifically over Miss Jenny's bed), Faulkner symbolically replicates the scopic control long wielded by men over women's leisure (indeed, over their very bodies) that now characterized the contemporary scene with a fresh intensity.[4]

It is this patriarchal and supervisory control—given fresh sanction by play theory's zeal for superintendence—that I would suggest Faulkner's final version of *Sanctuary* trenchantly critiques by reproducing the very cultural attitudes toward women's leisure and women's bodies that conspire to crush Temple Drake. As a representation of a woman under the additional and sometimes paradoxical burdens of her caste, race, and region, Temple succumbs to the pervasive ideologies of control that both form and disable her. Unlike Miss Jenny, who is immobilized by her age and infirmity and thus kept safely out of harm's way, Temple is an active participant in the rush and roar of the 1920s. Faulkner's extensive revisions, moreover (whose major effect, Joseph Blotner reminds us, is to "make Temple's story central"), direct our attention to the one woman in the novel who is the object of every male gaze—and whose utter destruction we are then forced to watch.[5]

Sanctuary creates this spectacle in order to reveal the self-destructive, narcissistic impulses inherent in the Roaring Twenties. It depicts a fictional world in which there is virtually no productive work and few productive energies—a southern world whose primary female character seeks to define herself through leisure but discovers instead that she is constrained (and finally defeated) by the very codes she seeks to master. By enacting for its readers a particularly horrific version of the leisure nightmare of the 1920s, and then by mocking all contemporary symbols of potential liberation, *Sanctuary* insists that for women (and perhaps even for men) there is finally no escape from these codes, even after one has recognized their controlling power. Faulkner's novel presents its readers with a deliberately vicious collapse, a moral implosion that drags virtually every character into its roaring black hole. It mounts a devastating critique of control, that is, by refusing to mitigate its effects.

By focusing, metaphorically speaking, on a different figure in Miss Jenny's room, however, Faulkner's contemporary Zora Neale Hurston tells a very different story about the same scene. In *Their Eyes Were Watching God*, Hurston, too, indicts the scopic control of women's bodies at work and at play, and with equal power shows the devastating effect that the ideologies behind that control can have on her protagonist's physical and psychic selves. After years of restrictive surveillance, Janie Crawford feels "cold" and "beaten down."[6] But rather than leave her there, stooped (like Saddie, as it were) to her demanded labors, Hurston helps Janie do what both Saddie and Temple cannot: get out. Instead of narrating a tale of implosive collapse, *Their Eyes Were Watching God* recapitulates a history of negotiation within constraints that eventually leads to an escape from them. Under Hurston's guidance, Janie's southern world, unlike Temple's, gradually discovers its productive energies, even, remarkably, its own control. If *Sanctuary* enacts the 1920s leisure nightmare, *Their Eyes Were Watching God*, in the end, reconstructs that decade's leisure dream.

The history that Hurston's novel recapitulates is not just Janie's but also that of the African American laborer she comes most closely to resemble, the domestic servant. By aligning Janie's escape from supervisory control with the early-twentieth-century transformation of live-in work to day work, *Their Eyes Were Watching God* affirms that under certain circumstances African American women could achieve a measure of control over their work, their time, and ultimately their own bodies, and that, rightly applied, play theory's endangered leisure ethic could indeed yield constructive, communal play. To be sure, Hurston's history is not without its limitations. Free time for any woman depends on factors—including sexual reproduction—that are often out of her control. Communal play, too, can self-destruct, sabotaged by jealousy and violence. But where *Sanctuary* imagines a trap, waiting to be sprung, *Their Eyes Were Watching God* sees a vision worth holding on to, worth working to rediscover. What follows is an exploration of these two southern visions as competing commentary on a particularly oppressive—and hopeful—age.

■

Any consideration of the control over the labor and leisure of southern women in the 1920s and 1930s must be measured against crucial developments taking place in the country as a whole. As we have seen, these two critical decades marked the consolidation on a national scale of what we now recognize as staples of the modern American leisure society, including motion pictures, automobiles, radio, the five-day work week, and professional sports.[7] But as the sober gospel of work gradually yielded to a "noisy gospel of play," new problems arose.[8] Who, for example, would monitor these new nonwork forms? Commentators from all arenas in the 1920s were afraid that without proper guidance, Americans would rush headlong into vice. This was not a new concern, as we have also seen—but it was powerfully exacerbated in the 1920s both by the wider availability of inexpensive recreations and by the cultural acceptance of the leisure ethic itself. Supervision, in contrast, long a central tenet of play theory, was regarded as the key to shoring up what George Cutten in 1926 called the "instability of morality."[9] What Cutten should have said was the *visibility* of morality, for what he and other panicked critics proposed was an increase in the scopic control that society wielded over people's play. By supervising leisure—by making it both intensely good and intensely visible—America could resist the moral degeneration that sank Rome.

The rise of modern advertising, paradoxically, helped establish the control that Cutten sought, although not precisely in ways he would have encouraged. For while advertisements in part hyped the passive spectacles that Cutten and others abhorred, they also spoke directly to consumers' therapeutic concerns, presenting them with images of the selves they might use their ever-increasing free time to shape. The dialectic that emerged between workers' new emotional needs and the strategies of advertisers thus helped channel Americans' increased leisure into the consumption of products that would enable the creation of those selves. Toothpastes guaranteed the dazzling smiles that made new romance possible. A brisk game of tennis left one looking fit. The motive power of a new car translated easily from machine to owner. And so on. Self-fulfillment (guided by intensive, internalized self-observation) was only a few carefully planned (and then endlessly repeated) shopping trips away.

And yet these dialectics become more problematic when we try to break terms like "worker" or "American" into their constitutive genders, races, classes, and even regions. The assumption that American women, for example, view their leisure in the same way that American men do fails to take into account that "men's notions of what constitutes a working day"—and thus what constitutes nonwork time—are likely to be very different from women's.[10] As T. J. Jackson Lears points out, moreover, women and men have not historically been depicted in or solicited by advertisements in the same way. Not only were images of (typically young, white) women increasingly prominent in local and national advertisements in the 1920s and 1930s, those images all too frequently bore little relation to the products being offered. Lears cites as an example a 1928 *Good Housekeeping* ad that features a skimpily dressed woman selling Drano. Such "detached" images, Lears contends, promised women "therapeutic feelings of emotional or sensuous excitement" rather than product performance; but the "therapeutic imperative" itself (the drive to "construct a pleasing 'self' by purchasing consumer goods"), Lears argues, actually "helped to domesticate the drive toward female emancipation" by offering women a "fake liberation through consumption."[11] One may question the degree of hegemonic control exerted by the advertisers (or by mainstream culture more generally), yet it seems clear that while men were urged to seek liberation in the play sphere—a space somewhere between work and home—women, as we have seen, were carefully guided (back) to a domestic sphere that for many, and particularly for African American women, had always represented work.

The American South presents an equally problematic case. As Daniel Rodgers admits, for example, his model of work's transvaluation into play at the turn of the century describes an industrial and therefore northern archetype.[12] Not only was the South predominantly agrarian well into the twentieth century, but southern attitudes toward work and leisure have traditionally presented a counterpoint to northern ones. Where the Puritan ethic defined work as an end in itself, the southern version had always considered labor a means to another end, namely "life." What this life consisted of, as C. Vann Woodward points out, depended on one's point of view. To a nineteenth-century southerner, the North's industrial expansion represented "ant-like busyness and grubby materialism." The "Southern Ethic," on the other hand, rejected Yankee "busy work" for the leisure of "human culture, spiritual reflection, contemplation, friends, family, nature—those things that made life worth the effort."[13] Above all, (white) southerners were not supposed to look as if they were working. From their vantage point, northern observers painted a far less idyllic picture of southern leisure. Their South was incorrigibly lazy, a slack subcivilization characterized by "idleness, indolence, slothfulness, languor, lethargy, and dissipation."[14]

The rapid industrialization of the New South in the early decades of the twentieth century gave the leisure-laziness myth a special urgency. In many quarters, southerners began to sound more and more like their Yankee counterparts. The "Atlanta Spirit" of the 1920s praised material expansion and enlisted traditionally Puritan notions about work in the drive to "build a new civilization" in the South. Southern industrialists reconceived their region as "a new frontier," a "land of promise" roused from lethargic slumber. Chamber of Commerce slogans such as "Mississippi Is Awake!" bubbled through the South.[15] But many southerners wondered what rough beast was slouching toward Atlanta to be born. In 1930, for example, the twelve Vanderbilt essayists behind the polemical collection *I'll Take My Stand: The South and the Agrarian Tradition* declared that industrialization threatened the very "essence of the Southern Ethic."[16] No matter how loudly new southern businessmen protested that they could balance growth with the gracious values of the Old South, proponents of agrarianism championed a return to a golden age of leisurely work untainted by frenzied materialism. The fight to maintain southern distinctiveness through leisure, however, became increasingly difficult in the face of a postwar proliferation of "American" standards through mass culture. By the 1930s, regional folkways were struggling to resist national forms, including chain stores, chain theaters, and radio networks.[17] If the Vanderbilt Agrarians felt especially embattled in 1930, they had good cause to.

But their golden age, like most mythical constructs, reflected a South that had only really existed in the minds of privileged white males like the Agrarians themselves. The much-praised leisure of the antebellum gentleman farmer, for example, rested quite literally on the bent backs of southern black slaves whose work was anything but leisurely and whose leisure seemed far from redemptive. Nor did emancipation appreciably relieve African Americans from degrading labor or provide them with welcome recreations; one could even argue that black workers in the postbellum South remained potent visual markers of southern white leisure. Southern white women present a somewhat different case. While the nineteenth-century cult of true womanhood circumscribed women's activity throughout the country, in the South the range of permissible behavior was always more severely limited. Even though southern white women "generally provided the domestic labor force for southern household management," for example, they were idealized as pampered "ladies" who did not work.[18] In the

1920s, however, southern white women, empowered in part by the Nineteenth Amendment (an advance that southern states fought bitterly, fearing its effects on black enfranchisement), moved rapidly into public life and began formulating their own opinions about how they might work and play. in modern times. But these women found their liberation no less controlled by patriarchal values than did their sisters to the north. Southern white women who attempted self-definition or fulfillment through either play or work typically did so from a position of economic, social, and sexual dependence. Despite clear advances in women's freedom, the flapper age was a potentially perilous one for women in the South, given the incompatibility of independence and mobility with the ideal of Southern womanhood. No agrarian could be entirely comfortable with the "new woman" emerging below the Mason-Dixon line.

■

It was in this climate of change and reaction that Faulkner—often seen as sympathetic to the agrarian attack on materialism[19]—reshaped *Sanctuary* to bring the story of Temple Drake into bolder relief. By paring back Horace Benbow's "cloyingly introspective" musings, Faulkner heightened Temple's narrative visibility without substantially altering her fictional behavior.[20] Appearing earlier in the novel and less mediated by Horace's sexually conflicted narcissism, Temple's story becomes more imaginatively available to the reader. These changes have in all likelihood also influenced critical opinion of Temple. Many readers, for example, have found it easy to pin her down in 1920s catch phrases, characterizing her as a "juvenile good-timer" who personifies "flapperhood" and eventually becomes "a gangster's moll."[21]

If *Sanctuary* encourages superficial readings such as these, it does so in complicated ways and for strategic purposes. Temple certainly seems to epitomize the 1920s flapper. She wears makeup and short skirts; she smokes cigarettes and drinks gin; she attends university dances and goes for drives with

Oxford's young town boys. Even young Bory Sartoris refers to her as a "jelly," mimicking a sexually crude slang expression he has probably heard used by Gowan Stevens, one of Temple's frequent dates and, at the novel's opening, a suitor for Bory's widowed mother Narcissa's hand.[22] What complicates *Sanctuary*'s presentation of Temple, however, are precisely statements like Bory's that veer toward the pornographic; for despite Temple's seemingly provocative behavior, Faulkner refuses to represent her "flapperhood" apart from male (even prepubescent male) perceptions of it. *Sanctuary* thus insists that Temple's identity—her appearance, personality, behavior—is actively constructed by male gazes.[23] Consider, for example, the weight Faulkner gives to external perceptions of Temple in the opening pages of chapter 4, the chapter that not only introduces but, for many critics, also morally indicts her. Temple makes her entrance in the chapter's first sentence as an explicitly visual (and grammatical) object: "Townspeople taking after-supper drives through the college grounds or an oblivious and bemused faculty-member or a candidate for a master's degree on his way to the library *would see Temple*, a snatched coat under her arm and her long legs blonde with running, in speeding silhouette" (29, emphasis added). While "townspeople" might include men, women, and children, and the paradoxically "oblivious" yet watchful faculty member is not specifically identified as male, the master's candidate is, and the overall effect of these lines is to construct Temple less as an individualized woman than as a male-watched moving shadow. That Faulkner emphasizes her speed could suggest that she is both literally and metaphorically a "fast" woman, but the sentence actually follows the predominantly male gaze as it follows Temple—and has followed her, over and over, as the deliberately iterative "[they] *would see*" suggests.

The rest of the paragraph then explicitly introduces the potential for violence inherent in the more potent gaze of frustrated male desire. Temple's running takes her to a waiting car owned by one of the "town boys," whom the university "men"—who are "not permitted to keep cars"—look "down upon . . . with superiority and rage" (29). Their rage is not directed at Temple, but the potential for its transference to her is made clear at chapter's end, when Gowan, though not exactly town boy or college man, turns on Temple in jealous anger: "You're pretty good, aren't you? Think you can play around all week with some badger-trimmed hick that owns a ford, and fool me on Saturday, dont you?" (39). Moreover, in the chapter's opening paragraph Faulkner subtly attributes the rage that the college men feel not to superiority, but to inferiority. The collegians are not only without cars; they also lack hats and trousers. Like children (or even like women) they wear "knickers." Even the town "boys" wear pants.

In the next paragraph the tables are turned, for on weekends Temple dates university men, not town boys. But Faulkner does not alter the essential scopic focus: on those occasions "the town boys . . . watched her enter the gymnasium upon black collegiate arms" (29–30). Temple is still a visual object, and although she may be partly responsible for being on display, Faulkner consistently emphasizes the desire of the watchers, not Temple's own pleasure at being watched. And once again Faulkner links the male gaze to incipient violence: the town boys lounge outside the gym— still watching Temple—"in attitudes of belligerent casualness" (29).

I focus on this chapter in detail because critics typically misuse it to "prove" Temple's calculated coquetry. Instead of noting that the operative verb in each of the four paragraphs that introduce Temple to the reader is some form of "watch," with Temple as its object, these critics emphasize the descriptions of her "bold painted mouth" and "cool, predatory" eyes (30), even though these adjectives appear to be the town boys', not the narrator's. Faulkner further complicates these impressions of Temple by placing a "soft chin" beneath her "bold" mouth and making her eyes not just predatory but "discreet" (30). Temple would appear, then—even to the equally predatory town boys—to give off conflicting signals. But rather than conclude that these signals justify her later violation, I would argue that Faulkner wants us to see Temple's *dis*play as a form of role play, her freedom (she can date either college men or town boys) and her body (legs, mouth, chin, eyes) as partially acted gestures, rather than entirely willful actions.[24] I do not mean that Temple is a mindless dupe of certain male-guided social constructions of gender—that she acts like a tramp simply because men want her to. I do claim, however, that Faulkner's language foregrounds a Temple who is scarcely imaginable outside of the male gaze that both play theory and broader cultural suspicions about the immorality of unsupervised recreation actively encouraged in the 1920s.[25] *Sanctuary* asks its readers to evaluate the effect of that gaze on a young woman's ability to control her body, her leisure, her time.[26]

■

If 1920s advertising frequently encouraged women to see themselves as sexual objects to be viewed and then consumed by men, it reinforced that objectification in myriad ways. Stuart Ewen argues, for example, that women in the 1920s were encouraged to see their "personality and looks" as essentially "commodified skills" and to treat their appearance as a "central category of their job[s]" as women. Advertisements further encouraged women to think of themselves as currency; in the metaphor of two 1920s sociologists, a modern woman had to choose how best to "spend" her personality "to bring the family and herself the greatest satisfactions."[27] Temple's looks, too, are metaphorically paid out by the end of those Saturday evening dances: "Her face was quite *pale*, . . . her hair in *spent* red curls. Her eyes . . . *blank*" (30, emphasis added). Faulkner's description suggests that Temple is both defined and defeated by the codes that encourage women to view themselves as commodities on display, whose "satisfying" self-exchange it is each woman's "job" to perform.

One could argue that advertising and the proliferation of consumer products in the 1920s sought to give women (and men) more control over their time and their bodies. The availability of inexpensive beauty aids, for example, allowed many women to create the new selves they had always wanted but could not afford. Mass consumption, perhaps, conferred autonomy instead of denying it. In her 1929 book *Selling Mrs. Consumer*, Christine Frederick argued that women in the 1920s were no longer "wards" of their fathers and husbands, but increasingly (and visibly) independent, educated, and sophisticated consumers, resolved to free themselves from domestic burdens and "to enjoy more of the good things of life." The consumption of new time-saving household devices in particular, she claimed (Frederick was a systems manager par excellence), would give women the leisure to pursue their extradomestic desires.[28]

But the data suggest that Frederick was wrong. Despite the rise of labor-saving devices, housework in 1930 was still more than a full-time job.[29] Moreover—and more pertinent to Temple, an unmarried woman—even those products that promised women control through self-enhancement subtly reinforced patriarchal codes of self-evaluation. Messages of liberation were undermined, that is, by ad copy and pictorials that offered as the goal of women's attractiveness not increased self-control or freedom, but male appreciation. The mirrors and mirror-like surfaces that dominate *Sanctuary*'s claustrophobic interior spaces suggestively reproduce the art direction of 1920s magazine ads that depict women (much like Temple) in poses of self-critical observation.[30] Temple's insistent recourse to her compact while at Frenchman's Bend—cited by some as evidence that she subconsciously desires violation and signals as much by endlessly reapplying her makeup—is perhaps better explained either as a form of denial (a way of reassuring herself of an orderly world composed of habitual gestures) or as her belief that her appearance is "her only tool with which to control men."[31] In either case, Temple's recurring self-observation suggests that she has internalized a male-oriented system of control, that she is trapped and defined by the male gaze—even when the gaze is her own.

At least Temple controls her compact. And yet the novel lets her control little else; she is both figuratively and literally an object manipulable by others. At the Saturday evening dances, we recall, she enters the gym "upon black collegiate arms." At Frenchman's Bend, Ruby Lamar, the common-law wife of head bootlegger Lee Goodwin, calls Temple "putty face" (63), referring literally to Temple's heavy makeup, but also suggesting that her face is infinitely malleable, that it can be reshaped at will, and not necessarily Temple's own. Later Temple's head is described as turning "like one of those papier-mâché Easter toys filled with candy" (73), figuring Temple as a decorative plaything, empty but for sweets and waiting to be violated by force. Moreover, Temple never controls the spaces she inhabits. She is a passenger in Gowan's car, a prisoner in Miss Reba's Memphis brothel, a parrot-like witness in the courtroom, and finally the ward of her father in Paris, where he even pays for the park bench on which she sits.

Ruby upbraids Temple at Frenchman's Bend for not running away, but Temple seems psychologically incapable of freeing herself—or even of recognizing the need for escape. Indeed, *Sanctuary* repeatedly mocks supposedly visible symbols of female liberation to underscore Temple's inability to realize that the world she is thrust into at the Bend requires acts of liberation she cannot imagine, let alone enact. While the act of smoking, for example, was in the 1920s "perhaps the one most potent symbol of [a] young women's testing of the elbow room provided by her new sense of freedom and equality," at Frenchman's Bend Temple keeps asking for cigarettes but cannot bring herself to smoke them.[32] Although she is not described as a woman who smokes in her opening appearance in chapter 4, by chapter 7 she asks Ruby, "May I have one?" But instead of smoking, Temple watches the cigarette "crush slowly in her fingers" (57), much as her own emotional control begins to dissolve. She finally "[drops] the crushed cigarette" (58)—as though symbolically unable to make any gesture of self-determination or independence—and picks up instead Ruby's baby boy, protesting her courage in stuttering phrases that fail to reassure: "'I'm not afraid,' Temple said. 'Things like that dont happen. Do they? . . . And besides, my father's a ju-judge. The gu-governer comes to our house to e-eat—'" (59). Only at Miss Reba's—after she has been raped, abducted, and imprisoned—does Temple smoke; and then she does so only in mannish imitation of Popeye, puffing swiftly, jerkily.[33]

A second symbol of female liberation that *Sanctuary* mocks is women's athletics, which in the early decades of the century had begun to offer many women "greater activity and a wider range in their means of self-expression and fulfillment."[34] In the beginning of the novel Temple is figured almost as an athlete, constantly running, springing, and jumping, activities that (along with tennis, swimming, and other sports) were believed to regenerate, if not emancipate, the female body. A health or physical education specialist of Faulkner's day would have encouraged Temple to run even more, thereby increasing not only her vigor and bodily control, but also her confidence, self-respect, and courage.[35] These characteristics, however, are exactly what her running seems to cost her: Temple's athleticism fails to regenerate or emancipate her, and the novel may even blame Temple's brutalization at Frenchman's Bend on her constant motion. As Ruby later insists to Horace, "If she'd just stopped running around where they had to look at her. She wouldn't stay anywhere" (169). Temple herself seems self-reproachful when she later recounts her night at the Bend: "I'd look at my legs and I'd think about how much I had done for them. I'd think about how many dances I had taken them to—crazy, like that. Because I thought how much I'd done for them, and now they'd gotten me into this" (227–28). Certain women's sports experts also believed that physical activity would relieve the female athlete "from sex strain" through the "sublimation" of her sexual "impulses."[36] Temple's running certainly doesn't arouse her (critics who believe she secretly craves the rape notwithstanding). But it does arouse the male spectators.

That sort of arousal was explicitly what the 1923 National Conference on Athletics and Physical Recreation for Women and Girls sought to eliminate from women's play. The conferees resolved that collegiate women athletes—unlike their male counterparts—should "be protected from exploitation for the enjoyment of the spectator."[37] To reduce male spectatorship in particular (and thus the indirect male control of women's sports), athletic directors in the 1920s discouraged intercollegiate competition among women, preferring instead segregated intramural contests and recreational "play days." Thus by the time of Temple's matriculation at Ole Miss, her own athletic opportunities would already have been greatly limited.[38] And yet as though in parody of the 1923 committee's intentions—or of their ineffectiveness in preventing more general cultural expressions of exploitive male "onlooking"—Faulkner depicts Temple as an athletic young woman constantly under the destructive spectatorial gaze of men.

Dancing is yet a third symbol of female liberation that is mocked in *Sanctuary*. Although Temple dances early in the novel, and in so doing may participate in a form of liberating recreation, it is hard to say whether she directs her movements or is merely passed "in swift rotation" from one partner to the next (30). Once she leaves the relative safety of the university, moreover, her bodily movements become increasingly constricted. Indeed, except for her running, Temple's primary physical motion after Gowan's car crashes at Frenchman's Bend (and before she dances again at the Grotto with Popeye) is an agonized "writhing" (94). This writhing—or "flinching" (92), "thrashing" (107), "arching" (147), "cringing" (154)—comes to constitute not self-liberating motion but something remarkably like a debased burlesque. Described by *Sanctuary*'s narrator as "long legged, thin armed, with high small buttocks—a small childish figure no longer quite a child, not yet quite a woman" (94), and having in Miss Reba's opinion "a boy's name" (153), Temple closely resembles the "boyish, nearly androgynous body of the slender, postpubescent" Ziegfeld girl. During her night at Frenchman's Bend, Temple actually enacts burlesque's most common non-dancing disrobing act—getting ready for bed—as Goodwin's assistant, Tommy, watches through the window.[39] When the men at Frenchman's Bend finally approach her, Temple, reacting to both the intimate display and the potential violation of her body, convulses involuntarily, as though performing an unwitting and spasmodic "cooch" dance or "shimmy" for their erotic pleasure. Although Temple is actually trying to evade the men's eyes (and hands), as she tries later to explain to Horace at Miss Reba's, her bodily movements parody those of a dancer on stage: "my skin started jumping away from it [Popeye's "nasty little cold hand"] like those little flying fish in front of a boat. It was like my skin knew which way it was going to go before it starting moving, and my skin would keep on jerking just ahead of it like there wouldn't be anything there when the hand got there" (229).

In particular, the cooch, a late-nineteenth-century elaboration of the belly dance, "linked the sexual display of the female performer and the scopic desire of the male patrons in a more direct and intimate fashion than any previous feature of burlesque." By the 1920s, when the cooch was being performed to the accompaniment of jazz and was known as the shimmy, the dancers would "twist, writhe, squirm and shake, each to her own inventive obscene devices."[40] When Temple is brought to Miss Reba's, where periods of quiet alternate with music from "a mechanical piano" (166), she is forced to perform for Popeye's perverse satisfaction. Once again, her attempt to evade display and/or violation contorts her body into the motions of a grotesque (and almost literally inverted) dance: "He came and looked down at her. She writhed slowly in a cringing movement, cringing upon herself in as complete an isolation as though she were bound to a church steeple. She grinned at him, her mouth warped over the rigid, placative porcelain of her grimace" (167).

In this description Faulkner further inverts the traditional physical relationship between performer and observer by placing Popeye above Temple in order to look down at her body instead of up to it, even though Temple imagines herself (bound to a "church steeple") in a more elevated location.[41] Ironically, this inversion—along with Popeye's repeated silencing of Temple (typically by clamping his hand over her mouth)—mimics the most significant historical development in American burlesque. As Robert Allen reports, burlesque was originally a highly charged and transgressively powerful "union of charismatic female sexuality and inversive insubordination." Female performers, beginning with Lydia Thompson and her "British Blondes" in the late 1860s, not only displayed their bodies but also acted out subversive skits of their own creation, mocking social constructions of gender through "intricate punning humor." By the late nineteenth century, however, as male producers, writers, and agents took control of burlesque, the female performers' power "to reordinate the world" was severely limited. Male producers bifurcated the burlesque into silent, feminine sexual display on the one hand, and verbal, male-dominated humor on the other.[42]

Shows that had once played as middle-class theater to mixed-gender audiences now looked out at shadowy, male-dominated, working-class crowds. Women who were denied the power to speak performed a burlesque that devolved into ever more lurid and explicit sexuality.

This historical context thus not only offers us a figurative (and cultural) explanation for Temple's degradation from collegiate respectability into brothel disrepute, it reminds us that in *Sanctuary* women's dancing is not merely mocked as an impotent symbol of liberation but appropriated and reconfigured as a performance for a specifically male audience. Faulkner's narrative recapitulation of the collapse of burlesque into silence and sleaze thus highlights the disempowering degradation of Temple, as she, like the transgressive burlesque dancers before her, comes under increasingly threatening male scopic control.[43]

■

Although Temple is watched by nearly everyone in the novel, as well as by readers outside it, the most potent male control is concentrated in Popeye. The first sentence in the novel introduces Popeye watching Horace drink from a spring. That Horace returns the gaze and finds himself locked in an extraordinary two-hour stare-down (Popeye's black, "rubber knob" eyes silently holding Horace in place [6]) signals Faulkner's focus on the power of vision to control movement. Popeye's gaze is of course itself empowered by his concealed "artermatic pistol" (21), but it is significant that in weighing several options for the novel's opening Faulkner selected this emblematic scene. Although the first time Temple encounters Popeye he does not look at her (instead Tommy gapes at her "scrambling," "running" figure "in slow astonishment" [40]), Temple soon comes to feel Popeye's eyes on her at nearly every turn, each time in a more degrading position. After she runs in horror from blind old Pap Goodwin, only to fall abjectly into "a litter of ashes and tin cans and bleached bones," she sees Popeye "watching her from the corner of the house, his hands in his pockets and a slanted cigarette curling across his face" (45–46). Later that night, still smoking, he will take one hand from its pocket, slip it under Temple's raincoat, and fondle her breast, although here his face is "turned a little aside" (79). The next morning, Temple discovers a man (presumably Popeye) watching her relieve herself in the woods, even though she has run far from the house to evade observation. Virtually no moment of Temple's "free" time is free from Popeye's gaze.

Nor is that gaze in any way impotent. Tommy is an impotent voyeur; if he is aroused, he doesn't activate his desire. Horace as well: he has complex sexual feelings for his stepdaughter, Little Belle, and his longing gazes at her photograph produce both arousal and nausea. But he remains an essentially introspective, powerless figure in the text, neither competent enough to win Goodwin's trial (or to prevent his ghastly lynching), nor decisive enough to resolve the marital crises that engulf him. Popeye, however, contrary to critical consensus, is not in aggregate an impotent man. Of course he is sexually impotent—at least to the degree that he cannot copulate. But he is certainly capable of potent sexual arousal. When assaulting Temple at Miss Reba's, for example, his "bluish lips" protrude labiophallically, eventually emitting "a high whinnying sound like a horse" (167). Popeye ejaculates sound, not semen, but he clearly has some type of orgasm. More important, Popeye's actions, sexual and otherwise, have an undeniably powerful effect on other characters in the novel. He kills Tommy, rapes Temple, indirectly causes Goodwin's death, and convinces Horace that "you cannot haggle, traffic, with putrefaction" (134). He is, in short, the most "potent," dangerous man in the text, violently collapsing the aestheticized distance between impotent voyeur and powerful agent.

Faulkner plays with reader's expectations of Popeye throughout the novel.[44] Only a particularly prescient reader would uncover Popeye's physical impotence before either Temple's elliptical taunt in chapter 24 ("You're not even a man! . . . when you cant even—When you had to bring a real man in to—" [244]) or Miss Reba's more elaborate exposition in the next chapter (271–73). Miss Myrtle even jokes that perhaps Popeye "went off and got fixed up with one of these glands, these monkey glands, and it quit on him" (271). If we follow this particular jest to its origins, we discover another revealing nexus of contemporary attitudes toward bodies, work, and leisure symbolically relevant to *Sanctuary*. In the 1920s popular conception, "monkey glands" were thought to be transplanted into impotent humans (generally men) to rejuvenate their sexuality. (There is a grain of truth behind the myth, but doctors were experimenting with human testicular transplants, not animal glands.) Eugen Steinach, the most prominent "regeneration" researcher of thé period, claimed to have developed successful surgical techniques for the restoration of not merely physical desire, but also the "love of, and ability to, work."[45] Though he did not use monkeys, Steinach did experiment on rats, which according to his reports behaved strikingly like the violent, "erect" rat Temple encounters in the crib at Frenchman's Bend (98). After Steinach's surgery, formerly meek, impotent rats became "hungry and playful," then charged about aggressively, fighting other male rats and copulating with females in heat—even, on occasion, forcing those not in heat to perform coitus.[46] In a novel like *Sanctuary*, then, which mocks all its principal characters' attempts at rejuvenation, we might say that Faulkner's bootleggers (who show no love of work) act like a cageful of Steinach's rats, with Pap as the original, symbolic, desiccated old rat, and Popeye as the grotesque embodiment of the rat that rapes. Just as *Sanctuary* mocks symbols of female liberation through recreation, so too does it ridicule contemporary attempts at male regeneration. In this novel, all forms of potential liberation collapse into impracticability.

What Popeye briefly becomes after abducting Temple from Frenchman's Bend is a perverted version of her friend, or beau. We see this first at the filling station, where "side by side, almost of a height, they appeared as decorous as two acquaintances stopped to pass the time of day before entering church" (147), and then at Miss Reba's, where Temple is referred to as Popeye's "girl" (152). But whereas Temple could previously exert a measure of control over her dates, such as whom she went out with, if not where, she has absolutely no control over her body or her leisure once she is raped at the

Bend. Even potentially sympathetic onlookers fail to come to her aid. At the filling station, for example, although Temple must look as though she has been brutally mistreated (she does, after all, have blood "all over the back of [her] coat" [147]), the station attendant does nothing to help her. When Popeye emerges from the "dingy confectionery" only to discover the car empty, we believe (or perhaps only hope) that Temple has gotten away at last. But the attendant "[jerks] his thumb toward the corner of the building" to indicate Temple's hiding place (146). Raped and abducted by one male, she is then casually exposed by a second. Are all men complicit in the surveillance of women's bodies? Are all women's bodies analogously controlled?

■

These questions might be out of order if Temple were an anomaly in Faulkner's text; that is, if other women in *Sanctuary* were either free from such control or at least more capable of regulating their own bodies in work and/or play. For then we might say that Faulkner's critique is limited to a particular social class, or a certain "type" of woman. Indeed, if other women in the novel are able to negotiate the social spaces they inhabit without concomitant observation and violation by the men in their lives, it becomes much easier to side with those critics who insist that Temple "gets . . . what 'has been coming to her!'"[47] Faulkner does present other women who appear to exercise some control over their bodies and their time. Horace's sister Narcissa, for example, is consistently described as impregnable or impervious, suggesting a physical and emotional control that Temple lacks. Horace's wife, Belle, also appears very much in control of her body and time, removing herself to her mother's in Kentucky when Horace walks out, for example. Miss Reba runs her own brothel and claims to have most of Memphis's professional men at her beck and call.

But none of these women is free from violation or restrictive surveillance. Narcissa's "impregnability" suggests that despite her apparent desire for young male companionship she will continue to live "a life of serene vegetation like perpetual corn or wheat in a sheltered garden" (110, 111). Belle's magazine-and-chocolate idleness hardly offers an encouraging model for the more active Temple. And Miss Reba's blustery insistence that she can put men who cross her "in jail three times over" notwithstanding (154), she becomes Popeye's eager dupe in his plan to incarcerate Temple, abetting the violation of her own codes of respectability in the process. As for the text's younger women, Little Belle, one might argue, is a more savvy version of Temple, one who "finds" men herself and takes them home at her leisure (15). And Minnie, Miss Reba's maid, can be read as an independent working woman who controls Temple's access to the outside world. Yet Little Belle's eponymous identification with her mother and her violent (though imaginary) violation by her stepfather, Horace (as he merges her body with Temple's and then fantasizes their collective rape), and Minnie's having been both abandoned and robbed by her husband suggests that the narrative regards neither of these women as any more capable of controlling her own body than Narcissa, Belle, or Miss Reba.

Which leaves Ruby.[48] Ruby is interesting because she is the only woman in *Sanctuary* whose actions Horace defends. From his first arrival at Frenchman's Bend, Horace watches Ruby as carefully as the other men watch Temple. He seems intrigued by the possibility that she is a woman with her "whole life before [her], practically" (18), in evident contrast to his middle-aged wife. His fascination does not prevent him, however, from figuratively violating her in an eery anticipation of Popeye's cold fondling of Temple several days later. As Ruby stands motionless inside the hall door, her arms "folded across her breast" as Temple will later fold hers, Horace suddenly "fumbled [his hand] across her cheek . . . his hand upon her face, touching her flesh as though he were trying to learn the shape and position of her bones and the texture of the flesh" (18). Later in the novel, Horace will defend Ruby's right to stay overnight in Jefferson when various "church ladies" seek her removal on the grounds that she is not married to the father of her child (188). Horace, too, as much as professes to admire her love for Goodwin, her maternal instincts, and her "practical wisdom" (210).

It seems particularly odd, however, that the only woman who engenders Horace's respect—that is, until the end of the novel, when he discovers that she is willing to prostitute herself to him "on demand" to pay for her husband's legal services (289)—can be read on another level as a parodic indictment of a type of woman even more vigorously "advertised," as we have seen, in Faulkner's day: the modern housewife. If we consider Ruby's actual position at Frenchman's Bend, we quickly realize that she inhabits a hellish inversion of the spaces pictured in the ads that Christine Frederick so admired. Instead of working effortlessly in a gleaming, modernized kitchen paid for by a hard-working and admiring husband, Ruby is the battered, unmarried mother of a bootlegger's baby, overworked and poorly dressed, who, as Popeye mocks, lives "down in the country," "chopping her own firewood," "cooking for a dummy and a feeb" in a grease-spattered kitchen (10, 11). "You can quit. I'll take you back to Memphis Sunday. You can go to hustling again," he sneers (9). Though she has escaped the life of a Memphis prostitute, Ruby is ultimately no more capable of regulating her body or leisure than Temple or the other women in the novel. The social space she inhabits—a debased version of the happy homemaker's loving and emancipatory kitchen—is as rigidly controlled by men as the spaces in which Temple finds herself.

This is not, as we might be tempted to say, authorial misogyny. It is instead a devastating and multipronged critique—of the supervisory control of women's bodies by men (given sanction by play theory's rage for superintendence); of the crippling internalization of the self-regulatory impulse (given alluring visual form by advertisements); and of the liberating kitchen fantasies of household systems specialists like Frederick—that leaves no way out for women *or* men. Faulkner mounts a critique of control, in other words, by making that control pervasive and unassailable. This is a strikingly modernist challenge to the whole notion of playing "for keeps," a deliberate affront to play theory's semipious constructions of "right" recreation that refuses to depict the supervised self as stable, whole, or unalienated.

Of course it is not the only way to mount such a critique. One might similarly challenge male scopic control, self-negating yearnings imposed by others, and the myth of emancipation through housework but also simultaneously (and in purposeful contrast) reclaim and narrate a model history that imagines a way out. And in the process make the individual imagination (in a different modernist gesture) that which saves us from those semipious assertions in the first place. As we will see, what I am describing is Zora Neale Hurston's own effort in *Their Eyes Were Watching God*, a novel that, like *Sanctuary*, critiques the scopic control of women's bodies but also imagines a self-liberation from superintendence while breathing fresh life into play theory's thwarted dream of constructive, communal leisure. This is not necessarily a better response than Faulkner's, but it is a markedly different one, and by attending to the differences we can more clearly evaluate the strategies of engagement available to American writers who confronted the early century anxiety over the "problem" of leisure, particularly for women. And because the narrative and historical turn from *Sanctuary* to *Their Eyes Were Watching God* is prepared for, in a sense, at Frenchman's Bend I return there briefly before moving ahead into Hurston's recuperative text.

■

What seems to bother Horace the most about Ruby's debased status at Frenchman's Bend is not that she is doing women's work but that she is "doing a nigger's work" (113). A woman who has "owned diamonds and automobiles too in her day, and bought them with a harder currency than cash" (113), Horace feels, should not be subjected to such degrading toil. "You are young yet; you could go back to the cities and better yourself without lifting more than an eyelid," he tells Ruby the first time they meet (18). In many ways Horace is right, and his commentary (including its unreflective racism) accurately reflects the racialized division of labor in the early twentieth century. Despite gaining access in the 1920s to jobs and industries previously closed to them, African Americans typically found their labors restricted to the most demeaning tasks, while young white women like Ruby were indeed heading "to the cities," where they made a better living doing easier work. White women in particular were the beneficiaries of the early-century feminization of clerical work. Though nineteenth-century offices had been staffed predominantly by men, the introduction of the typewriter transformed clerical work into women's work. These may also have been dead-end jobs; yet white women poured out of domestic service into clerical positions, where their white skin gained the favor of employers who were looking for front-office company representatives as well as talented typists. While in 1900 only 7 percent of all employed white women were clerical workers (but 30 percent were household servants), by 1930 clerical employment accounted for 25 percent of white women's work and domestic service only 12 percent.[49]

African American women did not benefit equally from the feminization of white-collar working space. One could argue that they were in some ways harmed by it. Not only was clerical work virtually an impossible option for African American women (0.1 percent of African American women had such positions in 1900, only 0.6 percent in 1930),[50] the vacuum created by white women's flight from domestic service—a form of employment characterized by intense scopic control—was filled primarily by African Americans. As David Katzman explains, by 1930 "domestic service had changed from the major form of female employment to an occupation statistically unimportant among all but black women."[51] Thus, hired household labor, even more than agricultural work (only 25 percent of African American women worked on farms in 1930, down from 44 percent in 1900), was decidedly "black" work when Horace was complaining about Ruby.

By 1937, when Hurston published *Their Eyes Were Watching God*, the Depression had made work both harder to perform and harder to come by. According to Jacqueline Jones, while the 1930s saw work opportunities decrease for all women, African American women were hit hardest, losing "what little they already had more swiftly and surely than did whites." Moreover, as Jones explains, the relatively high percentage of working

African American women in the 1930s "obscures the highly temporary and degrading nature of their work experiences. Specifically, most of these women could find only seasonal or part-time employment; racial and sexual discrimination deprived them of a living wage no matter how hard they labored; and they endured a degree and type of workplace exploitation for which the mere fact of having a job could not compensate." Even the altruistic gestures of the New Deal failed to improve the lot of black women workers. Special exceptions to programs like the National Industrial Recovery Act (1933) and the Social Security Act (1935)—federal legislation that was supposed to keep a protective eye on all American wage earners—eliminated more than 90 percent of black women from more generally extended economic safeguards. This nexus of factors—indifferent "supervision" and legislated invisibility foremost among them—"inhibited meaningful change in the status of black women, relegated as they were to the fringe of a developing, though crippled economy."[52]

It was in this climate of stasis and invisibility that Hurston shaped the fictional life of Janie Crawford, a life that reached from (roughly) the end of Reconstruction to the stock market crash. (Janie's age is as difficult to pin down in Hurston's novel as Hurston's own has been.)[53] Born to a seventeen-year-old mother who was herself born about the time that Sherman took Atlanta, Janie's approximate birthdate is 1881. The model for the storm that drives Lake Okeechobee over its levees at the end of the novel is probably the devastating hurricane of 1928, which killed more than 2,000 persons, 75 percent of whom were black and predominantly Bahamians living, like Janie and Tea Cake, near Belle Glade.[54] This may not be the storm that Hurston had in mind—she may not have had any actual storm in mind—but it is the one her audience (even ten years later) would likely recall when they read her text, and its date squares with Janie's age (around forty) at the end of the novel.

I suggest that Hurston's text, offering its own clear historical markers, brings into play several crucial decades of African American working women's history, including, strategically, the Depression—the specific economic and social moment during which she wrote and from the immediate perspective of which her readers absorbed Janie's story. I would further argue that Hurston has Janie narrate the story of her *whole* life in answer to her best friend Pheoby's more specific questions about her *recent* absence, not merely to show that Janie now possesses an "understandin'" (19) of the relationship of her past to her present but to link Janie's self-development (and here we turn back to the central issue) to important historical changes in the status of supervised African American working women.[55] Like Temple, though more specifically like black domestic servants, Janie's control over her labor, leisure, and body is constrained by ever more panicky ideologies of superintendence. Unlike *Sanctuary*, however, *Their Eyes Were Watching God* narrates through Janie a series of surprisingly successful negotiations within and then apparent escape from those ideologies. In what follows, we track this history, these negotiations, and that escape, though not without asking some hard questions about the opportunities for evasion within such strategies. We want to be sure that we are in the land of possibility, not utopia.

■

Much as Faulkner presents Temple as an object of visual investigation in her first appearance in *Sanctuary*, Hurston brings Janie into *Their Eyes Were Watching God* before a gallery of prying eyes, prefaced, ominously, by the explicitly male "Watcher" of the novel's opening paragraph (9). When Janie returns from "burying the dead," we are told, "The people all saw her come" and "remember[ed] the envy they had stored up from other times. . . . They made burning statements with questions, and killing tools out of laughs. It was mass cruelty" (9–10). Janie's visibility, like Temple's, engenders violence. But it is Janie (recalling Faulkner's faculty member) who acts oblivious and bemused. Although the crowd watches her intensely (the men noticing her "firm buttocks," "great rope of black hair," and "pugnacious breasts," the women her "faded shirt and muddy overalls" [11]) and talks about her long after she has faded from sight, Janie claims not to give the townspeople a second thought: "If God don't think no mo' 'bout 'em than Ah do, they's a lost ball in de high grass" (16). The town wants to know Janie's "business" (17); Janie dismisses them in playful metaphor. Unlike Temple, she is not controlled by the town's collective gaze. But this, after all, is the mature Janie, back from "burying the dead." Although as we will see, Janie is constrained during earlier parts of her life by the watchful, typically male eyes of others, at this point she is both the primary observer and the definer of her own experience. The narrative signals as much when the second chapter opens with this declaration: "*Janie saw* her life like a great tree in leaf" (20, emphasis added).

The life that Janie saw, until her second husband Joe's death, however, consists of attempt after attempt to delimit either her body, her labor, or her free time, all under the watchful eye of someone implicated in the regulatory systems of patriarchal control. Once again, unlike Temple, however, Janie responds to each attempt with her own forms of resistance, however meager. Janie's early years are spent under the strict surveillance of her grandmother, Nanny, who watches to see that the sexual assaults that violated her body (and her daughter's body) are not reenacted on Janie's. Janie, though perhaps unaware of Nanny's plan, resists it by trying to construct a self of her own choosing, by controlling her own time and learning how to respond to her own body. She spends "every minute that she could steal from her chores" lying "under a blossoming pear tree," out of Nanny's sight, gazing up at its "glistening leaf-buds" (23). When, freed from "her former blindness," she lets a local boy kiss her, Nanny, unfortunately, is watching. She calls Janie into the house and insists that she marry Logan Killicks, a local farmer.

In her determination to control Janie's body, Nanny reveals her complicity with white ideologies. Used "for a work-ox and a brood-sow" by her owners in slavery (31), Nanny nonetheless believes, as Sherley Williams has argued, that only "money or the protection of good white people" can shield black women from a life of hard labor.[56] Nanny also implicitly endorses the dominant cultural attitude concerning the "threat" of leisure, believing that unsupervised free time—particularly for African American women—leads straight to drunkenness or promiscuity. When Janie protests that she is not interested in the drab Killicks, for example, Nanny suggests that she will end up like her mother, "drinkin' likker and stayin' out nights" (37). "So you don't want to marry off decent like, do yuh? You just wants to hug and kiss and feel around with first one man and then another, huh?" (28).

Killicks also attempts to control Janie's body, work, and leisure. To him, Janie is "powerful independent" (51) and, by implication, lazy: "If Ah kin haul de wood heah and chop it fuh yuh, look lak you oughta be able tuh tote it inside," he grumbles (45). When Killicks later demands that Janie stop "foolin' round in dat kitchen" and come help him work outside, she refuses: "Youse in yo' place and Ah'm in mine" (52). Her response seems at first to reinforce the patriarchal assumption that a woman's place is in the home, but we can also read it as an attempt to resist additional burdens of labor and maintain control over the spaces that she already inhabits. Historians report that most rural southern black women at the turn of the century (when Janie lives with Killicks) worked in both kitchen and field, and so not only cooked, cleaned, sewed, and laundered but also (as Killicks seems to hope) collected firewood and hoed. When Janie refuses to work a mule or help Killicks move his manure pile, she accomplishes what few African American women before her could—namely, escape the "manual labor so physically arduous it was usually considered men's work."[57]

Janie does not take up the plow as Joe Starks's wife either. But it is Joe who (at first) thwarts her attempts at self-definition by controlling her body and time more thoroughly than either Nanny or Killicks did. Like Nanny, Joe is captivated by white values. He quickly assumes proprietary control over the town of Eatonville, becoming its "Mayor—post master—landlord—storekeeper," and paints his huge new house a "gloaty, sparkly white," making those around it look "like servant's quarters." Residents who work on civic projects at his bidding murmur "hotly about slavery being over" (75). Joe protests to Janie that he merely wants to see the other blacks in Eatonville work more and play less, much as Booker T. Washington had insisted in *Up from Slavery* (1901). "Ah wish mah people would git mo' business in 'em and not spend so much time on foolishness," Joe explains (98).

Joe's attitude toward Janie's work is complicated. On the one hand, his intention from the start is to alleviate her burden. When Janie tells him at their first meeting that Killicks has left her cutting potatoes while he has gone off to buy a mule for her to work, Joe acts outraged. "You behind a plow! You ain't got no mo' business wid uh plow than uh hog is got wid uh holiday!" he exclaims. "You ain't got no business cuttin' up no seed p'taters neither. A pretty doll-baby lak you is made to sit on de front porch and rock and fan yo'self and eat p'taters dat other folks plant just special for you" (49). In relation to labor, it would seem, Janie should occupy a position analogous to the one held by *Sanctuary*'s Judge Drake, who (as Temple recalls) would sit "on the veranda, in a linen suit, a palm leaf fan in his hand, watching the negro mow the lawn" (57). It soon becomes clear to Janie, however, that the metaphorical "front porch" on which she is meant to sit is so high up that she will never be able to get down. She would like, for example, to "indulge" with the other townspeople in "mule talk," or what Henry Louis Gates calls the "rhetorical play" of the porch.[58] Joe explains that such activity would be inconsistent with her place: "You'se Mrs. Mayor Starks, Janie. . . . They's jus' some puny humans playin' round de toes uh Time" (85). Oddly, Joe's original conception of the porch separated Janie from other people who would work for her; here, however, he wants to keep her from people who just play. Thus Joe, like the play reformers, distinguishes relaxing leisure (porch sitting) from degrading labor (potato planting) as well as dignified idleness from wasteful play.[59]

But Joe does not alleviate Janie's burden entirely. Though he keeps her from the fields, his conception of the dignified idleness of the porch still includes not only the duties of a housewife but also a full-time, six-day-a-week job in his store. Of course one could rightly observe that as a sales clerk, Janie occupies a very privileged position relative to other black women; as with clerical work, fewer than 1 percent of working African American women held jobs in sales by 1930. Even if one preferred to classify Janie as an extradomestic servant, the number of black women in similar positions was only 8 percent.[60] But the life that Janie sees from this position is hardly one of privilege. It is rather one in which she primarily plays the role—and completes the labors—of a live-in domestic servant, under the constant watch (and reproach) of her employer-husband.

She plays this role even in the store, Joe's public home. He bosses her curtly and ridicules her for not performing tasks to his satisfaction. He also severely limits her free time, not just by making her work but also by denying her access to public entertainment. The scopic control Joe exercises over Janie mirrors the power that white employers had over their own servants. One African American servant complained in 1904, for example, of restrictions that Joe lays equally on Janie. "We are bossed eternally; [our employers] ask us where we are going, where we have been, and what we did, and who our friends are."[61] Besides a lack of freedom, other servants complained of fatigue, loneliness, and boredom, precisely the states that Joe's rigid system of supervision presses on Janie. Not only does the store give her "a sick headache" (86), her mundane life, year after year, beats her down into "a rut in the road" (118). Female companions do not provide much relief either; even Pheoby, who is identified as Janie's best friend in the opening chapters, does not reappear in the novel until chapter 7, twenty years into Janie's life in Eatonville.

What is especially paradoxical about Joe's control of Janie's time and body is his attempt to render her both visible and invisible at the same time. Her position high up on the imaginary porch not only connotes distance from the more "common" folk but also permits their observation of her. Joe wants Janie to "overlook the world," but also wants the world to look Janie over (98). Her comparatively easy job is a sign both of privilege and of Joe's status: he is wealthy enough to "afford" a wife who does not need to work for a wage, much as he can afford to buy Matt Bonner's mule just "tuh let 'im rest" (91). Thus Janie must be seen. But at the same time Joe is intensely jealous of the way that other men look at Janie. So he forces her to tie her long black hair up under a head rag to prevent them from either seeing or "figuratively wallowing in it" (87). This concealment of Janie's beauty appears counterproductive; it hides one of the attributes that might most emphatically reaffirm Joe's lofty (male) status—hides it in fact under a customary sign of poverty. But it also visually reestablishes Joe's domination over Janie and more firmly defines her role as his servant. As David Katzman explains, the "ideal" live-in domestic servant (much like Janie, as Joe has fashioned her) "would be invisible and silent, responsive to the demands but deaf to the gossip, household chatter, and conflicts, attentive to the needs of mistress and master but blind to their faults."[62] It is perhaps not surprising then that Janie's most powerful act of resistance occurs when she engineers a startlingly public turning of the tables, accompanied by a verbal dexterity heretofore invisible. In retaliation for Joe's degrading comments about her body, Janie suddenly exposes him to the shocked gaze of the community, making his "faults" visible by talking "under" his clothes (122). That Janie accomplishes all this by "playin' de dozens" (123) signifies a prime moment of self-assertion as well as her desire (and ability) to take control of an explicitly playful, visible, and, for the most part, male medium.

Before this moment, Janie's only other forms of resistance are the silent pictures in her own mind. At first she occasionally "stuck out into the future, imagining her life different from what it was. But mostly she lived between her hat and her heels" (118). Until one day "she sat and watched the shadow of herself going about tending store and prostrating itself before Jody while all the time she herself sat under a shady tree with the wind blowing through her hair and her clothes. Somebody near about making summertime out of lonesomeness" (119). Creating for herself a mental representation of what she feels is missing from her marriage—liberty, friendship, and delight—Janie's longings mirror those of other servants, who were all too aware that the homes in which they slaved were not their own. "Home is the place where the loved ones live," explained one domestic in

1910, "a place of freedom, with the companionship of equals on equal terms. Home is not the kitchen and back bedroom of a house belonging to another."[63] In *Their Eyes Were Watching God*, then, home is not Joe Starks; home is Tea Cake Woods.

■

The shift in Hurston's novel from the scopic control of Joe to the "companionship of equals on equal terms" with Tea Cake is rightly read as one of the more consequential liberations in twentieth-century literature. Janie's ability to strike out against patriarchal control and then articulate an independent selfhood gives her a compelling presence in American letters.[64] But what is crucial to observe here are the specific ways that Hurston recovers and then inscribes into the novel two strategies of escape available to the class of workers to which Joe has consigned Janie, whose successful self-liberation affirms the value of a historical, not merely personal, transformation and vividly marks Hurston's strategic divergence from Faulkner's method of critiquing systems of scopic control.

The first strategy that an oppressed and unhappy live-in domestic servant might devise to liberate herself from unwelcome scopic control, and one that Janie mimics twice in the novel, is leaving her employer. This was frequently the only strategy available. As Katzman observes, given servants' scant economic power, "only a change of mistress could alter their working conditions."[65] And they did not stop at one change. Much as Janie leaves Killicks and then Joe (imaginatively at first, then physically once he is dead), unsatisfied domestics "continued to move in search of better jobs and living conditions."[66] The second liberating strategy involved reconceptualizing the limits and duties of domestic service itself. What live-in domestics found particularly oppressive about their work was not that it was a dead end—but that it quite literally had no end, either to its work or to its requirement of self-display. As one southern African American domestic put it in 1912, "I live a treadmill life. . . . You might as well say that I'm on duty all the time—from sunrise to sunrise, every day in the week."[67] These jobs meant exhausting, supervised labor, and they virtually foreclosed leisure— a limitation that many southern black women encountered in their own families even before they became servants. "By [age] four, you'd be doing feeding and a little field work," reported one woman of her 1890s North Carolina childhood; "by six you'd be doing small pieces in a tub every wash day and you'd bring all the clear water for the rinsing clothes. By eight, you'd be able to mind children, do cooking, and wash. . . . By ten, you'd be trained. . . . Work, work, work. No play, 'cause they told you, 'Life was to be hardest on you—always.'"[68] Many servants did have Sundays and one evening off per week; Janie herself does not work in the store on Sunday. But over the years, live-in servants insisted on their right to daily, self-structured free time, and many eventually earned enough money to rent rooms of their own and hire themselves out as day laborers, controlling their own work and leisure hours. By 1920—thanks largely to the efforts of domestics themselves—"the modern system of domestic service in the form of day-work," not live-in service, "had become entrenched."[69]

Janie's determined shift from Killicks to Joe to Tea Cake both literally and figuratively reenacts this momentous transformation of African American women's work. While life with her first two husbands consists of endless chores for other people—"a waste of life and time," Janie feels (86)— by the time she meets Tea Cake she is beginning to set her own hours. After Joe dies, for example, Janie keeps the store "in the same way," except in the evenings, when "she sat on the porch and listened and sent Hezekiah in to wait on late custom" (137). When she is ready, Janie further shortens her working hours, visiting with Pheoby or "once in a while [she just] sat around the lakes and fished" (143). Janie's "freedom feeling" (139), if partly enabled by her financial independence, is possible only once she releases herself from her live-in servant's job. When Tea Cake begins to court her, Janie spends even more time in recreation; by the time they join the migrant laborers on the Everglades muck Janie both experiences and articulates the joys of a self-supervised schedule of work and leisure: "Clerkin' in dat store wuz hard," she tells Tea Cake, "but heah, we ain't got nothin' tuh do but do our work and come home and love" (199).[70]

In addition to narrating (and embodying) this specific history, Janie's strategic transformation thus also brings to fictional life early-twentieth-century play theory's conception of leisure as a crucial site for both self and community regeneration in the face of the degradation of work. Although Janie does not particularly value the work that Joe requires her to perform, she is at least willing to lie to herself that Joe (and his desires) are worth "something in [her] mouth." "He's got tuh be," Janie avers, "else Ah ain't got nothin' tuh live for" (118). But as Joe's demands gradually deaden her soul, Janie's labors leave her painfully fragmented, split (like modern laborers, the play reformers held) into the "shadow" self that works in the store and the "she herself" that imagines "summertime" under a tree (119). Only through regenerative play will Janie reintegrate self and shadow. It is significant that she meets Tea Cake at the store, for example, for she discovers in that first encounter that she can be the woman who works and the woman who imagines "summertime" simultaneously. When Tea Cake shows her how to play checkers (a game previously Joe's exclusive province), she is thrilled that "Somebody wanted her to play. Somebody thought it natural for her to play" (146). Learning the game also raises Janie's self-esteem in ways that her work never could. Believing formerly that the game "wuz too heavy fuh [her] brains," Janie seems pleased when Tea Cake (having seen her play) assures her that she has "good meat on [her] head" (147).

Once Janie discovers that a regenerative ethic grounded in leisure—what Joseph Lee would call "Play the Restorer"—is more fulfilling than an ethic of self-denial through work, her play escalates.[71] She moves not toward leisured isolation, but toward partnered, intensely communal play, rising from listening by herself to tales on the porch, to coupled play with Tea Cake, to the "Dancing, fighting, singing, crying, laughing, winning and losing" in the jooks on the muck with all the "hordes of workers" (197, 196). In its movement toward larger and larger groups, Janie's play development duly resembles the recreation theorists' evolutionary models. And yet

Hurston's representations of play beyond the self signally revalue the reformers' own conceptions in at least two ways. First, Hurston's vision of group play on the muck rejects play theory's central notion that a corporate and ultimately national belonging is the true goal of group loyalty. Indiscriminately composed of African Americans, Native Americans, and "Bahaman workers" (228), muck play instead creates and sustains a diverse community of autonomous subgroups, separate from the white "bossman" (230) but also, when the hurricane comes, ready to split back along its constituent cultural lines. Hurston offers this model of fluid composition, decomposition, and recomposition (even the dances and parties form and reform every night, depending on who is around) as the basis for a truly regenerative group belonging.

Second, Hurston proposes an intensely beneficial play grouping that the recreation reformers seem oddly reluctant to discuss: the lovingly partnered play of emotionally and physically attached couples. In the long list of the benefits of self-construction through play—all the different physical, mental, moral, and civic advantages—there is no mention of play's power to create, strengthen, or sustain the bond between human pairs, or what Janie calls the "love game" (171). There may be several reasons for this omission. For one, the play reformers seem uncomfortable talking about human sexuality, unless it is to inveigh against "sex vice" or self-abuse, and to praise play's role in the development of a loving relationship might seem too suggestive for impressionable adolescents or young adults. Or the omission may be more strategic. Since the reformers saw the popular entertainment industry as their chief competition for American bodies and minds, and regarded that industry as already obsessed with what Jane Addams called "the newly awakened susceptibility of sex," play theorists may have wanted to distance play from love and romance entirely. Addams alone among the major reformers campaigned in her writing for organized recreation as a way to "stifle the lust for vice" while still praising human sexuality for "suffus[ing] the world with its deepest meaning and beauty."[72] Yet another possibility is that the play reformers were suspicious of intense attachments that might rival the state for the play-built individual's ultimate affections. As we have seen, play theory's developmental models jump quickly from individualized recreation to "gang" membership and group loyalty, eager, it would seem, to press ahead to play reform's final goal, obedient citizenship. An intensely bonded couple, like Janie and Tea Cake, just might not need the state; but on such recusals play theory as a successful civic doctrine would founder.

There are limits, to be sure, to Hurston's representations of both communal recreation and partnered play. Tea Cake's decision to beat Janie in order to relieve his fears of losing her to someone else, but more pointedly "to show" the others on the muck that "he was boss" (218), complicates any claim for the novel's endorsement of a loving partnership through work and play, particularly when Tea Cake's desire for "control" (220) through specifically visual means (the bruises on Janie's face) links him to all the other male figures who have sought to supervise Janie's body. Janie's apparent acceptance of the act ("the helpless way she hung on him made men dream dreams" [218]) further complicates matters. For although Hurston conspicuously omits Janie's reaction to the incident—indeed, Janie disappears from the remainder of the chapter, the only time in the novel that this happens[73]—there are no overt signs that she loves Tea Cake any less. The *text* seems less enamored of Tea Cake; his beating of Janie is almost immediately followed by the hurricane, Tea Cake's dog bite, his madness, and his death. It is almost as though the text says that after such a beating, the recreational joy on the muck cannot continue.[74] But Janie neither says that nor appears to feel it. Her subordination to Tea Cake—based largely, as she puts it, on her belief that he "made somethin' outa" her when her marriage to Joe had left her "dead" (247)—is represented as self-willed and freely chosen.

There are also limits to the novel's valorization of the regenerative group recreation on the muck. Although I do not agree with Jennifer Jordan that the novel ultimately depicts Janie's failed attempt to integrate herself into the black community, I do believe that the jealousy, anger, and violence that surface on the muck make Janie wary of uncritical acceptance of communities per se. Her wariness is perhaps first indicated when the flirtatious

Nunkie makes eyes for Tea Cake. Whereas Janie had previously enjoyed working beside Tea Cake, and the two of them, by "romping and play- ing . . . behind the boss's back," had gotten "the whole field to playing off and on," Nunkie's advances spoil Janie's work and her fun (199). Janie's sus- picions lead to blows between Tea Cake and herself, and later to Tea Cake's more serious beating.[75] Hurston's own collection of African American folk- lore, *Mules and Men* (1935), had anticipated the breakup of a jook/"job" community (197) in much the same way. In the closing pages of Part One ("Folk Tales"), Hurston describes a violently jealous quarrel—one that she is at the heart of—that turns bloody. The final paragraph reads:

> Slim stuck out the guitar to keep two struggling men from blocking my way. Lucy was screaming. Crip had hold of Big Sweet's clothes in the back and Joe was slugging him loose. Curses, oaths, cries and the whole place was in mo- tion. Blood was on the floor. I fell out of the door over a man lying on the steps, who either fell himself trying to run or got knocked down. I don't know. I was in the car in a second and in high just too quick. Jim and Slim helped me throw my bags into the car and I saw the sun rising as I ap- proached Crescent City.[76]

Thus much like Janie's, Hurston's own immersion into communal play had ended (if we trust her tale) in isolation and flight (albeit into the rising sun). But in *Their Eyes Were Watching God*, Hurston imagines for Janie a com- pensating return to companion and community (Pheoby and Eatonville) that Hurston's own story conspicuously lacks. While we may question the extent of Hurston's valorization of community in *Their Eyes Were Watching God*, we do know from *Mules and Men* that the ending Hurston offers Janie makes a stronger gesture toward social interconnectedness than the ending she offered herself.

■

We may still want to object, however, that the selfhood Hurston constructs for Janie is strikingly inconsistent with certain other histories we possess.

Are there details that the text must *re*press in order to *ex*press Janie's tale? Does knowing, for example, that migratory labor during the Depression "represented an extreme form of farm workers' displacement," the squalid camps themselves a symbol of "the black agricultural worker's descent into economic marginality"—and not "fun and games," as Jordan points out—make us not only doubt Hurston's representations but perhaps even regard them as wholesale evasions?[77] Does knowing that black towns like Eatonville were in large respect labor farms for neighboring white towns that catered to wealthy northerners wintering in Florida dissipate the haze of nostalgia enveloping Hurston's youthful recollections?[78] What if we discover that even as the national fertility rate dropped steadily throughout the early century, in 1940 the average rural southern black woman still had 5.5 children? Does Janie's twenty-plus years of conceptionless sexuality constitute the grossest evasion of all? Can Hurston narrate Janie's successful escape from patriarchal control over her body and her leisure only by glossing over these details?

Past readers such as Alain Locke and Richard Wright, who publicly lamented what they saw as the novel's lack of socially responsible protest, certainly thought so. Jordan, more recently, agrees, and specifically criticizes Hurston's representation of migrant labor as diverting play. "Hurston creates a dream relationship that allows Janie freedom to do the things that are amusing and to avoid the burdens of responsibility," Jordan argues. "She works much harder in Joe Starks's store," for example, while her "stoop labor is the equivalent of two weeks at summer camp."[79] Jordan is right to contrast these periods of Janie's life on the basis of her attitude toward the work, but I believe that Janie's attitude is precisely what is at stake, the sense of self-worth and self-control that are called up in her by the demands, duties, and expectations of the labor. This is not to say that the novel suggests that workers merely need attitude adjustments (too often the claim of the play theorists themselves) or that migrant labor was fun, but instead that to Janie, in contrast to the soul-deadening, intensely supervised work of the store, her work on the muck offers a far more satisfying combination of self-directed work, play, and loving companionship. Moreover, as Robert Hemenway suggests, *Their Eyes Were Watching God* does inscribe the "'smouldering resentment' of the black South" against white domination and forced labor.[80] It also observes the migrant workers themselves with an unflinching gaze:

> Some came limping in with their shoes and sore feet from walking. . . . Permanent transients with no attachments and tired looking men with their families and dogs in flivvers. All night, all day, hurrying in to pick beans. Skillets, beds, patched up spare inner tubes all hanging and dangling from the ancient cars on the outside and hopeful humanity, herded and hovered on the inside, chugging on to the muck. People ugly from ignorance and broken from being poor. (196)

Hurston may not foreground these critiques, but neither does she evade them, even if Janie does not locate in herself such tiredness, soreness, and pain.

The charge that Hurston undermines Janie's achievement of bodily control by willfully ignoring the possibility of pregnancy is somewhat harder to address. Children in general are suspiciously absent from the novel, excepting Janie herself, the youth of the "flivver" families, and the children who visit Matt Bonner's mule's "bleaching bones now and then in the spirit of adventure" (97). The ubiquitous breast-feeding baby one sees in the Farm Security Administration photographs from the Depression is even more conspicuously absent.[81] And yet can we not say that in certain respects Janie figuratively gives birth to herself, that by narrating her life story over again from the beginning she gradually brings to term the "jewel" of personal and sexual autonomy that as a girl she had found "down inside herself" (138) but had had to suppress when Nanny brokered her to Killicks? Or could we argue more literally that by not becoming pregnant Janie may actually exercise the ultimate control over her own body? Although the novel does not quite admit that Janie practices birth control, the mere fact that she avoids conception despite three husbands (each of whom, at some point, she appears to engage sexually) speaks strongly not to evasion but to confrontation and even mastery. Janie finally—however she does it—achieves the freedom that many insist comes only from "women's control over the means of reproduction."[82]

■

The control that Janie gains over her own story, her blossoming into what we might call "visible" speech and self-explanatory analysis, most clearly marks the imaginative difference between *Their Eyes Were Watching God* and *Sanctuary*. By this I mean not only the distinctions we may draw between Janie's and Temple's imaginations, but also the differences between Hurston's and Faulkner's imaginative decisions in crafting their contrapuntal explorations of this volatile period. What each work ultimately affirms is the imagination's central role in deflecting and then controlling the gazes that threaten to violate each and every one of us. Ironically, it is the play theorists themselves, whose supervisory logic Hurston and Faulkner implicitly critique, who would be among the first to applaud such affirmation.

Although at times Temple seems crippled simply by her inability to project herself into another's situation—to understand, for example, how her behavior at Frenchman's Bend might appear to someone else—she does relate a remarkable sequence of imaginative projections while talking to Horace at Miss Reba's. Horace even suspects that her whole tale (in which she imagines herself first as a bride in a coffin, then as a schoolteacher, then as an old man) might be a fiction, thinking that she tells it not merely with "a sort of naive and impersonal vanity" but "as though she were making it up" (226). In a sense she is making it up; whether what she tells Horace represents the fantasies she employed at Frenchman's Bend, or merely those she employs when he asks her to tell him what happened, they are nonetheless her creations. In other circumstances their complexity might indicate a fertile imagination, but here—particularly since Temple shows little sign of imaginative engagement elsewhere—they seem more the effects of trauma than evidence for sustaining (or sustainable) invention. What is striking is

Temple's inability to make any of the fantasies work, even though she is in imaginative control of them. Even when at the very last she wills herself into becoming an old man and believes she has the genitalia to prove it, she falls asleep before she can verify the transformation. It is as though the novel does, in the end, show Temple a possible route out of its implosive horrors, but withholds from her the ability to seize it.

That this way out is also play theory's—which in the end analogously called on the creative imagination to free laborers from the "dreary empti-ness and waste of life" in the modern world[83]—can be seen even more clearly in *Their Eyes Were Watching God.* Janie's imaginative powers, unlike Temple's, are genuinely reconstitutive: her mental self-division into woman and shadow, for example, enables her to survive her lonely, loveless mar-riage to Joe. Indeed, for Janie, imagination becomes a welcome addiction. "It was like a drug," the narrator explains. "In a way it was good because it reconciled her to things" (119). Janie's drug-like state may seem inappropri-ately evasive; "indifference," which she comes to feel, hardly seems like a positive emotion. But the play of "summertime" (119) that she creates in her head not only prevents her from being laid waste by Joe's wintry attitude; it also allows her to recognize the incarnation of that summertime when he appears in the person of Tea Cake. This is, moreover, quite in line with Joseph Lee's first play prescription for combating the emptiness of modern industrial labor. In the face of systems that threaten to "sterilize" our souls, Lee urged, people should nurture the "creative instinct"; doing so would give them "a nature that is not so easy to defeat."[84] Janie's maintenance of a healthy fantasy world accomplishes exactly that.

It also enables Janie to craft a version of her life story that produces ac-tion. For despite the contention that Hurston ultimately denies Janie her voice in the novel by usurping narrative control at crucial moments (the telling of stories on the muck, for example, or during Janie's testimony in court), the fact remains that Pheoby, Janie's auditor, is no longer the same person after her tale. "Ah done growed ten feet higher from jus' listenin' tuh you," she says. "Ah ain't satisfied wid mahself no mo'. Ah means tuh make

Sam take me fishin' wid him after this" (284). Pheoby learns through Janie's agency one of the text's most important lessons: the efficacy of partnered work and play. Thus Janie's imagination helps regenerate not only herself but also her dearest friend.

Hurston signals that regeneration by giving her narrative a form that Faulkner seems to have had in mind when he first drafted *Sanctuary*. Janie's tale ends where it begins, both literally and metaphorically, and Janie's closing gesture of pulling the horizon around her like a shawl recapitulates the circular motion that best represents the shape of her story. Faulkner's original version of *Sanctuary*, while not offering quite as complete a gesture, does begin and end with convicted killers awaiting death, as though to urge some connection, some way of making sense out of the otherwise horrific narrative. Play theorists, who cherished the symbolism of children's ring games, would likely have appreciated such purposeful gestures of wholeness and closure. But in the final version of *Sanctuary*, Faulkner quite deliberately breaks that circle. Where the original ends by springing the trapdoor to the hangman's gibbet, thus killing Popeye and perhaps offering readers some satisfaction in seeing Temple's rapist punished in the novel's last stroke, the revised novel hangs Popeye but then shifts to Temple, hopelessly bored in Europe and still subject to the familiar (and crippling) mechanisms of supervisory control: still watched over by her father, still fumbling with her compact—still unimaginatively engaged with the world. Whereas Hurston's ending wraps Janie and the narrative up together, in a modernist gesture that offers, with play theory, the power of art to heal alienation, Faulkner's ending intentionally unravels, just as Temple herself appears "to dissolve into the dying brasses" and "on into the sky" (333). Once again, and in its own brutal challenge to the bland assurances of play reform, *Sanctuary* points to the possibility of salvation but refuses the actual consolation of it. Ironically, yet fittingly, then, the text that tells of a moral collapse expands into the "embrace of . . . death" (333), while the novel that narrates an expansive life collapses into an enduring "peace" (286).

Afterword

H URSTON'S RECOVERY of the history of African American domestic labor circles us back, of all places, to Walden Pond. Where Thoreau despaired
of including lowly Irish laborers in his project of "free labor" and "unrelaxed
play," waving away the very real presence of those immigrants who, like little Johnny Riordan, were achieving a "greater independence," Hurston
finds redemptive value in shaping her protagonist's story according to a servant-class tale of self-transformation—in the service, moreover, of an inspiring fusion of work and play that Thoreau himself would likely have admired. The passage of time, perhaps, makes all the difference; writing in the
1930s, looking back over the tumultuous decades of the nation's economic
and social transformation, Hurston could see histories of successful resistance to the confining structures of market relations that in the 1840s were
only aborning. Of course Thoreau would also have been appalled at how
much more necessary such resistances had become. His generation may
have witnessed the fall from the farmer to the operative, but it was Hurston's that watched the operative collapse into the drudge.

The play theorists' forceful response to that collapse is a useful new context for reading nineteenth- and early-twentieth-century American literature. In grappling with the social consequences of the rise of corporate capitalism and the advent of modern leisure, American writers from Thoreau
to Hurston have necessarily also grappled with the ideals and assumptions
of the recreation reform movement. Seeking to redirect American energy
from the impoverishing factory floor to the revivifying neighborhood playground, play theorists addressed almost every troubling facet of modern
life: urban slums, racial conflict, industrial labor, ethnic assimilation, mass
production, juvenile delinquency, the new woman, the loss of the frontier,

illicit amusements. In this context of national wrangling over the disposition of American bodies at work and at rest—a conversation that play theory helped to shape—literary writers published their own narratives of laboring and leisuring American selves.

But as we have seen, the texts put forth by American writers frequently take issue with the core philosophy of play theory. For all its good intentions, the play theorists' vision of re-creative play, their heady alternative to modern labor's assault on the self, proved too deeply indebted to the values of the very system it sought to repair. The writers in this study suspected as much—that the way out was only a way back in—even before recreation reform had formulated a national ideology. Though Thoreau's project of self-cultivation, for example, mimics in many of its details Catharine Beecher's prescriptions for a "healthy" domestic economy, it expressly rejects her endorsement of standardization and overconsumption. Twain's approval of active recreations like camping stops pointedly short of promoting an already overcommodified Yosemite. After the turn of the century, American writers offered new stories to counter the theorists' popular narrative of right recreation; they challenged, for example, its conception of leisure as the new "frontier" for Americanizing immigrants (Cahan and Rölvaag); its infatuation with traditional gender roles (Gilman and Ferber) and "ideal" bodies (Johnson and Fitzgerald); its race- and class-segregated playgrounds (Dreiser and Wright); and its insistence on a personal freedom tempered by surveillance (Faulkner and Hurston). But play theory's deep flaw, these writers argued (a flaw reflected, in fact, in each critique), was its commitment to an ideology of teamwork that drew its metaphorical energies from the production- and profit-minded ethos of corporate capitalism, a system that did not, except under the compulsion of law, have the interests of its players (or workers) foremost in mind. The cure for a fragmented selfhood would not be found, in other words, in a program of revitalized national belonging, particularly if the real-world model for that belonging tended to exacerbate, rather than alleviate, fragmenting inequalities of gender, class, and race. Where, after all, did the "corporate personality" leave Sam Clemens,

David Levinsky, Clyde Griffiths, Bigger Thomas, Temple Drake, Per Hansa, Jay Gatz, or the ex-colored man? It left them largely isolated, atomized, and lonely, feeling little sense of belonging and often considerable disappointment, even betrayal, over the play- and work-built selves they had tried to shape.

This encapsulation of the arguments mounted against play theory by the writers in this study, however, risks calcifying the give and take of cultural debate into a stark tale of (evil) hegemony and (heroic) resistance. I have tried to communicate through the very structure of this book—in which each chapter takes up a focal pair of texts—that the story of the role of leisure in modern life is more complicated, and more interesting, than that. The writers I discuss in each chapter are engaged in dialogue not only with the play theorists but also with each other (or in the case of Twain, with himself). In some cases, one writer's resistance brings into relief another's accommodation, as we saw Wright's unsparing critique of the segregationist logic of play theory call into question Dreiser's optimistic relaxation of that critique in the final pages of *An American Tragedy*. In others, the comparisons bring to light the complexities of both accommodation and resistance. Thoreau might challenge the nationalist project of a Beecher or Channing, for example, yet still echo the nativist exclusions of the dominant culture. Cahan and Rölvaag might puncture the recreation theorists' romance of assimilation, but *Giants in the Earth*, in the end, can also endorse the healing power of constructive play. Gilman and Ferber might together protest Progressive Era redefinitions of women's work, but from almost opposite ideological positions. Thus these serial pairings illuminate the multiple ways that American writers encountered, understood, and in turn reshaped contemporary ideas of leisure and labor.

If the rise of corporate capitalism and recreation reform did much to mold those ideas, then it was the Depression's fate to unsettle them. Ironically, in many ways the social upheaval of the 1930s suggested that the literary writers had been right all along. For despite Americans' eager embrace of organized play, when the economic props (such as they were) were removed, play degenerated quickly as well. That was not the reformers' fault, of course. But to read the despairing descriptions in 1930s leisure handbooks of the "maladjustment" resulting from increased idleness is to wonder what good directed play had ever done, or whether a philosophy of leisure truly separate from capitalist ideals—if such a philosophy were indeed possible—might have better fortified Americans in the face of capitalism's collapse.[1]

One of the lessons of this study, however, is that ideas of play will always be troubled by ideas of work. Wishing that they were separate may do play a disservice, particularly if one is after, as I am here, a more thoroughly contextual understanding of representations of leisure and recreation. What one might wish to do instead, as some of the writers in this book suggest, is imagine a new "common consciousness," not one patterned on the corporate needs of a capitalist economy but one shaped into a radically different form that encourages both exhilarating work and meaningful play: the self-propagating gynecocracy of Herland, for example; or the partnered play of Janie and Tea Cake; or the fluid boundaries of the communities on the muck. Start from there, Gilman and Hurston seem to say, and see where it takes you. Or, as other of the writers suggest, one might instead insist on an inviolable self-ownership within the larger collective, flawed though that collective be. Recall Thoreau's mid-century reluctance to give up his hard-won (if painfully exclusive) rhetorical and social autonomy; Twain's resistance to late-nineteenth-century corporate capitalism unless artisan-led; Emma McChesney's refusal in the 1910s to "drown" her identity in the "music of the orchestra"; and Bigger's powerful Depression-era sense of self-reliance and even self-creation through murder. Perhaps that is how to wrest autonomy, creativity, and agency from a world in which neither work nor play seems consistently able to provide them.

Could one shape the same insistences or imaginings today? That question is fascinating to ask from this sociopolitical moment, as we race to dismantle the work (and thus also leisure) protections designed and implemented in the 1930s and after. Where the New Deal sought to buffer American workers from the harshest turns of the capitalist cycle, today we press, for example, to end welfare "as we know it" in the name of nineteenth-century injunctions against idleness and profligacy. It should come as no surprise that the attack on sinful public amusements has re-erupted in tandem with these injunctions, or that public figures can simultaneously decry the perils of ill-spent leisure and protest the raising of the minimum wage.

Even children's recess is under threat.[2] We are turning back the clock on work as well, as ongoing corporate downsizing (even, ironically, in the wake of startling new mega-mergers) looks yearningly back to the leaner and more competitive days of entrepreneurial capitalism, if in the name of escalating stock values instead of (in Luther Gulick's evocative phrase) "corporate morality." If job security is the basis of a true leisure—and if we need leisure, as Thoreau insisted, for a true integrity—where are we now? In a devastating paradox: we have reached "the end of work" (in which human labor, Jeremy Rifkin claims, "is being systematically eliminated from the production process"); but we are also "the overworked American" (facing work hours, argues Juliet Schor, that have been rising ominously since the 1940s). The Progressive Era dream, in other words, gone to smash. Where the play reformers and their optimistic peers believed that, any day now, we would all work less and enjoy work more, we now apparently work more hours and feel less secure doing it. I am not ready to adopt Rifkin's tone of impending catastrophe (a "change so vast in scale," he says, "that we are barely able to fathom its ultimate impact");[3] I think we're better fathomers (and imaginers) than that. But I am not convinced that, given the view from here, my own decision to end this book with Hurston's redemptive vision is not just whistling in the dark.

That said, a look at the imaginative engagements of post-Depression American writers with mid- to late-twentieth-century changes in labor and leisure might help explain how we have arrived where we are, and where to go from here. Dreams of renewal through earnest play did not end with Hurston, to be sure. We might tag along with Humbert Humbert or Sal Paradiso, for instance, to measure (however problematically) the postwar celebration of national mobility, with Depression panic safely past and jobs, for most, secure once more. Or assay, a little further ahead, more dystopian visions of desiring selves-in-motion—Maria Wyeth's view, say, from the freeways of Los Angeles in Joan Didion's *Play It as It Lays*. Or tap the raucous restlessness of a Benny Profane (in Thomas Pynchon's *V.*), or trace the seriocomic wanderings of Lipsha Morrissey through Louise Erdrich's North Dakota novels. Should we return to the children themselves? What might *The Bluest Eye*'s Pecola Breedlove tell us about the late-twentieth-century legacies of play theory's fantasies of assimilation and control? Or *The House on Mango Street*'s Esperanza Cordero about the stakes of neighborhood play? Finally, what is the fate of the gospel of play, or the ethic of work, or the desire for agency, in the postindustrial information age?[4] Is Rifkin right? Or can a text like Neal Stephenson's *Snow Crash*, for instance, imagine a fittingly cryptic way out? As apprehensive as contemporary events might make one, I like to think that the potential rewards of taking play seriously in American culture are still within reach, even in this (in its own way) oppressive, yet hopeful, age.

REFERENCE MATTER

NOTES

PREFACE

1. Glassberg, *American Historical Pageantry*, 54.

2. Some of the writers whose texts we will examine, in fact, had direct contact with the play reform movement. Wright, for example, briefly held a job at a South Side Boys' Club in Chicago; Hurston even appeared in the movement's national magazine after leading a presentation of African American "dances, work rhythms and games," including "survivals of African origin," at the 1934 National Folk Festival. See Chubb, "Folk Culture and Leisure," 279.

3. In seeking a more historical and contextual grounding for the study of play in American literature, I am nonetheless greatly indebted to the work of earlier scholars in opening up the field of leisure and representation to serious study. See, for example, the "sports" fiction studies of Higgs (*Laurel and Thorn*), Berman (*Playful Fictions*), Messenger (*Sport and the Spirit of Play in American Fiction* and *Sport and the Spirit of Play in Contemporary American Fiction*), and Oriard (*Dreaming of Heroes*), and the more theoretically minded "game-play" analyses of Rath ("Game-Play in Fiction" and "Game, Play, Literature"), Spariosu (*Literature, Mimesis and Play*), and R. Rawdon Wilson (*In Palamedes' Shadow*). Recent literary studies that take a more contextual interest in play and leisure—though without this study's attention to the specific histories of play theory and corporate capitalism—include Newbury's "Healthful Employment" (since incorporated into his fuller study of labor and writing, *Figuring Authorship in Antebellum America*); Brown's essays on Stephen Crane and 1890s amusement culture ("Interlude" and "American Childhood and Stephen Crane's Toys"), now incorporated into his *Material Unconscious*; and Oriard's *Sporting with the Gods*, a monumental history of "the rhetoric of play and game in American culture" that has been especially enabling for this book.

On work and representation in the antebellum period I am indebted to the studies of Bromell (*By the Sweat of the Brow*) and Weinstein (*The Literature of Labor*); in the postbellum and more modern periods to such studies as Seltzer's *Bodies and Machines* and Banta's *Taylored Lives* (this last a book that provides what might be called the "work theory" counterpart to my own interrogation of culturally influential theories of play). Several historial studies have also been invaluable, from Rodgers's classic *Work Ethic in Industrial America* to more recent investigations into the nature and meanings of class-based recreations in the late nineteenth and early twentieth centuries, including Rosenzweig's *Eight Hours for What We Will*, Couvares's *Remaking of Pittsburgh*, and Peiss's *Cheap Amusements*. My understanding of the history of the turn-of-the-century recreation reform movement in particular has benefited from the work of Cavallo (*Muscles and Morals*), Goodman (*Choosing Sides*), and Guttmann (*A Whole New Ball Game*). Finally, I have been guided throughout this project by Gareth Stedman Jones's double injunction that (1) leisure be studied in relation to, not in isolation from, work; and (2) that we broaden our analytical categories beyond "class expression versus social control," seeking instead (in Peiss's words) "a much richer and more complex picture of cultural change as a multidimensional set of interactions, in which hegemonic intentions are accommodated, resisted, and reshaped in a variety of ways." See G. Jones, "Class Expression Versus Social Control," and Peiss, *Cheap Amusements*, 8.

4. Seltzer, *Bodies and Machines*, 4.

5. In dividing *The Leisure Ethic* into its three sections, I have drawn in part on Herbert Gutman's periodization of industrializing America. Gutman argues that between 1815 and 1843 the United States was still a predominantly preindustrial country; that from 1843 to 1893 a "profound tension" existed between preindustrial social structures and industrial capitalism's modernizing institutions; and that after 1893 the United States was a "mature industrial society" (*Work, Culture, and Society in Industrializing America*, 13). My first period, stretching from Thoreau's mid-1840s sojourn at Walden to Twain's early 1880s return to the Mississippi, corresponds roughly to Gutman's second; and my second period (1880–1920) to his third. My third period, 1920–1940, takes us to the moment when American leisure hours—after years of steady increase—had finally begun to level off. See Schor, *The Overworked American*, 1–5.

6. Texts like Rölvaag's *Giants in the Earth* and Ferber's *Emma McChesney & Co.*, moreover, complicate simple categories like mainstream and alternative: Rölvaag's novel, though quite critical of "mainstream" thought, was a Book of the Month Club selection; Ferber's novel, though written by a woman, had a wide readership among "mainstream" men.

7. Lee, *Play in Education*, 476.

INTRODUCTION

1. Lee, *Play in Education*, 435–36. Gulick, *A Philosophy of Play*, xiv. Historians have disputed both the impetus behind the emergence of modern leisure and the precise quality of the value shift that the ascendancy of play implied, but most agree that play changed, in part, because work changed. Rodgers, for example, argues that as the new demands of turn-of-the-century industrial labor devalued individual work skills and industrial overproduction slowly eroded the "ascetic legacies" of the Protestant work ethic, the net effect was a slide "toward more hedonistic moral calculi" (*The Work Ethic in Industrial America*, 29, 123). Lears, while agreeing with Rodgers in principle, emphasizes more psychosocial factors in explaining the transvaluations of work and leisure. In a society where an integrated and autonomous self seemed increasingly impossible to achieve (let alone maintain) through labor, Americans, Lears argues, gradually exchanged their "Protestant ethos of salvation through self-denial" for a "therapeutic ethos stressing self-realization in this world" ("From Salvation to Self-Realization," 4). For a broad account of changing conceptions of and attitudes toward recreation, leisure, and sport at the turn of the century, see Higham, "The Reorientation of American Culture in the 1890s."

2. Oriard, *Sporting with the Gods*, xi.

3. Seltzer, *Bodies and Machines*, 60.

4. Lee, *Play in Education*, viii.

5. According to the play theorists, constructive play would solve a host of national problems. Here is Gulick writing in the *Playground* in 1904: "Dependency is reduced by giving men more for which to live. Delinquency is reduced by providing a wholesome outlet for youthful energy. Industrial efficiency is increased by giving individuals a play life which will develop greater resourcefulness and adaptability. Good citizenship is promoted by forming habits of co-operation in play. People who play together find it easier to live together and are more loyal as well as more efficient citizens. Democracy rests on the most firm basis when a community has formed the habit of playing together" (quoted in Cavallo, *Muscles and Morals*, 37). Not even Gulick's curiously monotonous, passive sentences can obscure the optimism of his vision.

6. Newbury, "Healthful Employment," 687.

7. Blackwell, *The Laws of Life*, 29, 28, 25.

8. Ibid., 33, 32, 47, 176.

9. Newbury argues persuasively that mid-century health and exercise reforms operated in large part to help members of the emergent middle class "distinguish themselves" from the working-class identities they had left behind, paradoxically

by claiming for themselves the physical, moral, and spiritual virtues of manual labor ("Healthful Employment," 693).

10. Blackwell, *The Laws of Life*, 172; Gulick, *Physical Education by Muscular Exercise*, 57.

11. Curtis, *Education Through Play*, 20; Lee, *Play in Education*, 43.

12. Frobisher, *The Blood and Breath*, 31; hereafter cited parenthetically.

13. If Frobisher's gushing preface sounds like an advertisement, of course it was one, and it was not lonely: sprinkled throughout the handbook are testimonials from satisfied users, plus long excerpts of praise from journals and newspapers. These interpolated testimonials could create jarring textual juxtapositions. On one page, for example, Frobisher's rhapsodic description of oratory's role in creating the "PERFECT MAN" by "adding truth, taste, sensibility and imagination, and other glorious attributes," is rudely undercut by the prosaic plug from the *Dubuque News* for "SOMETHING NOBBY.—Gum-elastic, or India-rubber, is a wonderful thing . . . ' (*The Blood and Breath*, 65).

14. Even thirty years before the founding of the Playground Association of America (PAA)—as the urgent call on *The Blood and Breath*'s back cover for "First-class Agents in every County in the United States" to market and promote the Pocket Gymnasium attests—*The Blood and Breath* was trying to draw Americans into a national discourse on health, fitness, and patriotism.

15. Lee, *Play in Education*, 140.

16. Newbury, "Healthful Employment," 693.

17. Lee, *Play in Education*, xiii.

18. The play reformers not only operated under the sign of the culture of management; they also actively managed people and institutions. Gulick, for example, served as director of the physical education program at the Springfield YMCA in the late 1880s; principal of Pratt Institute High School in Brooklyn from 1900 to 1903; director of physical education for the New York City school system from 1903 to 1906, where he also created and directed the Public School Athletic League and served as president of the American Physical Education Association; president of the PAA from 1906 to 1910; director of the Russell Sage Hygiene Department from 1907 to 1913; and founder of the Camp Fire Girls in 1912. (Gulick also took a medical degree in 1889.) Curtis directed the New York City playground system from 1898 to 1901 (after completing a Ph.D. in child psychology in 1898 with G. Stanley Hall at Clark University) and then ran the Washington, D.C., system beginning in 1905. Lee founded the Massachusetts Civic League and took over for Gulick as president of the PAA in 1910, a post he held until his death in 1937. (See Cavallo,

Muscles and Morals; Dorgan, *Luther Halsey Gulick*; and Boyer, *Urban Masses and Moral Order in America*.)

19. Curtis, *Education Through Play*, 14, 15.

20. Lee, *Play in Education*, 463, 478, 476, 494. Symptomatic of what many of the writers in this study ultimately see as play theory's fatal attraction to the values and structures of capitalism, however, in the end Lee can only conceive of this "overflow" of play in terms of market relations. "We must provide a market [for this overflow]," he claimed. "What gives life is not self-absorption but self-forgetfulness, not composing yourself as a beautiful image before the glass, but subordination to some outside end. What brings power and happiness is the thing required of you, something you have to do, making good, satisfying a market, not doing parlor tricks" (470).

21. From the start, play reformers looked beyond the children on their playgrounds toward reorganizing the life of the nation as a whole. Thus the list of play's benefits, though specific, could be staggeringly long. Consider the following inventory from a 1920s history of the play movement: (1) Physical: general health, "personal preparedness" (strength, speed, agility, endurance), beauty of form, and grace of movement; (2) Mental: control over the body's reflexes and sensorimotor skills; knowledge of one's environment, ideas gained from association with others, insights into human nature, and adjustments to "practical situations of life"; memory, imagination, and reason; (3) Moral: courage, self-initiative, decisiveness, perseverance, determination, self-reliance, self-control, self-restraint, thoroughness, aggressiveness, ambition, enthusiasm, and reliability; kindness, unselfishness, friendliness, truthfulness, justice, honesty, thoughtfulness, generosity, courtesy, service, tolerance, and sociability; loyalty, cooperation, freedom, obedience, morality, and optimism. As another sign of just how seriously the recreation reformers took play: where else would one find a movement's products touted as mother-, judge-, doctor-, and *coroner*-approved, as was the Everwear playground apparatus advertised in the *Playground* in the 1920s?

22. Gulick, *A Philosophy of Play*, 234; Curtis, *Education Through Play*, 63. The limits of Lee's tolerance for "free play"—and evidence that the play theorists were often as interested in productive work as in re-creative leisure—can be seen in his leaflet *The Tramp Problem*. Prepared for the Massachusetts Civic League, it contends that tramps are a "national evil" and should be "sent to the State Farm, where they may learn to work" (15). Contends a two-stanza poem on the leaflet's cover: "Dirt without work / Delights the shirk, / The tramp or hobo flagrant; / Work without dirt / Rewards desert / And terrifies the vagrant. // Then let us stick / By

spade and pick, / By hammer and macadam; / The ancient test / Is still the best / The Lord applied to Adam."

23. In *Choosing Sides*, Goodman offers the most severe critique of play reform as a conscious program of social control. Other historians have taken a more moderate view, including Cavallo and Guttmann. "[The play reformers'] conception of disciplined play was indeed meant to socialize boys and girls into the more or less rationalized modern world," argues Guttmann. "They did not, however, intend team games to eradicate individual initiative, nor did they imagine that organized play was the basis for industrial exploitation" (*A Whole New Ball Game*, 89). This measured critique is worth keeping in view; play reform was a broad and complex project, not merely an instance of middle-class hegemony. Nonetheless, the play theorists need not have been committed to an out-and-out project of "industrial exploitation" to have "imagined" some pretty dreadful things about individual agency in their play-built polis. I will try to avoid the at times one-sided critique of Goodman, but I will not be as quick to wave away the "imaginings" of play theory as Guttmann.

24. Gulick, *A Philosophy of Play*, 213, 222.

25. Curtis, *Education Through Play*, 8, 9.

26. Lee, *Play in Education*, 335, 336, 391.

27. Gilman, *Human Work*, 389.

28. See, for example, Gilman's 1908 essay, "A Suggestion on the Negro Problem."

29. Lee, *Play in Education*, 452. Lee drops into "Chinaman" dialect, for example, in chapter 26 and tells Irish jokes in his epilogue. According to Cavallo, Lee's membership in the Immigration Restriction League "disturbed" Curtis and Gulick but did not prevent them from asking him to join their effort to found the PAA in 1906 (*Muscles and Morals*, 35). In his own 1902 book, *Constructive and Preventive Philanthropy* (with an introduction by Jacob Riis), Lee describes the league's efforts to push a literacy bill through Congress in hope of preventing a further increase in the "squalid imported population" from the "lower and peasant classes of Europe" (8). Of those immigrant children who did end up on city playgrounds, Lee had this to say: "Our courage has risen, our humanity has expanded, to feel that these new-comers are Americans, and that, whether they are or not, they must be. And we are going to make them so" (235).

30. Lee, *Play in Education*, 191, 206, 229, 213, 211.

31. See Roediger, *The Wages of Whiteness*, 104, and Lott, *Love and Theft*, 53. The descriptions of one game in Lee's handbook would suggest that "Indians" were un-

derstood in explicitly racial terms even by children. "It is a little more exciting to be a white man pursued by an Indian than merely to be Jimmie chased by Mary Ann" (*Play in Education*, 297). Before the more generic "cowboy and Indian" terminology had evolved, then, one had "white man and (red) Indian."

32. Roediger, *The Wages of Whiteness*, 116.

33. Lee, *Play in Education*, 406, 402.

34. Dorgan, *Luther Halsey Gulick*, 37.

35. Lee, *Play in Education*, 469, 317.

36. Girl Scouts, *Campward Ho!*

37. Forbush, *Manual of Play*, 133.

38. Lee saw particular merit in stories of "heroic fiction," which one may read, tell to someone else, or act out in play. "These various methods of imagining are not very different in effect," Lee explained. "If there is greater intensity in the more active method, there is greater freedom in the other. As you sit looking in the fire while your mother reads, you can always be Robin Hood yourself—or Sir Galahad, Tom Sawyer, Tom Brown, Heidi, Sir Lancelot, Sir Lamarack, or Sir Bors de Ganis, as the case may be" (306–7).

39. In the table of contents for *Play in Education*, for example, Lee inserts this telling parenthetical note: "This and subsequent descriptive chapters are intended to present a portrait, not a photograph, and therefore include the element of interpretation as well as that of reporting" (xvii). That the play reformers attributed considerable power to storytelling is perhaps best illustrated in the extended discussion in Richardson and Loomis's *Boy Scout Movement Applied by the Church*. In the chapter "Recreational and Moral Value of Stories," the authors comment, "Certain definite transformations take place while the boy's mind follows the development of [a] story. It is being led. The moral or providential path is not of its own choosing" (369). Thus "every leader should thoroughly master a few of the very choicest suitable stories and be prepared to compete successfully with others less worthy" (370). Hall had himself suggested in *Adolescence* that "ephebic literature"—"true pictures" of the young that appeal to the young—"should be recognized as a class by itself, and have a place of its own in the history of letters and in criticism" (1: 530, 589). Or in the history of fundraising: Goodman reports that the play reformers used narratives they collected to gather money for the PAA, packaging "'true stories' of children who had stopped whining, sailed boats, and learned team play as a result of playgrounds" in PAA mailings to prospective donors (*Choosing Sides*, 66).

40. The phrases "work's century" and "play's century" are Oriard's (*Sporting with the Gods*, 422).

CHAPTER 1

1. Thoreau, *Walden*, 84; hereafter cited parenthetically.

2. Sumner, *The True Grandeur of Nations*, 5, 6.

3. Ibid., 6.

4. R. Richardson, *Henry Thoreau*, 55, 57.

5. Exceptions here include Neufeldt's "Thoreau's Enterprise of Self-Culture," L. Johnson's "Revolution and Renewal," and the discussions of Thoreau and particularly *Walden* in Oriard's *Sporting with the Gods* (esp. 373–78) and Bromell's *By the Sweat of the Brow* (213–39).

6. See Oriard and Bromell's studies for related claims about Thoreau's reconception of work and play. Oriard demonstrates that Thoreau (unlike Emerson) "envisioned a transcendent dialectic in which work and play are transformed by their fusion" (*Sporting with the Gods*, 369), while Bromell (though more interested in the distinctions between mental and manual labor) argues that labor, for Thoreau, "becomes a kind of sport, or play" (*By the Sweat of the Brow*, 229). My reading brings the anxious disruptions of mid-century immigration into the picture in order to identify a sociopolitical and rhetorical urgency constituent to Thoreau's rethinking of labor and leisure. Where Bromell argues, for example, that in *Walden* "Thoreau's politics are finally an ecological politics, focusing on the human situation in nature rather than the human situation in the polis" (231), I suggest in what follows that the politics of Thoreau's reconception of work and play, more than we have yet suspected, have a great deal to do with shifting mid-century notions of citizenship and the polis. For a brief biographical review of Thoreau's thoughts about play, see also Daher, "Leisure, Play and Labor in Thoreau."

7. *The Journal of Henry David Thoreau*, ed. Torrey and Allen, 6: 158 (March 8, 1854). Unless otherwise noted, all other journal passages in this chapter are taken from the first four published volumes of the Princeton University Press edition of Thoreau's journal (covering the years 1837–52) and are cited parenthetically as *PJ*, followed by volume and page number.

8. Channing, "Self-Culture," 14, 21, 19.

9. Thoreau, "The Commercial Spirit of Modern Times," 117.

10. Channing, "Self-Culture," 17, 20.

11. Ibid., 14.

12. Quoted in Betts, "Mind and Body in Early American Thought," 793, 799. Bancroft and Cogswell further claimed that they were "the first in the new continent to connect gymnastics with a purely literary establishment" (793).

13. G. Lewis, "The Beginning of Organized Collegiate Sport," 223.

14. Betts, "Mind and Body in Early American Thought," 800.

15. Emerson, *Selections*, 81, 301, 402.

16. Thoreau, "The Commercial Spirit of Modern Times," 117.

17. Residents of Concord, however, suspected that the seemingly idle Thoreau was up to no good. According to Canby, memories of Thoreau in Concord were not flattering. His neighbors saw him as "shiftless," a "Harvard graduate who wore old clothes, wouldn't choose a career, and could be met loafing wherever there were pines, ponds, or rivers" (*Thoreau*, 211). On Thoreau's defense of "unceasing play," see also Oriard's related discussion of Thoreau's "dialectic of *earnest play*" in *Sporting with the Gods* (374, original emphasis). On Thoreau's "hardwon" struggle to "confront and re-evaluate the meaning of his body" in *Walden*, see Bromell, *By the Sweat of the Brow*, 224–32.

18. Quoted in R. Richardson, *Henry Thoreau*, 55.

19. Martineau, *Society in America*, 3: 156; C. Beecher, *Letters to the People*, 8, 121; Adams, *History of the United States*, 1: 42.

20. "Why We Get Sick," 642, 646, 643.

21. Commentators also attributed the decline in American health to the rise of infectious diseases introduced into North America from Europe. In 1832, for example, the United States suffered the first of two deadly antebellum cholera epidemics. See Rosenberg, *The Cholera Years*, 42.

22. Laurie, *Artisans into Workers*, 16; Rodgers, *The Work Ethic in Industrial America*, 19.

23. Quoted in Rodgers, *The Work Ethic in Industrial America*, 5–6, original ellipsis and emphasis.

24. Riess, *City Games*, 13.

25. Hardy, *How Boston Played*, 43.

26. The first chapter in Henry Ward Beecher's widely read *Lectures to Young Men, on Various Important Subjects* (1844), for example, tackled "Industry and Idleness." The industrious young man could still enjoy himself; the "purest pleasures" lay "within the circle of useful occupation" (43–44). But "mere pleasure,—sought outside of usefulness,—existing by itself,—is fraught with poison" (44). Public amusements, in particular, Beecher declared, encourage vice, indulgence, and dissipation.

27. Channing, "Address on Temperance," 100.

28. Higginson, "Saints, and Their Bodies," 586; Emerson, *The Complete Works*, 5: 134, 65, 69, 106, 65.

29. In his 1845 *Report to the Committee of the City Council* on the Boston census, Lemuel Shattuck acknowledges a decrease in cholera but notes with alarm a

rise in diseases of the respiratory and particularly digestive organs. He meticulously documents, for example, "a decided increase" in deaths due to "*Enteritis*, or inflammation of the bowels," in "Bowel Complaints," and in "Diseases of the Stomach and Bowels" (147).

30. Many Americans saw the frequency of disease among the poor not as a failure of public policy but as a sign of divine retribution. This hampered, as one might imagine, mid-century social reform efforts. See Rosenberg, *The Cholera Years*.

31. Sklar, *Catharine Beecher*, 151.

32. C. Beecher, *A Treatise on Domestic Economy*, 13, 8; hereafter cited parenthetically.

33. This connection is made even more explicit in Catharine Beecher's *Letters to the People*. In the *Treatise*, Beecher also encourages American women to reconceive their workday chores as exemplary forms of healthful muscular action, devoting an entire chapter to the physiological and moral benefits of "Domestic Exercise." In bed-making, sweeping, and dusting, she explained, "almost every muscle in the body will be called into vigorous activity; and this kind of exercise should be continued two or three hours." Not spent only dusting, of course: "Washing, ironing, starching, rubbing furniture, tending infants, and all employments that require stooping, bending, and change of position, are promoting the health of the muscles used, and of all the various organs of the body" (116).

34. According to Root and de Rochemont's *Eating in America*, American per capita consumption of meat was a whopping 178 pounds per year during the 1830s, a total not surpassed until 1970 (139).

35. Reynolds, *Beneath the American Renaissance*, 101.

36. Neufeldt, "Thoreau's Enterprise of Self-Culture," 239; Sklar, *Catharine Beecher*, 307 n.

37. Sklar, *Catharine Beecher*, 166.

38. For another reading of the sandbank, labor, and Thoreau's "fanciful etymology" (235), see Bromell, *By the Sweat of the Brow*, 235–36.

As the word labor disappears from *Walden*, a new word, I would argue, symbolically takes its place: re-creation. After using several forms of "recreate" (135, 136, 194, 206), meaning "to refresh," Thoreau shifts to "re-create," meaning "to create anew." One of these appears in "Spring" ("the sun shines bright and warm this first spring morning, re-creating the world" [314]), although the first edition of *Walden* printed "recreating" instead. Because Thoreau, however, had actually added the hyphen himself in draft VI, most editions print "re-creating" today. But in his private copy of the 1854 *Walden*, Thoreau also rehyphenated the word "recreate" that appears at the end of "Higher Laws" in the passage on John Farmer, changing "recreate" (which had been an end-of-line hyphenation) to "re-create." All of Thoreau's editors have rejected the suggestion that Thoreau did so because he actually meant to shift the meaning of the word, and to this day every edition retains "recreate." But I believe that shifting the meaning is precisely what Thoreau had in mind. After all, "rec-reate" is proper syllabification for the word if it means "refresh"; why would Thoreau suddenly syllabify the word incorrectly? More signally, as we will see, it seems precisely John Farmer's re-creation that the passage in "Higher Laws" offers. I believe Thoreau was thus manipulating the meanings of the term "recreation" more deliberately (and earlier) in his texts than his editors have understood, and in a way that once again marks him as prescient—not until the turn of the century would the twitch of a hyphen so punningly rehabilitate a word that in Thoreau's day was more commonly linked to the trifling term "amusement." See Trench, *On the Study of Words*, 219.

39. Gross, "Culture and Cultivation," 45.

40. See Fanning, *The Irish Voice in America*, 74; Hardy, *How Boston Played*, 28; and Laurie, *Artisans into Workers*, 25–26. Ironically, it was the arrival of the Irish at mid-century that also jeopardized Beecher's program of domestic economy, in which she urged American women to perform their own housework in order to avoid "aristocratic" idleness. For as "the growth of middle-class wealth widened the demand for female domestic servants" (Wilentz, *Chants Democratic*, 110)—and Irish immigrants more than plugged the gap—fewer middle-class American women found themselves without domestic help. By 1850, as Christine Stansell has shown in *City of Women*, three out of every four serving women in New York City were Irish (cited in Roediger, *The Wages of Whiteness*, 145).

41. Gross, "Culture and Cultivation," 53.

42. Handlin, *Boston's Immigrants*, 82; Gross, "Culture and Cultivation," 43.

43. Hardy, *How Boston Played*, 28–29. Fears about the Irish were not new in the late 1840s—indeed, the memory of the Charlestown Convent Fire and subsequent riot in 1837 burned bright in the minds of Boston natives and immigrants alike— but only after the beginning of massive famine emigration did such anxieties become distinctly national concerns. See, for example, Handlin, *Boston's Immigrants*, 187–89. That nativist alarm could take many forms is evidenced by the same *Harper's* columnist who railed against "a nation of invalids" in "Why We Get Sick"; in the same essay he also blamed ignorant Irish cooks for forcing indigestible dinners down the nation's throat: "We can hardly expect that Liebig should be familiar to the present generation of our cooks, who belong to 'the finest peasantry' of the world, whose practical knowledge was confined to the roasting of a potato, until, fresh from Kilkenny, a wider field opened to them in our kitchens, where, un-

der the stimulus of soap fat and ten dollars a month, they commenced spoiling our dinners and ruining our stomachs" (644).

44. Fanning, *The Irish Voice in America*, 74.

45. Potter, *To the Golden Door*, 466–67.

46. Handlin, *Boston's Immigrants*, 185.

47. Buckley, "Thoreau and the Irish," 400, 397; Ryan, "Shanties and Shiftlessness," 77–78.

48. Ryan, "Shanties and Shiftlessness," 77.

49. In *Dark Thoreau*, Bridgman poses similar questions but ventures no answers; see 108.

50. Sattelmeyer, "The Remaking of *Walden*," 58. The two indispensable sources for information about the successive drafts of *Walden* are Shanley's *Making of "Walden"* and Clapper's "Development of Walden."

51. See, for example, Handlin, *Boston's Immigrants*, 70–72; and Ware, *The Industrial Worker*, 106–48.

52. Tellingly, in the original journal entry Thoreau records that "*he* [i.e., Field] changed seats" (*PJ* 2: 177), but in the final text he changes the account to read "*we* changed seats" (208, emphasis added). For another reading of the fishing scene in "Baker Farm," see Sattelmeyer, "'The True Industry for Poets,'" 193–95.

53. In *Thoreau's Wild Rhetoric*, Golemba argues provocatively that Thoreau's "xenophobia" is part of a rhetorical strategy designed to give his persona sufficient "Yankee shrewdness" and unsentimental toughness to make *Walden* a more attractive text to its presumably xenophobic audience (176–77). I agree that Thoreau's incipient nativism is in part a rhetorical necessity; but, as we shall see, it is primarily *Walden*'s internal logic that requires these sentiments, not any constraints imposed by potential readers.

54. Shanley, *The Making of "Walden,"* 31.

55. Sattelmeyer, "The Remaking of *Walden*," 60.

56. The next stanza of the ballad suggests just how closely in the journal Thoreau's imagination linked Johnny Riordan and Irish railroad laborers with his own project of creative, serious play, best exemplified in his fascination with the "deep cut" of the sandbank in "Spring." The ballad continues: "I shall grow up / And be a great man / And shovel all day / As hard as I can. / Down in the deep cut / [line missing] / Where the men lived / Who made the Rail road" (*PJ* 3: 156).

57. In "The Bean-Field," for example, Thoreau specifies that his formative initial visit to Walden Pond occurred "when I was four years old" (155). In "Winter Animals," Thoreau's description of the hares that visit his cabin makes them sound at first suspiciously like destitute Irish children, coming "round my door at dusk

to nibble the potato parings which I had thrown out" (280); but he then reveals that the "poor wee thing[s], lean and bony" could "scud" over the snow with remarkable "elastic[ity]," thereby (much like Johnny) "asserting [their] vigor and the dignity of Nature" (281). And in the "Conclusion," after relating the anecdote about the little boy who tells the traveler that the swamp before him did have a hard bottom (the traveler, his horse "up to the girths" in muck, simply hadn't reached it yet), Thoreau says, "So it is with the bogs and quicksands of society; but he is an old boy that knows it" (330)—figuring himself, in a sense, as an adult version (an "old boy") of little Johnny.

58. *The Journal of Henry David Thoreau*, ed. Torrey and Allen, 3: 242.

59. For usefully contextualized discussions of Thoreau's interest in (and even complicity with) the market ideology that he professed to abhor, see Fink, *Prophet in the Marketplace* (esp. 260–69), and Gilmore, *American Romanticism and the Marketplace*, 35–51.

60. As Ware reports, "the progress of the Industrial Revolution destroyed, not only the semi-agricultural factory population, but the New England farm that made its independence real" (*The Industrial Worker*, 74). And Gross reminds us that "at the very moment Thoreau was striving to control his own life in the face of the market, the railroad was sweeping up the remaining old-time farmers on the outskirts into the triumphant new world of agricultural capitalism" ("Transcendentalism and Urbanism," 378).

61. Gross, "Culture and Cultivation," 44.

CHAPTER 2

1. Attendance figures for the Centennial Exposition are provided in Laurie, *Artisans into Workers*, 115. Twain's "tearing along" statement is cited in Kaplan, *Mr. Clemens and Mark Twain*, 197.

2. Laurie, *Artisans into Workers*, 114.

3. Ibid. On Howells's visit and reactions to the Centennial Exposition, see Banta, *Imaging American Women*, 524–25.

4. Twain, *Adventures of Huckleberry Finn*, 41.

5. Twain was by far the play theorists' favorite American fiction writer. Tom Sawyer had a particular appeal for Lee, who saw the "contagion" of Tom's spirit for work as a model for beneficial action. "Here, in the human body," Lee suggested (in a metaphor that took many turns before returning to that body), "are thousands of molecules sitting round waiting to see what kind of sport you have to offer them. Is your invitation worth accepting; is the kind of game going on there one that is

worth while to join? . . . The game of health is like getting up a dance or a picnic. You must go in with a vim if you would succeed. It is the big fire that spreads. Or it is like Tom Sawyer's method when he had to whitewash the fence. You remember that he put such artistic appreciation into his job, that the other boys, instead of pitying him, actually parted with their treasures for a chance to do his work for him. Now Tom Sawyer is the sort of microbe you must have in your system" (*Play in Education*, 493).

6. Between 1872 and 1883, Twain's major publications include *The Gilded Age* (1873), "Old Times on the Mississippi" (1875), *The Adventures of Tom Sawyer* (1876), *A Tramp Abroad* (1880), and *The Prince and the Pauper* (1882). In the decade after the publication of *Huckleberry Finn* (1885), however, he published only two major works, *A Connecticut Yankee in King Arthur's Court* (1889) and *The Tragedy of Pudd'nhead Wilson* (1894), and one virtually forgotten novel, *An American Claimant* (1892).

7. Twain, *Roughing It*, 33, vi; hereafter cited parenthetically.

8. Gillman, *Dark Twins*, 23. For a related yet different reading of Twain's "economic" allegiances in *Life* and their impact on the text's narrative structures, see Weinstein's account of *Life* as "torn" between competing ideals of "efficiency": that of the (full-speed ahead) engineer and that of the (digressive) humorist (*The Literature of Labor*, 129–40). Weinstein's claim that the narrator both "deplores" the engineer's ideal and nonetheless "celebrates [it] as the herald of progress" (136) dovetails with my reading of Twain's split affinities for "old ways" and "new ways," although we differ on the implications of Twain's representational turn in the closing chapters of the book; see esp. 139–40.

9. Rodgers, *The Work Ethic in Industrial America*, 14, 8, 10.

10. Heightening this apprehension in the early nineteenth century was the gradual increase in scope and availability of leisure-time amusements. As Americans moved off their farms into towns and cities, urban recreations multiplied. Relatively innocent (and generally outdoor) folk pastimes such as hunting, fishing, wrestling, and stool-ball were soon supplanted by the more worrisome contests purveyed in billiard parlors, at bowling alleys, and on racetracks. For new readings of Puritan attitudes toward leisure, see Struna, *People of Prowess*, and Daniels, *Puritans at Play*.

11. Rodgers, *The Work Ethic in Industrial America*, 22, 67, 27. See Kasson, *Civilizing the Machine*, 102–6, for a discussion of these changes in New England. The Lowell factory system, for instance, was already being transformed in the 1840s and 1850s by the same Irish immigrants who had made Thoreau so anxious. As Kasson explains, the "hierarchical and manipulative model" of factory work at Lowell (in which workers were merely "passive agents" [105]), coupled with the changeover

from a "circulatory" work force of young New England women to a permanent (almost proletarian) population of Irish laborers, made "the possibility of an integrated and harmonious republican community" seem, by the 1850s, further off than ever (104, 106).

12. Somers, *The Rise of Sports in New Orleans*, vi.

13. Kirsch, *The Creation of American Team Sports*, 6–7.

14. Spears and Swanson, *History of Sport and Physical Activity*, 141.

15. Rodgers, *The Work Ethic in Industrial America*, 95, 96.

16. Ware, *The Industrial Worker*, xviii.

17. The profligate spending, of course, is a terrific boost to production—witness the countless breast pins and whistles Brigham Young must order simply to keep peace in his household(s).

18. Twain, "Sandwich Islands Lecture," 14.

19. Twain himself, of course, was never too enthusiastic about "paradise," of this world or any other, as perhaps best evidenced by his broadsides against conventional pulpit notions of heaven. See, for example, the "Heaven" section of Baetzhold and McCullough's *The Bible According to Mark Twain*, which includes "Captain Stormfield's Visit to Heaven," "Captain Simon Wheeler's Dream Visit to Heaven," "A Singular Episode: The Reception of Rev. Sam Jones in Heaven," "Mental Telegraphy?," and "Etiquette for the Afterlife: Advice to Paine" (129–210).

20. Rodgers, *The Work Ethic in Industrial America*, 114.

21. Kaplan, *Mr. Clemens and Mark Twain*, 237; Neider, *The Complete Essays of Mark Twain*, 473.

22. See Benson, *Mark Twain's Western Years*, 32.

23. Sears, *Sacred Places*, 122–23, 176, 177.

24. Twain may avoid fanning the flames of the craze, but he does torch a grove of trees in the Lake Tahoe section (in what almost seems an eerie reenactment of Thoreau's little wildfire at Walden Pond). "Yosemite and the Big Trees," as Twain indicates on 125, had become a tourist's catch phrase for the sights of the region after mid-century.

25. Sears, *Sacred Places*, 123, 124.

26. As Sears observes in *Sacred Places*, Twain himself criticized the popular Yosemite paintings of Albert Bierstadt in a review of the latter's 1867 *Domes of the Yosemite*; see 134.

27. As much as we'd like to think that *Roughing It* provides an enduring portrait of "flush time" gambling houses, hurdy-gurdies, etc., their presence in the narrative is limited to roughly one paragraph in chapter 43.

28. Critics have long split *Roughing It* into two halves, with the break between

chapters 41 and 42. (See, e.g., Henry Nash Smith, "Mark Twain as an Interpreter of the Far West.") This is certainly an important turning point in the narrative, but I believe the book more clearly divides into three sections: chapters 1–25, 26–62, and 63–79. For although Sam's experiences as a prospector end after the blind lead, his experiences with mining do not. For an analysis of the role of play in the structure of *Roughing It*, see Michelson, "Ever Such a Good Time."

29. H. Smith, "Mark Twain as an Interpreter of the Far West," 223.

30. A subgroup of the mining community also possibly intended here by the phrase "dull slaves of toil" is the Chinese, who typically purchased and then worked the claims that no one else wanted (and were thus often perceived as drudges). This disadvantaged ownership was frequently the only type permitted Chinese miners on the frontier. See Chiu, *Chinese Labor in California*, and Saxton, *The Indispensable Enemy*, 46–60, for a fuller discussion.

31. Moss, "Silver Frolic," 7; Saxton, *The Indispensable Enemy*, 55.

32. See Chiu, *Chinese Labor in California* (esp. ix–xii and 1–30), for an excellent account of the consolidation of corporate mining in California, and Saxton, *The Indispensable Enemy*, 55, for an explanation of the rapidity with which that consolidation occurred in Nevada after 1859.

33. For a more traditional reading of this episode, see H. Smith, "Mark Twain as an Interpreter of the Far West."

34. Even Twain's second great missed opportunity—the chance to be partnered with a group of New York capitalists on a million-dollar development deal—proves in retrospect to have been much less lucrative for the small investor who took Twain's place than at first promised. See Twain's revealing footnote at the end of chapter 58.

35. On Sutro's reputation, see G. Smith, *The History of the Comstock Lode*, 109. In 1897, in an ironic turn of events, Sutro was one of a group of American millionaires who proposed putting up $12,000 to sponsor a Twain lecture at the Waldorf Hotel, for which the best seats would be auctioned off at "Jenny Lind prices." Had the lecture, which was intended to be an anniversary reenactment of Twain's 1867 Cooper Union debut, come to pass, its proceeds might have pulled Twain out of his financial morass. But Twain's wife, Livy, got wind of the arrangements and nixed the idea (Kaplan, *Mr. Clemens and Mark Twain*, 348).

36. Banta, "The Boys and the Bosses," 505.

37. The quotation here appears in the notes to the Library of America edition of *Innocents Abroad* and *Roughing It* (New York: Library of America, 1984), 989. Notes by Guy Cardwell.

38. Twain, *Mark Twain's Letters from Hawaii*, 271.

39. This phrase, which epitomizes the growing attitude toward "right" leisure at mid-century, appeared in an 1859 *Baltimore American and Commercial Daily Advertiser* article about the role of leisure in industrial society. See Click, *The Spirit of the Times*, 103.

40. See, for example, Kaplan on Twain's anxiety about being typed as a lyceum "mountebank" in the early 1870s (*Mr. Clemens and Mark Twain*, 147); Fetterley on Twain's "consistently ambivalent" attitude toward his career as a professional humorist ("Mark Twain and the Anxiety of Entertainment," 382); and Gillman on Twain's "essentially adversarial" relationship with his lecture audiences (*Dark Twins*, 30).

41. Kaplan, *Mr. Clemens and Mark Twain*, 94, 95, 97.

42. Gordon, Edwards, and Reich, *Segmented Work, Divided Workers*, 95–96.

43. Gutman, *Work, Culture, and Society*, 320.

44. Ross, *Workers on the Edge*, 233.

45. Laurie, *Artisans into Workers*, 114.

46. Ross, *Workers on the Edge*, 235.

47. Laurie, *Artisans into Workers*, 114–15.

48. Ross, *Workers on the Edge*, xvi; Gutman, *Work, Culture, and Society*, 54. Haydu reminds us in *Between Craft and Class* that the transition from craft manufacture to mass production was not simply a straightforward and inevitable shift in factory politics, but was instead "actively contested" by workers in the late nineteenth century (2).

49. See Kruse, *Mark Twain and "Life on the Mississippi,"* 5–7.

50. I argue here that *Life*, like *Roughing It*, is more logically split into three sections than two: chapters 1–21, 22–50, and 51–60. Even Weinstein's excellent reading of Twain's "practice of literary labor" in *Life* continues to see the text in two halves. See, e.g., *The Literature of Labor*, 140.

51. Twain's Mississippi embrace may even try to reach wider than is geographically possible. James Cox notes in "*Life on the Mississippi* Revisited" that Twain's apparent claim in the first chapter that the river draws water from as far east as Delaware is patently false—a fact Twain would certainly have known.

52. Kruse, *Mark Twain and "Life on the Mississippi,"* 123.

53. "Editor's Table," *Harper's Magazine*, 413, 415, 416.

54. Ibid., 417.

55. Twain, *Life on the Mississippi*, 15; hereafter cited parenthetically.

56. Messenger, *Sport and the Spirit of Play in American Fiction*, 87; Guttman, *From Ritual to Record*, 47.

57. In *The Literature of Labor* (esp. 130, 142–46) Weinstein reads the prepon-

derance of dead bodies in the text as part of a larger allegorical strategy in Twain's writing. "A pattern emerges whereby Twain appears to expend as much energy in figuring out ways to destroy his characters as he does in producing them. One arrives at the conclusion that only by erasing the products of his imaginative labor does Twain complete the labor process itself. Moreover, Twain's career permits us to witness the drama of the author as engineer who must now find the solution to the problem of inventing too many characters—or, more precisely, too many characters of the 'wrong' or allegorical type. These texts thus labor to undo the characterological labor that they have done" (130). I see Twain involved less in a drama of "author as engineer" than in one of author as artisan, and less anxious about the "inefficiency" of his "literary labors" (Weinstein, *The Literature of Labor*, 12) than about the decline of artisanal power and control.

58. Somers, *The Rise of Sports in New Orleans*, 72, 85.

59. Ibid., 87.

60. "Mule" itself may invoke race, as a derisive slang term for "mulatto." During Reconstruction, it was more common in the South for blacks to ride as jockeys at race tracks, and even to mingle in the stands. See Somers, *The Rise of Sports in New Orleans*, 96–97.

61. Gutman, *Work, Culture, and Society*, 51–52.

62. Twain, "Whittier Birthday Speech," 111.

63. Kaplan, *Mr. Clemens and Mark Twain*, 199, 238.

64. In this respect, *Life on the Mississippi* registers something like the tension between self and system that went unresolved in Frobisher's 1876 exercise book, *The Blood and Breath*. By the end of *Life*, however, Twain resolves this tension in favor (however provisionally) of self, specifically the artisanal self.

65. This particular chart was designed by Bixby himself, an example of one skilled artisan's ingenious adaptation to the changing economics of the river. By 1882 Bixby has also changed jobs from pilot to captain; but unlike the earlier days, in the new economy captains have more actual and apparent power than their pilot employees. Bixby's taking of the wheel—as a captain, not a pilot—to show the cub how to steer the boat demonstrates this power vividly.

66. See Roediger, "'Not Only the Ruling Classes to Overcome,'" 213.

67. Rock Island also, curiously enough, houses a "national armory and arsenal" (328), quite possibly built in the aftermath of the 1877 riots. Gutman reports that critics of the riots specifically urged the "building of armories in large cities" (*Work, Culture, and Society*, 52).

68. These northwestern cities (and, by extension, the people in them) are also noticeably figured as male. Twain emphasizes this gendered perception when writ-

ing of St. Paul, an emphasis suggested by the masculine name "Paul" itself, but then stressed beyond necessity to implicate the region's other vigorous cities as well. "St. Paul's strength lies in her commerce—I mean *his* commerce. *He* is a manufacturing city, of course—*all the cities of that region are*—but *he* is peculiarly strong in the matter of commerce. Last year *his* jobbing trade amounted to upwards of $52,000,000" (340, emphasis added). Twain's emphasis on the Northwest's masculinity seems intended to counter the South's more feminine aspect, particularly its "girly-girly romance" (265).

69. Twain's covert appreciation for the railroad at the end of *Life* recalls his more open praise of its wonders near the beginning of *Roughing It*, where he reprints a *New York Times* newspaper clipping extolling the speed and comfort of a westward "jaunt" by train (48).

70. See MacCannell, *The Tourist*, esp. chapter 5.

71. Ross, *Workers on the Edge*, xviii. Ross distinguishes among several different types of industrial laborers during this period, including the all-but-extinct artisan, the factory artisan (an artisan in spirit and training, but whose "constituent operations" covered a more restricted range [97]), the factory laborer, and the outworker.

72. The appendix also fittingly (if figuratively) returns us to the "undying head" of the Mississippi River itself, to which the narrator himself has just traveled upriver.

73. Foner, *Mark Twain*, 181, 174.

74. Banta, "The Boys and the Bosses," 516 n.

75. Laurie, *Artisans into Workers*, 36.

76. Kaplan, *Mr. Clemens and Mark Twain*, 246.

77. On the role of play in *Tom Sawyer*, and on theories of play in the study of both Twain and literature more generally, see Pinsker, *"The Adventures of Tom Sawyer."*

CHAPTER 3

1. Charles M. Robinson, "The Ideal Playground," Playground Association of America pamphlet, no. 22 (New York, 1909), 9. Quoted in Cavallo, *Muscles and Morals*, 25–26.

2. Riess, *City Games*, 53.

3. See, for example, Turner's own "The West and American Ideals" (1914), in *The Frontier in American History*, esp. 305–6. Even as unsparing a critic of turn-of-the-century capitalism as Charlotte Perkins Gilman could argue that "'Unskilled

labour' is a product of social evolution" and that industry evolves "on inevitable lines" (*Human Work*, 240, 242). The problem, of course, is that we have condemned certain groups of workers to these highly specialized and "unelevating" tasks (241). But "if we accept the working plan of organic evolution," Gilman claims, we will recognize the "race-advantage[s]" of a more cooperatively organized society: "If the development of Society is in the universal line of march; if it is, if not an 'object,' at least an observed tendency, for the loose scarce-human protosocial stuff to move on steadily toward an always-increasing degree of common intelligence, common activity, common enjoyment, common peace, and power, and love,—then every process which promotes this movement is advantageous" (277).

4. Riess, *City Games*, 127, 128, 45.

5. Veblen, *The Theory of the Leisure Class*, 137, 136.

6. Quoted in Riess, *City Games*, 45. By 1904, of course, Henry James found the park almost too filled with working-class patrons (See James, *The American Scene*, 117–18 and 174–85). For more on Olmsted's vision for Central Park, see Homberger, *Scenes from the Life of a City*, 260–93.

7. See Hardy, *How Boston Played*, 85–87. In his compact discussion of working-class playground reform and class-inflected urban spatial development in late-nine-teenth-century Worcester, Rosenzweig usefully reminds us not only that workers— never merely "inert" or "totally pliable" in the face of elite social uplift programs— took an active role in shaping their nonwork lives, but also that middle and upper-class park reformers had motivations "much more complex" than social control, including fire protection, public health, civic pride, and real estate development, plus "naturalistic visions of society and an infatuation with European public gardens" ("Middle-Class Parks and Working-Class Play," 32, 34, 32).

8. Riis, *How the Other Half Lives*, 5; hereafter cited parenthetically.

9. Readers may have seen this photograph printed in reverse in other publications, including the 1971 Dover edition of Riis's *How the Other Half Lives*, but according to the Museum of the City of New York this is the correct orientation of Riis's original photo.

10. Or, as the caption to a 1909 photograph in the *Playground* of a group of boys swimming exuberantly in an urban pool put it (quoting Jane Addams): "A boy is not likely to spend his time in a hot, stuffy alley shooting craps, when there is a swimming pool on the playground just around the corner" (*Playground* 3 [Dec. 1909]: 9).

11. For a historian's perspective on the explicit link between leisure and the frontier, see Paxson's 1917 essay, "The Rise of Sport." Paxson, a prominent frontier historian, argued that sport constitutes "a new safety valve" for a "new society" (145)

and that the "search for sport revealed a partial substitute for pioneer life" (167). In 1905, amidst much "public clamor" to abolish the deadly pastime of collegiate football, Turner himself helped keep the sport alive at the University of Wisconsin. See Betts, *America's Sporting Heritage*, 127–28.

12. Turner, *The Frontier in American History*, 293, 37; Curtis, *Education Through Play*, 24, 26, 45, 56, 54, 62.

13. Hall, *Youth*, 3–4.

14. Turner, *The Frontier in American History*, 2.

15. Cavallo, *Muscles and Morals*, 57.

16. Hall, *Youth*, 3, 6. For an excellent discussion of Hall's recapitulation theory in relation to turn-of-the-century conceptions of manhood, see Bederman, *Manliness and Civilization*, esp. 77–120.

17. Lee, *Play in Education*, 168.

18. Mero, *American Playgrounds*, 35.

19. Turner, *The Frontier in American History*, 259. The phrase "higher heredity" is Hall's (*Youth*, 3).

20. Turner, *The Frontier in American History*, 275.

21. Cavallo, *Muscles and Morals*, 43. Someone like the eminently self-directing young Jay Gatsby (out in the far western state of Michigan, no less) would seem to have fully internalized this sort of daily curriculum, as evidenced by his own jottings on the flyleaf of his copy of *Hopalong Cassidy*. We will examine young (and old) Gatsby in Chapter 5.

22. Gulick, *A Philosophy of Play*, 246–47. For further discussion of the effects of rigid time schedules on turn-of-the-century playgrounds, see Goodman, *Choosing Sides*, 105 ff.

23. Curtis, *Education Through Play*, 78; Lee, *Play in Education*, 462.

24. Of course today such conflations of product, trademark, and nation seem less remarkable, the way having been smoothed, perhaps, by the advent of twentieth-century advertising, whose central aim might be described as getting consumers to feel that they share the personality of the products they buy. But companies can still push consumer-citizens too far. Consider Nike's proposed (but quickly shelved) "uniform" for the 1996 Summer Olympic Games in Atlanta, which featured an American flag whose field of stars had been replaced by the Nike "swoosh." See Reid, "Replacing Old Glory's Stars."

25. Lee, "Play as Medicine," *Playground* 5 (1911): 294 (quoted in Cavallo, *Muscles and Morals*, 101). Here we may qualify Seltzer's description in *Bodies and Machines* of the "system of analogies between the individual and the national or collective body" (149) that he argues characterizes man- and nation-making at the turn

of the century. Where Seltzer identifies a "conflation" of the individual and the collective body and more specifically a "modeling of the nation on the male natural body" (152), built in part on the theories of adolescence developed by Hall, play theory tells a different story of how boys grow into nations—an evolutionary one. In play theory (also built on Hall's psychology), nations are aggregates of boys bound together in an ethic of obedience and self-sacrifice that has developed from—and also fundamentally altered—their earlier boyhood states. The individual body is thus not the model for the nation in play theory; individuals must transform themselves from anarchic "Injuns" into team-oriented "democrats" before the nation can come into existence.

26. That the play reformers saw the need for team games as not merely a social but a political imperative (and a desperate one at that) is clear in the following excerpt from a 1923 book review in the *Playground* of Elmer D. Mitchell's *Racial Traits in Athletics*. The reviewer quotes Mitchell, with approval: "Team games and democracy are inseparable, the one goes with the other as a training for free citizenship. It is interesting in this connection to note that people who have lived under despotic governments, when freed from any upper control, become most unruly and unorganized. . . . A parallel is found on the playground. It is the Hungarian, the Pole, the Russian Jew, who are disturbing factors in the maintenance of discipline. These nationalities have never had any practice in self-discipline, not even any experience in team play, and when allowed free rein, they gang together in destructive moods. To make orderly citizens of this material is a hope that the playground is striving to realize" (520).

27. Gulick, *A Philosophy of Play*, 42–43, xi.

28. Recognizing, of course, that the very notion of "whiteness" was in this period under constant revision. Even where American play seemed most to welcome ethnic difference, it sought to contain it. Recall, for example, the "folk dancing" that shares time with "team games" on the PAA play schedule. Such seemingly autonomous expressions of folk culture were common on the playground, but they tended to serve, like the well-trained playground child (or, indeed, American citizen), a larger (and de-ethnicized) purpose. Glassberg reports in *American Historical Pageantry*, for example, that when ethnic dances were translated to the playground they were frequently offered as prelude to a communal performance of an English maypole dance, to represent "the various nationalities eventually uniting as Americans within the framework of a white, Anglo-Saxon Protestant nation" (59–60). On the use of playgrounds by immigrant youth, see Cavallo, *Muscles and Morals*, 46; Couvares, *The Remaking of Pittsburgh*, 119; Rader, *American Sports*, 160; and Riess, *City Games*, 168. Rader suggests that the playgrounds "appealed most

to the children of old-stock families of the middle and upper-income ranks, young-sters who had been shaped by the same values espoused by recreation leaders" (160).

29. Turner, *The Frontier in American History*, 3–4, 23, 22, 28, 349.

30. Ibid., 10, emphasis added.

31. Fine, "Attitudes Toward Acculturation," 76.

32. See ibid., 76–83. This belief is dramatized at the end of *The Making of an American* when Riis explains how he finally knew that he was American "made." At "home," visiting his mother in Denmark, a sick Riis sees a ship flying an Ameri-can flag outside his window and feels such a sharp pang of recognition that he sud-denly realizes he's an American. Having metaphorically turned being "sick" at "home" into being "homesick" for America, he not only claims an identity but is cured as well (442–43). When Riis died in 1914, Theodore Roosevelt eulogized him as "the ideal American citizen" (*Outlook*, June 6, 1914: 284).

33. Antin, *The Promised Land*, xi.

34. I am indebted to John Lednicky for first bringing this article to my attention.

35. Hendrick, "The Jewish Invasion of America," 164, 127, 134.

36. Ibid., 165. If Hendrick's essay "previews" Cahan's, so too do some of its il-lustrations, which are intended to provide examples of "distinctive types" of Jews. One sketch of the "successful, aggressive Jew," for example—the "class of Jew that dominates the clothing business and kindred enterprises"—very nearly matches a later drawing of Levinsky. Compare Hendrick, "The Jewish Invasion of America," 140, with the May 1913 installment of Cahan's *McClure's* version of "The Rise of David Levinsky," 85.

37. Cahan, "The Autobiography of an American Jew," *McClure's* (July): 125.

38. Ibid. (April): 100; (May): 76.

39. Ibid. (July): 119

40. Ibid. (May): 75; (July): 117.

41. Chametzky, *From the Ghetto*, 127.

42. Cahan, *The Rise of David Levinsky*, 61; hereafter cited parenthetically.

43. Turner, *The Frontier in American History*, 38.

44. Ibid., 4.

45. Ibid.

46. Including, ironically, the open lands themselves. At the end of the novel, during Levinsky's discussion of the rampant land speculation in New York at the turn of the century, we discover that "vast areas of meadowland and rock were turned by [the speculators and developers], as by a magic wand, into densely pop-ulated avenues and streets of brick and mortar. Under the spell of their activity cities larger than Odessa sprang up within the confines of Greater New York in the

course of three or four years" (512). Unlike on Charles Robinson's ideal playground, however, here the magic spells turn open space into urban clutter.

47. The turn that Cahan engineers for Levinsky is also a rejection of systematic factory work, since the "little improvements" that Levinsky at first finds so exciting have the chief effect of making him work not only faster and more efficiently, but more repetitively.

48. Critics who do comment on the "Dora" section include Chametzky, who briefly but inconsequentially observes that Levinsky's romance is "artfully interspersed with his growing business affairs" (*From the Ghetto*, 132); and Sanders, who praises the Dora "episode" on its own but complains that the eventually frustrated union "does not fit well into the novel's scheme," which he sees as Levinsky's failure at love on consistently "spiritual grounds." For a reading of the relationship between the values of "hearth" and "marketplace" that more closely resembles my own, see Dembo, *The Monological Jew*, 88–92.

49. Levinsky's relationship with Dora also refigures his earlier attraction to Gussie, the hardworking and thrifty "good soul" whose "snug little" bank account twice tempts Levinsky to propose marriage (154)—the first time in the hope that she will put him through school, the second with the expectation that she will provide capital for his partnership with the designer Chaikin. Instead of being a counterbalance to business, Gussie (whom Levinsky repeatedly describes as physically unattractive) represents little more to him than a no-interest loan, even when they engage in "a delirium of love-making" at the Grand Street pier (199).

50. Cavallo, *Muscles and Morals*, 102. Instead, most play theorists "favored industrial concentration as a means of mimimizing the inefficiency and waste of competition and mitigating economic exploitation" (ibid., 102).

51. Cahan's own opinion on the "Anglo-Saxon" team games like baseball that the play theorists favored was one of moderate approval. "Let your boy play baseball and become excellent in playing the game," he wrote in reply to a concerned parent in the *Forward* in 1903. "It should not interfere with their studies and they should not become dragged down in bad company. . . . Mainly, let us not so raise the children that they should grow up foreigners in their own birthplace" (quoted in Goodman, *Choosing Sides*, 89).

52. The pleasure of the company, of course, is not enough to keep the young manufacturer Levinsky from accepting the bribes of larger firms or from stealing the very cloak designs off their racks, or, once he is established as a million-dollar clothes maker himself, to prevent him from monopolizing the raw materials market and selling to the lesser trade at a profit. Even in company, it seems, Levinsky is never quite of that company.

53. Cahan's decision to have Levinsky shout "'My Country'" seems a deliberate spoof of Antin's *Promised Land*, in which the chapter that most thoroughly describes her assimilation to America is titled "My Country."

54. Cahan suggests at the beginning of Book XI ("Matrimony") that Levinsky's sexual encounter with Dora produced, to his disappointment, no child.

55. As products of the Progressive Era zeal for improving the workplace, but more important of the internal logic of play reform itself, these company-sponsored programs sought to create healthier labor conditions while at the same time promoting a team spirit thought lacking on the specialized assembly lines of modern American industry. The team sense might come from a company newspaper, or company housing, or a company school—all early-twentieth-century examples of welfare capitalism—but a particularly potent (so the employers believed) and widespread source was group recreation. More and more firms after the turn of the century, for example, encouraged lunchtime exercise and even interdepartmental sports for their employees, and many sponsored semiprofessional company teams in industrial recreation leagues. See Brandes, *American Welfare Capitalism*. In *The Theory of Organized Play*, Bowen and Mitchell enthusiastically describe the increase in industrial athletic fields and gymnasiums and claim that play helps to "overthrow autocratic methods in industry" (344). As we shall see, this is a particularly naive claim, both for American society and for Levinsky.

56. Brandes, *American Welfare Capitalism*, 76, 78.

57. See ibid., 78, and Seymour, *Baseball*, 227. One can see the team logic undermined by industrial sponsors in other ways as well. Henry Ford, for example, printed up for distribution a 1909 article from the *Detroit News* called "Don't Die on Third" that invoked the rhetoric of team sport while disavowing its ideology. The article, written by William J. Cameron (whom Ford eventually hired as his company spokesperson, and who later ghosted Ford's famous 1925 *Encyclopaedia Brittanica* entry "Mass Production") praises the example of a baseball player who takes it upon himself to steal home with the winning run instead of waiting for a teammate to drive him in. "All the world's a baseball diamond," Cameron wrote, and from third base "you become either a splendid success or a dismal failure." The key is not to "die on third"; but since you can't count on your teammate for help, you should seize the individual initiative and "win the score that life is ready to mark up against *your* name" (n.p., emphasis added). I am indebted to Martha Banta for bringing this article to my attention.

58. Seymour, *Baseball*, 229. Even at the height of the welfare capitalism movement, major industrialists admitted that their main concern was always the work of their factories, not the welfare of their employees, and that any "play" that a

company might sponsor should not interfere with the job at hand. Ford himself declared in *My Life and Work* (1923) that "when we are at work we ought to be at work. When we are at play we ought to be at play. There is no use trying to mix the two. The sole object ought to be to get the work done and to get paid for it. When the work is done, then the play can come, but not before" (92). See also Goldman, *Meanings of Leisure in Corporate America*, 177–79.

59. In his dealings with his employees Levinsky also replicates the play reformers' pervasive ideology of supervision, as when he hires factory hands to spy on the "doings of the [cloak-makers'] organization" during a strike (521).

60. In the *McClure's* story there is an idealistic operative from Levinsky's native town who agitates for better wages and working conditions, but when Levinsky fires him there is no strike, just as there is no benefit society. See Cahan, "The Autobiography of an American Jew," *McClure's* (June): 147–48.

61. Ibid. (July): 128.

62. Turner, *The Frontier in American History*, 307.

63. Of course, as critics like Dembo have pointed out, we need to view Levinsky's soul-searching "declaration[s]" with suspicion (*The Monological Jew*, 90). Nonetheless, when critics of Cahan's novel argue that Levinsky's closing understanding of his failure requires a rejection of wealth and status per se, they generally fail to see that Levinsky seems far more discouraged by his specific route to success, and what that route says about him as a creative and intellectual person (or, better yet, fails to say), than by the material trappings of it. See, for example, Fine, "Attitudes Toward Acculturation," 84–85, and Marovitz, "The Lonely New Americans of Abraham Cahan," 197.

64. Cahan, "The Autobiography of an American Jew," *McClure's* (April): 92.

65. Cahan deepens this critique by emphasizing that Levinsky's business career follows the trajectory of American capitalism from the mid-nineteenth century to the early twentieth century, the arc from a craftsperson to an entrepreneurial to a corporate economy. Levinsky begins in the trade as an apprentice learning the art of cloak-making but is soon off on his own hook, fighting to compete in a volatile industry. By the end of the novel he virtually controls that industry, having solidified his position by investing in shares of its components— the mills, the department stores, the mail-order houses—in the very best style of consolidated corporate capitalism. Levinsky's "rise" is the country's "rise"; his story is America's story. And yet by emphasizing Levinsky's dissatisfaction with his story, Cahan also critiques the evolutionary model implicit in the very metaphor of Levinsky's "rise." At the end of the novel, Levinsky sees himself right back where he started—the poor yeshivah boy endlessly, repetitively rocking over the Tal-

mud. Here Cahan offers a counterimage to the more dominant American "restlessness" (which always wants to move ahead) foregrounded in the rest of the novel.

66. Turner, *The Frontier in American History*, 309.

67. The full titles of Rölvaag's two Norwegian volumes were *In Those Days: A Story of Norwegian Immigration in America* and *In Those Days: The Founding of the Kingdom* (see Reigstad, *Rölvaag*, 111).

68. Haugen, *Ole Edvart Rölvaag*, 95.

69. Reigstad, *Rölvaag*, 97.

70. Steensma, "Rölvaag and Turner's Frontier Thesis," 101.

71. *Giants in the Earth*, 35; Carter, *Solomon D. Butcher*, 42. Subsequent quotations from *Giants in the Earth* are cited parenthetically in the text.

72. Turner, *The Frontier in American History*, 4.

73. Ibid., 2.

74. Ibid., 37.

75. Lee, *Play in Education*, 52.

76. Gulick, *A Philosophy of Play*, 274, 270.

77. Butcher's photograph of the humorously deadpan, card-playing, and watermelon-hoisting sons of Zachariah Perry is a notable exception. See Carter, *Solomon D. Butcher*, plate 25.

78. This is not an unlikely possibility at all. Baseball historian Seymour confirms that the sport was an important part of rural life in the nineteenth century, even on isolated farms. See chapter 13, "Down-Home Baseball," of *Baseball*.

79. E. West, *Growing Up with the Country*, 247.

80. Lee, *Play in Education*, 171.

81. Turner, *The Frontier in American History*, 23.

82. In the next two novels of Rölvaag's trilogy, however, *Peder Victorious* (1929) and *Their Fathers' God* (1931), he explores the contact between the two cultures in far greater detail.

83. As Haugen suggests, Per Hansa "is imbued with the vision of his own life as a fairy tale and himself as its hero" (*Ole Edvart Rölvaag*, 87). Haugen's discussion refers primarily to the Norwegian folk tales of the heroic "Ashlad." I believe that by transplanting the action of his story to the United States Rölvaag also invokes a more specifically American paradigm of the romance of success.

84. This ending would also seem a rebuke to the close of Willa Cather's *O Pioneers!*, refiguring her narrator's optimistic gaze into the future as Per Hansa's dead stare. Compare Rölvaag's "ashen and drawn" ending with the last sentence of Cather's novel: "Fortunate country, that is one day to receive hearts like Alexandra's

into its bosom, to give them out again in the yellow wheat, in the rustling corn, in the shining eyes of youth!" (180).

85. Billington, *The Frontier Thesis*, 3. Not until the 1930s (after Turner's death in 1932) did historians begin to critique his thesis in earnest.

86. Haugen, *Ole Edvart Rölvaag*, 91; Rölvaag, letter to his family, March 27, 1924 (quoted in Reigstad, *Rölvaag*, 106).

87. Steensma, "Rölvaag and Turner's Frontier Thesis," 102.

88. Simonson, *Prairies Within*, 20, 7.

89. Lee, *Play in Education*, 494.

90. Ibid. Beret's piety is quite consonant, however, with instructions that more sectarian play reformers were giving their charges about the spiritual benefits of merging work and play. According to one religious scouting handbook, for example, the chief goal of church-organized scout troops is "the development of character through educational recreation," which should in turn "inevitably contribute to the better allegiance of boys to their own denominations and to their more determined effort to fulfil their religious obligations" (Richardson and Loomis, *The Boy Scout Movement Applied by the Church*, 16–17).

91. Turner, *The Frontier in American History*, 3, 11.

CHAPTER 4

1. Hillis, "The Serious Note in the Education of Women," 852, 853.

2. Ibid., 852, 854.

3. Ross, "Struggles for the Screen," 341.

4. Oppenheim, "Till To-Morrow," 471. The *Outlook* also reviewed Ferber's own work favorably. A 1914 assessment of her second Emma McChesney novel, *Personality Plus*, found the story "intensely modern, humorous, and shrewdly observant of business and of men and women" (*Outlook*, Sept. 23, 1914: 224).

5. As Heller and Rudnick suggest in their introduction to *1915, The Cultural Moment*, mainstream American culture's "almost infinite capacity to absorb— some would say co-opt—the radical edge of any new social, political, or cultural movement" was particularly evident in the 1910s (8).

6. See Guttmann, *A Whole New Ballgame*, chapter 7; Riess, *City Games*, chapter 5; and Bowen and Mitchell, *The Theory of Organized Play*, chapter 1.

7. Gulick, *A Philosophy of Play*, xiv. But as we have previously seen—and will see again in this chapter—play's ultimate relationship to work still lay at the core of the play theorists' philosophy.

8. Lee, *Play in Education*, 445, viii. Even when the play group targeted is de-

scribed as "children," the play reformers generally discuss only "boy" issues. The extent to which boys stood in for both genders in the teens is exemplified in an *Outlook* article "about children" called "Who Broke the Window?," which elaborates Professor G. W. Fiske's theory that human "race epochs" can be correlated to "boy epochs" of development (Jan. 11, 1913: 75–78). The "boy epochs" Fiske delineates also correspond closely to the developmental model that play theorists proposed in the 1910s.

9. Curtis, *Education Through Play*, 11. Patrick addressed this state of affairs head-on in his article "The Psychology of Relaxation" for *Popular Science Monthly* in 1914, arguing that men and women possess intrinsically different vectors of force, or "motives": "Possibly the objection may be made that . . . our attention has been directed too much to the plays of boys and that the plays of girls have been disregarded. An important distinction arises here. . . . The life of stress and effort and self-direction of which play is the antithesis is essentially masculine. Man represents the centrifugal motive; he stands for movement, change, variety, adaptation; for activity, tension, and effort. Woman represents the centripetal motive; she stands for passivity, permanence, stability, repose, relaxation, rest. She has greater measure and harmony. She has therefore less need of the release afforded by primitive forms of activity" (601).

10. Curtis, *Education Through Play*, 7, 227.

11. Mrozek, *Sport and American Mentality*, 137, 149.

12. Dye, *Gender, Class, Race, and Reform*, 5.

13. *Outlook*, Jan. 1, 1910: 17; Mott, *A History of American Magazines*, 3: 430.

14. Fessenden, "The Girl and the Camp," 164–65, 169; Coale, "Life in a Girls' Camp," 713; Northend, "How to Choose a Summer Camp for Boys or Girls," 1007.

15. Fessenden, "The Girl and the Camp," 173; *Outlook*, May 25, 1912: 158; Coale, "Life in a Girls' Camp," 716, 717, emphasis added.

16. Northend, "How to Choose a Summer Camp for Boys or Girls," 1005, 1004.

17. "The American Woman and Her Home," *Outlook*, Sept. 17, 1910: 111; "Home Making the Woman's Profession," *Outlook*, Dec. 16, 1911: 909.

18. *Outlook*, Dec. 16, 1911: 909. The very first article in the series "Home Making the Woman's Profession" emphatically signaled the subordination of liberation to duty and efficiency in its closing paragraph: "We do not realize that a home is more than a complicated force-pump for getting what *we* want out of life, that it is a machine by which we are to return to the community what it has a right to expect from us, and efficient or not according to its social output" (Martha Bensley Bruere, "What Is the Home For?," *Outlook*, Dec. 16, 1911: 914).

19. Chattle, "How to Make Play out of Work," Aug. 23, 1916: 997; Aug. 30, 1916: 1052; Sept. 13, 1916: 105.

20. Arco Wand vacuum cleaner advertisement, *Outlook*, Jan. 24, 1917: 157.

21. Earlier versions of the Arco Wand ad more clearly show adult women using the product and leave off the "fairy" talk, instead stressing cost (only $150 to install) and ease of use.

22. Mary L. Read, "What Every Mother Knows," *Outlook*, Feb. 3, 1912: 276. As Theodore Roosevelt himself opined in the *Outlook*, the "new woman" threatened the American "race" to the extent that she sacrificed "old" female values. "New" was fine—as long as nothing "old" really changed. "I am a very firm believer in the new woman," claimed Roosevelt, "but the only new woman in whom I believe is she who adds new qualities to, and does not try to substitute them for, the primal, the fundamental virtues of the 'old' woman—she who was the wife, the mother, the sweetheart, the sister, of the past" (Jan. 3, 1914: 33).

23. Gilman, "The Yellow Wall-Paper," 761, 762, 763, 762, 763; hereafter cited parenthetically.

24. For an excellent reading of the relationship between imagination, art, and gender in "The Yellow Wall-Paper," see Shumaker, "'Too Terribly Good to be Printed.'"

25. That housewives recognized this infantilization is made clear in a remarkable letter received by Theodore Roosevelt in 1913 and reprinted in the *Outlook* later that year in an installment of his "Chapters of a Possible Autobiography." In response to Roosevelt's call for American women to have large families (any woman who bore fewer than three children he declared sterile), the writer, who describes herself as "only one of thousands of middle-class respectable women who give their lives to raise a nice family," explains how intensive domestic work coupled with a lack of intellectual stimulus made her practically another child in her own home. "I have had nine children, did all my own work, including washing, ironing, housecleaning, and the care of the little ones as they came along, which was about every two years; also sewed everything they wore. . . . I also helped them all in their school work, and started them in music, etc. But as they grew older I got behind the times. I never belonged to a club or a society or lodge, nor went to any one's house scarcely; there wasn't time. In consequence, I knew nothing that was going on in the town, much less the events of the country. . . . My husband more and more declined to discuss things with me. . . . So here I am, at forty-five years, hopelessly dull and uninteresting, while he can mix with the brightest minds in the country. . . . No woman can keep up with things who never talks with any one but young children" (*Outlook*, June 28, 1913: 476–77). In Gilman's imaginary Herland,

such a woman might have chosen to become a "Colonel"—one of Herland's class of educated and athletic older women—rather than a full-time (and paradoxically infantilized) mother.

26. Haney-Peritz, "Monumental Feminism and Literature's Ancestral House," 101.

27. Gilman, *Herland*, 1; hereafter cited parenthetically. For a very interesting analysis of the connection between Gilman's feminism, her literary style, and the idiom of surveillance (the "look") in the novel, see Wilson, "Charlotte Perkins Gilman's Steady Burghers."

28. Sears, *Sacred Places*, 119.

29. Kasson, *Amusing the Million*, 12, 13.

30. Ibid., 18, 17.

31. Ibid., 11. Scharnhorst also argues that Gilman's "ideal metropolis" owes much to the principles of urban planning expressed at the Columbian Exposition. See *Charlotte Perkins Gilman*, 91–92.

32. Progressive theory (and the Herland theory) of child-raising differed significantly, however, from the official government position articulated in the pamphlets issued by the newly formed Children's Bureau beginning in 1913. According to Wolfenstein, mothers in the 1910s were told by the government *not* to play excessively with their babies because play "carried the overtones of feared erotic excitement" ("The Emergence of Fun Morality," 90).

33. Lee, for example, notes in *Play in Education* that children like "to walk along a board laid on the ground, as it is still quite a feat to walk such a straight and narrow path. . . . There should be banks or slanting boards, or something else of the cellar door variety, . . . in every playground to which small children are invited" (105–6).

34. Gilman, *The Living of Charlotte Perkins Gilman*, 29, 66, 67. Gilman was particularly influenced by the popular fitness books of William Blaikie, whose *How to Get Strong and How to Stay So*, she claims, was a "great help" to her in the "development of a fine physique" (64).

35. Cromie, "Eight Minutes' Common-Sense Exercise for the Nervous Woman," 730. In calling his exercise for women a "Turkish Towel" routine Cromie was drawing on the exoticizations of women's play (and physical display) that grew increasingly popular after the widely hailed appearance of belly dancers on the Midway Plaisance at the Columbian Exposition.

36. Lee, *Play in Education*, 6, 5.

37. Lyman Abbott, "A Journal's Autobiography," *Outlook*, Jan. 5, 1895: 9.

38. Glassberg, *American Historical Pageantry*, 1, 67.

39. Ibid., 60.

40. Herland's "pure stock" population is both fascinating and troublesome. Van says that "there is no doubt in [his] mind" that the Herlanders are "of Aryan stock" and that although they are "somewhat darker than our northern races" they are—or "were"—"'white'" and "were once in contact with the best civilization of the old world" (54). Located, judging by Van's cryptic comments, either in Africa or South America, the Herlanders simultaneously represent a "lost band" of old-world Nordic "whites" *and* the possibility of a new white imperialism in the southern hemisphere. In addition to signaling Gilman's troubled complicity with the racial assumptions of her day, the insistence on the Herlanders' purity reminds us that in play theory—ostensibly focused on the home scene—questions of international relations are never far away. There are some disturbing homologies between play theory's imperialist fantasies of domestic control and broader United States longings for dominion overseas, perhaps most strikingly merged and illustrated in a photograph of a group of armed American golfers with their Philippine caddies (who sit at the golfers' feet, in numerical order, according to the conspicuously numbered shirts that they wear) that appeared in the *Outlook* in 1916. Titled "Golf in the Philippines—Unruly Moros Make the Game Hazardous for American Players," the caption reads in part: "'The course is not in very good condition at present, but in the near future we expect to have one of the best courses in the Philippine Islands.'. . . . It will be noticed that some of the players carry revolvers (colloquially 'guns') in holsters on their belts. The term 'good shot,' familiar to every golfer, takes on a new meaning under these circumstances" (Mar. 15, 1916: 610–11).

41. Glassberg, *American Historical Pageantry*, 5.

42. Ibid., 135.

43. The cooks, however—alone among the three groups—do have a distinctly political message to convey: "Real Food—for Real People—for Real Pay," a plea consonant with Gilman's own calls for the reform of domestic food preparation. (And, appropriately, "revolutionarily" presented; the message reads right to left instead of left to right.) The scientists, to be sure, hold two flags, itself a political statement, though a comparatively inert one. Indeed, the lead flag droops sadly.

44. There was apparently some jockeying between the two organizations over which was founded first. *The Book of the Camp Fire Girls* claims 1911 as the group's originary moment, but Bowen and Mitchell report in *The Theory of Organized Play* that it was officially founded in March 1912, the same month that Juliette Low enrolled the first "patrols" of Girl Guides in Savannah, Georgia (*Scouting for Girls*, 1).

45. Davis and Gulick, "The Camp Fire Girls," 182, 189. Davis and Gulick's article suggests that "proper training in housework" also required a certain mental

disposition. "The reason a woman dislikes housework," they claimed, "is because she has let it master her, let it become humdrum; she has let the spirit of discovery and romance go out of it. Instead of making her mind bend to this she has gone into other things and let the home go" (189).

46. Camp Fire Girls, *The Book of the Camp Fire Girls*, 6.

47. "The Adventure of Home-Making," *Outlook*, May 25, 1912: 158.

48. See Bowen and Mitchell, *The Theory of Organized Play*, 121–22.

49. Indeed, facing the title page of *Scouting for Girls* is "The First Girl Scout in the New World," Magdelaine de Vercheres, who is pictured wearing a scout's hat and holding a rifle—an image one would never find in the Camp Fire Girls' handbook. I do not mean to wave away the potentially troubling implications of the production of nationalist bodies in the Girl Scouts, who were by no means free from complicity with contemporary theories of coercive control. My point is rather to clarify the Girl Scouts' cultural distinctiveness from the Camp Fire Girls, who were from the start more intimately connected to the play theorists' work and interests.

50. See *Scouting for Girls*, 545. The Girl Scouts also recommended, among others, Lester Ward's *Psychic Factors of Civilization and Applied Sociology*, John Stuart Mill's *The Subjection of Women*, Olive Schreiner's *Woman and Labor*, John Dewey's *School and Society*, and William James's *Principles of Psychology*. No books by Hall, Gulick, Lee, or Curtis are recommended.

51. Gilman, *Women and Economics*, 157.

52. By distinguishing child-raising from maternity, Gilman also resolves what Wimbush argues is a crucial concern for mothers: how to create social outlets when one is a full-time caretaker of children. Herland's redefinition of motherhood eliminates the "framework of constraints which shape and fragment women's social networks and leisure opportunities" by giving each woman a job of her own—and no woman the full-time position of mother and housewife (Wimbush, "Mothers Meeting," 73).

53. In "workshop," moreover, Gilman here adds the term that is missing from the narrator's similar description of her bedroom in "The Yellow Wall-Paper."

54. Gulick, "The New Athletic," *Outlook*, July 15, 1911: 600; Lee, *Play in Education*, 140, 335, 340.

55. Gulick, *A Philosophy of Play*, 93; Lee, *Play in Education*, 400, 401, 402.

56. "Capital and Labor Hand in Hand" (editorial), *Outlook*, Feb. 23, 1916: 410.

57. Mary Dewhurst, "Bridgeport and the Eight-Hour Day," *Outlook*, July 5, 1916: 555.

58. Robb, "Our House in Order," *Outlook*, May 28, 1910: 360; Martha Bensley Bruere, "First Aid to the Home Budget-Maker," *Outlook*, Sept. 21, 1912: 126.

In the author's note to her autobiography, *The Living of Charlotte Perkins Gilman*, Gilman identifies Bruere as a "close and tender friend."

59. A. Lane, *To Herland and Beyond*, 230.

60. Gilman, *The Living of Charlotte Perkins Gilman*, 303, 304–5, 308, 305.

61. Ferber, *Emma McChesney & Co.*, 12, 43, 77; hereafter cited parenthetically.

62. Oriard, *Sporting with the Gods*, 208. For another reading of Emma, see T. Spears, *100 Years on the Road*, 5–7.

63. Margaret Naumburg, "Maria Montessori: Friend of Children," *Outlook*, Dec. 13, 1913: 799.

64. "A Professional Woman of Yesterday and a Group of Professional Women of To-Day," *Outlook*, Oct. 1, 1919: 186–87. I do not mean to suggest that acting does not require intelligence, merely that in the popular conception actors (and particularly actresses) are more commonly associated with emotion than with intellect. Other nondomestic women who appeared in the pages of the *Outlook* in the 1910s were similarly belittled, particularly the English suffragettes whose militancy included disruptive acts of civil disobedience. The *Outlook* routinely denounced these women as savage, wild, and dangerously anarchistic. That the journal simultaneously praised women for getting in touch with their "wild" side through vigorous outdoor "boy" play and activities like camping did not seem to strike anyone as inconsistent.

65. "Maude Adams," *Webster's American Biographies*, ed. Charles Van Doren (Springfield, Mass.: Merriam, 1975) 10–11.

66. Schreiner, *Woman and Labor*, 81.

67. Veblen, *The Theory of the Leisure Class*, 59–60.

68. Miss Smalley's paean to work echoes Ferber's own attitude as later expressed in *A Peculiar Treasure*. "With millions of others I have been a work worshipper," Ferber declared. "Work and more work. Work was a sedative, a stimulant, an escape, an exercise, a diversion, a passion. . . . I've worked daily for over a quarter of a century, and loved it. I've worked while ill in bed, while traveling in Europe, riding on trains. I've written in woodsheds, bathrooms, cabins, compartments, bedrooms, living rooms, gardens, porches, decks, hotels, newspaper offices, theaters, kitchens. Nothing in my world was so satisfactory, so lasting and sustaining as work" (11).

69. According to Amott and Matthaei's *Race, Gender, and Work*, Emma would be part of the very small 3 percent of working white American women who held managerial positions during the 1910s (125). But what makes Emma's identity as a 1910s female craftsperson particularly ironic is that women were being brought into the workplace as unskilled laborers in the 1910s in a strategic effort to displace male

craftsmen, who were more likely to strike, unionize, and resist shop discipline. "During World War I," Haydu reports, "employers praised women workers for their willingness to do as they were told" (*Between Craft and Class*, 42).

70. The appearance of minstrel humor in Ferber's novel also coincides with a disturbing increase in such jokes in the *Outlook* during the 1910s, particularly after the journal added a humor section at the end of each issue, beginning in 1911.

71. Veblen, *The Theory of the Leisure Class*, 182.

72. Ibid., 148.

73. Peiss, *Cheap Amusements*, 178, 163, 164, 55.

74. Even during Emma's most vivid (and potentially homoerotic) recognition of sisterhood—when she meets Hortense, her kindred spirit in idleness, and kisses, "very tenderly, [her] pretty, puckered lips"—she insists that each woman must resolve her dilemma alone: "You're asking a great big question," she tells Hortense. "I can answer it for myself, but I can't answer it for you" (134).

75. One problem Emma does have, however, is with Jock and Grace's baby-raising style, which seems patterned more after the series of "play-is-too-exciting" 1910s government pamphlets (see note 32) than the "all-play-is-good-play" theories of the play reformers. When Emma first sees her granddaughter and reaches down to pick her up out of her crib, Grace prevents the encounter with what would surely have been a government-approved rationale: "'Not now!' Grace said hastily. 'We never play with her just before feeding-time. We find that it excites her, and that's bad for her digestion'" (224).

76. Tarbell's series, which originally ran in the *American Magazine* (like Ferber's early McChesney stories), argued that "learning, business careers, political and industrial activities—none of these things is more than incidental in the national task of woman. Her great task is to prepare the citizen" (*The Business of Being a Woman*, 81).

77. Ferber, *A Peculiar Treasure*, 173–74, 174.

78. In the final story of *Roast Beef Medium*, Emma tells T.A., "We've been good business chums, you and I. I hope we always shall be. I can imagine nothing more beautiful on this earth for a woman than being married to a man she cares for and who cares for her. But, T.A., you're not the man" (287–88).

79. Ferber, *A Peculiar Treasure*, 196. Ferber reports that Roosevelt, whom she met as a journalist at the 1912 Republican National Convention in Chicago, told her that he thought Emma "ought to marry again. What became of her first husband? Die? Or did she divorce him? You never said. Anyway, she's got to marry T. A. Buck. An immensely vital woman. She could manage business and marriage all right" (196).

80. Ibid., 174.

81. Ibid., 223. Ferber notes that in 1925 when she was doing research for her novel *Show Boat* (1926), she arrived unannounced dockside at the James Adams Floating Palace. Introducing herself to the owner as Edna Ferber, a writer, down from New York to write about show boats, he exclaimed "Well, my God! . . . Emma McChesney!" (*A Peculiar Treasure*, 291).

82. C. Wilson, "Charlotte Perkins Gilman's Steady Burghers," 184.

83. Gilman, *Forerunner*, Feb. 1916: 56 (quoted in Scharnhorst, *Charlotte Perkins Gilman*, 105).

84. Scharnhorst, *Charlotte Perkins Gilman*, 105.

CHAPTER 5

1. J. Johnson, *The Autobiography of an Ex-Coloured Man*, 126–27, 127; hereafter cited parenthetically. On *Chameleon* as one of the novel's possible titles see Fleming, *James Weldon Johnson*, 36.

2. D. Lewis, *When Harlem Was in Vogue*, 99.

3. A. Thompson, rev. of *Tales of the Jazz Age*, 706. Some in the younger generation of Harlem Renaissance writers, however, claimed Fitzgerald as an important model, although more for his notorious style of living than for his approach to literature. "If we were influenced by anyone, it was F. Scott Fitzgerald," reported Dorothy West in a recent interview with Deborah E. McDowell; "at least Wally [writer Wallace Thurman] was. He wanted to live dangerously and die romantically. Like Fitzgerald, he wanted to drink himself to death" (McDowell, "Conversations with Dorothy West," 273).

4. See F. Allen, "Coolidge Prosperity," 66–67, for a description of the difficulties faced in the otherwise prosperous 1920s by growers of staple crops such as wheat, corn, and cotton, as well as by coal miners, textile manufacturers, and shipbuilders.

5. On sporting goods, see Noverr and Ziewacz, *The Games They Played*, 67; on radios, see F. Allen, "Coolidge Prosperity," 70. On the rise of free time, Rodgers reports in *The Work Ethic in Industrial America* that even during the short span between 1914 and 1920 the number of hours worked per week, on average, fell off sharply from fifty-five to forty-eight, and that by 1920 one week's paid vacation had "become the norm for most white-collar employees" (106).

6. For a concise summary of the rise of the oligopolistic control of leisure, see Butsch, *For Fun and Profit*, 14–16.

7. D. Ewen, "Popular Music of the Decade," 142, 145.

8. Kellner, *The Harlem Renaissance*, 166; D. Ewen, "Popular Music of the Decade," 147.

9. See D. Ewen, "Popular Music of the Decade," 143–45.

10. Kellner, *The Harlem Renaissance*, xviii.

11. Huggins, *Harlem Renaissance*, 91–92. At least one contemporary observer, physician and writer Rudolph Fisher, offered a more optimistic view of white patronage of black culture. Noting in 1927 that "this interest in the Negro is an active and participating interest"—that whites are "actually playing Negro games"—Fisher hoped that this participation might signal a deeper, more cross-cultural understanding. "Maybe these Nordics at last," he speculates at the end of his essay, "have tuned in on our wave-length. Maybe they are at last learning to speak our language" (Fisher, "The Caucasian Storms Harlem," 398). For a discussion of play and the bohemian counterculture in the 1920s (including a brief reading of *The Great Gatsby*), see Oriard, *Sporting with the Gods*, 407–41.

12. D. Ewen, "Popular Music of the Decade," 149.

13. Hall, *Youth*, 3.

14. Bowen and Mitchell, *The Theory of Organized Play*, 35. At the same time, play theorists continued to caution strongly against the strain and overstimulation of too earnest a devotion to the pleasures of the body. According to Bowen and Mitchell, contemporary thrill-seeking, whether pursued in the dance hall, gambling den, poolroom, movie house, or grandstand, could leave the leisured American "in a far worse physical condition than could ever result from the monotony of long working hours in a factory" (37). One wanted to effect a safe return, as it were, to the primitive forms of play, to strike a body-strengthening balance somewhere between disuse and abuse.

15. Ibid., 2, 2–3.

16. Lee, *Play in Education*, 159, 159–60, 347. Lee also praises black Americans for their emotional fortitude: "the Negro never wholly loses hope nor his sense of the joy of living." He also suggests that African Americans are more proficient at self-expression through art, including music, than whites (468).

17. Lehman and Witty, *The Psychology of Play Activities*, 161, 162.

18. E. Mitchell, "Racial Traits in Athletics," 151, 152.

19. In taking on "primitive" energies only to contain and control them, play theory also came strikingly to resemble what Lott describes as the "simultaneous production and subjection" of the black male subject at the heart of antebellum blackface minstrelsy's "structure of racial feeling" (*Love and Theft*, 115).

20. Curtis, *Education Through Play*, 83, 81–82, 83, 6. On the widespread popularity of African Americans as targets at turn-of-the-century amusement parks, see Nasaw, *Going Out*, 93–94.

21. Lee, *Play in Education*, 484, 487.

22. Ibid., 487, emphasis added. Lee here uses the phrase "the city" to stand in for "society" because in this section of *Play in Education* he has been comparing American society to specific historical culture-places and their "corporate ideals": Athens, which produced philosophers and artists ("because every citizen's conception of the body politic—the real Athens of which the Parthenon and the Long Walls were but the material reflections—included philosophy and art" [487]); Sparta, which produced soldiers; Rome, which produced administrators; and Yale—which produces football players. In all, a frighteningly limited conception of the possible relations among individuals, the polity, and (national) culture.

23. Ibid., 489.

24. J. Johnson, *Black Manhattan*, 60. Johnson himself was an excellent athlete who played semipro baseball both in Jacksonville as a teenager and later at Atlanta University. See J. Johnson, *Along This Way*, 36–37; Levy, *James Weldon Johnson*, 32; and Seymour, *Baseball*, 561–65.

25. Seymour, *Baseball*, 546.

26. Rader, *American Sports*, 96–97, 104.

27. J. Johnson, *Black Manhattan*, 62.

28. Ibid., 75.

29. It may also be possible to argue that the phrase "down to" itself registers a diminishment, *from* Douglass *down to* "the newest song and dance team," especially in a novel in which Wendell Phillips's "Toussaint L'Ouverture" is spoken by someone nicknamed Shiny. But perhaps more positively the broad array of pictures on the wall attests to the wider range of cultural identities available to black Americans at the turn of the century, all the way "down to" the crucial realm of popular culture. (Douglass himself, Johnson reveals, had a picture of Peter Jackson in his study [*Along This Way*, 208].) Johnson's own career as a songwriter suggests that he recognized the political possibilities of popular forms; in 1899, after all, he wrote a "comic opera satirizing the new American imperialism" symbolized by the Spanish-American War (Fleming, *James Weldon Johnson*, 11). And although Fleming argues that this choice of subject "shows that Johnson had little idea of the place to which black performers and artists of his day were relegated on the musical comedy stage" (11–12), I would suggest that it indicates just how well Johnson understood those restrictions—and sought to challenge them. The fact that in a few short years Johnson would be writing campaign songs for none other than Theodore Roosevelt,

however—and eventually accepting consular postings from the same—keeps the question of Johnson's own political allegiances from being too easily categorized.

30. Sammons, *Beyond the Ring*, 39, 43, 39–40.

31. J. Johnson, *Along This Way*, 208.

32. Charters, *Nobody*, 10.

33. The novel even appears, at one point, to quote Bert Williams himself. When the narrator says that he "once heard a coloured man sum it up [i.e., being black in America] in these words: 'It's no disgrace to be black, but it's often very inconvenient'" (155), he is likely paraphrasing Williams's own famous pronouncement. I say likely, however, because the only reference I have found to Williams's statement puts it in 1918, six years too late to have been the source for the narrator's recollection—unless of course this saying was already attributable to Williams before then. The full text of the 1918 *American Magazine* statement is: "I have never been able to discover that there was anything disgraceful in being a colored man. But I have often found it inconvenient—in America" (E. Smith, *Bert Williams*, 147–48). Johnson, of course, knew Williams from his own days as a musical comedy lyricist in turn-of-the-century New York.

34. E. Smith, *Bert Williams*, 140. Notably, though, as Smith points out, Williams still could not appear on stage with white women.

35. On Williams's detachment, see Charters, *Nobody*, 59.

36. Scott, "Leisure Time and the Colored Citizen," 595, 596, emphasis added.

37. Fleming, *James Weldon Johnson*, 41.

38. "Bert Williams," 394.

39. Ibid. Although the obituary/editorial is unsigned, Kellner's *Harlem Renaissance* identifies Theophilus Lewis, the *Messenger*'s drama critic, as the author. Kellner also reports that Williams himself, "well aware of his audience's expectations" (388), refused white theatrical entrepreneur David Belasco's offer in 1922 to star him in a serious play.

40. Interestingly, however, as Peiss notes, at the same time that the ex-colored man goes to Coney Island, the commercialization of the park itself exemplified the hastening decline of white, "middle-class cultural hegemony." See *Cheap Amusements*, 136–38.

41. Hudgeons, *The Official Price Guide to Collectible Toys*, 98.

42. See O'Brien, *The Story of American Toys*, 44, and Hudgeons, *The Official Price Guide to Collectible Toys*, 100. As O'Brien reports, late-nineteenth-century mechanical banks did not limit themselves to depictions of blacks—one could also find the "Reclining Chinaman" and "Paddy and the Pig," for example—but African American stereotypes accounted "by far" for the majority of such racist de-

signs (43–44). Other minstrel-inspired banks included "Boys Stealing Watermelons," "Jolly Nigger," and the more expressly political "Stump Speaker," in which "the coin drops into the [black] politician's carpet bag, while his jaw wiggles in gratitude" (44). At least one bank, "Darktown Battery," featuring three black ballplayers, presented its characters inoffensively—"apart from its title," as O'Brien points out (44), and perhaps also their minstrelized expressions; see Hudgeons, *The Official Price Guide*, 101. At the time of *The Autobiography of an Ex-Coloured Man*'s republication in 1927, wind-up blackface minstrel toys had also become popular, including Louis Marx's "Spic and Span, 'The Hams What Am'" and Ferdinand Strauss's "Jazzbo Jim" and "Ham and Sam, the Minstrel Team" (O'Brien, *The Story of American Toys*, 111).

43. Even the narrator's decision to refer to his patron as his "benefactor" has negative overtones in the novel, since "benefactor" is the term the narrator had first used ironically to describe the Pullman porter who stole his money and some of his personal effects (84).

44. Toll, *Blacking Up*, 34.

45. Lott, "'The Seeming Counterfeit,'" 231.

46. Indeed, *The Autobiography* implicitly represents the narrator's musical labors as slavelike. "At times I became so oppressed with fatigue and sleepiness that it took almost superhuman effort to keep my fingers going," he reports. At these times, the narrator's benefactor "seemed to be some grim, mute, but relentless tyrant, possessing over me a supernatural power which he used to drive me on mercilessly to exhaustion" (121).

47. The novel only hints at this suspicion, although the draft manuscript declares it. See Fleming, *James Weldon Johnson*, 23.

48. And as Harris makes clear, an assembly like this one not only *is* a "social function"; it also *has* a social function, serving to police the boundaries of a racialized society. "Ritualized violence," Harris reports, "resulted when Blacks were accused of committing a specific offense, that is, stepping out of place, which is what any of the accusations or 'crimes' would amount to. Accusation was equated with guilt (the law was irrelevant) and punishment ensued to restore the 'threatened' white society to its former status of superiority" (Harris, *Exorcising Blackness*, x–xi).

49. Perhaps not even Johnson, who here shrewdly understands the ways in which a lynching or burning in turn-of-the-century America could take on the characteristics of a spectacular leisure event, would have predicted the excesses that nearly came to pass in the 1920s. Seymour reports, for example, that during the revival of the Ku Klux Klan in the later decade "one Klavern even tried to get the owner of the Cincinnati Reds to declare Sunday, July 20, 1924, Klan Day at the Park

and permit the Klan, 40,000 strong in the county and 100,000 in the area, to publicly present flowers to the managers and players of the two teams" (*Baseball*, 594).

50. The suggestion of minstrelsy in this scene of black identities violently called up and then destroyed once again recalls Lott's characterization of the "simultaneous production and subjection of black maleness" at the core of antebellum blackface performance (*Love and Theft*, 115).

51. Nelson, rev. of *The Autobiography of an Ex-Coloured Man*, 338.

52. Other Americans were more skeptical about projects such as the narrator's in the 1920s, particularly the attempt to produce "American" music from African American themes. In Harold Stearns's influential collection of essays, *Civilization in the United States* (1922), for example, music critic Deems Taylor argued that America's multiracial heritage precluded the folk songs of any particular group from creating a truly national musical culture. "If you insist that Negro music is the proper basis for an American school of composition," Deems wrote, "try telling a Southerner that when he hears *Swing Low, Sweet Chariot*, he is hearkening to the voices of his ancestors!" (211).

53. Fitzgerald, *The Great Gatsby*, 64, 65, 99; hereafter cited parenthetically.

54. I put the term "racial" in quotation marks here to suggest the ways that early-twentieth-century notions of race differed from our own; what we would today identify as ethnic differences, for example, many in the 1920s understood as racial differences.

55. Quoted in Bruccoli and Bryer, *F. Scott Fitzgerald in His Own Time*, 351.

56. Godden, "*The Great Gatsby*," 348; Veblen, *The Theory of the Leisure Class*, 126.

57. Godden, "*The Great Gatsby*," 359.

58. Veblen, *The Theory of the Leisure Class*, 141.

59. Ibid., 204, 205.

60. Curtis, *Education Through Play*, 19.

61. Bowen and Mitchell, *The Theory of Organized Play*, 182, 185. For more on Schiller's influence on American play theory, see Neumeyer and Neumeyer, *Leisure and Recreation*, 134 ff.

62. Lee, *Play in Education*, 59, 59–60.

63. Ibid., 60. Lee's sense of the relationship between the "child's nature" and the child him- or herself is often indistinct. At times he seems to posit an almost divine origin for human behavior, at others some more mysterious set of "underlying forces" (Lee, *Play in Education*, 188) which may or may not originate in the individual. "Play is the child," Lee announces in his introduction. "It is the letting loose of what is in him" (viii). What is "in him," however, may not be entirely of him.

For "a child's play is in a true sense self-assertion, but it is the assertion of a self deeper than the individual" (256), a self fully comprehended only as part of the larger social whole. And yet Lee still maintains that some "laws" of the self may not come from that "whole" at all, but are instead "of the individual alone" (257).

64. Gatsby's employment under Cody both mirrors and inverts that of the ex-colored man's under his benefactor. Like the narrator of Johnson's novel, young Gatsby serves as a glorified valet; like the ex-colored man, Gatsby, too, is learning to perform a racial identity. Where the ex-colored man's grueling performances of "black" music symbolically enslave him, however, Gatsby's training in the ways of the leisured white elite frees him, at least temporarily, from his lowly origins. And yet in the end Gatsby will be punished just as severely as the ex-colored man for crossing "racial" lines.

65. Lee, *Play in Education*, 308, 311, 312.

66. Although play theory posits "impersonation" as an important component in the proper social, emotional, and intellectual development of humans, Gatsby, we might say, crosses the line from impersonation to imposture. Instead of sympathetically projecting his self into the selves of others—"to enter by one sheer leap of intuition into the heart of the object of his study and act out from that" (Lee, *Play in Education*, 109)—Gatsby operates, as Nick says, from an "overwhelming self-absorption" (65) that permits, perhaps, little more than "an unbroken series of successful gestures" (1). And yet, as Lee suggests, one "cannot live by gesticulation of even the most satisfying sort" (485).

67. The recurrent but unnamed presence of these myriad bodies seems both intentionally and inversely to mirror the excessive naming of the leisure-class characters at the beginning of chapter 4, Nick's famous timetable list "of those who came to Gatsby's house that summer" (40). This mirroring itself conversely emphasizes the vague and typically unnamed labor that the members of the leisure class themselves perform. Many of them appear to be connected "with the movies in one way or another" (40), but the narrative rarely gets more specific than this.

68. Sometimes the appearances of these working-class bodies have a notably disembodied quality, as in Nick's description of the "machine in Gatsby's kitchen which could extract the juice of two hundred oranges in half an hour if a little button was pressed two hundred times by a butler's thumb" (26).

69. See Drake and Cayton's *Black Metropolis*, for example, for representative data on Chicago. In 1890 only 11 percent of the servant-class jobs in Chicago were held by blacks; by 1930 the figure was 34 percent (225).

70. Michaels, "The Souls of White Folk," 195, 194, 195. An earlier essay that treats similar issues, although less complexly than Michaels's, is Gidley's "Notes on

F. Scott Fitzgerald." I am also indebted to Michael Merrill for sharing his insights (and resources) on race, eugenics, and *The Great Gatsby* during my writing and revision of this chapter.

71. Breitwieser, "*The Great Gatsby*," 66, original emphasis.

72. Tom, by punching the not "entirely white" Myrtle in the nose, is also, if somewhat obliquely, a figure of the "great white hope" in the novel—the boxer whom white fight fans hoped would keep the heavyweight championship in white hands. Indeed, as Michael Merrill argues in an unpublished manuscript on Fitzgerald and eugenics, Tom's "hulking" brutality is also very compatible with Madison Grant's pseudoscientific description of "Nordics" in *The Passing of the Great Race* (1916).

73. For a reading of such minstrel caricaturing, see Breitwieser, "*The Great Gatsby*," 48.

74. Breitwieser argues convincingly that Fitzgerald likely had in mind Paul Whiteman's 1924 concert "Experiment in American Music," which opened with "a survey of jazz's origins in field blues and other African American genres" and closed "with the debut performance of 'Rhapsody in Blue.'" Breitwieser shows how Fitzgerald, through Nick, in passages the novelist later excised, perceives—"although in the mode of anxiety and nausea"—"real" black jazz (ibid., 62, 65).

75. Ibid., 56.

76. From this perspective, moreover, we may be able to see in the novel a potentially more radical understanding of the inextricable interweaving of different cultural systems in what we call "American" culture. For unlike the biracialist demagogue Lothrop Stoddard, who would admit in *Re-Forging America: The Story of Our Nationhood* (1927) that black Americans possess "many interesting cultural forms" but would also demand that blacks, in effect, keep them to themselves, *The Great Gatsby* seems to acknowledge the already irrevocable imbrication of American cultures. Fitzgerald may not affirm black culture, but he seems to do more than merely perceive it; he seems in fact to recognize it as an undeniable component of the American given. Black culture may appear in *The Great Gatsby* in dangerously appropriated (and "neutralized") forms (such as the "stiff, tinny drip of the banjoes on the lawn" at Gatsby's party [31]), or it may be anxiously and mockingly objectified (as in the rolling eyes of the three "modish negroes" in the limousine), or even unexpectedly exhibited and then erased (as in the exposure and subsequent murder of the not "entirely white" Gatsby), but it is woven into the narrative in such a way that Fitzgerald's tragic tale of 1920s labor and leisure would be inconceivable without it.

77. One possible exception here may be the cigar factory scenes in *The Autobi-*

ography of an Ex-Coloured Man, in which the narrator works side by side with Cuban Americans, simultaneously learning a trade, a language, and a culture (specifically the Cuban-American culture of political exile). His acquisition of Spanish even (ironically) accelerates his ascent into the business world of white America.

78. Many of Adams's other cartoons for the *Crisis* are more clearly critical of race, as signaled by more obviously sarcastic titles or by Adam's appended commentary. See, for example, Adams's drawing for the January 1911 issue of the *Crisis* of an African American woman with her head slumped on a newspaper headlined "NEGRO LYNCHED / Brute Struck White Man / Made Confession / Mob was quiet and orderly," her eyes directed absently toward a framed picture of a neatly dressed black man—perhaps her husband, perhaps even the victim. The drawing is titled "The National Pastime." An accompanying note observes, "Seventy-five per cent. of the Negroes lynched have not even been accused of rape."

79. According to Bruccoli and Bryer, the cartoon was "attributed to Fitzgerald [by Henry Dan Piper] on the basis of a clipping in the Fitzgerald Papers, Princeton University" (*F. Scott Fitzgerald in His Own Time,* 92).

80. Another possibility is that the cartoon is meant to depict a Princeton student and his servant. There is another cartoon in the same issue of the *Princeton Tiger* drawn by the same artist (and explicitly cocredited to Fitzgerald) that shows a similarly caricatured black servant bringing a meal to a table of white students. See "Kenilworth Socialism," in ibid., 92.

CHAPTER 6

1. Wright, *Native Son,* 317, 319; hereafter cited parenthetically.

2. Walter H. Page, "To Theodore Dreiser," July 19, 1900, rpt. in *Sister Carrie,* by Theodore Dreiser, ed. Donald Pizer (New York: Norton, 1970), 439.

3. Notman, "Talks with Four Novelists: Mr. Dreiser," 393.

4. We might even imagine Bigger's exclamation as Wright's rejoinder to Dreiser's "simple" desire to tell about "life as it is, the facts as they exist." Goddammit, *look,* Wright says—whose life? What facts? This makes all the difference. Wright's sense of whose life counts, however, often stops (like Dreiser's) at his male lead; working-class women, black and white, fare poorly in both texts.

5. The play theorists' enthusiasm for increased access to recreation, however, did lead them to support issues of importance to the working class, including the loosening of restrictions on Sunday leisure. See, for example, Lee, *Play in Education,* 467, 476–79.

6. Frobisher, *The Blood and Breath,* 16.

7. N. Richardson, *The Church at Play*, 29. On expenditures for leisure, see "Personal Consumption Statistics for Recreation: 1909–1970," *Historical Statistics of the United States, Colonial Times to 1970* (Washington, D.C.: U.S. Bureau of the Census, 1976), 401.

8. Addams, *The Spirit of Youth and the City Streets*, quoted in Cavallo, *Muscles and Morals*, 100. Addams, however, was less optimistic about other public entertainments, including the motion picture theaters that both Clyde and Bigger attend.

9. Quoted in Riess, *The American Sporting Experience*, 269.

10. Quoted in Thaman, *Manners and Morals*, 57. The phrase "sex slush" (106) originally appeared in a 1924 issue of the *Lutheran* (Aug. 4, 1924: 14).

11. Bowen and Mitchell, *The Theory of Organized Play*, 38.

12. Cutten, *The Threat of Leisure*, 93. Critics, though, argued that the construction of playgrounds had no measurable effect on juvenile crime. See, for example, Rosenzweig, *Eight Hours for What We Will*, 150.

13. Lynd and Lynd, *Middletown*, 399.

14. See ibid., 401, and Cozens and Stumpf, *Sports in American Life*, 100. Over time, the percentage of church-sponsored scout troops fell from a high of 90 percent in 1912 to less than 50 percent by 1942, not because church interest declined but because other community groups saw the benefits of organizing recreation (Cozens and Stumpf, *Sports in American Life*, 100).

15. N. Richardson, *The Church at Play*, 9, 27.

16. Ibid., 28. On the rise in car sales, see the *Statistical Abstract of the United States*, vol. 48 (Washington, D.C.: Department of Commerce, 1926), 366.

17. Lynd and Lynd, *Middletown*, 259. On the impact of increased automobile touring on the reorganization of work, recreation, and space in rural America in the early twentieth century, see Interrante, "You Can't Go to Town in a Bathtub."

18. Gillkey, "Recreation and the Church," 495.

19. Nash, *Spectatoritis*, 66.

20. Lingeman, *Theodore Dreiser*, 322.

21. Lynd and Lynd, *Middletown*, 266 n.

22. *Saturday Evening Post*, Aug. 30, 1924: 42; *Saturday Evening Post*, July 5, 1924: 40. The reformers, too, recognized the power of advertising. Consider this paragraph from La Porte's *Recreational Leadership of Boys*: "Attractive posters are often very effective in creating interest [in recreational programs]. The following examples are suggestive of types that are effective: 'Where does your child play?' (a dirty back yard contrasting with a cheery playground). 'Who is your child's hero?' (picturing a slouching cigarette smoker and a fine, upstanding athlete). 'Is your boy's

daddy his best playmate?' (picture of family play scene and lonely boy without a playmate). 'Pay for playgrounds or pay for prisons' (picture of each)" (51).

23. May, *Screening Out the Past*, 205.

24. *Historical Statistics of the United States*, 400. The same source reports annual major league baseball attendance at close to 10 million spectators. Baseball, too, had installed its own censor in 1921, Judge Kenesaw Mountain Landis, who banned eight Chicago White Sox players from the 1919 American League championship team for allegedly fixing the World Series, a scandal to which Fitzgerald links Meyer Wolfsheim, and by extension Gatsby, in *The Great Gatsby*.

25. Dreiser, *An American Tragedy*, 27; hereafter cited parenthetically.

26. In *Recreational Leadership of Boys*, La Porte particularly stresses the need for strong fathers: "If the father does his full duty, the boy will not be a problem" (9). This "full duty" includes being "cordial and friendly," and someone to whom the boy can talk "frankly and openly" (9). Asa Griffiths fails on each count.

27. Spears and Swanson, *History of Sport and Physical Activity*, 178. That Asa and Elvira's attitude may change somewhat after Clyde flees Kansas City is also carefully signaled by Dreiser. In Elvira's letter to Clyde at the opening of Book Two, for example, she reports that Esta wants to keep little Frank and Julia in school "just as long as we can" (164). Frank even has a paper route—this in a family that had banned newspapers from the home as "too worldly" when Clyde was growing up (18).

28. Mead, *Mind, Self, and Society*, 162, 155.

29. See Gulick, *A Philosophy of Play*, 90–92, and Rogers, *The Child and Play*, 15–17.

30. See, for example, Thaman, *Manners and Morals*, chapter 5.

31. Curtis, *Education Through Play*, 55.

32. Bowen and Mitchell, *The Theory of Organized Play*, 322, emphasis added.

33. Dreiser, "America and the Artist," 424.

34. For more on Dreiser's use of the *World*'s reports, see Pizer, *The Novels of Theodore Dreiser*, and Fishkin, *From Fact to Fiction*. Although both stress the sensational nature of the *World*'s reporting, neither quite emphasizes the gains made in sheer entertainment value by Dreiser's decision to eschew the more "serious" trial records, arguing instead that Dreiser's real interest in consulting news reports is either to recast "the shapelessness of fact" into the "form of fiction" (Pizer, 223) or to "root" his book "firmly in actuality" (Fishkin, 121). One way that *An American Tragedy* signals its interest in the sort of melodramatic spectacle that I see as central to the book is in having one of Clyde's lawyers offhandedly refer to "that Harry Thaw case" (599). To Dreiser's audience, the "Thaw case" would have represented

not just a sensational 1907 murder trial but also an entertaining (and scandalous) 1908 film, *The Great Thaw Trial*, which was publicly attacked by antivice crusaders (see Langford, *The Murder of Stanford White*, 56; May, *Screening Out the Past*, 43; and Ramsaye, *A Million and One Nights*, 475). Another revealing sign of this interest, I believe, is Dreiser's decision to make the murder weapon a camera instead of a tennis racket (the actual weapon in one of the real cases). Not because a camera "is a more probable object to bring in a rowboat" (Fishkin, *From Fact to Fiction*, 236 n.), but because the camera synecdochically registers the importance of movies, spectacles, and the cult of the image in 1920s society and culture.

35. Ramsaye, *A Million and One Nights*, xlvii. Dreiser's stylistic shortcomings in *An American Tragedy* have been the subject of much commentary, beginning perhaps with H. L. Mencken's assessment of parts of the novel as "dreadful bilge" (see "Dreiser," 503). Although recent critics have begun a partial rehabilitation of Dreiser's technique (see, for example, Lee Clark Mitchell's insightful essay on repetition and doubling, "'And Then Rose for the First Time'"), none of these studies quite makes visible Dreiser's narrative "playfulness." And though I agree with Fishkin that Dreiser "proves himself to be a master craftsman" in this novel, I offer a quite different reading of his use of present participles in the novel. See Fishkin, *From Fact to Fiction*, 130–32.

36. Ramsaye, *A Million and One Nights*, xlviii.

37. Nowhere is this active-passive conflict more evident (or consequential) than on Big Bittern, where, at the "moment of action—of crisis!"—when Clyde must decide whether to capsize the boat and drown Roberta—he is overcome by a "sudden palsy of the will," a "physical and mental indetermination" (491, 492). Clyde's eventual act, his "flinging out at her," seems ironically inactive, unwilled. Many critics have read this (supposed) nonaction as evidence that Clyde is ultimately a determined character, that he lacks self-will and is controlled by dynamic "forces beyond his awareness and control" (Fishkin, *From Fact to Fiction*, 131). Yet consider Dreiser's description of Clyde's "flinging out at her." It is "not even then with any intention to do other than free himself of her." The act is not without any intention *at all*—but rather without any intention to do *other* than "free himself." It is, I would argue, ultimately a self-willed act *to* free himself. Reprehensible, yes; passive—no.

38. Messenger, *Sport and the Spirit of Play in American Fiction*, 166.

39. See, for example, Lehan, *Theodore Dreiser*, 143–44, and Grebstein, "*An American Tragedy*," 62.

40. Messenger, *Sport and the Spirit of Play in American Fiction*, 169.

41. Standish, *Frank Merriwell at Yale*, 262.

42. "Play and Negro Progress," 22; Playground and Recreation Association of America, *The Normal Course in Play*, 29. Technically, it was the Playground and Recreation Association of America and not the PAA that published *The Normal Course in Play*. The PAA changed its name twice: first (in the 1920s) to the Playground and Recreation Association of America and then (in the early 1930s) to the National Recreation Association. To avoid confusion, I will continue to refer to the organization by its most commonly known name, the Playground Association of America (PAA).

43. Settle, "Recreation for Negroes in Memphis," 444. Settle's use of the phrase "take its place" also strikingly recalls Annie Hillis's limited prescription for American women in the 1910s (who must "find their place and fall in line," as we saw in Chapter 4) and Joseph Lee's narrow notion, reviewed in Chapter 5, that it is "only the places that the public conception calls for that exist" (*Play in Education*, 487).

On other occasions that blacks appear in the *Playground* before the 1920s—even when the point of their appearance seems to be to demonstrate a particular social advance in the field of recreation—the roles that they inhabit are carefully circumscribed. The cover of the January 1909 issue, for instance, features a picture captioned "No Race, No Creed, No Color—No. 14 School Playground, Rochester, New York." But the picture itself shows a dozen young white boys standing in a semicircle smiling down at one small black boy—who is seated incongruously in a wheelbarrow.

44. Playground and Recreation Association of America, *The Normal Course in Play*, 29. Play theorists were generally more eager to discuss the "color scheme" of play equipment than the racial composition of the playgrounds themselves. But some also called explicitly for segregation: "While the writer is a believer in the negro and in democracy, he is of the opinion that in nearly all sections where it is possible to have separate grounds for colored and white children, it is better to do so, for the reason that there is often prejudice on the part of white parents against having their children, especially the girls, play with colored children" (Curtis, *The Play Movement and Its Significance*, 85).

45. Settle, "Recreation for Colored Citizens," 598.

46. Rudwick, *Race Riot at East St. Louis*, 219.

47. Drake and Cayton, *Black Metropolis*, 66. See also Tuttle, *Race Riot*, for a thorough account of the prelude and aftermath of the riot.

48. Wright, "Big Boy Leaves Home," 245, 246, 247, 248.

49. As he did in "Big Boy Leaves Home," Wright also makes Bigger's first crime—his accidental suffocation of Mary—turn on the unexpected proximity of his black body to her white one. Much as Big Boy and his friends know that merely

to be caught naked near the white woman is enough to convince an onlooker that sexual improprieties have been threatened, so too does Bigger stuff the pillow over Mary's mouth for fear that being discovered late at night alone by her bed would trigger the same reaction.

50. See Oriard for a persuasive reading of the Boys' Club's ping-pong tables as part of the novel's "rhetoric of game playing" in relation to the "systematic control [by whites] of the mechanisms for achieving success" (*Sporting with the Gods*, 315–16). In "How Bigger Was Born," Wright claims that getting a job at the actual South Side Boys' Club, "an institution which tried to reclaim the thousands of Negro Bigger Thomases from the dives and alleys of the Black Belt," was one of two events that made him "sit down and actually start work" on *Native Son*. Wright is as skeptical about the power of such clubs in his essay as in the novel: "Here I felt for the first time that the rich folk who were paying my wages did not really give a good goddamn about Bigger, that their kindness was prompted at bottom by a selfish motive. They were paying me to distract Bigger with ping-pong, checkers, swimming, marbles, and baseball in order that he might not roam the streets and harm the valuable white property which adjoined the Black Belt. I am not condemning boys' clubs and ping-pong as such; but these little stopgaps were utterly inadequate to fill up the centuries-long chasm of emptiness which American civilization had created in these Biggers. I felt that I was doing a kind of dressed-up police work, and I hated it" (xxvi–xxvii).

51. Bigger's attraction to mass culture (he reads pulp magazines, for example, in addition to going to the movies) supports Lizabeth Cohen's contention in *Making a New Deal* that in Chicago blacks more than any other American racial or ethnic group in the 1920s and 1930s were oriented toward the mass consumption trends of those decades, thus fulfilling "the hopes of the mass culture proponents who prophesied a unified consumer market during the twenties" (154). As Cohen explains, black receptivity to mass culture "grew out of a surprising source, a faith in black commercial endeavor not so very different from ethnic people's loyalty to ethnic businesses" (148). Believing that blacks should patronize black businesses, black consumers made a number of black-owned companies extremely successful. But the lack of bank capital made a self-sustaining black economy virtually impossible, and black consumers by necessity remained dependent on white businesses for survival. In *Native Son*, when Bigger is on the run from the police, he has to buy bread at a chain store (at an inflated price) because he cannot find a black bakery (233–34).

52. In *12 Million Black Voices*, Wright derides the kitchenette as "our prison, our death sentence without a trial, the new form of mob violence that assaults not only

the lone individual, but all of us, in its ceaseless attacks" (212). These filthy apartments breed disease, crime, and hopelessness, all the while piling up "mountains of profits for the Bosses of the Buildings." The kitchenette is thus "the funnel through which our pulverized lives flow to ruin and death on the city pavements, at a profit" (215).

53. Bigger's capture, in which the police in turn try to shoot, grab, and finally knock him off the water tower, is a particularly ironic version of what the play organizers called "tag games," which symbolized "hunting and warfare . . . , the main activities being chasing and flight, ending in capture or escape. Capture is usually indicated by 'tagging,' which means touching with the hand; sometimes one is captured by hitting him with a thrown object, or it may be required that a runner be actually held, at least long enough to tag him three times" (Bowen and Mitchell, *The Practice of Organized Play*, 86).

54. This too, as we have seen, had been Dreiser's critique: "Amid the plenty of the nation, the individual may well starve . . . " (Dreiser, "America and the Artist," 424).

55. For a related account of *Native Son*'s divergence from Dreiser's novel, see Hakutani, "*Native Son* and *An American Tragedy*."

56. When I say "Bigger's crime" I mean his murders of both Mary Dalton and Bessie, just as the book often uses the phrase in this way (e.g., 348–49). The courtroom speakers, however, often insistently collapse both murders into one "crime," the killing of Mary Dalton, allowing her death to signify both murders and nearly to overwhelm and erase the killing of Bessie. See the beginning of Max's defense, for example, at 353 ff.

57. See Walker, *Richard Wright, Daemonic Genius*, 121–25, for a description of how Wright asked to be supplied with newspaper clippings from the Robert Nixon case, which functioned for Wright much as the Chester Gillette case did for Dreiser. Also see Kinnamon, *The Emergence of Richard Wright*, 120–26, for a fuller discussion of the Nixon case.

58. Wright, "How Bigger Was Born," xxvii.

59. As Fishkin points out, Dreiser's text presents a special case: "Few writers of fiction have elicited the amount of literal reader participation that Dreiser elicited in this volume" (*From Fact to Fiction*, 133). One critic has even hypothesized a whole category of "anagogic" literary games, which include the "cooperative competition that encompasses both the writer's act of creation and the reader's act of augmentative re-creation" (Foust, "The Rules of the Game," 10). Given the context we have been examining, we should broaden this classification in Dreiser's case to include the re-creative acts of both reader and writer.

60. Some in Dreiser's day might nonetheless have said that the space Dreiser created was a dangerous one. In "I Find the Real American Tragedy," Dreiser relates that several newspapers described the Robert Edwards murder case of 1934 as "an exact duplicate of *An American Tragedy.*" These same papers asked Dreiser whether in his opinion "the novel had brought about the murder" (295).

CHAPTER 7

1. Faulkner, *Sanctuary: The Original Text*, 42.

2. As a further irony, "Saddie" is actually a nickname for "Saturday," given to Saddie by Horace himself. See Faulkner, *Sanctuary: The Original Text*, 44.

3. Sundquist, *Faulkner*, 45–46.

4. By scopic control I mean to implicate the superintendent forms of looking and onlooking to which the broad cultural acceptance of play theory's supervisory logic gave legitimacy. We might, after Laura Mulvey (and Eric Lott), call this the "supervisory gaze," though I also mean to keep in play the various meanings of the word scope, including (1) extent or range of view, outlook; and (2) opportunity or freedom for movement or activity. (See Mulvey, "Visual Pleasure and Narrative Cinema." Discussing the dynamic of mastery at work in minstrelsy, Lott suggests that one "might, after Laura Mulvey, call [it] the pale gaze" [*Love and Theft*, 153].) The surveillance that I track in this chapter is one that restricts activity (or extent, or range) in the paradoxical name of the greater freedom thought to be conferred by the properly recreated self.

5. Blotner, *Faulkner: A Biography*, 675.

6. Hurston, *Their Eyes Were Watching God*, 74, 118; hereafter cited parenthetically.

7. See Fox, "Epitaph for Middletown," 103. Of these, the five-day work week was the last to arrive. As Roediger and Foner report, as late as 1932 only 5.4 percent of American businesses had adopted the five-day week for their employees (*Our Own Time*, 245).

8. Rodgers, *The Work Ethic in Industrial America*, 29.

9. Cutten, *The Threat of Leisure*, 90.

10. Deem, *All Work and No Play?*, 4.

11. Lears, "From Salvation to Self-Realization," 22, 27.

12. See Rodgers, *The Work Ethic in Industrial America*, xiii–xiv.

13. Woodward, "The Southern Ethic in a Puritan World," 42; Reed and Hunnicut, "Leisure," 1207.

14. Woodward, "The Southern Ethic in a Puritan World," 42.

15. Tindall, *The Emergence of the New South*, 70–71, 98.

16. Woodward, "The Southern Ethic in a Puritan World," 42. Though similar in many respects, the twelve essays in *I'll Take My Stand* did not present exactly the same case. For a detailed discussion of the similarities and differences among the contributors (ten of whom were Vanderbilt faculty, students, or alumni), see Conkin, *The Southern Agrarians*.

17. See Cohen, *Making a New Deal*, 142.

18. Clinton, "Women in the Land of Cotton," 112, 113.

19. As Sundquist rightly observes, "*Sanctuary*, one might say, should have appeared as a chapter of the agrarian manifesto *I'll Take My Stand* (1930), for Faulkner would spend the next decade of his career, as Allen Tate there suggests a Southerner must do, taking hold of his tradition 'by violence'" (*Faulkner*, 59). For a detailed discussion of "agrarian play" and "Faulknerian sport" in Faulkner's writing more generally, see Oriard, *Sporting with the Gods*, 258–64.

20. Polk, "Afterword," 300.

21. W. Lewis, "A Moralist with a Corn Cob," 324; Frazier, "Gothicism in *Sanctuary*," 52; Canfield, "Introduction," 8.

22. Faulkner, *Sanctuary*, 26; hereafter cited parenthetically. "Jelly" is a 1920s African American slang term for sex, or the sexual parts, from "jelly roll" (sexual intercourse). See Kellner, *The Harlem Renaissance*, 431.

23. For a persuasive reading of Temple as shaped by Horace's perceptions, for example, see D. Cox, "A Measure of Innocence."

24. See ibid. for a summation of the disturbing critical viewpoint that Temple deserves her violation.

25. In his many revisions to the novel's opening, Faulkner at one point even began with Temple being observed by the town boys. For a discussion of the different opening scenes that Faulkner considered, see Canfield, "Introduction," 3.

26. Powerfully, and unsettlingly, the novel also implicates its readers' own gazes in this economy of superintendence. As Sundquist argues, "the assumed objectivity of the aesthetic of observation" is "exactly what is at stake in the novel," as Horace's narcissism in particular "is patently a figure for that of the reader" (*Faulkner*, 51). *Sanctuary*'s "endlessly creative elaboration of scenes and metaphors of observation and voyeurism induces a kind of paralysis that is at once repelling and enticing" (51). Tanner further suggests that Faulkner's refusal to narrate the central scenes of violence, particularly Temple's rape at Frenchman's Bend, crucially "shifts the burden of creation away from Faulkner and toward the reader," "making the reader do his work for him"; but that even this "distanced perspective" collapses as the novel subtly encourages the reader's "imaginative participation" in its horrific violence ("Reading Rape," 561, 569, 581, 573).

27. S. Ewen, *Captains of Consciousness*, 178.

28. Frederick, *Selling Mrs. Consumer*, 31. For a discussion of Frederick as a domestic systems manager extraordinaire, see Banta, *Taylored Lives*, 235–40.

29. See, for example, S. Ewen, *Captains of Consciousness*, 163.

30. Ibid., 177.

31. D. Cox, "A Measure of Innocence," 309.

32. Fass, "Smoking and Dancing as Symbols of Liberation," 172.

33. This development also seems to figure Temple not as an independent woman lighting a "torch of freedom" (the late 1920s commercial image of a liberated smoker) but as a fallen woman, corrupted by the peril of too much freedom, too much leisure.

34. Mrozek, *Sport and American Mentality*, 136–37.

35. See, for example, Bowen and Mitchell, *The Theory of Organized Play*, chapters 14–17, and Bowers, *Recreation for Girls and Women*, xvii–xxii.

36. Bowers, *Recreation for Girls and Women*, xvii. Others, however, still believed that female athleticism inhibited one's "adaptability to motherhood." See Guttmann, *A Whole New Ball Game*, 148.

37. Spears and Swanson, *History of Sport and Physical Activity*, 232.

38. See Guttmann, *Women's Sports*, 136–42. In *A Whole New Ball Game*, Guttmann describes the 1920s as "a period of stagnation" for women's sports (148). Faulkner may have had this situation in mind again when he sent Flem Snopes's stepdaughter Linda to Ole Miss in the Snopes trilogy. One can only imagine Flem's relief to discover that male scopic opportunities at the university would have been carefully restricted by the time of Linda's matriculation in 1927. Indeed, the University of Mississippi was in the process of tightening up its rules on all variety of recreations and amusements in the mid-1920s, including smoking, dancing, drinking, and the use of automobiles—all crucial activities for Temple in *Sanctuary*. See Cabaniss, *A History of the University of Mississippi*, 151, and Sansing, *Making Haste Slowly*, 99.

39. R. Allen, *Horrible Prettiness*, 272, 244.

40. Ibid., 232; Zeidman, *The American Burlesque Show*, 110.

41. Barthes on "Striptease" is instructive here. Despite Temple's supposed sophistication, her evident inexperience at performing in the eroticized way that the men at Frenchman's Bend expect denies her "the alibi of art and the refuge of being an object"—the state that Barthes suggests professional strippers achieve—and instead "imprison[s] her in a condition of weakness and timorousness" (86). Later, at the Memphis brothel, Temple tries (figuratively) to mimic the "ritual gestures" of the professional stripper (whose "porcelain" grimace she affects [*Sanctuary*, 167])

perhaps in the hope of "taking refuge" in the "icy indifference of skilful practitioners" (Barthes, 86), but in vain. Though she writhes on her imaginary "church steeple," Popeye "jerk[s] the covers back" off her bed and "grip[s] the top of [her] gown (167). Unlike the professional stripper, Temple is not "desexualized," nor can she "negate [her] flesh" (Barthes, 84).

42. R. Allen, *Horrible Prettiness*, 281, 237, 238. Intriguingly, this context also gives us another way to look at the interpolative burlesque scenes that generically disrupt *Sanctuary's* gothic novel / detective story pacing. The Virgil and Fonzo Snopes rubes-in-the-whorehouse interlude in chapter 21 and the beerfest at Miss Reba's in chapter 25 have been explained by critics either as evidence of "soft spots" in the novel (Karl, *William Faulkner*, 371), as necessarily comic relief from the text's otherwise horrific tension (Frazier, "Gothicism in *Sanctuary*," 50), or as parodic commentary on social pretensions in fictional Jefferson (Kinney, "*Sanctuary*," 113–14). I would argue further that these narrative burlesques inscribe into the novel the crucial shift in performative burlesque away from women's control over their own bodies and words toward a "verbal humor" provided by male comedians (Fonzo, Virgil, Clarence) and the silent display of female bodies as "objects of sexual humor" (R. Allen, *Horrible Prettiness*, 240). Male readers, in particular, I believe, are intended to laugh at the too thin / too plump physiques of Miss Reba and her friends.

43. This is the closest that Faulkner comes to stepping outside his narrowly implosive focus on the 1920s. Like Hurston, as we will see shortly, Faulkner here recapitulates a particular historical process within his narrative, but only to emphasize its dissolution, not, like Hurston, to grant it potentially redemptive historical force.

44. Including, as Sundquist suggests, his race. While there is "no significant evidence that Popeye is part Negro," his insistent characterization as a "black man," Sundquist argues, moves beyond a theological or mythological invocation of his evil "darkness" toward an ambiguous but provocative insinuation of real world miscegenation—ignorable here but for Faulkner's powerful turn to southern racial history as the major topic of his fiction for the next ten years (*Faulkner*, 57–58).

45. Kammerer, *Rejuvenation and the Prolongation of Human Efficiency*, 185.

46. Haire, *Rejuvenation*, 42. After Steinach's surgical techniques were used on humans, his procedures were widely attacked as too sexually oriented. According to Haire, "To both [ascetics and libertines] came a vision of a new path opened to wild excesses of unbridled lust" (8).

47. W. Lewis, "A Moralist with a Corn Cob," 329.

48. Actually, it also leaves the jailer's wife and the crazy woman who lives at the

edge of town. That these marginalized women seem ironically the most self-controlled in the text suggests that Faulkner may indeed have a class-based critique in mind. Neither character, however, appears to have the power (or necessary visibility) to make her independence a model for other women in the novel.

49. Amott and Matthaei, *Race, Gender, and Work*, 127, 125.

50. Ibid., 158.

51. Katzman, *Seven Days a Week*, 93. A proportionately high 43 percent of employed African American women already worked as house servants in 1900, and by 1930 that percentage had risen to 54 percent (Amott and Matthaei, *Race, Gender, and Work*, 158).

52. J. Jones, *Labor of Love*, 196, 199, 198.

53. For many years Hurston's birthdate had been listed as 1901, but she is now believed to have been born in 1891 (Howard, "Zora Neale Hurston," 134). See also Hemenway, *Zora Neale Hurston*, 32 n., for a discussion of Hurston's own evasiveness on this matter.

54. Evans and Lee, *Pearl City, Florida*, 125.

55. Thus I would amend McKay's claim that Hurston's novel offers a reading of "black female growth and development against the history of the oppression of race and sex" ("'Crayon Enlargements of Life,'" 53). I argue that it also reads that growth within a history of the successful transformation of African American women's work.

56. Williams, "Foreword," xii.

57. J. Jones, *Labor of Love*, 88, 4.

58. Gates, *The Signifying Monkey*, 194.

59. Gates's analysis of Joe's insistance that Janie not indulge in "mule talk" is useful here: "It is this tension between work and play, between maintaining appearances of respectability and control against the seemingly idle, nonquantifiable verbal maneuvers that 'produce' nothing, which becomes the central sign of the distance between Janie's unarticulated aspirations and the material aspirations signified by Jody's desire to 'be a big voice,' a self-designation that Jody repeats with alacrity almost as much as he repeats his favorite parenthetical, 'I god'" (*The Signifying Monkey*, 195).

60. Amott and Matthaei, *Race, Gender, and Work*, 158.

61. Katzman, *Seven Days a Week*, 16.

62. Ibid., 188.

63. Ibid., 161.

64. See, for example, Wall, "Zora Neale Hurston," and McKay, "'Crayon Enlargements of Life.'"

65. Katzman, *Seven Days a Week*, 212.

66. J. Jones, *Labor of Love*, 155.

67. Katzman, *Seven Days a Week*, 25.

68. Clark-Lewis, *Living In, Living Out*, 42.

69. Katzman, *Seven Days a Week*, 94.

70. On the relation of Janie's "freedom feeling" to her financial independence, see Baker, *Blues, Ideology, and Afro-American Literature*, 56–60. One irony of the novel's recovery of the history of African American domestic labor is that in 1950 Hurston herself would be "discovered working as a maid in Rivo Alto, Florida. She claimed to be resting her mind and collecting material firsthand for a piece she intended to write about domestics; it is more probable that she needed the money" (Howard, "Zora Neale Hurston," 144).

71. Indeed, as Gates argues, in the second half of the novel, figures of play become "the dominant repeated figures . . . , replacing the text's figures of flowering vegetation" (*The Signifying Monkey*, 194). The figure of "tumbling mud-balls" trying to "show [their] shine" (139) is particularly important, given the play theorists' interest in physical recreations and more specifically their belief in the 1920s that "tumbling" was a physically and psychologically "invaluable" exercise for women and girls—one that produced "exhilaration," "self-satisfaction," "pride," and most crucially, "skill in the control of the body" (Cotteral and Cotteral, *Tumbling, Pyramid-Building, and Stunts for Girls and Women*, 2–3). The second half of the novel charts Janie's progress toward exhilaration, self-satisfaction, and especially bodily "control" in just such metaphors of physical recreation and exercise.

72. Addams, *The Spirit of Youth and the City Streets*, 26, 20, 16. Although Addams went further than her play reform peers in calling for a recognition of the importance of human sexuality, she did so in her own genres, not in any official play handbooks; thus when historians of the move to organize play wrote their studies in the 1920s they could neatly elide her views on the topic. Like Addams, Cabot in *What Men Live By* (another text that calls for healthy play but is not itself a play handbook) praises love's power, even when it takes the form of same-sex union, a remarkably progressive stand for the 1910s.

73. Even in chapter 6, which focuses on the eulogy for Matt Bonner's mule (from which Janie is pointedly excluded), the narrative returns to Janie at the end of the chapter.

74. For a review of the different readings of Janie's beating, see Jordan, "Feminist Fantasies," 109–10.

75. For another example of the limits of communal recreation, one might also cite the resentment of the black workers from the muck, who in their anger over

Tea Cake's death (and their exclusion from the judicial review of it) want to testify against Janie during her trial.

76. Hurston, *Mules and Men*, 179.

77. J. Jones, *Labor of Love*, 202, 205; Jordan, "Feminist Fantasies," 112.

78. Seidel, "The Artist in the Kitchen," 111.

79. Jordan, "Feminist Fantasies," 111.

80. Hemenway, *Zora Neale Hurston*, 240.

81. See, for example, W. Evans et al., *The Years of Bitterness and Pride*.

82. Boutilier and SanGiovanni, *The Sporting Woman*, 15. A tenuous case may be built from certain evidence that Janie knows something about birth control. At one point, while Janie is waiting through the seasons to fall in love with Killicks, the narrator tells us that "She knew things that nobody had ever told her" and that she "often spoke to falling seeds" (44). In all likelihood, the things she knew have to do with love (or possibly sexual arousal) rather than birth control, but the statement is provocative, particularly in light of Janie's return home at the end of the novel with a packet of "seeds" that Tea Cake had meant to "plant" (283)—a completion of the image with suggestive undertones of both knowledge and control.

83. Lee, *Play in Education*, 435.

84. Ibid., 453, 454.

AFTERWORD

1. Neumeyer and Neumeyer, *Leisure and Recreation*, 199. The social upheaval the Neumeyers describe sounds almost exactly like what organized play and "right recreation" were supposed to prevent: a "mounting tide of crime and delinquency, drunkenness and vice," an "increase of insanity and nervous breakdowns," a "renewed energy to reform the social order," an "increasing number of wandering individuals who move across the country as tramps, hobos, and migrants," and "[increased] efforts to seek pleasure and thrills . . . to get relief from boredom and distress" (199).

2. As the *New York Times* reports, elementary school districts "across the country" have begun to eliminate recess "as a waste of time that would be better spent on academics"—a trend that has "provoked alarm, even indignation, among authorities on child development" (Apr. 7, 1998: A1).

3. Rifkin, *The End of Work*, 3, 5.

4. Now that the personal computer, with its capacity for games, E-mail, and recreational Web surfing, has made the office desk a potential play station, we have a new national debate over the demarcation of work time from play time. Not sur-

prisingly, employers are eager to hew to strict divisions—i.e., no play at work—while many employees are loath to give up the new work-play rhythms they have forged. Aptly enough, some critics "fear the move to more closely control computer use is a step toward breaking down skilled, autonomous work into its component parts—an information age equivalent to replacing craftwork with the assembly line" (Amy Harmon, "On the Office PC, Bosses Opt For All Work, and No Play," *New York Times*, Sept. 22, 1997: D11). Will our generation see the fall from the cyber-operative to the cyber-drudge?

BIBLIOGRAPHY

Adams, Henry. *History of the United States of America During the Administrations of Thomas Jefferson and James Madison.* Ed. Earl N. Harbert. Vol. 1. New York: Library of America, 1986.

Addams, Jane. *The Spirit of Youth and the City Streets.* New York: Macmillan, 1909.

————. *Twenty Years at Hull House.* 1910. New York: Signet-NAL, 1981.

Adelman, Melvin L. *A Sporting Time: New York City and the Rise of Modern Athletics, 1820–1870.* Urbana: University of Illinois Press, 1986.

Allen, Frederick Lewis. "Coolidge Prosperity" [1931]. In Solomon, 65–82.

Allen, Robert C. *Horrible Prettiness: Burlesque and American Culture.* Chapel Hill: University of North Carolina Press, 1991.

Amott, Teresa L., and Julie A. Matthaei. *Race, Gender, and Work: A Multicultural Economic History of Women in the United States.* Boston: South End, 1991.

Antin, Mary. *The Promised Land.* Boston: Houghton Mifflin, 1912.

Appleton, L. Estelle. *A Comparative Study of the Play Activities of Adult Savages and Civilized Children: An Investigation of the Scientific Basis of Education.* Chicago: University of Chicago Press, 1910.

Attwell, Ernest T. "Community Recreation and the Negro." *Opportunity* 1 (May 1923): 7–9.

————. "Playgrounds for Colored America." *The Playground* 15 (Apr. 1921): 84–89.

Baetzhold, Howard G., and Joseph B. McCullough. *The Bible According to Mark Twain.* Athens, Ga.: University of Georgia Press, 1995.

Baker, Houston, Jr. *Blues, Ideology, and Afro-American Literature: A Vernacular Theory.* Chicago: University of Chicago Press, 1984.

Banta, Martha. "The Boys and the Bosses: Twain's Double Take on Work, Play, and the Democratic Ideal." *American Literary History* 3 (Fall 1991): 487–520.

————. *Imaging American Women: Idea and Ideals in Cultural History.* New York: Columbia University Press, 1987.

————. *Taylored Lives: Narrative Productions in the Age of Taylor, Veblen, and Ford.* Chicago: University of Chicago Press, 1993.

Barthes, Roland. "Striptease." In *Mythologies*, trans. Annette Lavers, 84–87. New York: Hill and Wang, 1972.

Bassett, John E. "*Roughing It*: Authority Through Comic Performance." *Nineteenth Century Literature* 43 (Sept. 1988): 220–34.

Bederman, Gail. *Manliness and Civilization: A Cultural History of Gender and Race in the United States, 1880–1917.* Chicago: University of Chicago Press, 1995.

Beecher, Catharine E. *Letters to the People on Health and Happiness.* 1855. New York: Arno, 1972.

———. *A Treatise on Domestic Economy.* 1841. New York: Source Book, 1970.

Beecher, Henry Ward. *Lectures to Young Men, on Various Important Subjects.* 2d ed. Salem, Mass.: John P. Jewett, 1846.

Benson, Ivan. *Mark Twain's Western Years.* Stanford, Calif.: Stanford University Press, 1938.

Berman, Neil David. *Playful Fictions and Fictional Players: Game, Sport, and Survival in Contemporary American Fiction.* Port Washington, N.Y.: Kennicat Press, 1981.

"Bert Williams." Editorial. *The Messenger* 4 (Apr. 1922): 394.

Betts, John Rickards. *America's Sporting Heritage: 1850–1950.* Reading, Mass.: Addison-Wesley, 1974.

———. "Mind and Body in Early American Thought." *Journal of American History* 54 (Mar. 1968): 787–805.

Billington, Ray Allen, ed. *The Frontier Thesis: Valid Interpretation of American History?* New York: Holt, Rinehart and Winston, 1966.

Blackwell, Elizabeth. *The Laws of Life, with Special Reference to the Physical Education of Girls.* 1852. New York: Garland, 1986.

Blotner, Joseph. *Faulkner: A Biography.* 2 vols. New York: Random House, 1974.

Boutilier, Mary A., and Lucinda SanGiovanni. *The Sporting Woman.* Champaign, Ill.: Human Kinetics, 1983.

Bowen, Wilbur P. *The Teaching of Play.* Springfield, Mass.: F. A. Bassette, 1913.

Bowen, Wilbur P., and Elmer D. Mitchell. *The Practice of Organized Play: Play Activities Classified and Described.* New York: A. S. Barnes, 1929.

———. *The Theory of Organized Play: Its Nature and Significance.* New York: A. S. Barnes, 1923.

Bowers, Ethel. *Recreation for Girls and Women.* New York: A. S. Barnes, 1934.

Boyer, Paul. *Urban Masses and Moral Order in America, 1820–1920.* Cambridge, Mass.: Harvard University Press, 1978.

Brandes, Stuart D. *American Welfare Capitalism, 1880–1940*. Chicago: University of Chicago Press, 1976.

Breitwieser, Mitchell. "*The Great Gatsby*: Grief, Jazz, and the Eye-Witness." *Arizona Quarterly* 47 (Autumn 1991): 17–70.

Bridgman, Richard. *Dark Thoreau*. Lincoln: University of Nebraska Press, 1982.

Bromell, Nicholas. *By the Sweat of the Brow: Literature and Labor in Antebellum America* (Chicago: University of Chicago Press, 1993).

Brown, Bill. "American Childhood and Stephen Crane's Toys." *American Literary History* 7 (1995): 443–76.

———. "Interlude: The Agony of Play in 'The Open Boat.'" *Arizona Quarterly* 45 (Autumn 1989): 23–46.

———. *The Material Unconscious: American Amusement, Stephen Crane, and the Economies of Play*. Cambridge, Mass.: Harvard University Press, 1996.

Bruccoli, Matthew J., and Jackson R. Bryer, eds. *F. Scott Fitzgerald in His Own Time: A Miscellany*. Kent, Ohio: Kent State University Press, 1971.

Buckley, Frank. "Thoreau and the Irish." *New England Quarterly* 13 (Sept. 1940): 389–406.

Budd, Louis J. *Our Mark Twain: The Making of His Public Personality*. Philadelphia: University of Pennsylvania Press, 1983.

Butsch, Richard, ed. *For Fun and Profit: The Transformation of Leisure into Consumption*. Philadelphia: Temple University Press, 1990.

Cabaniss, James Allen. *A History of the University of Mississippi*. University: University of Mississippi Press, 1949.

Cabot, Richard C. *What Men Live By*. Boston: Houghton Mifflin, 1914.

Cahan, Abraham. "The Autobiography of an American Jew: The Rise of David Levinsky." *McClure's Magazine* 40 (Apr. 1913): 92–106; 41 (May-July 1913): 73–85, 131–52, 116–28.

———. *The Rise of David Levinsky*. 1917. New York: Harper and Row, 1960.

———. *Yekl: A Tale of the New York Ghetto*. New York: D. Appleton, 1896.

Caillois, Roger. *Man, Play, and Games*. Trans. Meyer Barash. London: Thames and Hudson, 1961.

Cameron, W. J. *Don't Die on Third*. Dearborn, Mich.: Henry Ford Museum, 1909.

Camp Fire Girls, Inc. *The Book of the Camp Fire Girls*. Rev. ed. New York: Camp Fire Girls, 1933.

Canby, Henry Seidel. *Thoreau*. Boston: Houghton Mifflin, 1930.

Canfield, J. Douglas. "Introduction." In Canfield, ed., 1–13.

————, ed. *Twentieth Century Interpretations of Sanctuary: A Collection of Critical Essays*. Englewood Cliffs, N.J.: Prentice-Hall, 1982.

Carter, John. *Solomon D. Butcher: Photographing the American Dream*. Lincoln: University of Nebraska Press, 1985.

Cather, Willa. *O Pioneers!* 1913. Boston: Houghton Mifflin, 1988.

Cavallo, Dominick. *Muscles and Morals: Organized Playgrounds and Urban Reform, 1880–1920*. Philadelphia: University of Pennsylvania Press, 1981.

Chametzky, Jules. *From the Ghetto: The Fiction of Abraham Cahan*. Amherst: University of Massachusetts Press, 1977.

Channing, William Ellery. "Address on Temperance." *The Works of William E. Channing, D. D.*, 99–116. Boston: American Unitarian Association, 1877.

————. "Self-Culture." In *The Works of William E. Channing, D. D.*, 12–36. Boston: American Unitarian Association, 1877.

Charters, Ann. *Nobody: The Story of Bert Williams*. New York: Macmillan, 1970.

Chattle, Ellen. "How to Make Play out of Work." *The Outlook*, Aug. 23, 1916: 997; Aug. 30, 1916: 1052–53; Sept. 6, 1916: 44–45; Sept. 13, 1916: 105.

Chiu, Ping. *Chinese Labor in California, 1850–1880: An Economic Study*. Madison: State Historical Society of Wisconsin, 1967.

Chubb, Percival. "Folk Culture and Leisure." *Recreation* 28 (Sept. 1934): 278–79, 307.

Churchill, Allen. "Era of Wonderful Nonsense" [1967]. In Solomon, 129–32.

Clapper, Ronald Earl. "The Development of Walden: A Genetic Text." Ph.D. diss. University of California, Los Angeles, 1967.

Clark-Lewis, Elizabeth. *Living In, Living Out: African American Domestics in Washington, D.C., 1910–1940*. Washington, D.C.: Smithsonian Institution Press, 1994.

Click, Patricia C. *The Spirit of the Times: Amusements in Nineteenth-Century Baltimore, Norfolk, and Richmond*. Charlottesville: University Press of Virginia, 1989.

Clinton, Catherine. "Women in the Land of Cotton." In Gerster and Cords, eds., 107–20.

Coale, Anna Worthington. "Life in a Girls' Camp." *The Outlook*, July 25, 1914: 710–17.

Cohen, Lizabeth. *Making a New Deal: Industrial Workers in Chicago, 1919–1939*. New York: Cambridge University Press, 1990.

Conkin, Paul K. *The Southern Agrarians*. Knoxville: University of Tennessee Press, 1988.

Cotteral, Bonnie, and Donnie Cotteral. *Tumbling, Pyramid-Building and Stunts for Girls and Women.* New York: A. S. Barnes, 1927.

Couvares, Francis G. *The Remaking of Pittsburgh: Class and Culture in an Industrializing City, 1877–1919.* Albany: State University of New York Press, 1984.

Cox, Dianne Luce. "A Measure of Innocence: *Sanctuary's* Temple Drake." *Mississippi Quarterly* 39 (Summer 1986): 301–24.

Cox, James M. *"Life on the Mississippi* Revisited." In *The Mythologizing of Mark Twain*, ed. Sara deSaussure Davis and Philip D. Beidler. University: University of Alabama Press, 1984.

Cozens, Frederick W., and Florence Scovil Stumpf. *Sports in American Life.* Chicago: University of Chicago Press, 1953.

Cromie, William J. "Eight Minutes' Common-Sense Exercise for the Nervous Woman." *The Outlook,* July 25, 1914: 730–35.

Curtis, Henry S. *Education Through Play.* New York: Macmillan, 1915.

———. *The Play Movement and Its Significance.* New York: Macmillan, 1917.

Cutten, George Barton. *The Threat of Leisure.* New Haven, Conn.: Yale University Press, 1926.

Daher, Michael. "Leisure, Play and Labor in Thoreau." In *Play as Context*, ed. Alice Taylor Cheska, 159–67. West Point, N.Y.: Leisure, 1981.

Daniels, Bruce C. *Puritans at Play: Leisure and Recreation in Colonial New England.* New York: St. Martin's, 1995.

Davis, Hartley, and Mrs. Luther Halsey Gulick. "The Camp-Fire Girls." *The Outlook,* May 25, 1912: 181–89.

Deem, Rosemary. *All Work and No Play? A Study of Women and Leisure.* Philadelphia: Open University Press, 1986.

Dembo, L. S. *The Monological Jew: A Literary Study.* Milwaukee: University of Wisconsin Press, 1983.

Dorgan, Ethel Josephine. *Luther Halsey Gulick, 1865–1918.* New York: Columbia University Teacher's College, 1934.

Drake, St. Clair, and Horace R. Cayton. *Black Metropolis: A Study of Negro Life in a Northern City.* Rev. and enl. ed. Chicago: University of Chicago Press, 1993.

Dreiser, Theodore. "America and the Artist." *The Nation* (April 15, 1925): 423–24.

———. *An American Tragedy.* 1925. New York: Signet-NAL, 1981.

———. "I Find the Real American Tragedy." *Mystery Magazine* 11 (February 1935). In *Theodore Dreiser: A Selection of Uncollected Prose*, ed. Donald Pizer, 291–99. Detroit: Wayne State University Press, 1977.

Dulles, Foster Rhea. *America Learns to Play: A History of Popular Recreation, 1607–1940*. New York: D. Appleton–Century, 1940.

––––––. *A History of Recreation: America Learns to Play*. 2d ed. New York: Appleton-Century-Crofts, 1965.

Dye, Nancy S. "Introduction." In *Gender, Class, Race, and Reform in the Progressive Era*, ed. Noralee Frankel and Nancy S. Dye, 1–9. Lexington: University Press of Kentucky, 1991.

"Editor's Table." *Harper's New Monthly Magazine* 26 (Feb. 1863): 412–18.

Emerson, Ralph Waldo. *The Complete Works of Ralph Waldo Emerson*. Vol. 5, *English Traits*. Ed. Edward Waldo Emerson. Centenary Edition. Boston: Houghton Mifflin, 1876.

––––––. *Selections from Ralph Waldo Emerson: An Organic Anthology*. Ed. Stephen E. Whicher. Boston: Houghton Mifflin, 1957.

Evans, Arthur S., and David Lee. *Pearl City, Florida: A Black Community Remembers*. Boca Raton: Florida State University Press, 1990.

Evans, Walker, et al. *The Years of Bitterness and Pride: Farm Security Administration, FSA Photographs, 1935–1943*. New York: McGraw-Hill, 1975.

Ewen, David. "Popular Music of the Decade" [1974]. In Solomon, 142–63.

Ewen, Stuart. *Captains of Consciousness: Advertising and the Social Roots of the Consumer Culture*. New York: McGraw-Hill, 1976.

Fabre, Michel. *The Unfinished Quest of Richard Wright*. Trans. Isabel Barzun. New York: William Morrow, 1973.

Fanning, Charles. *The Irish Voice in America: Irish-American Fiction from the 1760s to the 1980s*. Lexington: University Press of Kentucky, 1990.

Fass, Paula S. "Smoking and Dancing as Symbols of Liberation" [1977]. In Solomon, 172–88.

Faulkner, William. *Sanctuary*. 1931. New York: Vintage, 1987.

––––––. *Sanctuary: The Original Text*. Ed. Noel Polk. New York: Random House, 1981.

Ferber, Edna. *Emma McChesney & Co*. New York: Frederick A. Stokes, 1915.

––––––. *A Peculiar Treasure*. New York: Literary Guild of America, 1939.

––––––. *Roast Beef Medium: The Business Adventures of Emma McChesney*. New York: Frederick A. Stokes, 1913.

Fessenden, Elizabeth M. "The Girl and the Camp." *The Outlook*, May 27, 1911: 163–73.

Fetterley, Judith. "Mark Twain and the Anxiety of Entertainment." *Georgia Review* 33 (Summer 1979): 382–91.

Fine, David M. "Attitudes Toward Acculturation in the English Fiction of the

Jewish Immigrant, 1900–1917." In *American Mosaic: Multicultural Readings in Context*, ed. Barbara Roche Rico and Sandra Mano, 76–86. Boston: Houghton Mifflin, 1991.

———. *The City, The Immigrant, and American Fiction, 1880–1920*. Metuchen, N.J.: Scarecrow, 1977.

Fink, Steven. *Prophet in the Marketplace: Thoreau's Development as a Professional Writer*. Princeton, N.J.: Princeton University Press, 1992.

Fishburn, Katherine. *Richard Wright's Hero: The Faces of a Rebel-Victim*. Metuchen, N.J.: Scarecrow, 1977.

Fisher, Rudolph. "The Caucasian Storms Harlem." *American Mercury* 11 (Aug. 1927): 393–98.

Fishkin, Shelley Fisher. *From Fact to Fiction: Journalism and Imaginative Writing in America*. Baltimore: Johns Hopkins University Press, 1985.

Fitzgerald, F. Scott. *The Great Gatsby*. 1925. New York: Charles Scribner's Sons, 1953.

Fleming, Robert E. *James Weldon Johnson*. Boston: Twayne, 1987.

Foner, Philip S. *Mark Twain: Social Critic*. New York: International Publishers, 1958.

Forbush, William Byron. *Manual of Play*. Philadelphia: George W. Jacobs, 1914.

Ford, Henry. *My Life and Work*. Garden City, N.Y.: Doubleday, Page, 1923.

Foust, Ronald. "The Rules of the Game: A Para-Theory of Literary Theories." *South Central Review* 3 (Winter 1986): 5–14.

Fox, Richard Wightman. "Epitaph for Middletown: Robert S. Lynd and the Analysis of Consumer Culture." In Fox and Lears, 103–41.

Fox, Richard Wightman, and T. J. Jackson Lears. *The Culture of Consumption: Critical Essays in American History, 1880–1980*. New York: Pantheon, 1983.

Frazier, David L. "Gothicism in *Sanctuary*: The Black Pall and the Crap Table." In Canfield, ed., 49–58.

Frederick, Christine. *Selling Mrs. Consumer*. New York: Business Bourse, 1929.

Frobisher, J. E. *The Blood and Breath: A System of Exercise for the Lungs and Limbs*. New York: Goodyear's Rubber Curler, 1876.

Gates, Henry Louis, Jr. *The Signifying Monkey: A Theory of African American Literary Criticism*. New York: Oxford University Press, 1988.

Gerster, Patrick, and Nicholas Cords, eds. *The Old South*. Vol. 1 of *Myth and Southern History*. 2d ed. Urbana: University of Illinois Press, 1989.

Gidley, M. "Notes on F. Scott Fitzgerald and the Passing of the Great Race." *Journal of American Studies* 7 (Aug. 1973): 171–81.

Gillkey, Rev. Charles W. "Recreation and the Church." *The Playground* 17 (Dec. 1923): 495–98.

Gillman, Susan. *Dark Twins: Imposture and Identity in Mark Twain's America.* Chicago: University of Chicago Press, 1989.

Gilman, Charlotte Perkins. 1915. *Herland.* New York: Pantheon, 1979.

———. *Human Work.* New York: McClure, Phillips, 1904.

———. *The Living of Charlotte Perkins Gilman: An Autobiography.* New York: D. Appleton-Century, 1935.

———. "A Suggestion on the Negro Problem." *The American Journal of Sociology* 14 (July 1908): 78–85. Rpt. in *Charlotte Perkins Gilman: A Nonfiction Reader,* ed. Larry Ceplair, 176–83. New York: Columbia University Press, 1991.

———. *Women and Economics: A Study of the Economic Relation Between Men and Women as a Factor in Social Evolution.* Ed. Carl N. Degler. 1898. New York: Harper and Row, 1966.

———. "The Yellow Wall-Paper." *The Heath Anthology of American Literature.* Ed. Paul Lauter et al. Vol. 2, 761–73. Lexington, Mass.: D. C. Heath, 1990.

Gilmore, Michael T. *American Romanticism and the Marketplace.* Chicago: University of Chicago Press, 1985.

Girl Scouts. *Campward Ho!: A Manual for Girl Scout Camps.* New York: Girl Scouts, 1920.

———. *Scouting for Girls: Official Handbook of the Girl Scouts.* New York: Girl Scouts, 1920.

Glassberg, David. *American Historical Pageantry: The Uses of Tradition in the Early Twentieth Century.* Chapel Hill: University of North Carolina Press, 1990.

Godden, Richard. "*The Great Gatsby*: Glamor on the Turn." *Journal of American Studies* 16 (Dec. 1982): 343–71.

Goldman, Robert Lawrence. *Meanings of Leisure in Corporate America, 1890–1930.* Ann Arbor: University Microfilms International, 1977.

Golemba, Henry. *Thoreau's Wild Rhetoric.* New York: New York University Press, 1990.

Goodman, Cary. *Choosing Sides: Playground and Street Life on the Lower East Side.* New York: Schocken, 1979.

Gordon, David M., Richard Edwards, and Michael Reich. *Segmented Work, Divided Workers: The Historical Transformation of Labor in the United States.* New York: Cambridge University Press, 1982.

Gorn, Elliott J. *The Manly Art: Bare-Knuckle Prize Fighting in America.* Ithaca, N.Y.: Cornell University Press, 1986.

Grebstein, Sheldon N. "*An American Tragedy*: Theme and Structure." In *The Twenties: Poetry and Prose; Twenty Critical Essays*, ed. Richard E. Langford and William E. Taylor, 62–66. Deland, Fla.: Everett Edwards, 1966.

Green, Eileen, and Sandra Hebron. "Leisure and Male Partners." In Wimbush and Talbot, 37–44.

Groos, Karl. *The Play of Man*. Trans. Elizabeth L. Baldwin. New York: D. Appleton, 1912.

Gross, Robert A. "Culture and Cultivation: Agriculture and Society in Thoreau's Concord." *Journal of American History* 69 (June 1982): 42–55.

———. "The Great Bean Field Hoax: Thoreau and the Agricultural Reformers." *Virginia Quarterly Review* 61 (Summer 1985): 483–97.

———. "Transcendentalism and Urbanism: Concord, Boston, and the Wider World." *Journal of American Studies* 18 (Dec. 1984): 361–81.

Gulick, Luther H. *The Efficient Life*. 1907. Rpt. New York: Doubleday, Page, 1913.

———. *Manual for Physical Measurements in Connection with the Association Gymnasium Records*. New York: International Committee of the YMCA, 1892.

———. *Mind and Work*. New York: Doubleday, Page, 1908.

———. *A Philosophy of Play*. New York: Charles Scribner's Sons, 1920.

———. *Physical Education by Muscular Exercise*. Philadelphia: P. Blakiston's Son, 1912.

Gutman, Herbert G. *Work, Culture, and Society in Industrializing America: Essays in American Working-Class and Social History*. New York: Knopf, 1976.

Guttmann, Allen. *From Ritual to Record: The Nature of Modern Sports*. New York: Columbia University Press, 1978.

———. *A Whole New Ball Game: An Interpretation of American Sports*. Chapel Hill: University of North Carolina Press, 1988.

———. *Women's Sports: A History*. New York: Columbia University Press, 1991.

Haire, Norman. *Rejuvenation: The Work of Steinach, Voronoff, and Others*. New York: Macmillan, 1925.

Hakutani, Yoshinobu. "*Native Son* and *An American Tragedy*: Two Different Interpretations of Crime and Guilt." In *Critical Essays on Richard Wright*, ed. Yoshinobu Hakutani, 167–81. Boston: G. K. Hall, 1982.

Hall, G. Stanley. *Adolescence; Its Psychology and its Relations to Physiology, Anthropology, Sociology, Sex, Crime, Religion, and Education*. 2 vols. 1904. Rpt. New York: D. Appleton, 1928.

———. *Aspects of Child Life and Education*. Boston: Ginn, 1907.

———. *Youth: Its Education, Regimen, and Hygiene*. New York: D. Appleton, 1909.

Hampton, Benjamin B. *A History of the Movies.* New York: Covici-Friede, 1931.

Handlin, Oscar. *Boston's Immigrants: A Study in Acculturation.* Rev. ed. Cambridge, Mass.: Harvard University Press, 1959.

Haney-Peritz, Janice. "Monumental Feminism and Literature's Ancestral House: Another Look at "The Yellow Wallpaper." In Meyering, ed., 95–108.

Hardy, Stephen. *How Boston Played: Sport, Recreation, and Community, 1865–1915.* Boston: Northeastern University Press, 1982.

Harris, Trudier. *Exorcising Blackness: Historical and Literary Lynching and Burning Rituals.* Bloomington: Indiana University Press, 1984.

Haugen, Einar. *Ole Edvart Rölvaag.* Boston: Twayne, 1983.

Haydu, Jeffrey. *Between Craft and Class: Skilled Workers and Factory Politics in the United States and Britain, 1890–1922.* Berkeley: University of California Press, 1988.

Heller, Adele, and Lois Rudnick, eds. *1915, The Cultural Moment: The New Politics, the New Woman, the New Psychology, the New Art & the New Theatre in America.* New Brunswick, N.J.: Rutgers University Press, 1991.

Hemenway, Robert E. *Zora Neale Hurston: A Literary Biography.* Urbana: University of Illinois Press, 1977.

Hendrick, Burton J. "The Jewish Invasion of America." *McClure's Magazine* 40 (March 1913): 125–65.

Higginson, Thomas Wentworth. "Saints, and Their Bodies." *Atlantic Monthly* 1 (March 1858): 582–95.

Higgs, Robert J. *Laurel and Thorn: The Athlete in American Literature.* Lexington: University Press of Kentucky, 1981.

Higham, John. "The Reorientation of American Culture in the 1890s." In *The Origins of Modern Consciousness,* ed. John Weiss, 25–48. Detroit: Wayne State University Press, 1966.

Hillis, Annie P. "The Serious Note in the Education of Women." *The Outlook,* April 11, 1910: 851–55.

Homberger, Eric. *Scenes from the Life of a City: Corruption and Conscience in Old New York.* New Haven, Conn.: Yale University Press, 1994.

Hounshell, David A. *From the American System to Mass Production, 1800–1932: The Development of Manufacturing Technology in the United States.* Baltimore: Johns Hopkins University Press, 1984.

Howard, Lillie P. "Zora Neale Hurston." In *Afro-American Writers from the Harlem Renaissance to 1940,* ed. Trudier Harris, 133–45. Vol. 51 of *Dictionary of Literary Biography.* Detroit: Gale, 1987.

Howe, Irving. *World of Our Fathers.* New York: Harcourt Brace Jovanovich, 1976.

Howe, Irving, and Kenneth Libo. *How We Lived: A Documentary History of Immigrant Jews in America, 1880–1930.* New York: New American Library, 1979.

Hudgeons, Thomas E., III, ed. *The Official Price Guide to Collectible Toys.* 3d ed. Westminster, Md.: House of Collectibles, 1985.

Huggins, Nathan Irvin. *Harlem Renaissance.* New York: Oxford University Press, 1971.

Huizinga, Johan. *Homo Ludens: A Study of the Play Element in Culture.* 1950. Boston: Beacon, 1955.

Hurston, Zora Neale. *Mules and Men.* 1935. New York: Harper and Row, 1990.

———. *Their Eyes Were Watching God.* 1937. Urbana: University of Illinois Press, 1978.

Interrante, Joseph. "You Can't Go to Town in a Bathtub: Automobile Movement and the Reorganization of Rural American Space, 1900–1930." *Radical History Review* 21 (Fall 1979): 151–68.

James, Henry. *The American Scene.* 1907. Bloomington: Indiana University Press, 1968.

Johnson, George Ellsworth. *Education by Play and Games.* Boston: Ginn, 1907.

Johnson, James Weldon. *Along This Way.* New York: Viking, 1933.

———. *The Autobiography of an Ex-Coloured Man.* 1912. New York: Hill and Wang, 1960.

———. *Black Manhattan.* 1930. New York: Arno, 1968.

Johnson, Linck C. "Revolution and Renewal: The Genres of *Walden.*" In *Critical Essays on Henry David Thoreau's "Walden,"* ed. Joel Myerson, 215–35. Boston: G. K. Hall, 1988.

Jones, Gareth Stedman. "Class Expression Versus Social Control? A Critique of Recent Trends in the Social History of 'Leisure.'" *History Workshop* 4 (Autumn 1977): 162–70.

Jones, Jacqueline. *Labor of Love, Labor of Sorrow: Black Women, Work, and the Family, from Slavery to the Present.* New York: Vintage, 1986.

Jordan, Jennifer. "Feminist Fantasies: Zora Neale Hurston's *Their Eyes Were Watching God.*" *Tulsa Studies in Women's Literature* 7 (Spring 1988): 105–17.

Kammerer, Paul. *Rejuvenation and the Prolongation of Human Efficiency: Experiences with the Steinach Operation on Man and Animals.* New York: Boni and Liveright, 1923.

Kaplan, Justin. *Mr. Clemens and Mark Twain: A Biography.* New York: Simon and Schuster, 1966.

Karl, Frederick R. *William Faulkner: American Writer.* Boston: Faber and Faber, 1989.

Kasson, John F. *Amusing the Million: Coney Island at the Turn of the Century.* New York: Hill and Wang, 1978.

———. *Civilizing the Machine: Technology and Republican Values in America, 1776–1900.* 1976. New York: Penguin, 1984.

Katzman, David M. *Seven Days a Week: Women and Domestic Service in Industrializing America.* New York: Oxford University Press, 1978.

Kazin, Alfred. *On Native Grounds: An Interpretation of Modern American Prose Literature.* New York: Harcourt, Brace, 1942.

Kellner, Bruce, ed. *The Harlem Renaissance: A Historical Dictionary for the Era.* New York: Methuen, 1984.

Kinnamon, Kenneth. *The Emergence of Richard Wright: A Study in Literature and Society.* Urbana: University of Illinois Press, 1972.

Kinney, Arthur F. "*Sanctuary:* Style as Vision." In Canfield, ed., 109–19.

Kirsch, George B. *The Creation of American Team Sports: Baseball and Cricket, 1838–72.* Urbana: University of Illinois Press, 1989.

Kruse, Horst H. *Mark Twain and "Life on the Mississippi."* Amherst: University of Massachusetts Press, 1981.

Lane, Ann J. *To Herland and Beyond: The Life and Work of Charlotte Perkins Gilman.* New York: Pantheon, 1990.

Lane, Lauriat, Jr. "The Double in *An American Tragedy.*" *Modern Fiction Studies* 12 (Summer 1966): 213–20.

Langford, Gerald. *The Murder of Stanford White.* Indianapolis: Bobbs-Merrill, 1962.

La Porte, William R. *A Handbook of Games and Programs for Church, School, and Home.* New York: Abingdon, 1922.

———. *Recreational Leadership of Boys.* New York: Methodist Book Concern, 1927.

Laurie, Bruce. *Artisans into Workers: Labor in Nineteenth-Century America.* New York: Hill and Wang, 1989.

Lears, T. J. Jackson. "From Salvation to Self-Realization: Advertising and the Therapeutic Roots of the Consumer Culture, 1880–1930." In Fox and Lears, 3–38.

Lee, Joseph. *Constructive and Preventive Philanthropy.* New York: Macmillan, 1902.

———. *Play in Education.* New York: Macmillan, 1915.

———. *The Tramp Problem.* Leaflet no. 4. Boston: Massachusetts Civic League, 1910.

Lehan, Richard. *Theodore Dreiser: His World and His Novels.* Carbondale: Southern Illinois University Press, 1969.

Lehman, Harvey C., and Paul A. Witty. *The Psychology of Play Activities.* 1927. New York: Arno, 1976.

Levy, Eugene. *James Weldon Johnson: Black Leader, Black Voice.* Chicago: University of Chicago Press, 1973.

Lewis, David Levering. *When Harlem Was in Vogue.* New York: Knopf, 1981.

Lewis, Guy. "The Beginning of Organized Collegiate Sport." *American Quarterly* 22 (Summer 1970): 222–29.

Lewis, Wyndham. "A Moralist with a Corn Cob." *Life and Letters* 10 (June 1934): 312–28.

Lingeman, Richard. *Theodore Dreiser: An American Journey, 1908–1945.* New York: G. P. Putnam's Sons, 1990.

Lott, Eric. *Love and Theft: Blackface Minstrelsy and the American Working Class.* New York: Oxford University Press, 1993.

———. "'The Seeming Counterfeit': Racial Politics and Early Blackface Minstrelsy." *American Quarterly* 43 (June 1991): 223–54.

Lynd, Robert S., and Helen Merrell Lynd. *Middletown: A Study in American Culture.* New York: Harcourt, Brace, 1929.

Lynn, Kenneth S. "*Roughing It.*" In *Mark Twain: A Collection of Critical Essays,* ed. Henry Nash Smith, 40–46. Englewood Cliffs, N.J.: Prentice-Hall, 1963.

McAleer, John J. *Theodore Dreiser: An Introduction and Interpretation.* New York: Holt, Rinehart, 1968.

MacCannell, Dean. *The Tourist: A New Theory of the Leisure Class.* 1976. New York: Schocken, 1989.

McDowell, Deborah E. "Conversations with Dorothy West." In *The Harlem Renaissance Re-examined,* ed. Victor A. Kramer, 265–82. New York: Arno, 1987.

McKay, Nellie. "'Crayon Enlargements of Life': Zora Neale Hurston's *Their Eyes Were Watching God* as Autobiography." In *New Essays on "Their Eyes Were Watching God,"* ed. Michael Awkward, 51–70. New York: Cambridge University Press, 1990.

Marovitz, Sanford E. "The Lonely New Americans of Abraham Cahan." *American Quarterly* 20 (Summer 1968): 196–210.

Martineau, Harriet. *Society in America.* Vol. 3. London: Saunders and Otley, 1837.

Matthiessen, F. O. *Theodore Dreiser.* New York: Wm. Sloane, 1951.

May, Lary Linden. *Screening Out the Past: The Birth of Mass Culture and the Motion Picture Industry.* New York: Oxford University Press, 1980.

Mead, George H. *Mind, Self, and Society from the Standpoint of a Social Behaviorist.* Ed. Charles W. Morris. 1924. Chicago: University of Chicago Press, 1962.

Mencken, H. L. "Dreiser." In *A Mencken Chrestomathy*. New York: Knopf, 1949.

Mero, Everett B., ed. *American Playgrounds: Their Construction, Equipment, Maintenance and Utility*. 3d ed. New York: Baker and Taylor, 1909.

Messenger, Christian K. *Sport and the Spirit of Play in American Fiction: Hawthorne to Faulkner*. New York: Columbia University Press, 1981.

———. *Sport and the Spirit of Play in Contemporary American Fiction*. New York: Columbia University Press, 1990.

Meyering, Sheryl L., ed. *Charlotte Perkins Gilman: The Woman and Her Work*. Ann Arbor: UMI Research Press, 1989.

Michaels, Walter Benn. "The Souls of White Folk." In *Literature and the Body: Essays on Populations and Persons*, ed. Elaine Scarry, 185–209. Selected Papers from the English Institute, 1986. New Series, no. 12. Baltimore: Johns Hopkins University Press, 1988.

Michelson, Bruce. "Ever Such a Good Time: The Structure of Mark Twain's *Roughing It*." *Dutch Quarterly Review of Anglo-American Letters* 17 (1987): 182–99.

Mitchell, Elmer D. "Racial Traits in Athletics." *American Physical Education Review* 27 (Mar.–May 1922): 93–99; 147–152; 197–206.

Mitchell, Lee Clark. "'And Then Rose for the First Time': Repetition and Doubling in *An American Tragedy*." *Novel: A Forum on Fiction* 19 (Fall 1985): 39–56.

———. "Verbally *Roughing It*: The West of Words." *Nineteenth Century Literature* 44 (June 1989): 67–92.

Mizruchi, Susan. *The Power of Historical Knowledge: Narrating the Past in Hawthorne, James, and Dreiser*. Princeton, N.J.: Princeton University Press, 1988.

Moers, Ellen. *Two Dreisers*. New York: Viking, 1969.

Morgan, Angela. "Work: A Song of Triumph." *The Outlook*, Dec. 2, 1914: 757.

Moss, George. "Silver Frolic: Popular Entertainment in Virginia City, Nevada, 1859–1863." *Journal of Popular Culture* 22 (Fall 1988): 1–31.

Mott, Frank Luther. *A History of American Magazines*. Vol. 3, *1865–1885*. Cambridge, Mass.: Harvard University Press, 1938.

Mrozek, Donald J. *Sport and American Mentality, 1880–1910*. Knoxville: University of Tennessee Press, 1983.

Mulvey, Laura. "Visual Pleasure and Narrative Cinema." In *Visual and Other Pleasures*, 14–26. Bloomington: Indiana University Press, 1989.

Nasaw, David. *Going Out: The Rise and Fall of Public Amusements*. New York: Basic Books, 1993.

Nash, Jay B. *Spectatoritis*. New York: Holston House, 1932.

Neider, Charles, ed. *The Complete Essays of Mark Twain*. Garden City, N.Y.: Doubleday, 1963.

Nelson, Alice Dunbar. Review of *The Autobiography of an Ex-Coloured Man*, by James Weldon Johnson. *Opportunity* 5 (Nov. 1927): 337–38.

Neufeldt, Leonard N. "Thoreau's Enterprise of Self-Culture in a Culture of Enterprise." *American Quarterly* 39 (Summer 1987): 231–51.

Neumeyer, Martin H., and Esther S. Neumeyer. *Leisure and Recreation: A Study of Leisure and Recreation in Their Sociological Aspects*. New York: A. S. Barnes, 1936.

Newbury, Michael. *Figuring Authorship in Antebellum America*. Stanford, Calif.: Stanford University Press, 1997.

———. "Healthful Employment: Hawthorne, Thoreau, and Middle-Class Fitness." *American Quarterly* 47 (Dec. 1995): 681–714.

Northend, Mary Harrod. "How to Choose a Summer Camp for Boys or Girls." *The Outlook*, April 28, 1915: 1001–7.

Notman, Otis. "Talks with Four Novelists: Mr. Dreiser." New York *Times Saturday Review of Books*, June 15, 1907. In *Theodore Dreiser: A Selection of Uncollected Prose*, ed. Donald Pizer, 163–64. Detroit: Wayne State University Press, 1977.

Noverr, Douglas A., and Lawrence E. Ziewacz. *The Games They Played: Sports in American History, 1865–1980*. Chicago: Nelson Hall, 1983.

O'Brien, Richard. *The Story of American Toys, from Puritans to the Present*. New York: Abbeville, 1990.

Oppenheim, James. "Till To-Morrow." *The Outlook*, Feb. 24, 1912: 465–71.

Oriard, Michael. *Dreaming of Heroes: American Sports Fiction, 1868–1980*. Chicago: Nelson-Hall, 1982.

———. *Reading Football: How the Popular Press Created an American Spectacle*. Chapel Hill: University of North Carolina Press, 1993.

———. *Sporting with the Gods: The Rhetoric of Play and Game in American Culture*. New York: Cambridge University Press, 1991.

Patrick, G. T. W. "The Psychology of Relaxation." *Popular Science Monthly* 84 (June 1914): 590–604.

Paxson, Frederic L. "The Rise of Sport." *Mississippi Valley Historical Review* 4 (Sept. 1917): 141–68.

Peiss, Kathy. *Cheap Amusements: Working Women and Leisure in Turn-of-the-Century New York*. Philadelphia: Temple University Press, 1986.

Pettit, Arthur G. *Mark Twain and the South*. Lexington: University Press of Kentucky, 1974.

Phillips, William L. "The Imagery of Dreiser's Novels." *PMLA* 78 (Dec. 1963), 572–85.

Pinsker, Sanford. "*The Adventures of Tom Sawyer*, Play Theory, and the Critic's Job of Work." *Midwest Quarterly* 29 (1988): 357–65.

Pizer, Donald. *The Novels of Theodore Dreiser: A Critical Study*. Minneapolis: University of Minnesota Press, 1976.

"Play and Negro Progress." *Opportunity* 2 (Jan. 1924): 22.

Playground and Recreation Association of America. *The Normal Course in Play: Practical Material for Use in the Training of Playground and Recreation Workers.* Ed. Joseph Lee. New York: A. S. Barnes, 1925.

Polk, Noel. "Afterword." In *Sanctuary: The Original Text*, ed. Noel Polk, 293–306. New York: Random House, 1981.

Poole, Ernest. "Abraham Cahan: Socialist—Journalist—Friend of the Ghetto." *The Outlook*, Oct. 28, 1911: 467–78.

Potter, George. *To the Golden Door: The Story of the Irish in Ireland and America.* Boston: Little, Brown, 1960.

Rader, Benjamin G. *American Sports: From the Age of Folk Games to the Age of Spectators.* Englewood Cliffs, N.J.: Prentice-Hall, 1983.

Ramsaye, Terry. *A Million and One Nights: A History of the Movies.* 2 vols. New York: Simon and Schuster, 1926.

Rath, Sura P. "Game-Play in Fiction: A Critical Paradigm." *Diogenes* 136 (Winter 1986): 128–41.

———. "Game, Play, Literature: An Introduction." *South Central Review* 3 (Winter 1986): 1–4.

Reed, John Shelton, and Benjamin J. Hunnicutt. "Leisure." In *Encyclopedia of Southern Culture*, ed. Charles Reagan Wilson and William Ferris, 1207–10. Chapel Hill: University of North Carolina Press, 1989.

Reid, Ron. "Replacing Old Glory's Stars with Dollar Signs?" *Philadelphia Inquirer*, Feb. 6, 1996: D1.

Reigstad, Paul. *Rölvaag: His Life and Art.* Lincoln: University of Nebraska Press, 1972.

Review of *Racial Traits in Athletics*, by Elmer D. Mitchell. *The Playground* 17 (Dec. 1923): 520.

Reynolds, David S. *Beneath the American Renaissance: The Subversive Imagination in the Age of Emerson and Melville.* Cambridge, Mass.: Harvard University Press, 1989.

Richardson, Norman E. *The Church at Play: A Manual for Directors of Social and Recreational Life.* New York: Abingdon, 1922.

Richardson, Norman E., and Ormond E. Loomis. *The Boy Scout Movement Applied by the Church*. New York: Charles Scribner's Sons, 1915.

Richardson, Robert D. *Henry Thoreau: A Life of the Mind*. Berkeley: University of California Press, 1986.

Riess, Steven A. *The American Sporting Experience: A Historical Anthology of Sport in America*. New York: Leisure Press, 1984.

————. *City Games: The Evolution of American Urban Society and the Rise of Sports*. Urbana: University of Illinois Press, 1989.

————. *Touching Base: Professional Baseball and American Culture in the Progressive Era*. Westport, Conn.: Greenwood, 1980.

Rifkin, Jeremy. *The End of Work: The Decline of the Global Labor Force and the Dawn of the Post-Market Era*. New York: Putnam's, 1995.

Riis, Jacob A. *How the Other Half Lives: Studies Among the Tenements of New York*. 1890. New York: Dover, 1971.

————. *The Making of an American*. 1901. New York: Macmillan, 1917.

Robb, Juliet Everts. "Our House in Order." *The Outlook*, May 28, 1910: 354–60.

Rodgers, Daniel T. *The Work Ethic in Industrial America, 1850–1920*. Chicago: University of Chicago Press, 1974.

Roediger, David R. "'Not Only the Ruling Classes to Overcome, but Also the So-Called Mob': Class, Skill and Community in the St. Louis General Strike of 1877." *Journal of Social History* 19 (Winter 1985): 213–39.

————. *The Wages of Whiteness: Race and the Making of the American Working Class*. New York: Verso, 1991.

Roediger, David R., and Philip S. Foner. *Our Own Time: A History of American Labor and the Working Day*. New York: Verso, 1989.

Rogers, James Edward. *The Child and Play*. New York: Century, 1932.

Rölvaag, O. E. *Giants in the Earth: A Saga of the Prairie*. Trans. Lincoln Colcord and O. E. Rölvaag. 1927. New York: Harper and Row, 1955.

Root, Waverly, and Richard de Rochemont. *Eating in America: A History*. New York: William Morrow, 1976.

Rosenberg, Charles E. *The Cholera Years*. Chicago: University of Chicago Press, 1962.

Rosenzweig, Roy. *Eight Hours for What We Will: Workers and Leisure in an Industrial City, 1870–1920*. New York: Cambridge University Press, 1983.

————. "Middle-Class Parks and Working-Class Play: The Struggle over Recreational Space in Worcester, Massachusetts, 1870–1910." *Radical History Review* 21 (Fall 1979): 31–46.

Ross, Steven J. "Struggles for the Screen: Workers, Radicals, and the Political Uses of Silent Film." *American Historical Review* 96 (April 1991): 333–67.

———. *Workers on the Edge: Work, Leisure, and Politics in Industrializing Cincinnati, 1788–1890.* New York: Columbia University Press, 1985.

Rudwick, Elliott M. *Race Riot at East St. Louis: July 2, 1917.* Carbondale: Southern Illinois University Press, 1964.

Ryan, George E. "Shanties and Shiftlessness: The Immigrant Irish of Henry Thoreau." *Éire-Ireland: A Journal of Irish Studies* 13 (Fall 1978): 54–78.

Rybczynski, Witold. "Waiting for the Weekend." *Atlantic* 268 (August 1991): 35–52.

Sammons, Jeffrey T. *Beyond the Ring: The Role of Boxing in American Society.* Urbana: University of Illinois Press, 1988.

Sanborn, Margaret. *Mark Twain, The Bachelor Years: A Biography.* New York: Doubleday, 1990.

Sanders, Ronald. *The Downtown Jews: Portraits of an Immigrant Generation.* 1969. New York: Dover, 1987.

Sansing, David G. *Making Haste Slowly: The Troubled History of Higher Education in Mississippi.* Jackson: University Press of Mississippi, 1990.

Sattelmeyer, Robert. "The Remaking of *Walden.*" In *Writing the American Classics,* ed. James Barbour and Tom Quirk, 53–78. Chapel Hill: University of North Carolina Press, 1990.

———. "'The True Industry for Poets': Fishing With Thoreau." *ESQ* 33 (1987): 189–201.

Saxton, Alexander. *The Indispensable Enemy: Labor and the Anti-Chinese Movement in California.* Berkeley: University of California Press, 1971.

Scharnhorst, Gary. *Charlotte Perkins Gilman.* Boston: Twayne, 1985.

Schor, Juliet B. *The Overworked American: The Unexpected Decline of Leisure.* New York: Basic Books, 1991.

Schreiner, Olive. *Woman and Labor.* New York: Frederick A. Stokes, 1911.

Scott, Emmett. "Leisure Time and the Colored Citizen." *The Playground* 18 (Jan. 1925): 593–96.

Sears, John F. *Sacred Places: American Tourist Attractions in the Nineteenth Century.* New York: Oxford University Press, 1989.

Seidel, Kathryn Lee. "The Artist in the Kitchen: The Economics of Creativity in Hurston's 'Sweat.'" In *Zora in Florida,* ed. Steve Glassman and Kathryn Lee Seidel, 110–20. Orlando: University of Central Florida Press, 1991.

Seltzer, Mark. *Bodies and Machines.* New York: Routledge, 1992.

Settle, T. S. "Recreation for Colored Citizens—Needs and Methods." *The Playground* 18 (Jan. 1925): 597–98, 612–13.

———. "Recreation for Negroes in Memphis." *The Playground* 9 (1915–16): 441–44.

Seymour, Harold. *Baseball: The People's Game.* New York: Oxford University Press, 1990.

Shanley, J. Lyndon. *The Making of "Walden," with the Text of the First Version.* Chicago: University of Chicago Press, 1957.

Shattuck, Lemuel. *Report to the Committee of the City Council Appointed to Obtain the Census of Boston for the Year 1845.* 1846. New York: Arno, 1976.

Shumaker, Conrad. "'Too Terribly Good to be Printed': Charlotte Perkins Gilman's 'The Yellow Wallpaper.'" In Meyering, ed., 64–74.

Simonson, Harold P. *Prairies Within: The Tragic Trilogy of Ole Rölvaag.* Seattle: University of Washington Press, 1987.

Sklar, Kathryn Kish. *Catharine Beecher: A Study in American Domesticity.* New Haven, Conn.: Yale University Press, 1973.

Smith, Eric Ledell. *Bert Williams: A Biography of the Pioneer Black Comedian.* Jefferson, N.C.: McFarland, 1992.

Smith, Grant H. *The History of the Comstock Lode, 1850–1920.* 1943. Reno: Nevada State Bureau of Mines and Mackay School of Mines, 1964.

Smith, Henry Nash. "Mark Twain as an Interpreter of the Far West: The Structure of *Roughing It.*" In *The Frontier in Perspective*, ed. Walker D. Wyman and Clifton B. Kroeber, 205–28. Madison: University of Wisconsin Press, 1957.

Solomon, Barbara H., ed. *Ain't We Got Fun? Essays, Lyrics, and Stories of the Twenties.* New York: Mentor-NAL, 1980.

Somers, Dale A. *The Rise of Sports in New Orleans: 1850–1900.* Baton Rouge: Louisiana State University Press, 1972.

Spariosu, Mihai. *Literature, Mimesis and Play: Essays in Literary Theory.* Tübingen: Narr, 1982.

Spears, Betty, and Richard A. Swanson. *History of Sport and Physical Activity in the United States.* 2d ed. Ed. Elaine T. Smith. Dubuque, Iowa: Wm. C. Brown, 1983.

Spears, Timothy J. *100 Years on the Road: The Traveling Salesman in American Culture.* New Haven, Conn.: Yale University Press, 1995.

Standish, Burt L. [Gilbert Patten]. *Frank Merriwell at Yale.* Philadelphia: David McKay, 1903.

Stansell, Christine. *City of Women: Sex and Class in New York, 1789–1860.* New York: Knopf, 1986.

Stearns, Harold E., ed. *Civilization in the United States: An Inquiry by Thirty Americans.* 1922. Westport, Conn.: Greenwood, 1971.

Steensma, Robert. "Rölvaag and Turner's Frontier Thesis." *North Dakota Quarterly* 27 (Autumn 1959): 100–104.

Stoddard, Lothrop. *The Rising Tide of Color Against White World-Supremacy.* New York: Scribner's, 1920.

Struna, Nancy L. *People of Prowess: Sport, Leisure, and Labor in Early Anglo-America.* Urbana: University of Illinois Press, 1996.

Sumner, Charles. *The True Grandeur of Nations: An Oration Delivered Before the Authorities of the City of Boston, July 4, 1845.* Philadelphia: Henry Longstreth, 1846.

Sundquist, Eric J. *Faulkner: The House Divided.* Baltimore: Johns Hopkins University Press, 1983.

Tanner, Laura E. "Reading Rape: *Sanctuary* and *The Women of Brewster Place.*" *American Literature* 62 (Dec. 1990): 559–82.

Tarbell, Ida M. *The Business of Being a Woman.* New York: Macmillan, 1913.

Thaman, Mary. *Manners and Morals of the 1920's: A Survey of the Religious Press.* Westport, Conn.: Greenwood, 1954.

Thompson, Anita B. Review of *Tales of the Jazz Age,* by F. Scott Fitzgerald. *The Messenger* 5 (May 1923): 706.

Thompson, E. P. "Time, Work-Discipline, and Industrial Capitalism." *Past and Present* 38 (December 1967): 56–97.

Thoreau, Henry David. "The Commercial Spirit of Modern Times." In *Early Essays and Miscellanies,* ed. Joseph J. Moldenhauer et al., 115–18. Princeton, N.J.: Princeton University Press, 1975.

———. *Journal 1: 1837–1844.* Ed. Elizabeth Hall Witherell et al. Princeton, N.J.: Princeton University Press, 1981.

———. *Journal 2: 1842–1848.* Ed. Robert Sattelmeyer. Princeton, N.J.: Princeton University Press, 1984.

———. *Journal 3: 1848–1851.* Ed. Robert Sattelmeyer et al. Princeton, N.J.: Princeton University Press, 1990.

———. *Journal 4: 1851–1852.* Ed. Leonard N. Neufeldt and Nancy Craig Simmons. Princeton, N.J.: Princeton University Press, 1992.

———. *The Journal of Henry David Thoreau.* Ed. Bradford Torrey and Francis H. Allen. 14 vols. Boston: Houghton Mifflin, 1906.

———. *Walden.* Ed. J. Lyndon Shanley. Princeton, N.J.: Princeton University Press, 1971.

Tindall, George Brown. *The Emergence of the New South, 1913–1945.* Baton Rouge: Louisiana State University Press, 1967.

Toll, Robert C. *Blacking Up: The Minstrel Show in Nineteenth-Century America.* New York: Oxford University Press, 1974.

Trench, Richard Chenevix. *On the Study of Words.* New York: Redfield, 1852.

Turner, Frederick Jackson. *The Frontier in American History.* 1920. New York: Holt, Rinehart and Winston, 1962.

Tuttle, William M., Jr. *Race Riot: Chicago in the Red Summer of 1919.* New York: Atheneum, 1970.

Twain, Mark. *Adventures of Huckleberry Finn.* 1885. New York: Laurel-Dell, 1974.

———. *The Adventures of Tom Sawyer.* 1876. New York: Grosset and Dunlap, 1946.

———. *The Autobiography of Mark Twain.* Ed. Charles Neider. 1959. New York: Harper and Row, 1975.

———. "Dinner Speech." In *Mark Twain Speaking,* ed. Paul Fatout, 110–15. Iowa City: University of Iowa Press, 1976.

———. *Life on the Mississippi.* 1883. New York: Signet-NAL, 1961.

———. *Mark Twain's Letters from Hawaii.* Ed. A. Grove Day. Honolulu: University of Hawaii Press, 1975.

———. *Roughing It.* 1872. New York: Signet-NAL, 1962.

———. "Sandwich Islands Lecture." In *Mark Twain Speaking,* ed. Paul Fatout, 4–15. Iowa City: University of Iowa Press, 1976.

Vallin, Marlene Boyd. "Mark Twain, Platform Artist: A Nineteenth-Century Preview of Twentieth-Century Performance Theory." *Text and Performance Quarterly* 9 (1989): 322–33.

Veblen, Thorstein. *The Theory of the Leisure Class.* 1899. New York: Penguin, 1979.

Walker, Margaret. *Richard Wright, Daemonic Genius: A Portrait of the Man, a Critical Look at His Work.* New York: Warner, 1988.

Wall, Cheryl A. "Zora Neale Hurston: Changing Her Own Words" [1982]. In *Zora Neale Hurston: Critical Perspectives Past and Present,* ed. Henry Louis Gates, Jr., and K. A. Appiah, 76–97. New York: Amistad, 1993.

Ware, Norman. *The Industrial Worker, 1840–1860: The Reaction of American Industrial Society to the Advance of the Industrial Revolution.* 1924. Chicago: Ivan R. Dee, 1990.

Warren, Robert Penn. *Homage to Theodore Dreiser.* New York: Random House, 1971.

Weinstein, Cindy. *The Literature of Labor and the Labors of Literature: Allegory in Nineteenth-Century American Fiction.* New York: Cambridge University Press, 1995.

West, Elliott. *Growing Up with the Country: Childhood on the Far Western Frontier.* Albuquerque: University of New Mexico Press, 1989.

West, Michael. "Scatology and Eschatology: The Heroic Dimensions of Thoreau's Wordplay." *PMLA* 89 (October 1974): 1043–64.

Whipple, Edwin P. "Loafing and Laboring." *North American Review* 153 (July–Dec. 1891): 32–43.

White, Hayden. "Literature and Social Action: Reflections on the Reflection Theory of Literary Art." *New Literary History* 11 (Winter 1980): 363–80.

"Why We Get Sick." *Harper's New Monthly Magazine* 13 (October 1856): 642–47.

Wiggins, David K. *Glory Bound: Black Athletes in White America.* Syracuse, N.Y.: Syracuse University Press, 1997.

Wilentz, Sean. *Chants Democratic: New York City and the Rise of the American Working Class, 1788–1850.* New York: Oxford University Press, 1984.

Williams, Sherley Anne. "Foreword." *Their Eyes Were Watching God.* 1937. Urbana: University of Illinois Press, 1978.

Williamson, Joel. *New People: Miscegenation and Mulattoes in the United States.* New York: Free Press, 1980.

Wilson, Christopher P. "Charlotte Perkins Gilman's Steady Burghers: The Terrain of *Herland.*" In Meyering, ed., 173–90.

Wilson, R. Rawdon. *In Palamedes' Shadow: Explorations in Play, Game, and Narrative Theory.* Boston: Northeastern University Press, 1990.

Wimbush, Erica. "Mothers Meeting." In Wimbush and Talbot, 60–74.

Wimbush, Erica, and Margaret Talbot, eds. *Relative Freedoms: Women and Leisure.* Philadelphia: Open University Press, 1988.

Wolfenstein, Martha. "The Emergence of Fun Morality." In *Mass Leisure,* ed. Eric Larrabee and Rolf Meyersohn, 86–96. Glencoe, Ill.: Free Press, 1958.

Woodward, C. Vann. "The Southern Ethic in a Puritan World." In Gerster and Cords, eds., 41–66.

Wright, Richard. "Big Boy Leaves Home." In *Richard Wright: Early Works,* 239–75. New York: Library of America, 1991.

———. "How Bigger Was Born." Introduction to *Native Son.* 1940. New York: Harper and Row, 1989.

———. *Native Son.* 1940. New York: Harper and Row, 1989.

———. *Richard Wright: Early Works.* New York: Library of America, 1991.

———. *12 Million Black Voices.* 1941. In *Richard Wright Reader,* ed. Ellen Wright and Michel Fabre, 144–241. New York: Harper and Row, 1978.

Zeidman, Irving. *The American Burlesque Show.* New York: Hawthorn Books, 1967.

INDEX

In this index an "f" after a number indicates a separate reference on the next page, and an "ff" indicates separate references on the next two pages. A continuous discussion over two or more pages is indicated by a span of page numbers, e.g., "57–59." *Passim* is used for a cluster of references in close but not consecutive sequence.

Library of Congress Cataloging-in-Publication Data

Gleason, William A.
   The leisure ethic : Work and play in American literature,
1840–1940 / William A. Gleason.
      p.   cm.
   Includes bibliographical references and index.
   ISBN 0-8047-3399-6 (cloth) — ISBN 0-8047-3434-8 (pbk.)
      1. American literature—19th century—History and criticism.   2. Leisure—
United States—History—19th century.   3. American literature—20th century—
History and criticism.   4. Literature and society—United States—History.
5. Leisure—United States—History—20th century.   6. Recreation in literature.
7. Leisure in literature.   8. Work in literature.   9. Play in literature.   I. Title.
PS217.L44G58   1999
810.9'355—dc21   98-35016
                                                                                                      CIP

♾ This book is printed on acid-free, recycled paper.

Original printing 1999
Last figure below indicates year of this printing:
08   07   06   05   04   03   02   01   00   99